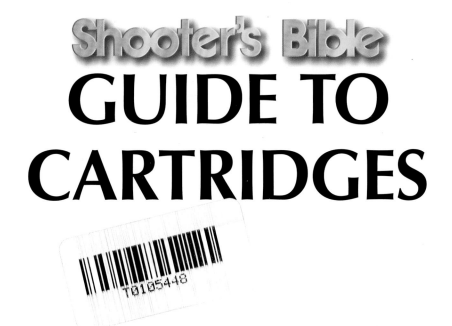

Shooter's Bible
GUIDE TO
CARTRIDGES

Compiled and Edited by W. Todd Woodard

Skyhorse Publishing

Skyhorse Publishing books may be purchased in bulk at special discounts for sales promotion, corporate gifts, fund-raising, or educational purposes. Special editions can also be created to specifications. For details, contact:
Special Sales Department
Skyhorse Publishing
307 W. 36th Street, 11th Floor
New York, NY 10018

www.skyhorsepublishing.com

10 9 8 7

Library of Congress Cataloging-in-Publication data is available on file.
ISBN: 978-1-61608-222-2

Printed in China

**Got cartridge comments, corrections, or conversations? "Like" the Shooter's Bible Guide to Cartridges page on Facebook or email the author at wtoddwoodard@gmail.com.**

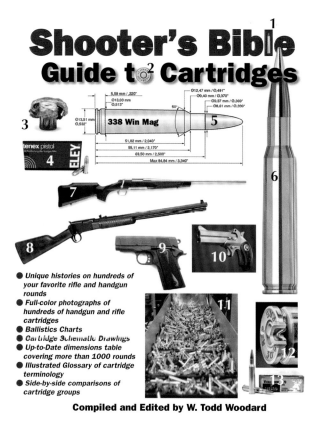

Shooter's Bible
Guide to Cartridges

Compiled and Edited by W. Todd Woodard

- Unique histories on hundreds of your favorite rifle and handgun rounds
- Full-color photographs of hundreds of handgun and rifle cartridges
- Ballistics Charts
- Cartridge Schematic Drawings
- Up-to-Date dimensions table covering more than 1000 rounds
- Illustrated Glossary of cartridge terminology
- Side-by-side comparisons of cartridge groups

**On The Cover: 1, Norma 470 Nitro Express PH. 2, Weatherby 257 W'by Mag headstamp. 3, Remington Core-Lokt bullet mushroom. 4, Eley Tenex 22 LR pistol ammo & box. 5, Norma 338 Win Mag cartridge diagram. 6, Hornady 50 BMG Silvertip. 7, Browning RMEF X-Bolt White Gold rifle. 8, Henry Pump Action 22 LR. 9, Colt Defender New Agent. 10, Bond Arms Ranger Derringer. 11, Norma factory case production line. 12, Remington Centerfire Primer Cutaway. 13, Federal 270 Win 130gr Vital-Shok Nosler Partition ammo and box.**

Note: Every effort has been made to record specifications and descriptions of guns and ammunition accurately, but the Publisher can take no responsibility for errors or omissions.

Contents

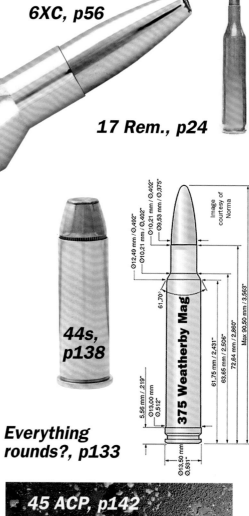

6XC, p56

17 Rem., p24

44s, p138

375 Weatherby Mag

Everything rounds?, p133

45 ACP, p142

Primer, 19

Foreword

Being something of a skeptical loner, I don't take to most people right off the bat, but when Todd Woodard and I first met decades ago, there was just something about him that made me want to know more. Which is kind of strange, since on the surface we appear to be different guys. I'm slender, hyper, going Mach 3 all the time, and tend to speak when I should listen. On the other hand, Todd is a big, quiet guy who moves a lot slower, at least physically, which makes a lot of folks underestimate his intellect and tenacity, both of which he possesses in large quantities.

Todd put those two personal qualities to great use in his competitive shooting days, first analyzing his guns and cartridges, then shooting and shooting and shooting until he was sure he had the very best rifle/load combination possible for the task at hand. Once that was behind him, Todd applied those same qualities to his professional life. He knew to get anywhere in our highly-competitive business, he would have to give up his beloved Texas and move to, and work in, the nightmare of New York city, where he was a staff editor at *Field & Stream.* That led to other gigs, and for more than two decades Todd has been the man behind the scenes of several highly-successful hunting, firearms, and shooting-related publications. It also allowed him to return home, to Texas, and work for himself.

Perhaps that's one of the reasons I both like and admire him so much. While our professional careers in the outdoor writing business seem to have mirrored each other's in many ways, the one that sticks out in my mind is that we both have often been the "man behind the mirror," toiling in the trenches and doing the heavy lifting while others grabbed the spotlight. Then, when we'd had enough of the corporate world and decided to strike out on our own, we both took slightly different paths—Todd back to Texas and the world he loves most, that of firearms and ammunition and ballistics—me to Alaska and the world of hunting, guiding and high adventure. Yet we remained connected on both a personal and professional level. We both have worked for and edited several different magazines and newsletters over the years, many of which are sadly no longer with us, but whenever I needed material on guns, shooting, and ballistics, he was my first call simply because I knew he knows his stuff as well as —and in many cases, more so—than many of the more well-known gun writers out there, and that he would deliver to me high-quality work on time, every time.

The other thing I have always admired about Todd is his integrity. When he writes about something, he doesn't simply rewrite a company press release or mimic the rhetoric of some slick PR guy. Simply stated, he will not make it up. If he tells you a certain handgun has a tendency to jam in the heat of battle, it is because it has done so in his own hands. If he says, in his experience, a certain specific cartridge produces tack-driving groups from a specific rifle, it is because he has personally shot those groups. In this, his work ethic reminds me of a famous quote from Ronald Reagan when discussing his dealings with the old Soviet Union—"Trust, but verify."

That's what you'll find in these pages—no fancy rhetoric, no rewritten press releases, no unverified stories told by some other gun writer who, truth be told, spends most of his time behind a desk or, when in the field, having someone else hold his hand and tell him to "shoot that one." Instead you'll find solid information about the favorite cartridges American hunters and shooters most prefer, spiced with personal anecdotes gleaned from decades of hands-on experience.

Like Reagan, I am a "trust, but verify" kind of guy. But when Todd Woodard tells me something—especially about guns and ammunition and ballistics, as well as trends in the shooting business—I tend to believe him because, even to this day, he continues to do the heavy lifting.

That's why the **Shooter's Bible Guide to Cartridges** should find a special place in the library of all serious hunters and shooters. It has in mine.

—*Bob Robb*
Tucson, Arizona
December 2010

Introduction

I have been in the business of publishing material on guns and hunting for more than 20 years now, which is not remarkable in any way except, perhaps, in durability. During that time, I have edited and written about the topics of guns and cartridges from the platform of my own bias and predilections—mainly, what has worked for me, and what I've seen work for others.

I admit I'm not a cartridge collector, though aspects of that hobby are interesting in small doses. No, I come at the issue of cartridges from the standpoint of the end-user, the antelope hunter faced with a 375-yard shot, or the handgunner with 15+1 rounds of 9mm in his SIG personal-defense rig, or the shotgunner playing a game of miss-and-out with friends on 70-yard passing clays. I always wonder what gets the job done, and, if it's possible to discern, what gets the job done best.

Those are interesting questions for me because all of us have opinions about what cartridge or shotshell works best for us in the arenas we play in. I was a competitive shooter at Texas A&M back when dinosaurs roamed, and I spent a lot of the university's money deciding what brand and lots of 22 LR ammo shot best in my Walther GX-1. According to my Hoppe's-stained shooting diary, I fired about 500 live rounds a week (triple that in dry-firing) 40 weeks a year, for five years. If I didn't perform during shootoffs on Thursdays, I didn't travel and compete. That I shot the same lot of Eley Match black box (not the more expensive Tenex red box) for three years was a decision I tested and verified and reverified, always looking for the batch of Federal UltraMatch or RWS RIfle Match that would work better.

Likewise, when I hunt deer, I continue to use my hand-built 25-06 Rem, which over the 30 years has gotten a Lothar Walther fluted barrel, a Timney trigger, Zeiss glass, and is now eating 115gr handloads assembled by a competition shooter whose reputation for precision is acknowledged among the local cognoscenti.

So when I apply this method of thinking to the general topic of writing about cartridges, how does it fit? What is it in the name of this book, the **Shooter's Bible Guide to Cartridges**, that suggests you're not looking for the *Encyclopedia Britannica of Little Known Brass?*

My answer, as you'll see in these pages, is to let the market—the reader—decide what I should cover. But how would I know that in advance? It's actually pretty easy: Shooters care about the things we buy, that we spend money on. There's a reason why the 30-06 Springfield has been around 100 years, and why it has spawned a host of downsized rounds such as the 270 Win and 25-06 Rem, to name just two. People like it. When people like something, they buy it, and then they buy more of it. So, if I'm willing to listen to you and deliver the product you want to read, rather than what I want to write, then we're happy.

Translated into coverage, then, here's how I've assembled the 40,000 words and 200-ish images in this book: I've concentrated on learning little-known facts about the "successful" cartridges, and I know they're successful because people like you and I continue to buy them. That's what makes the book you're holding the **Shooter's Bible Guide to Cartridges** rather than *Woodard's Big Book of Every Cartridge Known to Man, Most of Which You Don't Care About.*

So, while there are hundreds of cartridges in this book, I touch on many of them only in the most basic way, mainly to acknowledge they exist. But I know you care about them in only the most basic way, because your thutty-thutty is what you've invested in, thus, what you care about most. What you really want to know, I believe, is something remarkable about the 30-30 you own—its history, its use, its unique makeup, and why it continues to be among the most-purchased rounds in history.

As we go forward, I believe this book offers insights on cartridges that you may already own, and that the **Shooter's Bible Guide to Cartridges** helps you appreciate how smart you are to have purchased and relied on those rounds to protect yourself and your family, hunt with, and otherwise enjoy—because they're simply excellent products.

—Todd Woodard
Houston, Texas
May 20, 2011

Cartridge Glossary

Components of "ammunition," from the bottom: a primed case, propellant (powder), and a bullet. Drawing courtesy of Hornady.

Definitions used with permission of the Sporting Arms and Ammunition Manufacturers' Institute, SAAMI.org

Accidental Discharge (AD): An unexpected and undesirable discharge of a firearm.

Accuracy: A measurement of how widely dispersed a group of projectiles is.

Action: The combination of the receiver or frame and breech bolt together with the other parts of the mechanism by which a firearm is loaded, fired and unloaded.

Airgun: Uses compressed air or gas (carbon dioxide) to propel a projectile. Usually 17 to 22 caliber.

Air Space (Ullage): The volume in a loaded cartridge or shotshell not occupied by the propellant or the bullet, wads or shot.

Animal-Gut Cartridge: A primitive combustible cartridge consisting of a tubular sheath or sack filled with black powder. The sheath is made from thin, treated animal gut and is reasonably moisture proof.

Annular Ring: A circumferential crimp or indentation around the primer. In some military rounds, a dye was used in this ring for waterproofing and often to identify some characteristic of the cartridge.

Ammunition: Loaded cartridges consisting of a primed case, propellant and with or without one or more projectiles. In military parlance, *small-arms ammunition* have bores not larger than one inch. *Ball ammunition* means a cartridge with a full metal jacket or solid metal bullet. *Live ammunition* is an unfired cartridge or shotshell that is assembled with a live primer, propellant and projectile or shot charge. An *ammunition lot* is a term generally used by American sporting ammunition manufacturers for denoting same-day conditions used to load a batch of ammunition. *Match ammunition* is made specifically for match target shooting using special controls to assure uniformity. *Metallic ammunition*

Chart courtesy of SAAMI.

Ogive

Core

Copper Jacket

Boattail-shaped base

This 6.5 Grendel V-Max bullet from Hornady has a copper-jacketed bullet over a lead-alloy core. This hollow-point design has a cavity in the nose to improve expansion, and it's fitted with a polymer tip to improve aerodynamics and to resist damage in the magazine. This spitzer bullet has a sharp-pointed, long ogive. Photo courtesy of Hornady.

generally describes rimfire and centerfire ammunition. *Reference ammunition* is used in test ranges to evaluate test barrels, ranges and other velocity and pressure measuring equipment. *Patched ball ammunition* refers to a full metal jacketed bullet (FMJ). *Tracer ammunition* contains a compound in its base that burns during flight.

LEAD BUCKSHOT - CALCULATED PELLET COUNT PER POUND

Shot Name	Nominal Dia. in.	(mm)		APPROX. PELLETS PER POUND* Nominal Antimony Content (weight percent) 0.5% ("Soft") ("Hard")
No. 4 Buck	0.240	(6.10)		338
No. 3 Buck	0.250	(6.35)		299
No. 2 Buck	0.270	(6.86)		238
No. 1 Buck	0.300	(7.62)		173
No. 0 Buck	0.320	(8.13)		143
No. 00 Buck	0.330	(8.38)		130
No. 000 Buck	0.360	(9.14)		100

*Actual pellet counts per pounds in a shotshell will vary from the calculated values tabulated above due to variation in antimony content of the shot in the shell and tolerances in shot diameters.

One pound = 0.45 kilogram

Full Metal Jacket

 Jacketed Hollow Point

 Lead Hollow Point

 Lead Round Nose

 Semi-Jacketed Hollow Point

 Lead Semi-Wadcutter

 Soft Point Wadcutter Match

Lead Wadcutter Match

Photos courtesy of Remington

Annulus: The ring-like space between the top of the primer and the primer pocket or battery cup on the base of a cartridge. Colored lacquer is sometimes applied to this area to provide a visual seal.

Antimony: A metallic element used to alloy lead to increase hardness.

Anvil: An internal metal component in a cartridge primer assembly against which the priming mixture is pinched by the firing-pin blow.

Armor Piercing (Ammunition): Ammunition utilizing a projectile specifically designed to penetrate hardened, or armor-plated targets such as tanks, trucks, and other vehicles.

Attached Head: Early centerfire with the head of the cartridge attached to the body by riveting or other means. Circa 1860s and beyond. Example: .577 Snider.

Auto: Shorthand for autoloader or automatic firearm operation.

B

Back Bore: A shotgun, chambered for a specified gauge, whose barrel bore diameter is greater than the nominal specified for that gauge, but does not exceed SAAMI maximum.

Backthrust: The force exerted on the breech block by the head of the cartridge case during propellant burning.

Ballistic Coefficient: An index of the manner in which a particular projectile decelerates in free flight.

Ballistics: The science of projectiles in motion. *Interior Ballistics* deal with projectile movement inside the gun. Includes all aspects of combustion within the gun barrel, including pressure development and motion of the projectile along the bore of the firearm. *Exterior Ballistics* study projectile movement between the muzzle and the target. *Terminal Ballistics* are effects of the projectile in the target.

Barrel Length (interior ballistics): Measurement from the face of the muzzle to the base of the seated bullet or base of the case neck.

Barrel Vibration: Oscillations of a barrel as a result of firing. Barrel whip is the movement of the muzzle end that occurs as the projectile leaves.

Battery Cup: In a shotshell primer, the flanged metallic cup that contains and supports the primer cup and anvil.

BB: Spherical shot having a diameter of .180 in. used in shotshell loads. The term BB is also used to designate steel or lead air rifle shot of .175 in. diameter.

Big Bore: Centerfire cartridge with a bullet .30 in. or larger in diameter.

Body: The cartridge case part which contains propellant, or the tubular section of a shotshell

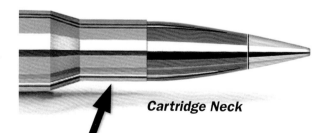
Cartridge Neck

that contains the propellant, wads and shot charge.

Rimfire Cartridge

Bore: The interior of a barrel forward of the chamber. *Bore axis* describes line through the center of the bore. *Bore constriction* means a reduction in the internal diameter of a firearm bore. *Bore diameter* in rifled barrels describes the minor interior diameter of a barrel, which is the diameter of a circle formed by the tops of the lands. Bore diameter in shotguns or muskets is the interior dimension of the barrel forward of the chamber but before any restrictive choke or expanded muzzle.

Bore Casting: Pouring a special alloy or material that has a low melting point into the bore or chamber of a firearm. The cast is used to study physical characteristics of the bore.

Bore Slugging: A process of determining the interior dimensions of a rifled barrel by measuring a lead ball which has been expanded to fill the bore.

Breech: The rear end of the barrel. A *breech block* is the mechanism that supports the head of the cartridge. The *breech face* is part of the breech block that rests against the head of the cartridge case or shotshell during feeding and firing. There are four major *breeching systems*. In the *belted chamber* design, the cartridge seats in the chamber on an enlarged band ahead of the extractor groove of the cartridge body. The *mouth chamber* design has the cartridge seated in the chamber on the mouth of the cartridge case. The *rimless chamber* seats the cartridge on the shoulder of the cartridge case. And in a *rimmed chamber* design, the cartridge seats in the chamber on the rim or flange of the cartridge case.

Buckshot: Lead pellets ranging in size from .20 to .36 in. diameter, normally loaded in shotshells.

Bullet: A non-spherical projectile for use in a rifled barrel. *Bullet jacket* is the metallic cover over the core of the bullet. *Bullet cores* are usually an alloy of lead, antimony and/or tin. *Bullet diameter* is the maximum dimension across the largest cylindrical section of a bullet. A *boattail bullet* has a tapered or truncated conical base. A *capped bullet* uses a standard lead bullet with a harder-metal nose. A *copper-jacketed* bullet has an outer jacket of copper or copper alloy over a lead-alloy core. An *expanding bullet* is used for hunting, providing controlled expansion upon impact. An *exploding bullet* contains an explosive in the nose, intended to explode on impact. A *flat-nose bullet* has a flattened front end at right angles to the axis. A *frangible bullet* is designed to break up upon impact to minimize ricochet or spatter. A *full-metal-jacket* (FMJ) bullet encloses most of the core, with the exception of the base, with another metal. A *hollowpoint bullet* has a cavity in the nose to improve expansion. The *bullet ogive* is the curved forward part of a bullet. A *partition bullet* has a jacket divided into two cavities, which enclose the forward and rear cores of the bullet. It is designed so the first cavity expands and the rear cavity holds together for penetration. A *roundnose bullet* has a radiused nose. A *semi-jacketed bullet* has a partial jacket that exposes a lead nose. Similarly, a *semi-jacketed hollowpoint bullet* has a partial jacket and the lead nose has a cavity. A *semi-wadcutter bullet* (SWC) employs a distinct shoulder and short truncated cone at the forward end. The conical extended nose, flat point, and sharp shoulder cut a full-diameter hole in the target. May also include a hollowpoint to facilitate expansion. *Soft-point bullets* (SP) expose a portion of the core at the nose of a jacketed bullet. Often abbreviated JSP or SP. They tend to expand more slowly than a hollowpoint bullet and are used where deeper penetration and expansion are needed. A *spire-point bullet* has a cone-shaped ogive. A *spitzer bullet* has a sharp-pointed, long ogive. From the German word *spitz*, meaning pointed. Most modern military bullets are of this type. A *steel-jacket bullet* uses plated or clad steel in place of gilding metal or copper. A *swaged bullet* is formed by ramming the bullet material into a die. A *truncated bullet* is a flat-nosed bullet design with a conical shape rather than a nose formed by a radius. The truncated-cone design uses a flat-nosed bullet with a conical shape rather than ogive formed by a curve or radius. A *wadcutter* bullet has a sharp-shouldered nose intended to cut target paper cleanly. A *wax bullet* is made from paraffin or other wax material, usually for short-range indoor-target shooting. A *heel-type bullet* has a rear section of reduced diameter; so when loaded, the front portion is flush with the case. *Sintered* bullets are formed by the high-pressure consolidation of powdered metal into a bullet form. Such bullets were made experimentally and loaded into .30-06 cases prior to WWII also adopted by Germany in 9mm during the war.

Bullet Jump: The distance a bullet must travel from the cartridge case to the rifling.

Bullet Upset: In interior ballistics, the change of bullet form due to chamber pressure. In exterior ballistics, the expansion of a bullet upon impact.

Bulk Density: The ratio of the weight of a given volume of powder versus the weight of the same volume of water.

Burning Rate (Burn Rate): An index of how fast burning propellant changes into gas.

C

Caliber: The approximate diameter of the circle formed by the tops of the lands of a rifled barrel, often expressed in hundredths of an inch or millimeters.

Cannelure: A circumferential groove generally of corrugated appearance cut or impressed into a bullet or cartridge case.

Cartouche: French equivalent for cartridge.

Cartridge: A single round of ammunition consisting of the case, primer and propellant with or without one or more projectiles. Also applies to a shotshell. The *cartridge case* is the main body of a single round into which other components are inserted to form a cartridge. Usually made of brass, steel, copper, aluminum or plastic. *Wildcat* is a nonstandard cartridge usually based upon modifications of an existing commercial cartridge case. A *bottleneck cartridge* has a distinct angular shoulder stepping down to a smaller diameter at the neck. A *centerfire cartridge* has its primer central to the axis in the head of the case. *Metric cartridges* are identified by their nominal bullet diameter and cartridge case length, both of which are given in millimeters, such as 7x57. A *rimfire cartridge* is a flange-headed piece containing the priming mixture inside the rim cavity, aka smallbore. *Rimless cartridge's* case head is the same diameter as the body. *Rimmed cartridges* have a rimmed or flanged head larger in diameter than the body of the case. *Semi-rimmed* means the case head is slightly larger in diameter than the case body and has an extractor groove forward of the head.

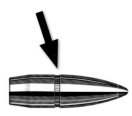

Cannelure

A *flechette cartridge* is loaded with one or multiple finned steel dartlike projectiles. A *Flobert cartridge* is a small-caliber (9mm or smaller) rimfire cartridge, usually used for indoor shooting in Europe. Many contain only primer compound. Caseless cartridges are modern designs wherein the "case" is molded solid propellant with an attached projectile and primer and is consumed in firing. *Combustible cartridges* were early ammunition which contained propellant in a nitrated paper casing. The entire envelope was consumed when the round was fired.

Cartridge Neck: Reduced-diameter cylindrical portion of a cartridge case, extending from the bottom of the shoulder to the case mouth.

Case: aka cartridge case or shotshell case. A *belted case* has an enlarged band ahead of the extractor groove, common on magnum-type cartridges. A *straight case* has little or no taper along its length. A *solid-drawn case* is formed from a metallic disc that has been subjected to an alternating series of progressive draws and anneals, resulting in a finished cartridge case. *Solid-head cases* are modern construction where the head is formed from comparatively thick metal to withstand the higher pressures of modern loads. *Folded-head cases* have their bases folded to form the rim and primer pocket.

Nickel-Plated: Cartridge cases, bullets, or primers which have been electroplated with nickel. Bright, silvery appearance.

Case Capacity: How much propellant will fit in a cartridge case with a fully seated bullet.

Case Extractor Groove: An annular groove cut in rimless, semi-rimmed cartridge or belted cases, forward of the head, for the purpose of providing a surface that the gun extractor may grip to remove the case from the chamber. Also called *cannelure*.

Case Fire-Forming: Changing the external shape of a cartridge case by firing in a chamber of the desired configuration.

Case Head Expansion: An enlargement of the cartridge case head diameter on firing.

Case Mouth: The opening in the case into which the projectile or shot is inserted.

Case Shoulder: The angled or tapered section of a bottleneck cartridge case connecting the main body of the case to the smaller-diameter neck.

A selection of brass cases. Most are straightwall designs. Two have bottleneck shapes, with the left case in front having a sharp shoulder angle. Photo courtesy of Hornady.

Case Split: A longitudinal rupture in the wall of a cartridge case or shotshell.

Case Stretching: The elongation in the body of a cartridge case during firing.

Case Taper: The gradual reduction in diameter of a cartridge case from head to shoulder or mouth.

Casting: A process for making lead bullets by pouring molten metal into a mold.

Chamber: In a rifle, shotgun or pistol, the rearmost part of the barrel that has been formed to accept a specific cartridge or shell when inserted, or the holes in the cylinder of a revolver. *Chamber leade* is the conical part of the bore between the chamber and the rifling.

Coefficient Of Form: A numerical term indicating the general profile of a projectile.

Cook-Off: High temperatures in a firearms chamber (usually machine guns) causing firing of a cartridge without operation of the firing mechanism.

Copper Units of Pressure (CUP): Measurement of pressure using a piston fitted into a hole drilled in the chamber. Upon ignition, gases drive the piston into a calibrated copper slug. The amount of calibrated deformation is then checked on standardized tables, which give resulting pressures. Piezoelectric and strain-

Primer pocket in a centerfire case.

gauge measurements (PSI) have largely replaced CUP.

Copper Wash: A copper coating applied to a steel cartridge case for corrosion resistance.

Copper-Tubed Bullet: A lead hollowpoint bullet with a thin, closed-ended copper tube. Also called express bullet.

Cordite: A type of smokeless nitrocellulose powder. Used widely in British military and sporting cartridges.

Crimp: The closure of the mouth of a shotshell. A *rolled crimp* is performed by inverting the mouth of the tube over a top wad or slug. A *star crimp, aka rose crimp,* folds the sidewalls in a star-shaped pattern. A *stake crimp* is a rectangular crimp on the case neck or primer pocket. *Stab crimps* appear on the neck as a point or dot. Also called *point crimp.*

Crispin Cartridge: Rimfire cartridge where the fulminate is contained in an annular ring nearly midway between the base and mouth of the cartridge.

Cupfire Cartridge: A front-loading rimfire cartridge used in early pistols.

Cutaway Cartridge: A sectioned cartridge that shows interior construction.

Cylinder Gap: The opening or clearance between barrel and cylinder in a revolver.

D

Decapper: Tool used to remove primers from cartridge cases or shells.

Doubling: Unintentional firing of a second shot.

Double-Tap: Two very quick shots fired from a handgun with both directed by the sights.

Dram Equivalent (Dram Equiv): The accepted method of correlating relative velocities of shotshells loaded with smokeless propellant to shotshells loaded with blackpowder. The reference blackpowder load chosen was a 3-dram charge of blackpowder, with 1⅛ oz. shot and a velocity of 1200 fps. Therefore, a 3-dram equivalent load using smokeless powder would be with 1⅛ oz. of shot having a velocity of 1200 fps or 1.25 oz. of shot and a velocity of 1165 fps. A 3¼-dram-equivalent load might have 1⅛ oz. shot and a velocity of 1255 fps.

Draw Mark: A longitudinal scratch on a cartridge case caused by foreign material on either the draw punch or die during fabrication.

Drop Test (Sensitivity Test For Primed Shells Or Primers): A method of determining the sensitivity of primed cases held in a specified die and subjected to a range of specified firing-pin blows imparted by a freely falling ball.

The grooves cut into a Hornady DGS roundnose bullet by barrel rifling is called engraving. Photo courtesy of Hornady.

Dud: A popular term for a cartridge that fails to fire after its primer is struck by the firearm's firing pin.

Dum-Dum Bullet: Often misused as a term for any soft-nosed or hollowpoint hunting bullet. Derives from a British .303 cal. military bullet developed in India's Dum-Dum Arsenal circa 1897-1898.

E F

Engraving: 1. The grooves cut into a bullet by barrel rifling. 2. The forming of grooves in a bullet by the barrel rifling.

Energy: The following formula is used to obtain kinetic energy of a projectile: $E = WV2/14,000gc$ where: W = weight of projectile, in grains V = velocity, in feet per second gc = gravitational constant, 32.16 feet/second squared. Commonly expressed in the foot-pounds, joules or kilogram meters.

Extreme Spread: The distance between the centers of the two shots which are the farthest apart of a group of shots on a target.

Forcing Cone: The tapered lead from the shotgun chamber diameter to the bore diameter. The tapered lead from the bore diameter to the choke diameter. The tapered entrance to the bore in the rear of a revolver barrel.

Feed Throat: A component which guides a cartridge from the magazine to the chamber.

Flash Hole: A hole pierced or drilled through the center of the web in the primer pocket in a

Muzzle flash is formed by burning gunpowder gases exiting the muzzle of a firearm. Image courtesy of Fiocchi.

metallic cartridge case. The hole in the end of a battery cup primer used in shotshells.

Flash Suppressant: A material that is added to propellant for the purpose of reducing muzzle flash.

Foil: Part of a primer.

Frangible Projectile: A projectile that breaks up readily upon impact.

Free Bore: A cylindrical length of bore in a firearm just forward of the chamber in which rifling is not present. Associated with bullet jump.

Full-Length Resizing: The operation of reforming a fired cartridge case to approximately its original dimensions.

Fusing: The balling of lead shot due to gas leakage. The melting of the core of a jacketed bullet. The melting of a lead alloy bullet.

G

Gunpowder (Powder, Blackpowder, Semi-Smokeless, Pseudo Blackpowder, Smokeless): *Blackpowder* is a finely ground mixture of about 15% charcoal, 10% sulfur, and 75% potassium nitrate. Proportions vary. Undoubtedly known to early Chinese and Hindu people of India as an incendiary or a demolition device and not in "firearms." Earliest known use of it as propellant in firearms was by the Arabs, circa 1150, in their war with the Iberians. Blackpowder is classified as an explosive. It is characteristically graded by grain size such as Fg (coarse) or FFFFG (fine). It generates low pressures in gun chambers.

Semi-Smokeless Powder appeared in the late 1800s and early 1900s. It was a mixture of blackpowder and gun cotton (nitrocellulose). Hazardous. Discontinued in the late 1940s. Pseudo Blackpowder: Pyrodex and similar products are modern substitutes for blackpowder. Classified as a flammable solid, not as an explosive. In firearms, Pyrodex can be substituted volume-for-volume for blackpowder charges. *Smokeless powder* contains mainly nitrocellulose (single base) or both nitrocellulose and nitroglycerine (double base). *Single-Base Powder:* a smokeless propellant for ammunition whose principal ingredient is colloided nitrocellulose. The nitrogen content of the nitrocellulose is usually between 13.1% and 13.2%. *Double-Base Smokeless Powder:* A propellant composed of colloided nitrocellulose and nitro-

glycerin as its base as opposed to single-base powder, which has colloided nitrocellulose only as its base material. The percentage of nitroglycerin added ranges from a low of 3% to a high of 39%. Made of a nitrocellulose base (single-base powders typified by the Improved Military Rifle Powder, IMR, types) or a nitrocellulose and nitroglycerine mix (double-base, such as Bullseye). Triple-base powders incorporate nitroguanidine and similar ingredients, but are not in wide commercial distribution. Generally used in large caliber military ammunition.

Modern powders are available in tubular grains, spherical grains, and flakes. The grains of modern smokeless propellant powders are made in various sizes. The smaller the grain, the faster it burns. Flake powder is a type of smokeless propellant in the form of thin discs or cut squares. Non-Hygroscopic smokeless powder resists water absorption. Progressive burning powder is a smokeless propellant in which the burning rate is controlled by physical and/or chemical means.

Gas Check: A metallic cup attached to the base of some lead alloy bullets. An obturating cup used under the piston in crusher pressure testing.

Gas Cutting: An erosive effect in a firearm caused by the high-velocity, high-temperature propellant gases.

Gauge: A term used in the identification of most shotgun bores. (410 bore is an exception.) It is related to the number of bore diameter lead balls weighing one pound.

Gilding Metal: Alloys of 90 or 95 percent copper and the remainder zinc. Also termed Commercial Bronze. Neither name is recommended by Copper Development Association, Inc., instead Alloy No. 220 and Alloy No. 210, respectively, are recommended. Used extensively for the manufacture of bullet jackets.

Grain: A unit of weight (avoirdupois), 7000 grains per pound. A term sometimes applied to a single particle of propellant powder. More properly called a kernel.

Gun Cotton: Nitrated cellulose (either cotton linters, wood pulp or a mixture of the two), which is used for the manufacture of smokeless propellant. Chemical name is nitrocellulose.

H

Hardball: A slang term for Full Metal Jacketed pistol ammunition with no lead exposed at the tip.

Head: The end of the cartridge case in which

the primer or priming is inserted and the surface upon which the headstamp identification is imprinted.

Head Clearance: The distance between the head of a fully seated cartridge or shell and the face of the breech bolt when the action is in the closed position. Commonly confused with headspace. Headspace is the distance from the face of the closed breech of a firearm to the surface in the chamber on which the cartridge case seats.

Headstamp: Numerals, letters and symbols (or combinations) stamped into the head of a cartridge case or shotshell to identify the manufacturer, caliber or gage, and other additional information. *See photo at left.*

High Brass: Properly called "high cup," this slang refers to the length of the external metal cup on a shotshell. The brass head extends approximately three-quarters of an inch up the case measured from the base of the head. The brass head on low brass (low cup) shotshells extends about one-quarter inch or less up the case from the base. *See photo at left.*

Heel: The rear portion of a bullet. A heel cavity is a recess in the base of a bullet.

Hull: Slang term for a cartridge or shotshell case.

J K L

Jacket: The envelope enclosing the lead core of a compound bullet.

Kernel: A single particle of propellant powder.

Keyhole: An oblong or oval hole in a target

that is produced by an unstable bullet striking the target at an angle to the bullet's longitudinal axis.

Lacquered Case: Usually a steel case which has been coated with lacquer for corrosion protection. Often, German WWII or Soviet bloc military rounds. Includes waterproofing technique for shotshells.

Loading Density: The ratio of the weight of the powder charge to the capacity of the case. It is usually expressed as the ratio of the charge weight to the capacity the powder chamber in grains of water.

Land(s): Uncut surface of the bore of a rifled barrel.

Lapping: The process of polishing a metal surface such as the interior of a barrel with a fine abrasive substance.

Leade: That section of the bore of a rifled gun barrel located immediately ahead of the chamber in which the rifling is conically removed to provide clearance for the seated bullet. Also called throat.

Leading: The accumulation of lead in the bore of a firearm from the passage of lead shot or bullets. Also, metal fouling.

Load: The combination of components used to assemble a cartridge or shotshell.

Loading Density: The relationship, in a cartridge, of the volume of the propellant to the available case volume. Usually expressed as a percentage.

Long Rifle: Originally, the term was used in reference to long-barreled flintlock rifles. Now, the name given one type of a caliber 22 rimfire cartridge.

Loose Pack: Cartridges provided loosely packaged in cartons rather than being tightly organized.

M

Magnum: A term commonly used to describe a rimfire or centerfire cartridge, or shotshell, that is larger, contains more shot or produces higher velocity than standard cartridges or shells of a given caliber or gauge.

Meplat: A term for the blunt tip of a bullet, specifically the tip's diameter.

Mercurial: Refers to a primer composition containing a mercury compound. Non-mercurial primers are desired because traces of mercury in a fired cartridge case make it brittle and less useful for reloading.

Minie Ball: A conical-nosed lead bullet, slightly under bore diameter, incorporating a hollow base, designed to expand into the rifled bore upon firing for gas sealing purposes without the use of a patch.

Minute of Angle (M.O.A.): An angular measurement method used to describe accuracy capability. A minute of angle is one sixtieth of a degree, and subtends 1.047 inches at 100

Right: Better ingredients make better pizza? Papa John's ads say so, and in its own way, so does this Federal primer ad from 1995. Image courtesy of Federal Cartridge Co.

FEDERAL PRIMERS.
THE RELIABILITY IS WELL KNOWN.
THE RECIPE IS TOP SECRET.

In the primer mix area at Federal Cartridge Company, Gordy Dusterhoft and his colleagues make what is widely recognized as the world's most reliable ammunition primer.

Elk hunters in Montana know it. Trap shooters in Ohio know it. So do duck hunters in Louisiana, finicky reloaders, the U.S. Shooting Team — even our competitors know it.

What none of them knows, however, is the precise chemical formula we use to make our primers. Sorry, trade secret.

But in a very real sense, our formula for making the world's most reliable primer is this: stick with what you know works best, and put it in the hands of uniquely qualified people.

Gordy Dusterhoft and his colleagues make what many consider to be the world's most reliable primer.

by other manufacturers.

Primer assembly requires the optimum blend of human involvement and advanced automation to achieve critical tolerances down to 10,000ths of an inch.

During manufacturing we use our proprietary computerized vision system, which checks every primer to ensure proper assembly. Our people also check for precise dimensional tolerances, test for sensitivity and energy output, and finally conduct ballistics testing of the loaded round to gauge performance against engineering specifications.

We inspect every primer we make using a computerized vision system.

Primer Technician at Federal® is a coveted job — employees earn that position only after many years of proving their skills in other areas of the plant. That's important given the meticulous manufacturing process involved in making our primers.

Primer mix, for example, demands careful attention to the smallest details, in part because the basic lead styphnate formula we use is trickier to mix than the normal lead styphnate formula used

Like most of the people here at Federal, the people who make our primers aren't just ammunition experts. They're also hunters and shooters themselves. And they know that perhaps the most important ingredient in any successful hunt or shoot is a primer you can count on, every single time. So next time you take to the blind, or the range, or the woods or the trail, take Federal ammunition with you. Even if you aren't exactly sure what's in it, you can be absolutely sure of what you'll get out of it.

Cup, primer, and anvil are assembled to critical tolerances of 10,000ths of an inch.

FEDERAL®
STRICTLY MADE. STRICTLY TESTED. STRICTLY AMMUNITION.™

©1995 Federal Cartridge Company

Official supplier

yards, which for practical shooting purposes is considered to be one inch. A minute-of-angle group, therefore, equals 1 inch at 100 yards, 2 inches at 200 yards, etc.

Misfire: A failure of the priming mixture to be initiated after the primer has been struck an adequate blow by a firing-pin or the failure of the initiated primer to ignite the powder.

Mushroom: A descriptive term for a soft point, hollow point or special type of bullet point that is designed to expand to increased sectional diameter.

N O

Neck Annealing: A heating process used in cartridge case manufacture intended to relieve internal stresses in the neck area caused by cold working.

Neck Clearance: The dimensional difference between the diameter of the neck of a loaded cartridge case and the chamber.

Neck Radius: The curved surface between the neck and the shoulder of a cartridge case.

Neck Tension: The circumferential stress that the case neck exerts on the seated bullet, as a result of the interference fit provided by the case neck inside diameter and the bullet outside diameter.

Neck Thickness: Average thickness of the wall of a cartridge case surrounding the bullet.

Necking-Down: The use of case-forming dies to reduce both the outside and inside diameter of a cartridge case neck.

Non-Corrosive: A term applied to primers that contain no chemical compounds that could produce corrosion or rust in gun barrels, but does not necessarily protect from corrosion or rust.

Nose: The point or tip of a bullet.

Obturation: The momentary expansion of a cartridge case against chamber walls, which minimizes the rearward flow of gases between the case and the chamber wall when the cartridge is fired.

A mushroomed bullet. This is a Remington Core-Lokt round. Photo courtesy of Remington.

Ogive: The curved portion of a bullet forward of the bearing surface.

Oilproof: The treatment of a cartridge to minimize the entry of oil or water.

Overall Length: The greatest dimension of a loaded cartridge, i.e., from face of the head to the tip of the bullet for centerfire or rimfire or to the crimp for shotshells.

P

Paper Shell: Shotshells which are constructed with a body made from paper tubing.

Parabellum: The pistol, and especially the 9x19 mm cartridge for it, designed by George Luger and adopted by the German army in 1908.

Patched Ball (Muzzleloading): Round or conical lead projectiles that utilize cloth or other material to form a gas seal for the projectile.

PSI: Pounds per square inch.

Powder Chamber Capacity: As with most interior ballistics capacity measurements it is usually expressed in grains of water. It is determined by measuring the weight of water that a fired case from the test firearm can contain with a bullet seated to its normal depth. Note that this varies with different bullets or seating depth as well as the dimensions of the chamber, and the brand of case.

Percussion: A means of ignition of a propellant charge by a mechanical blow against the primer (modern) or cap (antique). A percussion cap is the ignition source for several types of muzzleloading firearms, usually consisting of a copper alloy cup containing the priming mix. It is placed on the nipple.

Pitch (Rifling): The distance a bullet must travel in the bore to make one revolution.

Point-Blank Range: The farthest distance that a target of a given size can be hit without holding over or under with the sights.

Powder Burning Rate: The speed with which a propellant burns. It is affected by both physical and chemical characteristics, as well as conditions under which it is burned.

Powder Charge: The amount of powder by weight in a cartridge case.

Powder Deterioration (Smokeless): The chemical decomposition of modern smokeless propellant. It can be accelerated by improper storage conditions.

Powder Fouling: Powder residue left in firearms after firing.

Powder Measure: A device to measure quantities of powder volumetrically.

Pressure: In a gun or cartridge, the force imparted to various components that is developed by the expanding gases generated by the deflagration of the propellant when fired.

Primer: A cartridge ignition component *(see photos above and bottom right)* consisting

of brass or gilding metal cup, priming mixture, anvil and foil disc, which fires the cartridge when struck with sufficient force. The *primer cup* is a brass or copper cup designed to contain priming mixture. *Primer pellet* is the explosive component of a primer. The *primer pocket* is a cylindrical cavity formed in the head of a metallic centerfire cartridge case, or in the head of a shotshell, to receive an appropriate primer or battery cup primer assembly. *Boxer primers* are an ignition component consisting of a cup, explosive mixture, anvil and covering foil or disc which together form the completed primer ready for assembly into the primer pocket of a cartridge case. One central flash hole is pierced through the bottom of the primer pocket into the propellant cavity of the case. Used in modern commercial centerfire ammunition made in Canada and the United States. Developed in the late 1860s by Col. E.M. Boxer of England. *Centerfire primers* have the cartridge initiator assembled central to the axis of the head of the cartridge case and which is actuated by a blow to the center of its axis, as opposed to a rimfire primer, which must be struck on the circumference of the cartridge head. *Corrosive primers* contained a priming mixture with compounds of chlorine and oxygen generally used in military ammunition made before 1952. The residues are hygroscopic and, therefore, promote rusting. *Battery-cup primer* is a flanged metal cup having a flash hole at the bottom end. Also, it's an ignition component using a battery cup as a holder for the other elements, usually found in shotshells. *Bar-anvil* refers to an inside-primed cartridge (patented by E.H. Martin approx. 1865), in which a short bar of iron is transverse to the base of the cartridge and secured by distinctive crimps. A *Berdan primer* is an ignition component consisting of a cup, explosive mixture and covering foil. The anvil is an integral part of the cartridge case head in the bottom center of the primer pocket. One or more flash holes are drilled or pierced through the bottom of the primer pocket into the propellant cavity of the base. Commonly found in European cartridges. Designed by Hiram Berdan. Starting in the early 1870s, this type of printing system was widely used for both military and sporting ammunition. *Benet priming* was developed by Col. S.V Benet commander of Frankford Arsenal in the late 1860s and used extensively in early U.S. military ammunition. A copper or iron cup was crimped inside the head of the case and served as an anvil. A *non-corrosive primer* does not contain chemical compounds that could produce corrosion or rust in gun barrels. It does not by itself prevent corrosion or rust. A *non-mercuric primer* does not contain compounds of mercury. A *rimfire primer* is found in the circumferential cavity or rim of rimfire ammunition.

Primer Seating: The insertion of a centerfire primer or battery cup in the head of a cartridge case or shotshell. Properly seated, it should be flush or below the face of the head.

Primer Flash: The illumination produced by the extremely hot gases which result from the very rapid build-up of pressure and temperature when the priming mixture detonates.

Primer Failures: Primer cratering occurs when there's a circumferential rearward flow of metal surrounding the indentation of a firing-pin in a fired primer cup. Primer leak is the escape of gas between the primer cup and head of the cartridge case, or shotshell head. Primer setback is a condition when a primer, or battery cup primer assembly, moves partially out of its proper location in the primer pocket of a metallic car-

tridge or shotshell during firing. *Primer blank* is a fired primer cup in which the firing-pin indent has been punched out by internal gas pressure. A *blown primer* is separated completely from the cartridge or shotshell after firing due to severe expansion of the primer pocket and head. A *dropped primer* is one that is separated completely from the cartridge or shotshell after firing without obvious distortion of the primer pocket and head. A *flattened primer* is a condition where the normally rounded corners of a fired primer cup are squared due to internal pressures; or a primer cup configuration in which the crown is flattened to alter sensitivity. A *loose primer* is does not fit properly in the primer pocket of a cartridge case or shotshell. A *pierced primer* is a fired primer which has been perforated by the firing-pin.

Priming Mixture: A combination of explosive and/or pyrotechnic type ingredients, which, when pressed into a cup or spun into the rim cavity of a rimfire shell, will explode or deflagrate from the impact of a firing-pin and ignite the propellant in a cartridge or shotshell.

Projectile: An object propelled from a firearm by the force of rapidly burning gases or other means.

Propellant: In a firearm, the chemical composition which, when ignited by a primer, generates gas. The gas propels the projectile. Also called powder, gunpowder, smokeless powder, blackpowder.

R

Reloading: The process of manually reassembling a fired cartridge case with a new primer, propellant and bullet or wads and shot. Also called handloading. Reloading components include primers, propellant powder, bullets, or shot and wads, used with fired cases to load ammunition. Reloading data are descriptions of recommended relationships of reloading components. Reloading dies are tools which hold and/or reform cartridge cases or shotshells during a reloading operation.

Rifling: Grooves formed in the bore of firearm barrel to impart rotary motion to a projectile. Rifling pitch is the distance the projectile must move along a rifled bore to make one revolution. Usually expressed as one turn in x inches (or millimeters).

Rim: The flanged portion of the head of a rimfire cartridge, certain types of centerfire rifle and revolver cartridges and shotshells. The flanged portion is usually larger in diameter than the cartridge or shotshell body diameter and provides a projecting lip for the firearm extractor to engage so that the cartridge or shotshell may be extracted from the chamber after firing. In a rimfire cartridge, the rim provides a cavity into which the priming mixture is charged. The *rim seat* is a counterbore in the rear end of a chamber or bolt face to support the head of a rimmed cartridge. A *cracked rim* is a radial rupture of the head and rim of a rimfire cartridge or shotshell. A *split rim* is a circumferential rupture of the rim of a rimfire cartridge or shotshell.

Rupture: A generally circumferential separation in the side wall of a cartridge case. May be complete or partial.

S

SAAMI: The acronym for the Sporting Arms and Ammunition Manufacturer's Institute.

Sabot: From the French word for shoe. A carrier in which a sub-caliber projectile is centered to permit firing the projectile in a larger bore firearm. In small arms or artillery, a cylindrical projectile of less than bore diameter is encased in a bore diameter sleeve that is discarded in flight after discharge. It is commonly used in large (.50 caliber or greater) diameter military ammunition to provide high-velocity armor defeating capabilities. Also found in shotgun slugs and some other specialized hunting ammunition.

Season Cracking: A term used for stress-corrosion cracking that involves metallic cases or shotshell cups with both residual stress and specific corrosive agents.

Seating: The positioning of a primer or bullet in a metallic cartridge case or a wad in a shot-

A microscope in the Norma factory examines the rim, the flanged portion of the head of a cartridge. The flanged portion is usually larger in diameter than the cartridge-body diameter.

Steel shot, left; copper shot, right.

In the French, a sabot is a shoe carved from a single block of wood. In the gun, it's a plastic sleeve into which a bullet fits. Diagram courtesy of Hornady.

shell. Seating depth is the longitudinal position of a bullet, primer or wad in a cartridge case.

Secant Ogive: A projectile nose with the curvature not tangent to the cylindrical bearing portion.

Sectional Density: The ratio of bullet weight to its diameter.

Shocking Power: A colloquial term used to describe the ability of a projectile to dissipate its kinetic energy effectively in a target.

Shoulder Radius: The curved surface between the body and the shoulder of a cartridge case.

Short: A type of 22 caliber rimfire cartridge.

Short Round: A cartridge in which the bullet is seated below the specified minimum length.

Shot: Spherical pellets used in loading shotshells. Commonly formed from lead but may be made from steel. Drop shot (soft shot) is lead shot containing less than 0.5% alloying metal. Chilled shot is lead shot containing more than 0.5% alloying metal to increase its hardness. Also called Hard Shot. Coated shot is copper or nickel-plated shot, coated to increase apparent shot hardness and reduce in-bore shot deformation. Dust shot is lead shot having a nominal diameter of .040 in. or smaller. Fused shot occurs when two or more shot pellets joined together during the process of manufacturing or during firing. Steel shot are soft steel pellets made specifically for use in shotshells. Bird shot is a general term used to indicate any shot smaller than buckshot, or individual projectiles of less than .24 in. diameter.

Shot Size: A numerical or letter(s) designation indicating the average diameter of a pellet. With numerical designations, the average pellet diameter may be determined as follows: Shot Size = (17 - Number Designation)/100. For example,

A shot wad contacts the shot load.

for No. 6 shot: (17-6)/100 = 0.11 in. The size of the shot is given as a number or letter—with the larger number the smaller the shot size. The size designation was originally based upon the size of a mesh through which the shot would pass. The finest size generally used is #9 which is approximately .08 in. in diameter and the largest common size is #2, which is approximately .15 inch in diameter. However, bird shot is available in a range of sizes from .05 in. (#12, also called dust shot used in .22 rimfire shotshells) to .21 in. (TT). Buckshot has individual projectiles of .24 in. in diameter or greater.

Shot Collar: A plastic or paper insert surrounding the shot charge in a shotshell to reduce distortion of the shot when passing through the barrel.

Shotshell: A round of ammunition contain-

A shot-protector wad is made of plastic and designed to reduce pellet deformation during barrel travel.

ing multiple pellets for use in a shotgun. A one-piece shotshell is a shotshell component having the body and basewad as a single unit with a metallic cup. Sometimes called unibody shell. Also, a complete round of ammunition having the body and basewad as a single unit without a head of a different material. A plastic shotshell is a complete round of ammunition having a plastic body, a basewad that may or may not be a single unit and a metallic head.

Shot Bridging: A wedging action of shot pellets in a tube causing a stoppage of flow in a

This is a Remington Accu-Tip shotgun slug capped by a polymer tip to improve aerodynamics. Photo courtesy of Remington.

shotshell loading operation.

Shot Column: The length of the shot load in a shotshell.

Shot String: The distance between the leading and trailing pellets of a shot charge in flight.

Shot Tower: A tall building in which molten lead alloy is dropped through a colander near the top of the tower into a tank of water at the bottom to produce spherical pellets.

Shoulder: The sloping portion of a metallic cartridge case that connects the neck and the body of a bottleneck-type cartridge.

Shoulder Split: A longitudinal rupture in side wall of the shoulder of a bottlenecked cartridge case.

Sizing: The reduction in diameter of a bullet by forcing it through a die of smaller diameter than the bullet. Also, the reduction in diameter of a cartridge case by forcing it into a die of smaller diameter than the case. A sizing die is a tool used to form a cartridge case or bullet to proper dimensions. Full-length sizing is the operation of reforming a fired cartridge case to approximately its original dimensions. Neck sizing is the operation performed by reloaders to reduce or restore the original neck diameter of a fired cartridge.

Skid Marks: Longitudinal rifling marks formed

This is a stem, a failure of a cartridge to feed in which the bullet jams against the top or bottom of the chamber.

on the bearing surface of bullets as they enter the rifling of the barrel before rotation of the bullet starts.

Slug: A term applied to a single projectile for shotgun shells. Also slang term for bullet. A Brenneke slug is a formed rifled slug with a wad assembly attached to its base by a screw for use in shotguns. A rifled slug is a single projectile with spiral grooves and hollow base, intended for use in shotguns.

Small Arms: Generally a military term. Fully-automatic weapon capable of being carried by a person and fired without additional mechanical support.

Smoothbore: Firearm with unrifled bore, typically a shotgun.

Spire Point: A projectile with a conical nose profile.

Spitzer: A pointed projectile with a profile characterized by a curved ogive and a small flat.

Squib: A cartridge or shell which produces projectile velocity and sound substantially lower than normal. May result in projectile and/or wads remaining in the bore.

Stem (Stemming): A failure of a cartridge to feed in which the bullet jams against the top or bottom of the chamber.

Stoppage: When a firearm stops firing due to a malfunction of either the gun mechanism or ammunition. This term is normally used in connection with automatic firearms, machine guns, etc.

Stopping Power: Inexact, misused term that refers to the ability of a small-arms cartridge to cause a living target to be incapacitated.

Stove-Piping: A failure to eject where the fired case is caught in the ejection port by the forward motion of the bolt The case protruding upward out of the ejection port is said to resemble an old fashioned stove pipe.

Subcaliber Tube: A tube which is placed in the bore of a firearm to enable the firing of smaller or lower powered ammunition.

T U V W X Y Z

Tipping: The instability of a bullet in flight. Keyholing.

Trap: A device to safely stop a bullet in flight. Usually found in indoor ranges behind the target area.

Trajectory: The curved path of a projectile from muzzle to target. A parabolic curve that crosses the line of the sight twice. A trajectory table describes the downrange trajectory of a projectile or of shotshell pellets, buckshot or rifled slugs. Flat trajectory is a relative term for minimal arching in the flight of a projectile. Generally, the faster the speed of the projectile, the flatter its trajectory. Midrange trajectory is the distance, measured in inches, that a projectile travels above the line of sight at a specific point in the trajectory that is half the distance between the firearm and a target.

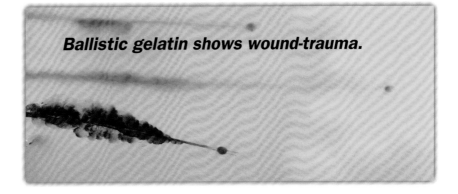

Ballistic gelatin shows wound-trauma.

Twist: The distance required for one complete turn of rifling usually expressed as a ratio, e.g., 1 in 10 inches. Twist gain is barrel rifling in which the rate of twist is faster at the muzzle than at the chamber end.

Velocity: The speed of a projectile at a given point along its trajectory.

Wad: The material between propellant and shot pellets in a specific shotshell. The *base wad* is a cylindrical component that is assembled into the head end of a shotshell. A *card wad* is a thin card-like disc placed over a shot load or powder. A *cup wad* is a powder and shot separator of a shallow cup design which when loaded with lips down acts to help seal powder gases and so protect the rear of the shot column. *Filler wads* are discs of various shapes and thicknesses used to adjust the volume of the contents of a shotshell. *Nitro wad* is an unlubricated, overpowder wad made of cardboard or felt. It is used with smokeless powder. Also called nitro card wad. An *overpowder wad* is a design of separators, made of various materials and used between the propellant powder and the shot pellets. A shot-protector wad is made of plastic and designed to reduce pellet deformation during barrel travel. The *top wad* is the closure disc over the top of the shot column held in place by a rolled crimp.

Web: The solid portion of a brass centerfire cartridge case between the inside of the case at the head and the bottom of the primer pocket. The smallest dimension of a smokeless powder kernel.

Window Shell: A manufacturer's sample cartridge with cutaway transparent window to show interior construction.

Wound Trauma Incapacitation: Correct term for the ability of a projectile to incapacitate an animal or human shot with a bullet.

Zero: The farthest distance from a firearm at which the bullet's path and the point of aim coincide.

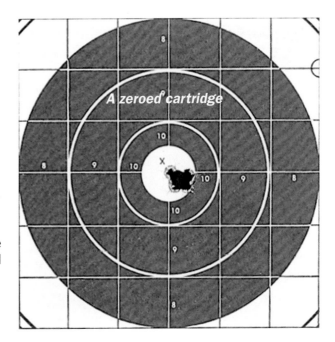

A zeroed cartridge

Definitions used with permission of the Sporting Arms and Ammunition Manufacturers' Institute, SAAMI.org

1: The Pipsqueaks

17 MACH2

17 Remington Fireball

17 Remington

17 HMR

25 Auto

4.6x30mm H&K

5.7x28mm FN

Perhaps the formal definition of "pip-squeak" doesn't quite fit here, because while these subcalibers are small, they aren't insignificant. There are both 17-caliber centerfire rounds and rimfire rounds, most notably the 17 Remington, 17 Remington Fireball, and the 17 Hornady Magnum Rimfire and 17 Mach 2, that are currently being loaded commercially. The class has a long and distinguished history.

The beginning of subcaliber rounds began with the French gunsmith and firearms designer Nicolas Flobert (1819-1894). According to the National Institute of Justice, "The French gunmaker Louis Nicolas Auguste Flobert developed target arms and low-powered cartridges. The ball was loaded in a thin copper case with a hollow rim folded into the base. Fulminate was smeared into the hollow rim, providing all of the power for the ball; no additional propellant was used." Flobert created a host of smallish schutzen rifles for indoor parlor shooting at ranges up to 10 meters. He primar-

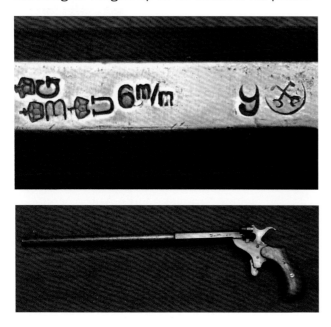

Nicolas Flobert was the original subcaliber wildcatter, working as small as 4mm in some bullets. This is a 6mm cyclist pistol, also called a sparrow pistol or VeloDog. Thousands were manufactured in France about 1895-1905 and exported all over Europe. This one has an ejector and a guillotine breech. A "U" surmounted with two crowns is the official punch of Bremen and means "untersucht" (tested). These were sold as premiums to any purchaser of a bicycle as a means to ward off dogs. That's a 26cm barrel. Photos courtesy of Alain Daubresse, owner of www.littlegun.be.

ily worked in 6mm calibers, but he trimmed some of them down to 4mm. Much later in the country in the 1920s, A.J. Jones was putting 12 and 14-caliber rounds into handbuilt cases, followed 25 years later by 17-caliber pioneers Charles O'Neil and Parker Otto (P.O.) Ackley. Ackley made perhaps the biggest stride for the 17 class, when, 65 or so years ago, he built the 17 Pee Wee (aka the Ackley Pee Wee), which was based on a 30 M1 carbine case necked down to .172 inch.

Some of the early wildcat cartridges were the 17 Javelina (Paul Marquart, A&M Gunshop, 1958), the 17-222 Remington (post-1950, when the 222 Remington was introduced), 17-222 Magnum (Dave Wolfe, 1960s), 17-223 Remington, 17 PPC (Bob Simonson, using a 37gr moly-coated boat-tail VLD bullet), and the 17 Mach IV wildcat (Vern O'Brien, 1962, a 221 Remington Fireball necked down to 17-caliber). Other variations include the 17 Hornet, 17 Bee, 17 Lovell, 17 Woods- man, 17 Pee Wee, 17 A&M, 17 Squirrel, 17 Ackley Hornet, 17 Ackley Bee, 17 Hebee (a 17 Ackley Bee improved), 17 CCM (Cooper Centerfire Magnum, Dan Cooper), 17 Landis Woodsman, 17-40, and 17-32 Jet.

For 20 years following Ackley's work, the development of .17-caliber wildcats was hampered because the choice of 17-caliber bullets available during the 1960s was limited. R.B. Sisk made 17-caliber bullets in 20-, 25-, and 30gr weights, as did Ted Smith and Walker Machine Tool Co. of Louisville, Kentucky. Cases necked down to accept the 17s included the 22 Hornet, the 218 Bee, 221 Remington, 222 Remington; 223 Remington, 222 Remington Magnum, 225 Winchester, and 22-250 Remington, and probably others.

The acceptance of small rounds improved in 1971 when Remington introduced the factory **17 Remington** cartridge. Officially a 223 Remington necked down to 17-caliber, the new 17 Remington was much closer to the 17-222 wildcat in dimensions and case capacity. It yielded muzzle velocities of more than 4,000 fps, making it compete with the 220 Swift, which for many years was the only other commercially loaded cartridge with a muzzle velocity above 4K.

In 2007, Remington doubled down on subcalibers when it created the **17 Remington Fireball** to compete with the 17 Mach IV wildcat

SELECTED LOADS & BALLISTICS

Remington 17 Remington Fireball UMC 25gr JHP

Range, Yards	Muzzle	100	200	300	400	500
Velocities (fps)	3850	3280	2780	2330	1925	1569
Energy (ft-lbs)	823	597	429	301	206	137
Trajectory (in.)	1.7	1.6	0	-3.0	-14.1	-34.7

Remington 17 Remington Fireball AccuTip-V 20gr JHP

Range, Yards	Muzzle	100	200	300	400	500
Velocities (fps)	4000	3380	2840	2360	1930	1555
Energy (ft-lbs)	710	507	358	247	165	107
Trajectory (in.)	1.6	1.5	0	-2.8	-13.5	-33.8

Remington 17 Remington AccuTip-V 20gr JHP

Range, Yards	Muzzle	100	200	300	400	500
Velocities (fps)	4250	3594	3028	2529	2081	1684
Energy (ft-lbs)	802	574	407	284	192	126
Trajectory (in.)	1.3	1.3	0	-2.5	-11.8	-29.2

For many years the only commercially loaded 17-caliber available, the 17 Remington remains the workhorse of the 17s, primarily with 25gr bullets, which can yield velocities of 4000 fps and up to 4300 fps with the 20gr bullets. Photos courtesy of Midway USA.

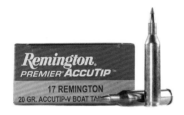

Curiously, the two .17-caliber centerfire rounds are currently offered side by side in the Remington commercial line. The Fireball is loaded with two bullets, the 25gr UMC Rifle bullet and the 20gr AccuTip-V. The 17 Remington comes loaded in only the 20gr AccuTip-V configuration in Remington's catalog. Cartridge photo courtesy of Remington; ammo and box photos courtesy of Midway USA.

round. In October 2006, Remington announced that they wanted to compete for part of the varmint market dominated by two .17-caliber rimfire cartridges, the 17 HMR and 17 Mach 2. The company rolled out the 17 Remington Fireball, based on the classic 221 Remington Fireball case, in the Premier AccuTip Line. When loaded with Remington's 20gr AccuTip-V bullet, the 17 Remington Fireball had a published muzzle velocity of 4000 fps, rivaling the velocity and trajectory of the 22-250 Remington out to 300 yards using 50% less powder and generating 86% less recoil. Spex were a bullet diameter of .172 in (4.4 mm), neck diameter of .206 in., shoulder diameter of .3673 in. and a base diameter of .3769 in. Case length was 1.420 in., and it used a small rifle primer.

Perhaps as important, the company chambered guns for the new pipsqueak. In 2007, Remington offered the new 17 Remington Fireball in the Model 700 CDL SF LTD Edition (Classic Deluxe Stainless Fluted), the Model 700 VSF (Varmint Synthetic Fluted) and the Model 700 SPS Varmint (Special Purpose Synthetic), the Model 700 SPS, and the compact Model Seven CDL.

For 2008, the company offered the Fireball in the UMC line with a 25gr JHP, and along the way, the 17 Fireball received a 2008 NRA Golden Bullseye Award for "Ammunition Product of the Year." That same year Remington added the Model 700 VSSF II and Model Seven CDL to its list of rifles chambered in 17 Remington Fireball, and in 2009, chambered the Model 700 VTR in 17 Fireball.

On the rimfire side, the **17 HMR** and **17 Mach 2** have shorter histories. Launched in 2002, the 17 HMR is the fastest rimfire in history, and its development was a team effort between Hornady, Marlin, and Ruger. The companies wanted a rimfire cartridge that would outperform the 22 WMR in veloc-

Hornady 17 HMR NTX 15.5gr Polymer Tip

Range, Yards	Muzzle	100	200	300	400	500
Velocities (fps)	2525	1829	1291			
Energy (ft-lbs)	236	119	59			
Trajectory (in.)	-1.5	0	-17.3			

Hornady 17 HMR V-Max Polymer Tip 17gr

Range, Yards	Muzzle	100	200	300	400	500
Velocities (fps)	2550	1901	1378			
Energy (ft-lbs)	245	136	72			
Trajectory (in.)	-1.5	0	-8.5			

Hornady 17 HMR XTP Polymer Tip 20gr

Range, Yards	Muzzle	100	200	300	400	500
Velocities (fps)	2375	1776	1304			
Energy (ft-lbs)	250	140	75			
Trajectory (in.)	-1.5	0	-9.9			

Federal 17 HMR V-Shok 17gr

Range, Yards	Muzzle	100	200	300	400	500
Velocities (fps)	2530	1804				
Energy (ft-lbs)	242	123				
Trajectory (in.)	-0.2	0				

Hornady 17 MACH2 NTX 15.5gr

Range, Yards	Muzzle	100	200	300	400	500
Velocities (fps)	2050	1450	1071			
Energy (ft-lbs)	149	75	41			
Trajectory (in.)	-1.5	0	-15.6			

Hornady 17 MACH2 V-Max 17gr

Range, Yards	Muzzle	100	200	300	400	500
Velocities (fps)	2050	1450	1071			
Energy (ft-lbs)	149	75	41			
Trajectory (in.)	-1.5	0	-15.6			

CCI 17 MACH2 V-Max 17gr

Range, Yards	Muzzle	100	200	300	400	500
Velocities (fps)	2010	1471				
Energy (ft-lbs)	152	82				
Trajectory (in.)	-0.1	0				

Hornady, Marlin, and Ruger gambled on the 17 HMR's development because it would become the first new rimfire cartridge since the semi-defunct 5mm Remington was launched in 1970.

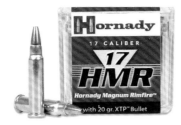

Ruger chambers the 17 HMR in the 77/17 bolt gun with a walnut stock or laminate. Both comes with 9-shot rotary magazines. The company also chambers the Single Six revolver in 17 HMR. Photos courtesy of the manufacturers.

ity and trajectory and fit existing rimfire rifle designs. Using the 22 WMR case as a parent, the trio necked the 22 WMR down to accept a .172-in.-diameter bullet with a maximum overall length of 1.35 inches, the same as the 22 WMR. The resulting bottleneck rimfire case had a 25-degree shoulder, and it had a 17gr Hornady V-Max bullet sitting on Hodgdon's Lil' Gun powder. In 2004 Hornady offered a second load using a 20gr XTP controlled-expansion bullet.

Other companies joined in, with the 2003-2004 announcements by CCI, Federal and Remington that they were commencing distribution of 17 HMR ammunition under their brand names.

There were issues with the use of 17 HMR ammunition in semi-automatic firearms. Steve Hornady wrote in September 2009, "We believe 17 HMR ammunition is manufactured to the highest standard of care and quality and performs within the specifications established for 17 HMR ammunition and is consistent with SAAMI standards for all ammunition.

"We are not firearms manufacturers and we believe the firearms manufacturers are solely the ones responsible for determining if and how they should market and sell a model

17 Javelina: Built on the 222 case. Case capacity between the Mach IV and the 17 Remington. Cases difficult to form, partially because shoulder must be pushed back, then case is necked down. Case must be trimmed after forming.

17-222: Similar to the 17 Remington (which limits its appeal) with a slightly longer neck. Formed by first running the 222 Remington case in a sizing die and finishing the operation by fireforming.

17 Jet: Based on the 22 Remington Jet case. Tedious case forming, 32-degree shoulder. Similar to the Mach IV.

17 Squirrel: Another version of the 22 Hornet case with the shoulder pushed back.

17-221: Early version of the 17 Mach IV with its shoulder angle moved back.

17 Mach IV: Introduced by the O'Brien Rifle Company in 1963. Predated 17 Remington by eight years. Formed by necking down the 221 Fireball to 17-caliber. OAL for both is 1.400 inches. Available bullets include 19gr Calhoon, 25gr Remington and Hornady designs.

17 Peewee/17-30 Carbine. Introduced in 1945 by Ackley. Similar to the 17 Ackley Bee.

17 Landis Woodsman. Eponymously named for 1950s-era Canadian writer C.S. Landis (Woodchucks and Woodchuck Rifles). Cartridge is based on 25-20 Winchester.

17 Ackley Bee. Efficient case. Drives 20- and 25gr bullets between 3550 and 3850 fps.

17 Ackley Hornet. The Hornet case holds this one back. Fireforming may damage cases.

or type of firearm. WE STRONGLY URGE YOU TO CONTACT THE MANUFACTURER OF YOUR FIREARM TO DETERMINE IF IT IS SAFE TO USE 17 HMR AMMUNITION IN YOUR SPECIFIC TYPE AND MODEL OF FIREARM.

"We specifically warn you: DO NOT USE 17 HMR AMMUNITION IN FIREARMS IF THE MANUFACTURER OF THAT FIREARM HAS STATED IT WILL NOT SAFELY FUNCTION WITH 17 HMR AMMUNITION. SERIOUS INJURY MAY RESULT.

"We specifically cannot tell you that a certain type firearm, be it semi-auto, bolt, lever, or otherwise, is safe or unsafe with this or any

Opposite: Several of the Pipsqueaks would be fine squirrel getters. Artwork by Weimer Pursell. © Winfield Galleries, LLC, St. Louis, Missouri. Used with permission. To view current artwork and pricing, log on to www.WinfieldGalleries.com.

The SS197SR, also known as the Sporting Round, is loaded with Hornady's V-Max polymer-tipped bullet and makes 2034 fps MV and 256 ft-lbs ME. Photo courtesy of Midway USA

other ammunition."

Hornady was likewise vital to the development of the 17 Mach 2, and it has springboarded off the success of the 17 HMR. The 17 Mach 2 is based on the CCI Stinger version of the 22 LR case with a 20-degree shoulder. SAAMI specifications call for a case length of .714 in. and the same 1.0-in. cartridge overall length as the 22 Long Rifle cartridge. Hornady engineer Dave Emary should be credited with the heavy lifting of the 17 HMR's development, seeing the sense of necking-down the 22 WMR case to the 17gr .172-caliber V-Max bullet, which averaged 2100 fps. Because that velocity is almost twice the speed of sound, it earned the "Mach 2" moniker. All in, the 17M2 is a practical step up from the 22 LR.

On the handgun side, one of the pipsqueaks that bridges the rifle/handgun classification is the **4.6x30mm H&K**, a proprietary cartridge designed for the compact, submachine-gun Personal Defense Weapon known as H&K MP7A1. The FMJ load uses a hardened armor-piercing steel core that can penetrate 22 layers of Kevlar or a Kevlar helmet at 50 yards. A joint product of the German arms-making company Heckler & Koch and British ammunition maker Radway Green, the round is proprietary in the sense that it's currently chambered only for the H&K MP7A1 PDW. It competes with the FN 5.7x28mm round, though when fired in the MP7, it falls behind the 5.7x28mm fired out of a P90. Also, the 4.6x30mm was designed to replace the 5.56x45mm NATO as a smaller, lighter armor-piercing cartridge. Quite a mission task, when the two rounds are compared. The 5.56x45mm M855 shoots a 62gr round with a MV between 2450 and 3100 fps, depending on barrel length. H&K's 4.6x30mm PDW shoots a 40gr round at 1900 fps. Still, as a package, the 4.6x30mm round in the compact, controllable select-fire MP7 package has appeal. The shooter can engage multiple attackers out to 200 meters with the .183-cali-

ber round, but stow the gun easily under a jacket, photographer's vest, tactical vest, or in a thigh holster.

FN Herstal of Belgium started the development of the **5.7x28mm** in 1986 as a submachine gun round for the FN P90 personal defense weapon (PDW) and FN Five-seven. The "5.7" part of the name might fool you since this does not use a .23-caliber. Instead, it uses .224-in.-diameter bullets like other 22 centerfires. Designed to replace the 9x19mm Parabellum, the 5.7x28mm is a bottlenecked cartridge similar to the 22 Hornet or 22 K-Hornet with a long, pointed bullet. Variations of the bullet itself include the SS190 AP bullet (armor piercing, 1994); the heavier SB193 for subsonic loads, the L191 tracer, and the SS192 with a soft core instead of a steel penetrator.

The **25 Automatic Colt Pistol** also goes by the shorter names of 25 Auto or 25 ACP. Metrically, it's known as the 6.35x16mmSR (for semi-rimmed), the 6.35mm, and the 6.35mm Browning. Regardless of known aliases, it's a semi-rimmed straight-wall pistol cartridge introduced by John Browning in 1908. It has been called the smallest centerfire pistol round in production, and that might be true depending on how the 4.6mm and 5.7mm rounds above are classified. The 25 ACP may be chambered in compact, lightweight guns, but its power is paltry—in the same class as the 22 LR rimfire. Still, several manufacturers still make the round, which means people are still buying guns for it. ●

2: 20 Is Plenty

204 Ruger

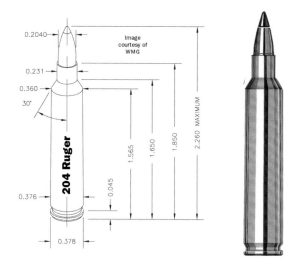

The **204 Ruger** was another collaboration between Ruger Firearms and Hornady Ammunition, and it became one of a few cartridges that top 4000 fps. Sitting mid-range between the pipsqueak .17s and the huge .22-caliber cartridge category, the niche it seeks to fill is as a dedicated varmint cartridge—basically, a low-recoil 22-250. Like the .17-caliber shooters, 204 owners can stay on the gun and target and see the bullet do its work through the scope. Yet it still shoots successfully out to 300 yards.

The six-year-old 204 Ruger is based on the 222 Remington Magnum, which gives it a capacity advantage over wildcats based on the 223 Remington case. Ackley's Handbook for Shooters and Reloaders contains information on a wildcat 20/222 almost 50 years ago that parallels what Hornady has done with the 204. Hodgdon information states that the 204 should be trimmed to 1.84 inches while RCBS says the 222 Magnum should be trimmed to 1.850 inches. The 222 Rem Mag uses a 23-degree shoulder, while chamber specs call for a 30-degree angle on the 204. Overall load length for the 204 is 2.26 inches, while the 222 Magnum is set at 2.22 to 2.28 inches. Both use the same .378-in. rimless base.

Velocities are topnotch: a Federal factory load (32gr Nosler Ballistic Tip) comes out the muzzle at 4030 fps. A Hornady 32gr V-Max runs 4225 fps; a Remington 32gr AccuTip, 4225 fps, a Winchester 32gr Ballistic Tip, 4050 fps; and a Winchester 34gr hollowpoint, 4025 fps, just to name a few.

This .20-caliber finds its best use on prairie

Bitterroot Valley Ammunition, top, is a small-volume loader compared to Winchester, bottom. The BVAC is produced in Montana. Photos courtesy of Cheaper Than Dirt.

dogs, and if the rodents are shot at sporting distances, being able to see the bullet hit around the target (first-shot misses are common) allows the shooter to either dial-in clicks

SELECTED LOADS & BALLISTICS

Bitterroot Valley (BVAC) 204 Ruger Hornady V-Max Bullet 32gr

Range, Yards	Muzzle	100	200	300	400	500
Velocities (fps)	3750	3229	2347			
Energy (ft-lbs)	999	740	391			

Bitterroot Valley (BVAC) 204 Ruger Hornady V-Max Bullet 40gr

Range, Yards	Muzzle	100	200	300	400	500
Velocities (fps)	3600	3210	2524			
Energy (ft-lbs)	1150	915	566			

Federal Premium 204 Ruger Sierra BlitzKing V-Shok 39gr

Range, Yards	Muzzle	100	200	300	400	500
Velocities (fps)	3750	3363	3008	2682	2377	2093
Energy (ft-lbs)	1218	979	784	623	489	379
Trajectory (in.)		0.8	0	-4.7	-14.1	-29.9

SELECTED LOADS & BALLISTICS

Federal Premium 204 Ruger Nosler Ballistic Tip 32gr

Range, Yards	Muzzle	100	200	300	400	500
Velocities (fps)	4030	3465	2968	2523	2119	1755
Energy (ft-lbs)	1154	853	626	452	319	219
Trajectory (in.)		0.7	0	-4.7	-14.9	-33.1

Hornady 204 Ruger NTX 30gr

Range, Yards	Muzzle	100	200	300	400	500
Velocities (fps)	4225	3632	3114	2652	2234	1856
Energy (ft-lbs)	1189	879	646	468	332	230
Trajectory (in.)	-1.5	0.6	0	4.2	-13.4	-29.6

Hornady 204 Ruger V-MAX 32gr

Range, Yards	Muzzle	100	200	300	400	500
Velocities (fps)	4225	3645	3137	2683	2272	1899
Energy (ft-lbs)	1268	944	699	512	367	256
Trajectory (in.)		0.6	0	-4.1	-13.1	-29.0

SELECTED LOADS & BALLISTICS

Hornady 204 Ruger V-Max 40gr

Range, Yards	Muzzle	100	200	300	400	500
Velocities (fps)	3900	3482	3103	2755	2433	2133
Energy (ft-lbs)	1351	1077	855	674	526	404
Trajectory (in.)		0.7	0	-4.3	-13.2	-28.1

Hornady 204 Ruger SP 45gr

Range, Yards	Muzzle	100	200	300	400	500
Velocities (fps)	3625	3188	2792	2428	2093	1787
Energy (ft-lbs)	1313	1015	778	589	438	319
Trajectory (in.)		1	0	-5.50	-16.9	-36.3

Remington 204 Ruger AccuTip-V 32gr

Range, Yards	Muzzle	100	200	300	400	500
Velocities (fps)	4225	3632	3114	2652	2234	1856
Energy (ft-lbs)	1268	937	689	500	355	245
Trajectory (in.)		0.6	0	-4.1	-13.1	-28.9

tasks. If your smallest powder funnel fits .22-cal cartridges, it will spill powder outside with the .20-caliber case mouth. Solution: Cut off a .17-caliber case and flare open the case. Then push it onto the too-big funnel throat, and the .17 case will step down the size to easily pour the powder into a 204 case. ●

SELECTED LOADS & BALLISTICS

Remington 204 Ruger Super-X HP 34gr

Range, Yards	Muzzle	100	200	300	400	500
Velocities (fps)	4025	3339	2751	2232	1775	1393
Energy (ft-lbs)	1223	842	571	376	238	146
Trajectory (in.)		0.8	0	-5.5	-18.1	-42.0

Remington 204 Ruger AccuTip-V 40gr

Range, Yards	Muzzle	100	200	300	400	500
Velocities (fps)	3900	3451	3046	2677	2336	2021
Energy (ft-lbs)	1351	1058	824	636	485	363
Trajectory (in.)		0.7	0	-4.3	-13.2	-28.1

Winchester 204 Ruger Super-X JHP Varmint 34gr

Range, Yards	Muzzle	100	200	300	400	500
Velocities (fps)		3339	2751	2232		
Energy (ft-lbs)	1223	842	571	376		

Winchester 204 Ruger Ballistic Silvertip 32gr

Range, Yards	Muzzle	100	200	300	400	500
Velocities (fps)		3482	2984	2537		
Energy (ft-lbs)	1165	862	632	457		

or hold off the dog to correct for a follow-up shot. But too much recoil moves the scope off the target, and the shooter can't see the splash and make immediate adjustments. Because the 204's small powder charge doesn't produce much kick, it becomes a good mixture of accuracy, low recoil, and reach.

Reloaders whose gear bottoms out at .22 caliber will find that reloading the .20-caliber is initially challenging, even for the most basic

3: Buzz, Buzz

218 Bee

The **218 Bee** uses standard .224 bullets in a necked-down and blown out 25-20 case with a 15-degree shoulder. The rimmed cartridge has an overall case length of 1.345 in. The 25-20 case can be reformed to the Bee's .22 caliber with a 218 Bee full-length resizing die. The Bee can also be formed from a 32-20 parent case, but the process requires an extra form die.

Sadly, the Bee may not be around as a factory load much longer. Of the major companies, only Winchester sells a 218 Bee factory load, using a 46gr hollowpoint with a muzzle velocity of 2760 fps and muzzle energy of 778 ft-lbs. According to Winchester's ballistic tables, with a 150-yard zero, that hits +1.5 in. at 100 yards and -4.2 in. at 200 yards.

Reloaders wishing to duplicate the factory load can use the Speer 46gr flat point bullet in front of 14.2 grains of IMR 4198 powder with a CCI primer. That produces a muzzle velocity of 2738 fps, according to Speer reloading data. The average Hornet case will hold about 14 grains of water filled to the top of the neck. The Bee will hold about 18, or 28% more.

If the Bee goes by the wayside, it will mark the end of a remarkable history. Winchester created the Bee in 1938 for the company's Model 92 lever-action rifle, a curious and flawed decision because varmint hunters prefer bolt actions. Also, the Bee faced a lot of competition in the field from more-established cartridges such as the 22 Hornet. Because the Bee was designed for a lever-action rifle, it was loaded to lower chamber pressure, which means it gives up velocity compared to the Hornet. Also, the Bee's blunt-nosed bullets put it at a ballistic disadvantage. Perhaps more damaging to the Bee's prospects was the introduction of the popular 222 Remington cartridge in 1950, along with several other wildcats.

As a result, the Bee has been chambered in only a handful of rifles, such as the Winchester Model 43, the Sako L46, the Kimber Model 82 single shot, Marlin's Models 90 and 1894, Ruger's 1-B, and the Winchester Model 92. ●

Because the Bee was designed for a lever-action rifle, it was loaded to lower chamber pressure, giving up velocity compared to the Hornet. But Winchester's 46gr load develops 2760 fps at the muzzle. Photo courtesy of Winchester.

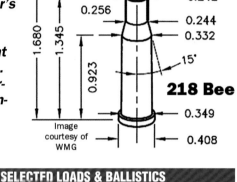

218 Bee

Image courtesy of WMG

SELECTED LOADS & BALLISTICS

Winchester 218 Bee Super-X Hollowpoint 46gr

Range, Yards	Muzzle	100	200	300	400	500
Velocities (fps)	2760	2103	1551	1156	961	850
Energy (ft-lbs)	778	451	246	137	94	74
Trajectory (in.)		3.3	0	-18.2	-62.4	

Conley Precision Cartridge 218 Bee V-Max 40gr

Range, Yards	Muzzle	100	200	300	400	500
Velocities (fps)	2900					
Energy (ft-lbs)	746					

Conley Precision Cartridge 218 Bee Nosler Solid Base 45gr

Range, Yards	Muzzle	100	200	300	400	500
Velocities (fps)	2800					
Energy (ft-lbs)	783					

Conley Precision Cartridge 218 Bee V-Max 50gr

Range, Yards	Muzzle	100	200	300	400	500
Velocities (fps)	2600					
Energy (ft-lbs)	750					

Previous page: Norman Hall painted this Western promotional poster, entitled "Dreams." The 218 Bee is a premier rabbit round. © Winfield Galleries, LLC, St. Louis, Missouri. Used with permission. To view current artwork and pricing, log on to www.WinfieldGalleries.com.

4: Remarkable Rimfires

One of the more interesting hypothetical questions posed for an apocalyptic nuclear future is, when the mushroom clouds start appearing on the horizon, what gun does the smart survivor grab when he/she is running out the door? For many who plan for WT-SHTF (when the * hits the fan), they'll grab not their AR-15, nor their 300 Win Mag nor even their trusty thutty-thutty. They plan to grab two bricks of 22 LR and a lightweight rifle. Why would some choose the 22 LR or its siblings in a bug-out rifle? The 22 rimfires are ubiquitous, lightweight for their round volume, quiet, and accurate inside their effective ranges. Remarkable, really. That's why the 22 LR is the most popular round manufactured in the world—to the tune of billions of rounds produced annually worldwide. The rounds also have the huge advantage of being used interchangeably in rifles, revolvers, pistols and semi-automatic pistols.

Of the 22 rimfires, the **22 Short** has been the most successful, at least if you measure success in terms of longevity. The diminutive cartridge is 154 years old, dating from its first use in an S&W pocket pistol in 1857. The **22 Long** came along 14 years later (1871) as a more powerful answer to the Short's paltry power—the Long is a combination of a Long Rifle case and the Short's 29gr bullet. The **22 Long Rifle**, introduced by Peters Cartridge in 1887, is the most popular of the 22 rimfire cartridges today. They all hail from ancient blackpowder designs and have an uncommon construction unique to the family.

If you pull a 22 round from its case, you'll see that the case and bullet head have the same diameter, but the portion that fits into the case (heel) has a reduced diameter. This tapered heel shape is markedly different from centerfire rounds, whose bullets fit into slightly larger cases. Also unlike centerfires, which have separate primers set into the center of the case head, the rimfire priming compound that ignites the power is contained inside the outer rim of the case.

The rimfire primer by itself is surprisingly powerful, which you can witness at a range by pulling a 22 bullet from its case and emptying the powder, then inserting the blank case into a

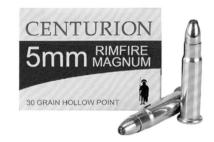

Helotes, Texas-based Centurion Ordnance imports the Centurion-branded 5mm Rem Mag. rimfire ammo from Aguila Ammunition in Mexico. Aguila makes a full line of ammunition, including the high-velocity Super Extra Short with a 29gr bullet and the 20gr Colibri load, which doesn't include gunpowder. It is intended for training purposes only, and develops MV of 375 fps and whopping muzzle energy of 6

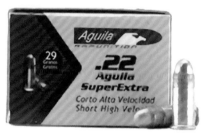

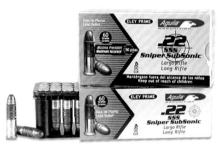

ft-lbs. The propellant is Eley's priming mixture. On the other end of the weight spectrum is the company's Sniper SubSonic round, which has a 60gr solid lead bullet. It has a MV of 950 fps and a 100-yard velocity of 802 fps, with a muzzle energy of 120 ft-lbs. It will function and cycle in most semi-automatic firearms, and spins best with 1:9 or 1:7 rifling twist. It too has Eley priming. Photos courtesy of CheaperThanDirt.com.

rifle or pistol chamber and firing it. The amount of sound and gases exiting the muzzle will raise your eyebrows. In fact, the primer is powerful enough to propel a bullet, as the French proved as far back as 1845. The very first rimfire ammunition, called the BB (bullet breech) Cap and used for parlor shooting, shot a round lead ball using only priming compound in the case.

While most of the 22 rimfire family remained fairly static over the years, the 22 LR continued to develop and is now available in target, standard-velocity, high-velocity, hyper-velocity, and shotshells loads. The standard LR load has a lubricated 40gr solid-lead roundnose bullet on it, and it develops a MV around 1140 fps (see the accompanying tables). Target loads, likewise with 40gr RN lead bullets, are usually coated with wax and have slightly lower velocities to keep them subsonic, reducing instability. High-velocity LR cartridges with 40gr copper-plated solid bullets run 1255 fps at the muzzle. Hollowpoints in that same load are slightly faster, around 1280 fps. Hyper-velocity loads, such as CCI Stingers and Remington Yellow Jackets, use 30gr to 33gr copper-plated hollowpoints that develop muzzle velocities of about 1500 fps.

Though the 22 Short and 22 Long Rifle are unquestionably the most popular rimfires available (the Long seems to be nearly obsolete), other rimfire variations—some quite old—manage to hang on. The BB Cap mentioned nearby

Several companies offer speeded-up 22 LRs, such as this Remington Yellow Jacket 33gr truncated-cone hollowpoint, a Hyper

Velocity round. MV velocity: 1500 fps; velocity at 100 yards: 1075 fps. Photos this page courtesy of the manufacturers.

Several companies load various weights of 22 Winchester Magnum Rimfire (WMR), including Hornady's Varmint Express 30gr V-Max, which has a polymer tip. Its muzzle velocity is 2200 fps, with a corresponding muzzle energy of 322 ft. lbs. Remington's Premier line has a 33gr AccuTip, MV 2000 fps; ME 293 ft-lbs, has a metal tip, which makes it unsuitable for guns with tubular magazines.

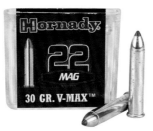

CCI Stinger 0050 22 LR Copper-Plated Hollowpoint 32gr

Range, Yards	Muzzle	25	50	75	100
Velocities (fps)	1640		1292		1066
Energy (ft-lbs)	191		119		81
Trajectory (in.)		0.1	0.7	0.0	-2.3

CCI Maxi-Mag HP +V 0059 22 Win. Mag. JHP 30gr

Range, Yards	Muzzle	25	50	75	100
Velocities (fps)	2200		1749		1375
Energy (ft-lbs)	322		204		126
Trajectory (in.)		-0.1	0.7	0.8	0.0

CCI Maxi-Mag HP 0024 22 Win. Mag. JHP 40gr

Range, Yards	Muzzle	25	50	75	100
Velocities (fps)	1875		1574		1319
Energy (ft-lbs)	312		220		155
Trajectory (in.)		0.1	1.0	1.1	0.0

CCI 22 Maxi-Mag TNT 0063 22 Win. Mag. TNT JHP 30gr

Range, Yards	Muzzle	25	50	75	100
Velocities (fps)	2200		1768		1405
Energy (ft-lbs)	322		208		131
Trajectory (in.)		-0.1	0.7	0.8	0.0

CCI 22 Maxi-Mag 0073 22 Win. Mag. Poly-Tip V-Max 30gr

Range, Yards	Muzzle	25	50	75	100
Velocities (fps)	2200		1866		1571
Energy (ft-lbs)	322		232		164
Trajectory (in.)		-0.2	0.5	0.6	0.0

CCI Segmented Hollowpoint 0064 22 LR 32gr

Range, Yards	Muzzle	25	50	75	100
Velocities (fps)	1640		1292		1066
Energy (ft-lbs)	191		119		81
Trajectory (in.)		0.1	0.7	0.0	-2.3

CCI 0028 22 Short Copper-Plated Hollowpoint 27gr

Range, Yards	Muzzle	25	50	75	100
Velocities (fps)	1105		961		868
Energy (ft-lbs)	73		55		45
Trajectory (in.)		0.3	0.0	-2.6	-7.9

CCI 22 Mag TNT Green 0060 22 Win. Mag. TNT Green HP 30gr

Range, Yards	Muzzle	25	50	75	100
Velocities (fps)	2050		1648		1317
Energy (ft-lbs)	280		181		116
Trajectory (in.)		0.0	0.9	1.0	0.0

CCI Segmented HP Sub-Sonic 0074 22 LR 40gr

Range, Yards	Muzzle	25	50	75	100
Velocities (fps)	1050		963		897
Energy (ft-lbs)	98		82		72
Trajectory (in.)		1.2	1.8	0.0	-4.3

still has factory loadings for it, as does the 30gr conical ball CB Cap, which contains some powder.

Olin/Winchester's line of 22 rimfire products is broad. It includes traditional standard-velocity 22 LR, but also the Super-X T22 Target 22 LR 40 Grain load, with a MV 1150 fps and a ME of 117 ft-lbs. The Hyper Speed 22 Long Rifle 40gr plated load works well on small game and pests. It has a MV of 1435 fps. The Winchester Limited Edition Oliver F. Winchester Commemorative Ammunition, 22 Long Rifle 40gr plated load, marked the 200th anniversary of Oliver F. Winchester birthday. The round was unusual because of the nickel-plated brass case and "OFW" on the head stamp. Ballistics Information: Muzzle Velocity, 1255 fps; Muzzle Energy, 140 ft-lbs. The 22 Winchester Rimfire (WRF) is a sparsely loaded choice, with a 45gr plated lead flat nose bullet hopping along at a muzzle velocity of 1300 fps with a muzzle energy of 169 ft.-lbs. This cartridge is made for Winchester

Model 1890 and 1906 rifles, but not for revolvers. Most 22 WRF revolvers have undersized bores that cannot use a jacketed bullet. Also, this WRF ammunition is not a 22 Magnum—it is a different cartridge, nor is it a 22 Winchester Automatic round. The Winchester Super-X 22 Long Rifle 25gr #12 shot shotshell is a short-range pest-getter. The Super-X 22 Winchester Magnum Rimfire (WMR) 28gr Jacketed Hollow Point is another namesake round that keeps hanging around. This load has a muzzle velocity of 2200 fps. Photos this page courtesy of Midway USA.

SELECTED LOADS & BALLISTICS

CCI Mini-Mag 0031 22 LR Copper-Plated Hollowpoint 36gr

Range, Yards	Muzzle	25	50	75	100
Velocities (fps)	1260		1104		1003
Energy (ft-lbs)	127		97		80
Trajectory (in.)		0.6	1.2	0.0	-3.2

CCI Gamepoint 0022 22 Win. Mag. JSP 40gr

Range, Yards	Muzzle	25	50	75	100
Velocities (fps)	1875		1614		1385
Energy (ft-lbs)	312		231		170
Trajectory (in.)		0.1	0.9	0.9	0.0

CCI Velocitor 0047 22 LR CPHP 40gr

Range, Yards	Muzzle	25	50	75	100
Velocities (fps)	1435		1230		1084
Energy (ft-lbs)	183		134		104
Trajectory (in.)		0.3	0.9	0.0	-2.5

CCI Small Game Bullet 0058 22 LR LFN 40gr

Range, Yards	Muzzle	25	50	75	100
Velocities (fps)	1235		1088		992
Energy (ft-lbs)	135		105		87
Trajectory (in.)		0.7	1.3	0.0	-3.3

CCI Sub-Sonic HP 0056 22 LR LHP 40gr

Range, Yards	Muzzle	25	50	75	100
Velocities (fps)	1050		963		897
Energy (ft-lbs)	98		82		72
Trajectory (in.)		1.2	1.8	0.0	-4.3

CCI Select 0045 22 LR LRN 40gr

Range, Yards	Muzzle	25	50	75	100
Velocities (fps)	1200		1056		964
Energy (ft-lbs)	128		99		82
Trajectory (in.)		0.8	1.4	0.0	-3.5

CCI Green Tag 0033 22 LR LRN 40gr

Range, Yards	Muzzle	25	50	75	100
Velocities (fps)	1070		977		908
Energy (ft-lbs)	102		85		73
Trajectory (in.)		0.3	0.0	-2.6	-7.6

CCI Pistol Match 0051 22 LR LRN 40gr

Range, Yards	Muzzle	25	50	75	100
Velocities (fps)	1070		977		908
Energy (ft-lbs)	102		85		73
Trajectory (in.)		0.3	0.0	-2.6	-7.6

CCI 0037 22 Short LRN 29gr

Range, Yards	Muzzle	25	50	75	100
Velocities (fps)	830		763		704
Energy (ft-lbs)	44		37		32
Trajectory (in.)		1.0	0.0	-4.7	-13.5

CCI 0027 22 Short CPRN 29gr

Range, Yards	Muzzle	25	50	75	100
Velocities (fps)	1080		946		857
Energy (ft-lbs)	75		58		47
Trajectory (in.)		0.3	0.0	-2.7	-8.1

CCI Maxi-Mag 0023 22 Win. Mag. TMJ 40gr

Range, Yards	Muzzle	25	50	75	100
Velocities (fps)	1875		1603		1366
Energy (ft-lbs)	312		228		166
Trajectory (in.)		0.1	0.9	1.0	0.0

CCI Mini-Mag 0030 22 LR CPRN 40gr

Range, Yards	Muzzle	25	50	75	100
Velocities (fps)	1235		1092		998
Energy (ft-lbs)	135		106		88
Trajectory (in.)		0.7	1.3	0.0	-3.3

CCI Long 0029 22 Long CPRN 29gr

Range, Yards	Muzzle	25	50	75	100
Velocities (fps)	1215		1019		908
Energy (ft-lbs)	95		67		53
Trajectory (in.)		0.1	0.0	-2.2	-6.8

CCI Short-Range Green 0952 22 LR HP 21gr

Range, Yards	Muzzle	25	50	75	100
Velocities (fps)	1650		1128		912
Energy (ft-lbs)	127		59		

CCI Standard Velocity 0032 22 LR LRN 40gr

Range, Yards	Muzzle	25	50	75	100
Velocities (fps)	1070		977		908
Energy (ft-lbs)	102		85		73
Trajectory (in.)		0.3	0.0	-2.6	-7.6

CCI CB 0026 22 Short LRN 29gr

Range, Yards	Muzzle	25	50	75	100
Velocities (fps)	710		656		607
Energy (ft-lbs)	32		28		24
Trajectory (in.)		1.6	0	-6.7	-18.8

CCI CB Long 0038 22 Long LRN 29gr

Range, Yards	Muzzle	25	50	75	100
Velocities (fps)	710		656		607
Energy (ft-lbs)	32		28		24
Trajectory (in.)		1.6	0	-6.7	-18.8

CCI 22 WRF 0069 JHP 45gr

Range, Yards	Muzzle	25	50	75	100
Velocities (fps)	1300		1125		1013
Energy (ft-lbs)	169		126		103
Trajectory (in.)		0.6	1.1	0	-3.1

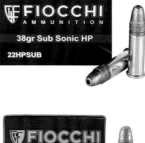

Eley Tenex has been the gold standard of competitive shooting for years, This Pistol 22 LR features special lubrication to increase cycle reliability in semi-automatic pistols and rifles (previously called Eley Tenex Semi-Auto). Muzzle Velocity: 1030 fps. A number of companies manufacture 22 LR target loads, which usually feature lower velocities and better consistency shot to shot. The Lapua Pistol OSP 22 LR 40gr lead roundnose is designed to reliably cycle the actions of semi-auto rimfire handguns. Muzzle Velocity: 902 fps. This RWS R-100 22 LR 40gr round is recommended for silhouette shooting with rifles and pistol, and have higher velocities to knock over steel animals at 50 and 100 meter. Muzzle Velocity: 1130 fps. Though Fiocchi has an Italian lineage, most Fiocchi ammunition is loaded at its plant in Ozark, Missouri. This Fiocchi Exacta Rifle Super Match 22 LR 40gr selection is produced in small lots and competes against Tenex. Muzzle Velocity: 1050 fps. A more affordable choice from Fiocchi is its Shooting Dynamics 22 LR Subsonic 38gr hollowpoint with a muzzle velocity of 1030 fps. Photos this page courtesy of Midway USA.

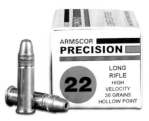

One way to get more velocity with the same powder charge is to lighten the bullet, as Armscor does with the 22 LR 36gr copper-plated hollowpoint. Uses: Plinking, small-game hunting. Muzzle velocity: 1260 fps; velocity at 50 yards: 1093 fps, velocity at 100 yards: 989 fps.

CCI Stinger 0050 22 LR Copper-Plated Hollowpoint 32gr

Range, Yards	Muzzle	25	50	75	100
Velocities (fps)	1640		1292		1066
Energy (ft-lbs)	191		119		81
Trajectory (in.)		0.1	0.7	0.0	-2.3

CCI Maxi-Mag HP +V 0059 22 Win. Mag. JHP 30gr

Range, Yards	Muzzle	25	50	75	100
Velocities (fps)	2200		1749		1375
Energy (ft-lbs)	322		204		126
Trajectory (in.)		-0.1	0.7	0.8	0.0

CCI Maxi-Mag HP 0024 22 Win. Mag. JHP 40gr

Range, Yards	Muzzle	25	50	75	100
Velocities (fps)	1875		1574		1319
Energy (ft-lbs)	312		220		155
Trajectory (in.)		0.1	1.0	1.1	0.0

CCI 22 Maxi-Mag TNT 0063 22 Win. Mag. TNT JHP 30gr

Range, Yards	Muzzle	25	50	75	100
Velocities (fps)	2200		1768		1405
Energy (ft-lbs)	322		208		131
Trajectory (in.)		-0.1	0.7	0.8	0.0

CCI 22 Maxi-Mag 0073 22 Win. Mag. Poly-Tip V-Max 30gr

Range, Yards	Muzzle	25	50	75	100
Velocities (fps)	2200		1866		1571
Energy (ft-lbs)	322		232		164
Trajectory (in.)		-0.2	0.5	0.6	0.0

CCI Segmented Hollowpoint 0064 22 LR 32gr

Range, Yards	Muzzle	25	50	75	100
Velocities (fps)	1640		1292		1066
Energy (ft-lbs)	191		119		81
Trajectory (in.)		0.1	0.7	0.0	-2.3

CCI 0028 22 Short Copper-Plated Hollowpoint 27gr

Range, Yards	Muzzle	25	50	75	100
Velocities (fps)	1105		961		868
Energy (ft-lbs)	73		55		45
Trajectory (in.)		0.3	0.0	-2.6	-7.9

CCI 22 Mag TNT Green 0060 22 Win. Mag. TNT Green HP 30gr

Range, Yards	Muzzle	25	50	75	100
Velocities (fps)	2050		1648		1317
Energy (ft-lbs)	280		181		116
Trajectory (in.)		0.0	0.9	1.0	0.0

CCI Segmented HP Sub-Sonic 0074 22 LR 40gr

Range, Yards	Muzzle	25	50	75	100
Velocities (fps)	1050		963		897
Energy (ft-lbs)	98		82		72
Trajectory (in.)		1.2	1.8	0.0	-4.3

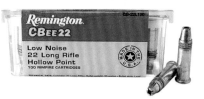

The CB loads have reduced power and noise. CCI's 22 CB Long shoots a 29gr RNL bullet as quietly as some pellet rifles. Muzzle velocity: 710 fps; velocity at 100 yards: 607 fps. Energy at 100 yards: 24 ft-lbs. The Remington 22 LR has a MV of 740 fps and a ME of 40 ft-lbs. Energy at 50 yards: 35 ft-lbs. Energy at 100 yards: 30 ft-lbs. Photos courtesy of the companies.

A more popular and more powerful cartridge is the **22 Winchester Rim Fire (WRF)**, introducing in 1890. The most common current loading has a .224-in.-diameter 45gr flat-point bullet with a full heel, rather than the tapered heel bullet of the 22 LR. It is also called the **22 Remington Special.** Also, the **22 WRF (or 22 Rem Sp)** can be fired in rifles chambered for the 22 WMR cartridge.

At one time, Winchester's **22 Winchester Magnum Rimfire (WMR) was o**nce the most powerful rimfire cartridge in the market. Introduced in 1959**, the 22 WMR** is a lengthened version of the 22 WRF case and shoots a 40gr FMJ or JHP bullet at 2000 fps MV.

Now it's being challenged by an old-is-new-again round, the **5mm Remington Rimfire Magnum,** originally introduced by Remington in 1970. The 5mm RRM is based on a necked-down 22 Magnum case, with a BD of .2045 in., the same as the .20-caliber 204 Ruger covered in an earlier chapter. The original Remington factory load's 38gr hollowpoint bullet had a MV of 2100 fps, which gave it a little more range than the 22 WMR. The major problem with the round wasn't its performance, but rather its expense and its lack of acceptance by other manufacturers. It was chambered in only a handful of rifles, notably the Remington bolt-action 591 and 592. Ballistically, it offers a lot compared to the 17 HMR, which shoots a 17gr bullet that's less than half the weight of the 5 RRM's 38gr pill, but which runs 400 fps faster (2550 fps MV). ●

5: First Varminter

WINCHESTER REPEATING ARMS COMPANY

NEW HAVEN, CONN., U.S.A.

MANUFACTURERS OF EVERY VARIETY OF

METALLIC AMMUNITION, PAPER AND BRASS SHOT SHELLS,

GUN WADS, PRIMERS, PERCUSSION CAPS, ETC.

ALSO THE

CELEBRATED WINCHESTER AND HOTCHKISS REPEATING RIFLES.

GOVERNMENT CONTRACTORS. CAPACITY OF WORKS, 2,000,000 CARTRIDGES PER DAY.

The original Hornet was called the 22 Winchester Center Fire and was introduced in 1885—one of the company's earliest cartridges, like those above. The Hornet smokeless wildcat was originated during the 1920s by army Captain G.L. Wotkyns, who upgraded the relatively slow 22 Winchester Center Fire (WCF) into a higher-velocity varmint cartridge.

22 Hornet

The **22 Hornet** is a very small cartridge, but when loaded with 45gr bullets at a velocity of 2700 fps, it's bad for critters and varmints out to about 200 yards. Total case length is 1.403 in., and the trimmed case length is 1.393 in. The .350-in.-head case accepts small rifle primers, and IMR 4227 is a favorite reloading powder. In Europe, the Hornet is known by the metric designation 5.6x35Rmm. The rimmed case makes it suitable for single-shot rifles and pistols. It was the smallest commercially available .22 caliber centerfire cartridge until the introduction of the FN 5.7x28.

The 22 Hornet fills the gap between such popular varmint/predator cartridges as the 22 WMR and the 223 Remington. The Hornet is easily eclipsed by the 222, 220 Swift, and the 22-250, but its low noise and almost no recoil make it suitable for shooting in areas where too much sound might bother the neighbors.

The original Hornet was called the 22 Winchester Center Fire (intr. 1885), a blackpowder cartridge that fired a lead bullet at about 1500 fps. The Hornet smokeless wildcat was originated during the 1920s by army Captain G.L. Wotkyns. He wanted to upgrade the relatively slow 22 Winchester Center Fire (WCF) into a higher velocity varmint cartridge. He necked the .226-in.-diameter WCF's tapered case down to accept 45gr .223-caliber bullets that would match the bore of the Model 1922 Springfield 22 LR rimfire rifle barrel.

After further development, it earned the distinction of being the first commercial varmint cartridge adopted by a U.S. manufacturer (1930). The Winchester 1930 load had a bullet diameter of .223 in., but today's 22 Hornets have .224-in. diameters.

Remington factory ammo uses a 45gr hollowpoint or a pointed soft point, both running 2690 fps at the muzzle and a -7.1 drop at 200 yards with a 100-yard zero. Winchester offers a 34gr Supreme jacketed hollowpoint with a MV of 3050 fps and a -6.6 drop at 200 yards with a 100-yard zero. Winchester also offers a 45gr soft point load and a 46gr hollowpoint (both with 2690 MV, -7.7 in. drop at 200 yards with 100-yard zero). Other load ballistics are included in the accompanying table.

Most rifles chambered for the round have a 1:16 twist and a bore-groove diameter of .223 to .224 in. The Hornet has always been chambered for bolt-action and single-shot rifles, so it has a reputation for being accurate. Some of the rifles that have been chambered in 22 Hornet were Winchester's Model 43, 54, and

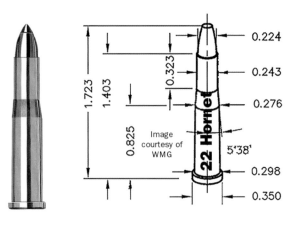

Illustrations courtesy of Hornady.

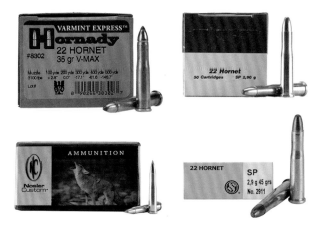

One of the surprising facets of the Hornet is its overseas popularity. Hornady and Nosler load the round domestically, but Prvi Partizan and Sellier & Bellot, among others, load the metric version as well. Images courtesy of Midway USA.

Only Sierra continues to offer .223-caliber 40gr and 45gr soft-nose Hornet bullets (right), but the standard 22 Hornet load data in the Sierra manual is for .224 bullets. Image courtesy of Sierra.

70. Savage offered Models 19, 23, 219, 24, and the 340.

Others included the Stevens 417, Sako's small-action L46, Krico's 300, the Brno ZKB, Herter's Plinker, Kimber's Model 82, and Charles Daly Model 10. Some of the best recent products in 22 Hornet are the CZ 527 bolt rifle with American Classic Stock, Ruger's Model 77/22H, Ruger's #1 single shot, T/C's Contender pistols, and Browning's bolt-action

Micro Hunter and Low Wall 1885 single-shot rifle. Two revolvers chambered for 22 Hornet are the massive Raging Bull double-action from Taurus and the BFR from Magnum Research Inc. The Hornet also found its way into the Anschütz Exemplar pistol.

Reportedly, the Hercules 2400 powder got that name because it would generate 2400+ fps from the Hornet rifles with 45gr bullets.

The Kilbourne Hornet (K-Hornet, 1940) is an Improved version of the round made by Lysle Kilbourne. The Improved Hornet has its shoul-

This is the T/C 1:12 twist 14-in. barrel for the Contender pistol. It's a popular silhouette choice with adjustable sights. Photo courtesy of Midway.

der pushed forward. Brass is fire-formed in a K-Hornet chamber from factory 22 Hornet bullets. The K-Hornet can be handloaded to higher velocities. ●

SELECTED LOADS & BALLISTICS

Hirtenberger 22 Hornet SP 45gr

Range, Yards	Muzzle	100	200	300	400	500
Velocities (fps)	2526	2029	1597	1256	1044	927
Energy (ft-lbs)	639	412	256	158	109	86
Trajectory (in.)		3.6		-17.6	-57.8	-128

Hornady 22 Hornet V-Max 35gr

Range, Yards	Muzzle	100	200	300	400	500
Velocities (fps)	3100	2271	1590	1126	923	806
Energy (ft-lbs)	747	401	197	99	66	50
Trajectory (in.)	-1.5	2.8	0	-17.1	-61.6	-146

Remington 22 Hornet Premier AccuTip 35gr

Range, Yards	Muzzle	100	200	300	400	500
Velocities (fps)	3100	2271	1591	1127	924	806
Energy (ft-lbs)	747	401	197	99	66	51
Trajectory (in.)		0	-1.6	-5.5	-13.0	-25.5

Remington 22 Hornet Express Pointed Soft Point 45gr

Range, Yards	Muzzle	100	200	300	400	500
Velocities (fps)	2690	2042	1502	1128	948	840
Energy (ft-lbs)	723	417	225	127	90	70
Trajectory (in.)		0	-2.1	-7.1	-16.0	-30.0

Remington 22 Hornet Express Hollow Point 45gr

Range, Yards	Muzzle	100	200	300	400	500
Velocities (tps)	2690	2042	1502	1128	948	840
Energy (ft-lbs)	723	417	225	127	90	70
Trajectory (in.)		0	-2.1	-7.1	-16.0	-30.0

SELECTED LOADS & BALLISTICS

Sellier & Bellot 22 Hornet Bullet SP 45gr

Range, Yards	Muzzle	100	200	300	400	500
Velocities (fps)	2346	1657	1175	947	825	732
Energy (ft-lbs)	650	275	138	90	68	54
Trajectory (in.)		5.8	0	-31.0	-97.9	-210.5

Sellier & Bellot 22 Hornet Bullet FMJ 45gr

Range, Yards	Muzzle	100	200	300	400	500
Velocities (fps)	2346	1657	1175	947	825	732
Energy (ft-lbs)	650	275	138	90	68	54
Trajectory (in.)		1.8	0	-31.0	-97.9	-210.5

Winchester 22 Hornet Super-X Hollowpoint 46gr

Range, Yards	Muzzle	100	200	300	400	500
Velocities (fps)	2690	2044	1505	1131	949	842
Energy (ft-lbs)	738	426	231	130	92	72
Trajectory (in.)	-1.5	0	-7.1	-29.9	-79.9	-168.4

Winchester 22 Hornet Super-X Soft Point 45gr

Range, Yards	Muzzle	100	200	300	400	500
Velocities (fps)	2690	2044	1505	1131	949	842
Energy (ft-lbs)	722	417	226	128	90	71
Trajectory (in.)	-1.5	0	-7.1	-29.9	-79.9	-168.4

Prvi Partizan 22 Hornet Soft Point 45gr

Range, Yards	Muzzle	100	200	300	400	500
Velocities (fps)	2427					
Energy (ft-lbs)	582					
Trajectory (in.)	NA					

6: Triple Deuces

The **222 Remington** was introduced by Remington in 1950 (in the Model 722, with 24- and 26-in. barrels) and was the first fully rimless 22 centerfire cartridge. The 222 Rem performs much like the 219 Zipper, fitting between the 22 Hornet and the 220 Swift. This case was an entirely new development, it was not based upon any then-existing cartridge. However, in many respects, it resembles a scaled-down version of the 30-06 Springfield.

Merle "Mike" Walker, a Remington employee who developed the button process for rifling barrels and the Remington Models 721, 722, 40X, and 40XBR rifles, is credited with birthing the 222 Rem, along with Homer W. Young. The original prototype looked very much like the 221 Fireball, detailed elsewhere in these pages. But at a 1.450 in. case length, the original was too short to feed reliably through the 722 action, Walker thought.

After further tinkering, the maximum case length turned out to be 1.700 in., with a trimmed case length of 1.690 in. The cartridge now takes a small rifle primer, and usually shoots 50gr to 55gr bullets most accurately with 1:14 twist rates. Bore groove diameter is .224 in. Heavier bullets need a faster twist than 1-in-14 twist.

The 222 Rem was first used in competition in 1951 and dominated for more than 20 years. Until the advent of PPC cartridges 25 years later, most shooters considered the 222 to be the most inherently accurate cartridge design. Reasons for that accuracy include a modest case volume for low recoil and a long neck. The long neck ensures concentricity in the case/bullet relationship.

Besides benchrest shooting, the 222 is a widely used varmint cartridge. In Europe, hunters use the 222 for small game up to the size of roe deer, which rarely exceed 70 pounds. With proper loads, it is very versatile and relatively nondestructive of hides and meat on fox, blackcock, roe deer and similar species.

Wildcats based on the 222 Rem include the 222-35, 222-40, and 222 Haney.

Based on the 222 Rem, the similarly named

Opposite page: Women campers might like the soft report of the 222 Rem in a handy rifle. This Winchester Rifle Poster (Model 1902-03) was painted by an unknown artist circa 1909. © Winfield Galleries, LLC, St. Louis, Missouri. Used with permission. To view current artwork and pricing, log on to www.WinfieldGalleries.com.

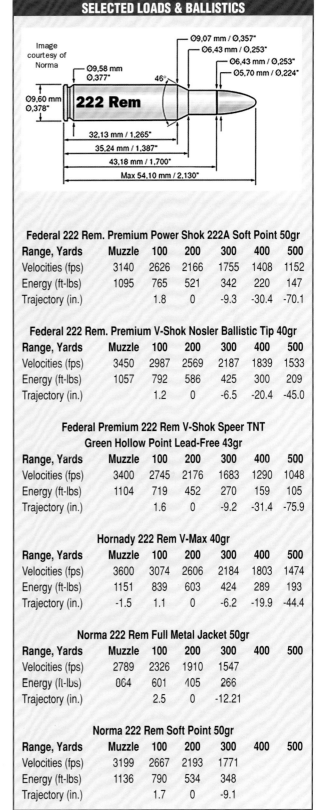

SELECTED LOADS & BALLISTICS

Image courtesy of Norma

222 Rem

Ø9.07 mm / Ø.357"
Ø6.43 mm / Ø.253"
Ø6.43 mm / Ø.253"
Ø5.70 mm / Ø.224"
Ø9.58 mm Ø.377"
46°
Ø9.60 mm Ø.378"
32.13 mm / 1.265"
35.24 mm / 1.387"
43.18 mm / 1.700"
Max 54.10 mm / 2.130"

Federal 222 Rem. Premium Power Shok 222A Soft Point 50gr

Range, Yards	Muzzle	100	200	300	400	500
Velocities (fps)	3140	2626	2166	1755	1408	1152
Energy (ft-lbs)	1095	765	521	342	220	147
Trajectory (in.)		1.8	0	-9.3	-30.4	-70.1

Federal 222 Rem. Premium V-Shok Nosler Ballistic Tip 40gr

Range, Yards	Muzzle	100	200	300	400	500
Velocities (fps)	3450	2987	2569	2187	1839	1533
Energy (ft-lbs)	1057	792	586	425	300	209
Trajectory (in.)		1.2	0	-6.5	-20.4	-45.0

Federal Premium 222 Rem V-Shok Speer TNT Green Hollow Point Lead-Free 43gr

Range, Yards	Muzzle	100	200	300	400	500
Velocities (fps)	3400	2745	2176	1683	1290	1048
Energy (ft-lbs)	1104	719	452	270	159	105
Trajectory (in.)		1.6	0	-9.2	-31.4	-75.9

Hornady 222 Rem V-Max 40gr

Range, Yards	Muzzle	100	200	300	400	500
Velocities (fps)	3600	3074	2606	2184	1803	1474
Energy (ft-lbs)	1151	839	603	424	289	193
Trajectory (in.)	-1.5	1.1	0	-6.2	-19.9	-44.4

Norma 222 Rem Full Metal Jacket 50gr

Range, Yards	Muzzle	100	200	300	400	500
Velocities (fps)	2789	2326	1910	1547		
Energy (ft-lbs)	864	601	405	266		
Trajectory (in.)		2.5	0	-12.21		

Norma 222 Rem Soft Point 50gr

Range, Yards	Muzzle	100	200	300	400	500
Velocities (fps)	3199	2667	2193	1771		
Energy (ft-lbs)	1136	790	534	348		
Trajectory (in.)		1.7	0	-9.1		

222 Remington Magnum (222 Magnum) is an interesting cartridge on its own. It's the parent round for the 204 Ruger, which shoots a 20-caliber (5mm) bullet in a necked down 222

Norma 222 Rem Soft Point 62gr

Range, Yards	Muzzle	100	200	300	400	500
Velocities (fps)	2887	2457	2067	1716		
Energy (ft-lbs)	1148	831	588	405		
Trajectory (in.)		2.1	0	-10.4		

Nosler Custom 222 Rem Ballistic Tip Varmint 40gr

Range, Yards	Muzzle	100	200	300	400	500
Velocities (fps)	3330	2879	2470	2097	1760	1465
Energy (ft-lbs)	985	736	542	390	275	191
Trajectory (in.)		0	-2.7	-11.2	-27.7	-55.5

Nosler Custom 222 Rem Ballistic Tip Varmint 50gr

Range, Yards	Muzzle	100	200	300	400	500
Velocities (fps)	3025	2631	2270	1940	1642	1385
Energy (ft-lbs)	1016	769	572	418	299	213
Trajectory (in.)		0	-3.6	-13.9	-33.6	-66.3

Nosler Custom 222 Rem. Mag. Ballistic Tip Varmint 50gr

Range, Yards	Muzzle	100	200	300	400	500
Velocities (fps)	3340	2919	2534	2181	1859	1570
Energy (ft-lbs)	1238	946	713	528	384	274
Trajectory (in.)		0	-2.6	-10.7	-26.1	-51.7

Prvi Partizan 222 Rem Soft Point 50gr

Range, Yards	Muzzle	100	200	300	400	500
Velocities (fps)	3140	2700	2305	1940		
Energy (ft-lbs)	1095	810	589	418		
Trajectory (in.)		0	-3.3	-13.1		

Remington Express 222 Rem. Pointed Soft Point 50gr

Range, Yards	Muzzle	100	200	300	400	500
Velocities (fps)	3140	2602	2123	1700	1350	1107
Energy (ft-lbs)	1094	752	500	321	202	136
Trajectory (in.)	0.7	0	-2.3	-6.5	-13.1	

Remington Express 222 Rem. HP Power-Lokt 50gr

Range, Yards	Muzzle	100	200	300	400	500
Velocities (fps)	3140	2635	2182	1777	1432	1172
Energy (ft-lbs)	1094	771	529	351	228	152
Trajectory (in.)	0.7	0	-2.2	-6.2	-12.5	

Remington Premier AccuTip-V 222 Rem. Boat Tail 50gr

Range, Yards	Muzzle	100	200	300	400	500
Velocities (fps)	3140	2744	2380	2045	1740	1471
Energy (ft-lbs)	1094	836	629	464	336	240
Trajectory (in.)	0.6	0	-1.9	-5.4	-10.7	

Winchester Super-X 222 Rem. Pointed Soft Point 50gr

Range, Yards	Muzzle	100	200	300	400	500
Velocities (fps)	3140	2602	2123	1700	1350	1107
Energy (ft-lbs)	1094	752	500	321	202	136
Trajectory (in.)	2.2	0	-10.0	-32.3	-73.8	

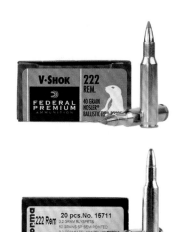

The Federal 222 Rem. 40gr Nosler has a point-blank trajectory out to 300 yards, where it drops -6.5 in. with a 200-yard zero. Norma's 50gr Soft Point isn't quite as good, dropping -9.1 in. @ 300 yards. Photos courtesy of Midway USA.

Rem Mag. The 222 Rem Mag is created by lengthening the case and shortening the neck of the 222 Rem. This increases case capacity about 20% more than the 222 Rem.

That makes the 222 Rem Mag and the 223 Rem near twins in velocity and accuracy, but the two aren't interchangeable. In overall case length, the 222 Magnum is almost 0.1 in. longer than the 223, and its body is slightly longer, too.

The **222 Magnum** was originally designed by Springfield Armory and Remington to become a small-caliber choice for a light infantry weapon in the early 1950s. Unofficially called the 22 Remington Experimental or 22 Special, Remington used a conventional 55gr SP hunting type bullet in the round. It lost the head-to-head contest with the 223 Rem as the military round, but it lived on as a commercial load until 1998—40 years from its introduction as a commercial varmint round in the 24-in.-barrel Model 722 in 1958. The last Remington factory load for the 222 Magnum drove a 55gr bullet at a muzzle velocity of 3240 fps.

A handload similar in performance uses 55gr 224-caliber Hornady spitzer bullet on top of Hodgdon BL-C(2) powder. The cartridge overall length is 2.325 in. The starting load is 24.5 grains (3021 fps; 38,000 CUP) and a max load of 26.5 grains runs 3240 fps with 46,800 CUP. Also, 60gr to 63gr bullets can make 3000 fps muzzle velocity with suitable powders. For instance, 30 grains of Hodgdon H414 develops 3085 fps.

Wildcats and variations on the 222 Rem Mag include the 5.6x50mm Mag, 22 Tom Cat (shoulder 30 degrees), the 22-40 (shoulder angle 40 degrees), and the 22-45 (shoulder angle 45 degrees). Expanded to 243, it spurred the 6x47, 6x47-40, and the 6x47-45. ●

The 4000-fps barrier is difficult for heavier rounds to achieve. That's why many of the rounds that reach this gaudy speed top out as the .22-caliber rounds—thicker bullets are too hard to drive through the air. But a handful of 4K 22s still exist, though they may reach that speed with only with handloads.

Among these rounds are the venerable **22-250 Remington,** which was originally a wildcat made by necking down the 250-3000 Savage to 22-caliber, which gave rise to its name. The parent case had been around since 1915, so it's reasonable to assume that many wildcatters made a 22-(caliber) 250 (case name) before J. E. Gebby, but he gets credit for developing the round because, in 1937, he copyrighted his design as the 22 Varminter. In 1965, Remington brought out the first commercial loads, and currently the round is second only to the 223 Remington in popularity as a varmint round.

Until the advent of the .17-caliber Pipsqueaks (see Chapter 1) and the 204 Ruger (Chapter 2), the **220 Swift** was known as the "fastest production cartridge ever made," and in some loads, it still may be. The Swift

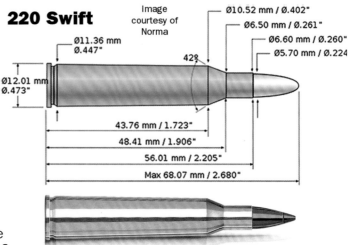

220 Swift

The Swift shoots best when loaded with a 55gr spitzer at 3800 to 3900 fps, but it takes a 50gr-or-lighter bullet to creep up to the 4000 fps and above range. Favorite reloading powders IMR 4064, H380, and IMR 4895. Dimension illustration courtesy of Norma; Cartridge illustration courtesy of Hornady

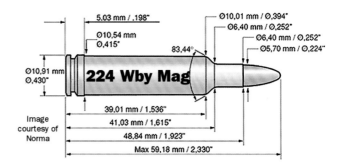

224 Wby Mag

Above, introduced in 1963, the 224 Weatherby Magnum is the only commonly available varmint cartridge with a belted case design.

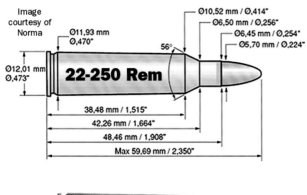

22-250 Rem

In most cases, the 22-250 is at its best when loaded with a 55gr spitzer bullet, but it usually won't develop 4K speeds with bullets bigger than 40 grains. According to the Hodgdon Data Manual, 26th Edition, H380 is an outstanding powder for the 22-250. Dimension illustration courtesy of Norma; Cartridge illustration courtesy of Hornady

Previous page: A more modern interpretation of the cartridge ad, this Federal pitch is from 1996.

could certainly back up that brag for 65 years after its 1935 introduction—a remarkable run. Like the 22-250, the 220 Swift (which uses 0.224-in.-diameter bullets) was based on the 250-3000 Savage parent case, and Grosvenor Wotkyns is credited with its development. However, the current version is based on a necked-down 6mm Lee Navy, a semi-rimmed cartridge dating from 1895 that, when topped with a 48gr .22-caliber bullet, would develop a MZ above 4100 fps. Currently, Norma sells the 220 Swift with a 50gr bullet at 4110 fps.

The **224 Weatherby Magnum** squeaks into the 4K group based on its ability to generate the requisite speed with a handload. The Sierra reloading manual lists a 40gr hollowpoint in the case running 4100 fps with a sufficient

Federal Premium 22-250 Rem. P22250D 43gr Speer TNT Green

Range, Yards	Muzzle	100	200	300	400	500
Velocities (fps)	4000	3252	2618	2065	1590	1224
Energy (ft-lbs)	1528	1010	654	407	241	143
Trajectory (in.)		0.9	0	-6.1	-20.8	-50.5

Hornady 22-250 Rem 40gr V-MAX

Range, Yards	Muzzle	100	200	300	400	500
Velocities (fps)	4150	3553	3032	2568	2148	1771
Energy (ft-lbs)	1529	1121	816	585	410	278
Trajectory (in.)		0.8	0	-4.5	-14.2	-31.7

Federal Premium P220B 220 Swift 40gr Nosler Ballistic Tip

Range, Yards	Muzzle	100	200	300	400	500
Velocities (fps)	4250	3694	3204	2766	2367	2003
Energy (ft-lbs)	1604	1212	912	679	498	356
Trajectory (in.)		0.5	0	-3.9	-12.4	-27.3

Hornady 220 Swift 50gr V-MAX Moly

Range, Yards	Muzzle	100	200	300	400	500
Velocities (fps)	3850	3384	2965	2583	2232	1910
Energy (ft-lbs)	1645	1271	976	741	553	405
Trajectory (in.)		0.8	0	-4.80	-14.8	-31.8

Winchester Super-X 220 Swift X220S 50gr PSP

Range, Yards	Muzzle	100	200	300	400	500
Velocities (fps)	3870	3310	2816	2373	1972	1616
Energy (ft-lbs)	1663	1226	881	625	432	290
Trajectory (in.)		0.8	0	-5.2	-16.7	-37.1

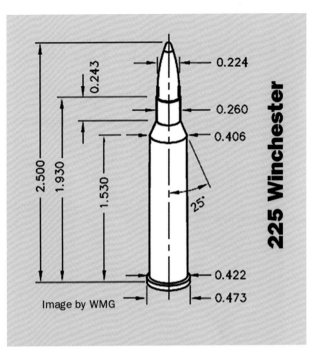

The 225 Winchester's forbear is the 219 Wasp, which, when lengthened, allowed the 225 to produce 22-250 velocities.

Weatherby 224 W'by Magnum 55gr SP

Range, Yards	Muzzle	100	200	300	400	500
Velocities (fps)	3650	3192	2780	2403	2056	1741
Energy (ft-lbs)	1627	1244	944	705	516	370
Trajectory (in.)		2.80	3.70	0	-9.8	-27.9

Winchester Super-X 225 Winchester X2251 55gr PSP

Range, Yards	Muzzle	100	200	300	400	500
Velocities (fps)	3570	3066	2616	2207	1838	1514
Energy (ft-lbs)	1556	1148	835	595	412	280
Trajectory (in.)		1.1	0	-6.2	-19.7	-43.6

charge of IMR 4198. It hails from Roy Weatherby's 1940s-era 220 Rocket, an improved version of the 220 Swift. Usually, 224 WM rifles shoot best with bullets 55 grains and up in weight. Currently, no other company chambers a rifle in this caliber.

The 224 Weatherby Magnum is almost a ballistic twin of the ***225 Winchester,*** which like the 224, makes the 4K cutoff only with handloads, and then, just barely. The Hodgdon manual has one 225 Winchester load making 4020 fps with a 40gr Speer bullet. Though the

225 Win is still factory-loaded by Winchester, it was eclipsed early on by the 22-250. Despite its wildcat status in June 1964, the 22-250 was introduced as a replacement for the 220 Swift, killing the 225 Win as well. ●

8: Nearly Twins

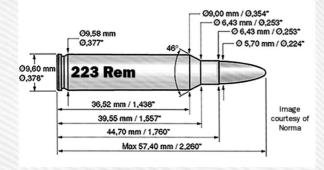

Image courtesy of Norma

The 5.56mm NATO and 223 Remington cartridges and chamberings are similar but not identical. Military cases are generally made from thicker brass than commercial cases; this reduces the powder capacity, and the NATO specification allows a higher chamber pressure. The 5.56mm NATO chambering, known as a NATO or mil-spec chamber, has a longer leade, which is the distance between the mouth of the cartridge and the point at which the rifling engages the bullet. The 223 Remington chambering has a shorter leade, and it is only required to be proof tested to the lower SAAMI chamber pressure. Dimension illustration courtesy of Norma; cartridge illustration courtesy of Hornady. Box image (circa 1975) courtesy of Federal Cartridge Co.

New AR-15 shooters—and there are hundreds of thousands of them in the last five years—face a bewildering set of choices when they consider buying a new rifle.

One of the first questions is about chambering. What's the difference between **223 Remington** and **5.56 NATO**, and can the rounds be shot interchangeably?

The confusion is understandable. The author recently shot three AR-15 rifles head to head, and their chambering designations illustrate how the 223 and 5.56mm NATO rounds coexist in the market.

The guns were a High Standard HSA-15 Flat-Top Carbine No. HSTX6551, and it carried the dual-caliber designation of 5.56 NATO/223 Rem It is a direct-impingement unit like the Stag Arms Model 2T, which had only the 5.56x45mm NATO chamber. Ruger's new SR-556FB gas-piston gun was chamber-marked

SELECTED LOADS & BALLISTICS

Federal Premium 223 Rem P223P 40gr Nosler Ballistic Tip

Range, Yards	Muzzle	100	200	300	400	500
Velocities (fps)	3700	3210	2770	2370	2010	1680
Energy (ft-lbs)	1215	915	680	500	360	250
Trajectory (in.)		0.9	0	-5.5	-17.3	-38.1

Federal Premium 223 Rem P223R 43gr Speer TNT Green

Range, Yards	Muzzle	100	200	300	400	500
Velocities (fps)	3600	2920	2330	1810	1390	1100
Energy (ft-lbs)	1235	810	515	315	185	115
Trajectory (in.)		1.3	0	-7.9	-27.1	-65.9

Federal 223 Rem P223Q 55gr Barnes Triple-Shock X-Bullet

Range, Yards	Muzzle	100	200	300	400	500
Velocities (fps)	3200	2750	2350	1980	1650	1360
Energy (ft-lbs)	1250	925	670	475	330	225
Trajectory (in.)	1.6	0	–8.0	–25.1	–55.5	

Federal 223 Rem GM223M 77gr Sierra MatchKing BTHP

Range, Yards	Muzzle	100	200	300	400	500
Velocities (fps)	2720	2480	2260	2040	1840	1650
Energy (ft-lbs)	1265	1055	870	710	580	465
Trajectory (in.)	1.7	-8.1	-24.1	-51.0		

Federal 223 Rem Power-Shok 223L 64gr Soft Point

Range, Yards	Muzzle	100	200	300	400	500
Velocities (fps)	3050	2680	2340	2030	1740	1490
Energy (ft-lbs)	1320	1020	780	585	430	315
Trajectory (in.)		1.7	0	-8.1	-24.7	-53.2

Federal American Eagle 223 Rem AEBP223G 50gr JHP

Range, Yards	Muzzle	100	200	300	400	500
Velocities (fps)	3325	2840	2400	2010	1650	1360
Energy (ft-lbs)	1225	895	640	445	305	205
Trajectory (in.)		1.4	0	-7.5	-24.0	-53.7

Fiocchi 223 Rem 223SFNT 45gr Frangible Sinterfire

Range, Yards	Muzzle	100	200	300	400	500
Velocities (fps)	3300	2630	2050	1556	1189	991
Energy (ft-lbs)	1087	691	419	242	141	98
Trajectory (in.)		0	-5.74	-18.77		

Hornady 223 Rem 40gr V-MAX

Range, Yards	Muzzle	100	200	300	400	500
Velocities (fps)	3800	3249	2762	2324	1928	1578
Energy (ft-lbs)	1282	937	677	479	330	221
Trajectory (in.)		0.9	0	-5.50	-17.6	-39.1

SELECTED LOADS & BALLISTICS

Remington 223 Rem R223R6 62gr Hollow Point Match

Range, Yards	Muzzle	100	200	300	400	500
Velocities (fps)	3025	2572	2162	1792	1471	1217
Energy (ft.-lbs.)	1260	911	643	442	298	204
Trajectory (in.)		1.9	0	-9.4	-29.9	-66.4

Remington 223 Rem RM223R1 69gr MatchKing BTHP

Range, Yards	Muzzle	100	200	300	400	500
Velocities (fps)	3000	2720	2457	2209	1975	1758
Energy (ft.-lbs.)	1379	1133	925	747	598	473
Trajectory (in.)		1.6	0	-7.4	-21.9	-45.4

Remington 223 Rem RM223R3 77gr MatchKing BTHP

Range, Yards	Muzzle	100	200	300	400	500
Velocities (fps)	2788	2539	2303	2081	1871	1675
Energy (ft.-lbs.)	1329	1102	907	740	598	480
Trajectory (in.)		2.0	0	-8.5	-25.1	-51.7

Winchester 223 Rem X223R 55gr Pointed Soft Point

Range, Yards	Muzzle	100	200	300	400	500
Velocities (fps)	3240	2747	2304	1905	1554	1270
Energy (ft.-lbs.)	1282	921	648	443	295	197
Trajectory (in.)		1.9	0	-8.5	-26.7	-59.6

Winchester 223 Rem S223LRF 35gr Ballistic Silvertip

Range, Yards	Muzzle	100	200	300	400	500
Velocities (fps)	3800	3251	2766	2330	1935	1586
Energy (ft.-lbs.)	1110	813	588	417	287	193
Trajectory (in.)		0.9	0	-5.5	-17.5	-38.9

Winchester 223 Rem USA2232 45gr Jacketed Hollow Point

Range, Yards	Muzzle	100	200	300	400	500
Velocities (fps)	3600	3033	2533	2085	1687	1356
Energy (ft.-lbs.)	1295	919	641	434	284	184
Trajectory (in.)		1.2	0	-6.7	-21.4	-48.7

5.56x45mm NATO-223 Rem.

Along with the gas-system decision, the prospective AR-buyer must also choose a chamber dimension that makes the most sense. If you want to shoot cheaper, easily procured ammunition that will function in nearly any AR, then choose rifles with 5.56mm NATO chambers. Here's why:

The 223 Remington is the most widely-used centerfire rifle cartridge in the developed world. In its 5.56x45mm military form, it is the primary issue ammunition for the U.S. Military and NATO forces. The 223 Remington began as the 222 Remington in the 1950s. When the US military was looking for a new high-speed small-caliber round to replace the 308

SELECTED LOADS & BALLISTICS

Lapua 223 Rem 4315040 55gr FMJ

Range, Yards	Muzzle	100	200	300	400	500
Velocities (fps)	3130	2747	2395	2070		
Energy (ft.-lbs.)	1196	922	701	523		
Trajectory (in.)		4	5	0		-55

RWS 223 Rem CM223 42gr Copper-Matrix NTF

Range, Yards	Muzzle	100	200	300	400	500
Velocities (fps)	3270	2938				
Energy (ft.-lbs.)	1069	863				

Silver State Armory 223 Rem 70gr Barnes TSX BT

Range, Yards	Muzzle	100	200	300	400	500
Velocities (fps)	2750					
Energy (ft.-lbs.)	1176					
Trajectory (in.)		2.9	0	-10		

Cor-Bon 223 Rem MPG22355-20 55gr Lead Free

Range, Yards	Muzzle	100	200	300	400	500
Velocities (fps)	3300					
Energy (ft.-lbs.)	1330					

Extreme Shock 223 Rem 22362FHVL20 62gr FHVL

Range, Yards	Muzzle	100	200	300	400	500
Velocities (fps)	3024					
Energy (ft.-lbs.)	975					

PRVI Partizan 223 Rem FMJ Boattail 62gr A-419

Range, Yards	Muzzle	100	200	300	400	500
Velocities (fps)	3051					
Energy (ft.-lbs.)	1276					

Brown Bear 223 Rem AR223HP 62gr HP (lacquered steel case)

Range, Yards	Muzzle	100	200	300	400	500
Velocities (fps)	3050					

SELECTED LOADS & BALLISTICS

Hornady 223 Rem 53gr HP with Cannelure

Range, Yards	Muzzle	100	200	300	400	500
Velocities (fps)	3330	2873	2460	2083	1742	1446
Energy (ft-lbs)	1305	971	712	510	357	246
Trajectory (in.)		1.4	0	-7.2	-22.5	-49.4

Hornady 223 Rem 55gr TAP FPD

Range, Yards	Muzzle	100	200	300	400	500
Velocities (fps)	3240	2854	2500	2172	1871	1598
Energy (ft-lbs)	1282	995	763	576	427	312
Trajectory (in.)		1.4	0	-7.0	-21.4	-45.9

Hornady 223 Rem 60gr TAP FPD

Range, Yards	Muzzle	100	200	300	400	500
Velocities (fps)	3115	2754	2420	2110	1824	1567
Energy (ft-lbs)	1293	1010	780	593	443	327
Trajectory (in.)		1.6	0	-7.5	-22.9	-48.9

Hornady 223 Rem 75gr BTHP Superformance Match

Range, Yards	Muzzle	100	200	300	400	500
Velocities (fps)	2930	2694	2470	2257	2055	1863
Energy (ft-lbs)	1429	1209	1016	848	703	578
Trajectory (in.)		1.2	0	-6.9	-20.7	-42.7

Nosler 223 Rem 60001 40gr BT

Range, Yards	Muzzle	100	200	300	400	500
Velocities (fps)	3700	3215	2784	2390	2030	1698
Energy (ft-lbs)	1216	918	688	507	366	256
Trajectory (in.)		0	-1.9	-8.3	-21.0	-41.0

PMC 223 Rem 64gr Pointed Soft Point

Range, Yards	Muzzle	100	200	300	400	500
Velocities (fps)	2775	2511	2261	2026	1806	
Energy (ft-lbs)	1094	896	726	583	464	
Trajectory (in.)		2.0	0	-8.8	-26.17	

Remington 223 Rem L223R8 50gr UMC Jacketed Hollow Point

Range, Yards	Muzzle	100	200	300	400	500
Velocities (fps)	3425	2899	2430	2007	1633	1324
Energy (ft-lbs)	1302	933	655	447	296	195
Trajectory (in.)		1.3	0	-7.3	-23.4	-52.7

Remington 223 Rem L223R3 55gr UMC Metal Case

Range, Yards	Muzzle	100	200	300	400	500
Velocities (fps)	3240	2759	2326	1933	1587	1301
Energy (ft-lbs)	1282	929	660	456	307	207
Trajectory (in.)		1.5	0	-8.1	-25.5	-57.0

Remington 223 Rem R223R1 55gr Pointed Soft Point

Range, Yards	Muzzle	100	200	300	400	500
Velocities (fps)	3240	2747	2304	1905	1554	1270
Energy (ft-lbs)	1282	921	648	443	295	197
Trajectory (in.)		1.6	0	-8.2	-26.2	-58.6

Winchester, Remington started with the 222 Remington, lengthening the case enough to boost powder capacity by about 20%. This occurred in 1958, and the round was dubbed the 222 Remington Magnum.

The cartridge was not accepted by the military, but it was introduced commercially. In 1964, the 5.56x45mm, also based on a stretched 222 Rem case (and very similar to the 222 Rem Magnum), was adopted along with the new M-16 rifle. As with the 222 Rem Magnum, the new military case achieved enhanced velocity by increasing case capacity with a longer body section and shorter neck. This military modification of the 222 Rem was originally called the 222 Special but was later renamed the 223 Remington. In military metric nomenclature, the round was called the 5.56x45mm.

It is loaded with a 0.224-inch-diameter jacketed bullet, with weights ranging from 40 to 90 grains, though the most common loading is 55 grains. The 5.56mm chamber specification has also changed over time since its adoption, as the current military loading (NATO SS-109 or US M855) uses longer, heavier bullets than the original loading did. This has resulted in a lengthening of the throat in the 5.56mm chamber.

Problems: Using 5.56mm NATO mil-spec cartridges (such as the M855) in a 223 Rem-chambered rifle can lead to excessive wear and stress on the rifle and may even be unsafe, and SAAMI (Sporting Arms and Ammunition Manufacturers' Institute) recommends against the practice. In our testing over the years, we've found that using commercial 223 Rem cartridges in 5.56mm NATO-chambered rifles work reliably, and we've not seen accuracy problems we can attribute to firing the shorter-leade 223 Rem in longer-leade 5.56mm-chambered guns. So, it makes sense to buy ARs chambered for 5.56mm rounds, which can shoot both 223 Rem and NATO ammo safely, and not to buy 223-caliber-chamber guns for general use (target shooting is a different matter), because they can't always shoot 5.56mm ammo safely.

Both versions are widely loaded commercially, both domestically and in foreign plants. Monarch brand ammunition, for instance, sold at Academy sporting-goods stores, is loaded by JSC Barnaul Machine-Tool Plant in Barnaul, Russia. The 223-stamped FMJ ammo with a Cyrillic-character headstamp has lacquered steel cases and non-corrosive Berdan primers. The website is www.ab.ru/~stanok.

Silver State Armory (SSA) sells 5.56mm ammo online at www.ssarmory.com. Samples we've shot recently have brass headstamped "R P" for Remington Peters, and per round it cost 55 cents. Of course, all the majors load several bullet weights and styles, and the cartridge is so popular that bulk packs, such as Federal's 100-round box, sells at Wal-Mart for $39.97/100, or 40 cents a round. It's the same round as the company's 223B load (www.federalpremium.com), with a full-metal-jacket boattail bullet. More loads are contained in the table adjacent. ●

9: The Sweet 6mms

One of the most flexible and shootable categories of rifles are the 6mm metric designations (244 caliber). What's puzzling about this metric category is how some very sweet cartridges, perhaps even superior ones for certain uses, just manage to hang on commercially despite their quality.

To start examining the overlooked 6mm metrics, we can travel back to 1955, when Remington engineers were developing the 244 Remington as a high-performance cartridge. When they necked down the parent 257 Roberts case, the round shot best with 75gr to 90gr bullets for deer in barrels with a rifling pitch rate of 1:12. Two problems arose: Deer hunters wanted to shoot 100gr bullets, not 90s, and the similar 243 Win would do that. Also, that the 243 was available in Winchester's sweet Model 70 Featherweight, whereas the 244 was offered in Remington's less comely Model 722, might have played a role.

Three years later, Remington started rifling its 244-caliber barrels with a 1:9 twist, which will stabilize 100gr and 105gr spitzer bullets. But the 244 Remington's brand was already damaged, so in 1963, Remington changed the 244's name to **6mm Remington.**

Get ready to be confused: The 243 Winchester was called the 6mm Winchester during its development, but when it was introduced in 1955, the company blessedly changed the name to the 243 Winchester. Having a 6mm Win and a 6mm Rem would have caused untold grief in the shooting market. The 243 is an offspring of the 308 Winchester case, and like its parent, the 243 has a reputation for excellent accuracy. As a result of its accuracy and easy-shooting nature, the 243 is chambered in more rifle models than any other cartridge, except the 30-06 Springfield. For small-game hunting, 70gr to

85gr 243 Win bullets are good choices, and for deer, 90gr to 100gr get the job done.

Another 6mm that's overlooked, except in the niche that birthed it, is the **6mm PPC** or **6PPC,** an acronymic formation of the names of its developers, Louis Palmisano and Ferris Pindell (Palmisano-Pindell-Cartridge). As a general cartridge, the stubby 6PPC has a 1.503-in.-long case only and a shoulder angle of 30 degrees, which makes it suitable for bolt-action or single-shot rifles. The short sharp-shouldered case doesn't feed well from a magazine.

Why is the 6PPC so accurate? Nobody knows for sure, but the effects of its design elements—a small primer, a small flash hole, nearly straight case body, case-size-to-bore ratio—provide very consistent velocities.

Most 6PPC shooters form their cases from Lapua 220 Russian brass, and both Sako and Norma make factory-formed 6PPC cases. Sako also builds a SAAMI-spec 6PPC round, called the 6PPC USA. In the 6mm PPC case, varmint shooters can use 6mm bullets from 50gr to 90gr, but the 6PPC shoots best with bullets under 80gr in 1:14 and 1:12-twist barrels.

Perhaps the **6mm Norma BR** will someday stop being overlooked, because it is an accurate and mild cartridge for target shooting or varminting. Supposedly, its original develop-

Left and center, the 6mm Rem's and 243 Win's thick-body shape recalls the outlines of its 308 Win parent cartridge. Image courtesy of Hornady.

Previous page: One of the 6mms, the .243 Winchester found its way into several lever-action rifles, a trend which continues today. Browning's BLR, for instance, is chambered in the round, which offers accuracy and soft-recoil characteristics in short actions. The artist for this Winchester advertising artwork called "Dinner Surprise" is unknown. © Winfield Galleries, LLC, St. Louis, Missouri. Used with permission. To view current artwork and pricing, log on to www.WinfieldGalleries.com.

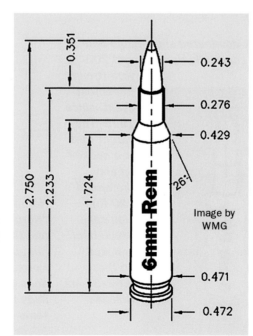

6mm Rem

0.351 · 0.243 · 0.276 · 0.429 · 26° · 2.750 · 2.233 · 1.724 · 0.471 · 0.472

Image by WMG

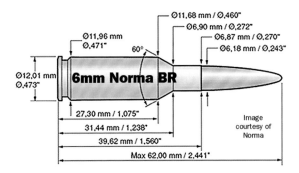

Best twist rates for the 6mm Norma Benchrest range from 1:8 to 1:12. Its accuracy potential is said rank behind only the 6 PPC and 22 PPC up to 200 yards, but the 6mm BR is superior at 300 meters and out. Both Lapua and Norma sell 6mm BR loaded ammunition made for 300m competition.

ment occurred because Americans shooting the Russian-affiliated 6PPC wanted a U.S.-made rival. Norma, together with members of the Swedish 300-meter national team, as the 6 BR, and its role was to supplant both the 243 Win (better accuracy) and the 308 Win (less recoil) for high-volume shooting (120+ rounds in a match). Almost every existing international 300-meter world record today has been set with this little cartridge, and it has been used to shoot 10-shot groups under 4 inches at 1000 yards, and it makes frequent appearances in NRA Match Rifle, NRA/CMP Service Rifle, and Palma matches.

The round, aka *6mm BR, 6BR Norma,* or *6BR*, was based on the original 6mm Remington Benchrest case. It is versatile, shooting bullets from 50gr to 108gr accurately

Below, the 6PPC has dominated short-range benchrest competition, especially the 100- and 200-yard Group Benchrest event, since 1975. The parent case is a necked-up and fireformed 220 Russian case, which itself is based on the 7.62x39mm Russian.

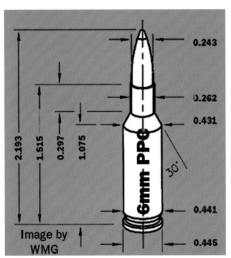

Image by WMG

Federal Premium 6mm Rem
P6D 85gr Barnes Triple-Shock X Bullet

Range, Yards	Muzzle	100	200	300	400	500
Velocities (fps)	3350	3044	275	2490	2238	2000
Energy (ft-lbs)	2118	1749	1436	1171	945	755
Trajectory (in.)		1.1	0	-5.7	-17.0	-35.3

Winchester 243 Win SXP243W 95gr XP3

Range, Yards	Muzzle	100	200	300	400	500
Velocities (fps)	3100	2864	2641	2428	2225	2032
Energy (ft-lbs)	2027	1730	1471	1243	1044	871
Trajectory (in.)		1.4	0	-6.4	-18.7	-38.0

Hornady 243 Win 58gr V-Max Moly

Range, Yards	Muzzle	100	200	300	400	500
Velocities (fps)	3750	3308	2909	2544	2206	1896
Energy (ft-lbs)	1811	1409	1090	833	627	463
Trajectory (in.)		0.8	0	-5.0	-15.4	-33.0

Northwest Custom Projectile 6mm PPC
No. 2797 95gr Barnes Triple Shock

Range, Yards	Muzzle	100	200	300	400	500
Velocities (fps)	2650					

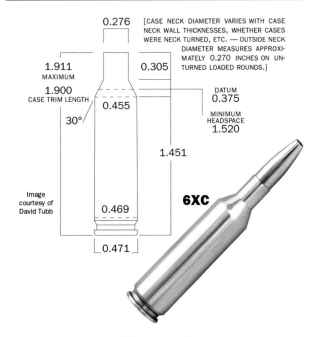

Norma now makes 6XC Brass (headstamped "Norma 6XC") with a large-rifle-sized primer pocket, and the company believes the 6XC may become the next dominant ISU 300 Meter cartridge in Europe. Norma also offers loaded factory ammunition, as does Tubb's Superior Shooting Systems Inc., which uses the 115gr DTAC bullet. Superior Shooting Systems Inc. also sells the Tubb 6XC brass made by Silver State Armory as well as the Norma brass.

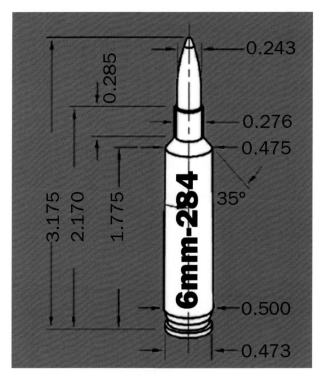

Dimensions on cartridge diagram: 0.285, 0.243, 0.276, 0.475, 0.500, 0.473, 35°, 3.175, 2.170, 1.775 — 6mm-284

Norma 6mm Norma BR 105gr Diamond Line Moly Coated HPBT

Range, Yards	Muzzle	100	200	300	400	500
Velocities (fps)	2789	2608	2435	2267	2110	1959
Energy (ft-lbs)	1813	1585	1380	1199	1037	895
Trajectory (in.)		1.7	0	–7.36	–21.9	–44

Norma 6XC 95gr Nosler BST

Range, Yards	Muzzle	100	200	300	400	500
Velocities (fps)	2953	2704	2469	2245		
Energy (ft-lbs)	1840	1543	1286	1064		
Trajectory (in.)		1.3	0	–6.5		

Conley Precision Cartridge 6mm-284 95gr Nosler Partition

Range, Yards	Muzzle	100	200	300	400	500
Velocities (fps)	3000					

Weatherby 240 Wby. 100gr Nosler Partition

Range, Yards	Muzzle	100	200	300	400	500
Velocities (fps)	3406	3136	2882	2642	2415	2199
Energy (ft-lbs)	2576	2183	1844	1550	1294	1073
Trajectory (in.)	2.8	3.5	0.	-8.4	-22.9	

with better ballistics than a 308, and burning about a third less powder with half the recoil, depending on the load.

The **6XC** has been said to be ultimate competitive round by David Tubb, who has won several Camp Perry across-the-course championships and one Long Range Championship using the 6XC. In particular, he says the 6XC is the best feeding round he has used. Tubb says the "original" 6mmX round with a 20-degree shoulder resulted from chambering a barrel using a 243 Winchester reamer held (stopped) 0.132 inches short of its intended depth. This was done to allow use of a 22-250 parent case, which was manipulated with a sizing die and fire-forming the case in the 6mmX chamber.

The **6mm-284** is similar to the 240 Weatherby Magnum in performance, and compared to the standard 6mm Remington, the 6mm-284 runs 100 to 150 fps faster in any 6mm bullet weight. Due to its sharp shoulder angle, when it is necked down to 6mm, the 284 Winchester case may collapse. (The 284 Winchester was introduced in 1963 by Winchester for use in its Model 88 lever action and Model 100 autoloading rifles.) But this hasn't kept the 6mm-284 from outstripping the popularity of the parent 284 Winchester cartridge, if the sale of reloading dies is any indication. Bullets weighing 70gr to 87gr make the 6mm-284 a deadly varmint cartridge, but bullets up to 105gr are commonly used.

With its big belted case, the **240 Weatherby** is the bully of the 6mms. Weatherby added the round to its Mark V rifle magnum line in 1968, and it closely resembles a 30-06 case with the trademark Weatherby belt and a similar capacity, or with a similar bullet size, the British 240 Apex. As the tables nearby show, it will outrun the 243 by 300 to 400 fps, adding about 100 yards of range to the 243. The 240 W'by Mag needs a long barrel to develop top-end performance, and though it's usually thought of as a varminter, 90gr to 105gr bullets makes it a fine deer and pronghorn cartridge. ●

The 240 Weatherby Magnum has the 30-06's outline and nearly the larger round's powder capacity.

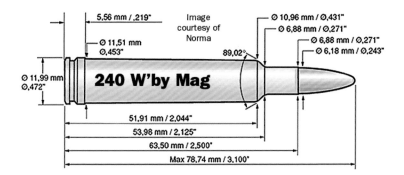

10: The Quarter Bores

Is the 25-35 WCF "The Kind That Gets 'Em?" Could be. It initially appeared in 1895 in the Winchester Model 1894 lever-action rifle. The artist for this Winchester Rifles & Ammunition poster is unknown, but it appeared circa 1904. © Winfield Galleries, LLC, St. Louis, Missouri. Used with permission. To view current artwork and pricing, log on to www.WinfieldGalleries.com.

We kick off the chapter on the quarter-bores—so named for the "25" in their names—with the earliest of the set, the **25-20 Winchester (25 WCF),** one of the few cartridges to survive the transition from black to smokeless powder. It became the first centerfire 25-caliber wildcat way back in 1882. The case was named the 25-20 Single-Shot, but that version of the round was too long to feed through the Model 1892 action. To shorten it by 0.3 inch, Winchester necked down the 32-20 to 25 caliber, making it suitable for chambering in the Model 92, and later the Model 43 bolt gun, Model 65, and Model 53, among others by Marlin, Remington, Sako, and Savage. Its long-standing appeal likely has to do with its mild manners when putting small

game in the larder, and it has probably killed a lot of deer, too, but its 60gr to 75gr flatnose bullets are underpowered for big game. Interestingly, the necked-down 25-20 became the 218 Bee in 1938. It was likely the appearance of the 22 Hornet in 1930 that put the 25-20 on the back shelf.

The **25-35 Winchester** (or in Europe, the **6.5x52Rmm**) has the unusual distinction of making its initial appearance more than 100 years before its reintroduction in a commercial rifle chambering. The 25-35 was introduced in 1895 in the Winchester Model 1894 lever-action rifle, then rechambered in the Model 94 Trails End Hunter variation again in 2005. Unlike the 25-20 covered above, the 25-35 Winchester works well for whitetail deer and

SELECTED LOADS & BALLISTICS

Remington Express 25-20 WCF R25202 86gr Soft Point

Range, Yards	Muzzle	100	200	300	400	500
Velocities (fps)	1460	1194	1030	931	858	797
Energy (ft-lbs)	407	272	203	165	141	121
Trajectory (in.)		0	-22.9	-78.5	-173	-315

Winchester 25-20 Winchester X25202 86gr Soft Point

Range, Yards	Muzzle	100	200	300	400	500
Velocities (fps)	1460	1195	1030	932	859	798
Energy (ft-lbs)	407	273	203	166	141	122
Trajectory (in.)		11.4	0	-44.1		

SELECTED LOADS & BALLISTICS

Winchester 25-35 Winchester X2535 117gr Soft Point

Range, Yards	Muzzle	100	200	300	400	500
Velocities (fps)	2230	1866	1545	1281	1096	984
Energy (ft-lbs)	1292	904	620	426	312	252
Trajectory (in.)		4.3	0	-19.0	-59.4	

Sellier & Bellot 6.5 x 52 R (25-35 Win.) SB33055 117gr SP

Range, Meters	Muzzle	100	200	300	400	500
Velocities (m/s)	673	551	451	369		
Energy (joules)	1721	1153	773	518		
Trajectory (cm)		0	-27.8	-104.4		

The Remington Express and the Winchester Super-X loads are identical 25-20 WCF 86gr soft points developing MV of 1460 fps and ME of 407 ft-lbs. The Ten-X 25-20 WCF puts an 85gr lead round nose flat point out at MV of 1350 fps and energy at 100 yards of 269 ft-lbs. Tenex says the load is safe for use in first-generation guns, and is appropriate for cow-boy action shooting. Photos this chapter courtesy Midway USA.

The Winchester Super-X Ammunition 25-35 WCF 117gr soft point is designed for rapid, controlled expansion. It has a MV of 2230 fps and ME of 1292 ft-lbs. The Sellier & Bellot ammunition is sold as its metric equivalent of 6.5x52mm Rimmed, but that's just 25-35 WCF under a different name. The 117gr soft point is ballistically similar to the Super-X, developing MV of 2208 fps and ME of 1267 ft-lbs. It's made by Companhia Brasileira de Cartuchos (CBC) in Sao Paulo, Brazil, which also manufactures and distributes Magtech and MEN ammunition and components.

antelope, and it compares well with the hotter 25-caliber rounds. For instance, sighted in at 200 yards with a 117gr round nose bullet, the slower 25-35 bullet drops 4.8 inches at 300 yards compared to a spitzer 117gr from a 25-06 dropping 2.8 inches at 300 yards (see accompanying table).

SELECTED LOADS & BALLISTICS

Remington Express 250 Savage R250SV 100gr PSP

Range, Yards	Muzzle	100	200	300	400	500
Velocities (fps)	2820	2504	2210	1936	1684	1461
Energy (ft-lbs)	1765	1392	1084	832	630	474
Trajectory (in.)		2.0	zero	-9.2	-27.7	-58.6

Winchester 250 Savage 100gr Super-X Silvertip

Range, Yards	Muzzle	100	200	300	400	500
Velocities (fps)	2820	2467	2140	1839	1569	1339
Energy (ft-lbs)	1765	1351	1017	751	547	398
Trajectory (in.)		2.4	0	-10.1	-30.5	-65.2

Remington and Winchester's 100gr loads don't make the 250 Savage get to 3000 fps, like the original name of 250-3000 promised. Both develop MV of 2820 fps and have ME of 1765 ft-lbs.

The Bitterroot Valley Ammunition ramps up the bullet weight to 120 grains, which puts the MV at 2400 fps and the ME 1534 ft-lbs. The downrange ballistics aren't bad for a 95-year-old codger, making velocity at 100 yards 2148 fps and velocity at 300 yards 1695 fps. That allows for a maximum point blank range of 201 yards with zero set at 172 yards.

Ponder the **250-3000 Savage's** name for a moment. Is there another cartridge with "3000" in its name, or even anything similar? An example doesn't come to mind. If we were

SELECTED LOADS & BALLISTICS

Federal Premium 257 Roberts +P P257B 120gr Nosler Part.

Range, Yards	Muzzle	100	200	300	400	500
Velocities (fps)	2800	2570	2350	2140	1940	1760
Energy (ft-lbs)	2090	1760	1470	1220	1005	820
Trajectory (in.)		1.9	0	-8.3	-24.0	-49.2

Hornady 257 Roberts +P 81353 117gr SST Superformance

Range, Yards	Muzzle	100	200	300	400	500
Velocities (fps)	2945	2705	2478	2262	2057	1863
Energy (ft-lbs)	2253	1901	1595	1329	1099	902
Trajectory (in.)		1.60	0.00	-7.30	-21.4	-43.8

Remington Express 257 Roberts +P R257 117gr SP Core-Lokt

Range, Yards	Muzzle	100	200	300	400	500
Velocities (fps)	2650	2291	1961	1663	1404	1199
Energy (ft-lbs)	1824	1363	999	718	512	373
Trajectory (in.)		2.6	zero	-11.7	-36.1	-78.2

Winchester 257 Roberts +P X257P3 117gr Power-Point

Range, Yards	Muzzle	100	200	300	400	500
Velocities (fps)	2780	2411	2071	1761	1488	1263
Energy (ft-lbs)	2009	1511	1115	806	576	415
Trajectory (in.)		2.6	0	-10.8	-33	-70

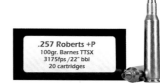

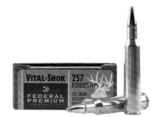

Hornady's Superformance rounds are loaded with proprietary propellants that increase the velocity ratings up to 200 feet per second compared to other popular brands. In this 257 Roberts +P 117gr InterLock Super Shock Tip (SST) bullet, that means muzzle velocity of 2945 fps. Federal Premium Vital-Shok's 257 Roberts +P 120gr Nosler Partition gets out the tube at 2780 fps The Double-Tap Ammunition's 100gr Barnes Tipped Triple-Shock X Bullet has a muzzle velocity of 3175 fps.

SELECTED LOADS & BALLISTICS

Federal Premium 25-06 Rem P2506G 85gr Nosler Ballistic Tip

Range, Yards	Muzzle	100	200	300	400	500
Velocities (fps)	3550	3230	2930	2640	2380	2130
Energy (ft-lbs)	2380	1965	1615	1320	1070	855
Trajectory (in.)		0.9	0	-5.0	-15.0	-31.2

Winchester 25-06 Rem S2506CT 110gr AccuBond CT

Range, Yards	Muzzle	100	200	300	400	500
Velocities (fps)	3100	2870	2651	2442	2243	2053
Energy (ft-lbs)	2347	2011	1716	1456	1228	1029
Trajectory (in.)		1.4	0	-6.3	-18.5	-37.6

Remington 25-06 Rem PRC2506RA 115gr Core-Lokt Ultra

Range, Yards	Muzzle	100	200	300	400	500
Velocities (fps)	3000	2751	2516	2293	2081	1881
Energy (ft-lbs)	2298	1933	1616	1342	1106	903
Trajectory (in.)		1.6	zero	-7.1	-20.7	-42.5

Federal Premium 25-06 Rem P2506E 115gr Nosler Partition

Range, Yards	Muzzle	100	200	300	400	500
Velocities (fps)	3030	2790	2550	2330	2120	1930
Energy (ft-lbs)	2345	1980	1665	1390	1150	945
Trajectory (in.)		1.5	0	-6.8	-20.1	-40.9

Hornady 25-06 Rem 81453 117gr GR SST

Range, Yards	Muzzle	100	200	300	400	500
Velocities (fps)	3110	2861	2626	2403	2191	1989
Energy (ft-lbs)	2512	2127	1792	1500	1246	1028
Trajectory (in.)		1.40	0	-6.4	-18.9	-38.6

The flexible 25-06 Rem handles a range of bullet weights, including Federal Premium V-Shok 85gr Nosler Ballistic Tips. It hurries out the barrel at 3550 fps and builds ME of 2378 ft-lbs. The Black Hills Gold 25-06 Rem ammo shoots 100gr Barnes Triple-Shock X Bullets (hollowpoint flat base 100% copper) at a MV of 3200 fps, producing ME of 2273 ft-lbs. The Winchester Supreme 115gr Ballistic Silvertips have a solid-base boattail design. The Ballistic Silvertip bullet is Lubalox coated. It cranks out 2392 ft-lbs of energy at the muzzle, running 3060 fps. Most makers produce 117- and 120gr 25-06 loads.

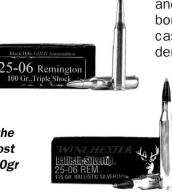

to construct one, it might be the 220-4000 instead of the 220 Swift, or the 243-3500, which is quite a mouthful. Looking at the 250-3000 Savage's nomenclature, then, we can deduce that the "3000" refers to 3000 fps, which these days is a fairly common muzzle velocity. But when the round was introduced in the Model 99 lever action rifle in 1915—1915!— as the brainchild of Charles Newton, it broke the 3000 fps barrier with an 87gr bullet. If you flip back a couple of chapters and review the ballistics of the Winchester and Remington 6mm cartridges, introduced during the 1950s with modern powders, you'll see how well the ballistics for the turn-of-the-century round compare. In current loads, the 250 Savage will push a 100gr bullet to more than 3000 fps, and velocities with 75gr bullets climb above 3400 fps.

Not a lot of individuals without eponymous companies get cartridges named for them, but the **257 Roberts** is one cartridge just named for a guy. N.H. (Ned) Roberts is the namesake wildcatter for whom this cartridge is named, and his idea, based on the 7x57mm Mauser, is basically the parent case sized down with a long neck and mild shoulder angle to accept .257-caliber bullets. The 1920s-era cartridge became popular as a varmint and deer cartridge, and in 1934, Remington made its own version by likewise necking down the 7x57mm case, but retaining the original Mauser case-body taper and shoulder. Even though the Roberts and Remington cartridges had major differences, Big Green kept the wildcat's cachet by calling the new cartridge the 257 Remington-Roberts. For decades ammunition companies loaded the 257 Roberts to low pressures, but current loads can drive 117- or 120gr boattails to 2800 fps, making it suitable for elk and caribou.

For many years, the **25-06 Remington** battled the 257 Roberts among deer hunters and pronghorn hunters who liked the quarter-bores' long-range performance. Looking at the cases, that suggested that the 25-06 was underperforming, since it's just a 30-06 necked down to handle .257-caliber bullets. The 25-06's large case capacity needed a slow-burning propellant like Du Pont IMR-4350, which came out during the early 1940s, or B.E. Hodgdon's H4831 in the late 1940s, which really solidified the round as a long-range wildcat round for 49 years. In 1969 Remington domes-

SELECTED LOADS & BALLISTICS

Weatherby 257 Wby. B25780TTSX 80gr Barnes TTSX

Range, Yards	Muzzle	100	200	300	400	500
Velocities (fps)	3870	3561	3274	3005	2753	2514
Energy (ft-lbs)	2661	2253	1904	1605	1346	1123
Trajectory (in.)		1.9	2.6	0.0	-6.4	-17.4

Weatherby 257 Wby. H257100SP 100gr SP

Range, Yards	Muzzle	100	200	300	400	500
Velocities (fps)	3602	3298	3016	2750	2500	2264
Energy (ft-lbs)	2881	2416	2019	1680	1388	1138
Trajectory (in.)		2.4	3.1	0.0	-7.7	-21.0

Weatherby 257 Wby. N257120PT 120gr Partition

Range, Yards	Muzzle	100	200	300	400	500
Velocities (fps)	3305	3046	2801	2570	2350	2141
Energy (ft-lbs)	2910	2472	2091	1760	1471	1221
Trajectory (in.)		3.0	3.7	0.0	-8.9	-24.3

The Weatherby 257 Weatherby Magnum 115gr Nosler Ballistic Tip shown at right has a ballistic coefficient of 0.453. It's shown full size. The Cor-Bon DPX Hunter 257 Weatherby Magnum 100gr Barnes Tipped Triple-Shock X Bullet Hollow Point gets downrange at 3200 fps. Nosler Custom's 120gr Partition Spitzer is loaded exclusively for Midway USA. The Custom line's brass is cut to the exact SAAMI specifications, chamfered, deburred and the flash holes are checked for proper alignment. Primers are inspected and hand seated. The powder is hand thrown and verified for consistency. Muzzle Velocity: 3135 fps. Weatherby cartridge and box photos courtesy of Weatherby.

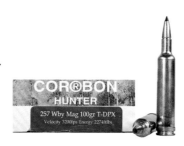

ticated it as a factory load. I have shot a lot of deer with my 25-06, and over the years, I stopped using 100gr spitzer bullets because they didn't shoot well in my gun. Regular old Remington Core-Lokt 120gr bullets were better, but I eventually settled on Winchester 115gr boattail Silvertips as the best balance of trajectory, accuracy, and terminal performance in my deer gun. I remain awfully fond of A.O. Niedner's quarter-bore round, even after 30 years.

Like the 240 Wby Mag in the 6mm class, the **257 Weatherby Magnum** is the top dog among the Quarters. In 1944, Roy Weatherby started with the roomy 300 H&H case to make the 257 W'by Mag, and it is a canyon-crossing hammer on deer, 'bou, and elk. Like the 25-06, it's best in a longer barrel (24 inches is enough for the 25-06, but the 257 needs 26 inches). Like other Weatherby rounds, ammo is expensive—$60 and up for 20 rounds, and in limited distribution. Nosler 120gr Partitions and Remington 120gr Core-Lokts are good game bullets for handloaders on top of H870 and IMR-7828 slow-burning powders. ●

11: The WSSMs

In 2003, with inspiration from high-velocity benchrest cartridges like the 6mm BR and 22 PPC, the **223** and **243 Winchester Super Short Magnums** (WSSM) were introduced. These calibers took the short-magnum concept—which originated with the 300 Winchester Short Magnum—one step further. The impressive speeds of the WSSM are achieved by putting a lightweight bullet on top of a short, fat, high-volume case. This basic concept resulted in muzzle velocities of 4100 fps with the 243 and up to 3850 fps with the 223. Then in 2004, the **25 WSSM** became the latest "short-fat" cartridge to roll off the East Alton, Illinois, assembly lines. (In November 2010, Olin announced it would move the Winchester center-fire production line to Mississippi.)

Oddly, when the observer looks at the ballistics of the WSSM trio, it's hard to call them "magnum" across the board, as least when compared to competing Weatherby Magnums, which are neither Short, nor Winchester. Certainly, two of the three WSSMs better existing "standard" cartridge specs, but they don't make top-of-the-heap "magnum" speeds. So their appeal is that they can be chambered in rifles with shorter actions and, perhaps, shorter barrels that don't need 24-in.-long tubes to maximize powder-burning length. Winchester Ammunition claims the short, fat design improves the interior ballistics of the cartridge

WSSM cartridges are notable for their short, fat cases and their short 2.36-in. overall lengths, which fit in shorter actions. Because of this, a super-short action size was designed for the Browning A-Bolt rifle. Although both cases are of the same 1.67-in. length, the .223 version has a longer neck and a shorter body than the 243 WSSM. All of the Winchester Super Short Magnums have 0.555-in. head diameters. Three loadings are being offered in each caliber (see table next page): For the 223 WSSM, a Supreme 55gr Ballistic Silvertip and Super-X 55gr Power Point are suitable for varminting. The 64gr Power Point would be enough for deer and antelope. Of the three 243 WSSM loads, the Supreme 55gr Ballistic Silvertip is right for varmints. The Supreme 95gr Ballistic Silvertip and a Super-X 100gr Power Point are also good deer loads. The 25 WSSM's introduction was notable not only because of the design, but it was the first quarter-bore introduced since the 257 Roberts in 1934. (Remington adopted the existing wildcat 25-06 back in 1969.) The 25 WSSM equals the ballistics of the 25-06 cartridge but with 14 percent less powder. Though their case shapes are vastly different, Winchester's WSSMs should perhaps offer a hat tip to the 6.5mm Rem Mag, a short magnum that predates them all by many years, and which drives a 120gr bullet to a MV of 3210 fps.

by exposing more propellant surface area to the primer, making ignition more consistent. Also, the beltless case allows headspacing off the PPC-inspired shoulder, which Winchester claims will improve accuracy.

To look further into the WSSM versus Standard Length versus Magnum debate, let's check a few competing cartridges loads from Winchester, Weatherby, and Remington to see how they stack up. Winchester currently offers three loads for the 223 WSSM, two of which are 55gr bullets. The MV for the 223 WSSM

Right: On the left is the 25 WSSM; on the right is the 25-06 Remington, based on the 30-06 Springfield case.

Below: The short fat design of the WSSMs hails from PPC benchrest cartridges. Cartridge photos this page courtesy of Winchester Ammunition.

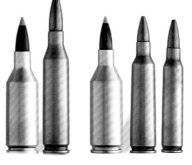

SELECTED LOADS & BALLISTICS

Winchester Super-X 223 WSSM X223WSS 55gr PSP

Range, Yards	Muzzle	100	200	300	400	500
Velocities (fps)	3850	3367	2934	2541	2181	1851
Energy (ft-lbs)	1810	1384	1051	789	581	418
Trajectory (in.)		0.8	0	-4.9	-15.1	-32.8

Winchester Super-X 223 WSSM X223WSS1 64gr Power Point

Range, Yards	Muzzle	100	200	300	400	500
Velocities (fps)	3600	3144	2732	2356	2011	1698
Energy (ft-lbs)	1841	1404	1061	789	574	410
Trajectory (in.)		1	0	-5.7	-17.7	-38.5

Winchester Supreme 223 WSSM SBST223SS 55gr Ballistic Silvertip

Range, Yards	Muzzle	100	200	300	400	500
Velocities (fps)	3850	3438	3064	2721	2402	2105
Energy (ft-lbs)	1810	1444	1147	904	704	541
Trajectory (in.)		0.7	0	-4.4	-13.6	-28.8

Winchester Supreme 243 WSSM SBST243SS 55gr Ballistic Silvertip

Range, Yards	Muzzle	100	200	300	400	500
Velocities (fps)	4060	3628	3237	2880	2550	2243
Energy (ft-lbs)	2013	1607	1280	1013	794	614
Trajectory (in.)		0.6	0	-3.9	-12	-25.5

Winchester Super-X 243 WSSM X243WSS 100gr Power Point

Range, Yards	Muzzle	100	200	300	400	500
Velocities (fps)	3110	2838	2583	2341	2112	1897
Energy (ft-lbs)	2147	1789	1481	1217	991	799
Trajectory (in.)		1.4	0	-6.6	-19.7	-40.5

Winchester Supreme 25 WSSM S25WSSCT 110gr AccuBond CT

Range, Yards	Muzzle	100	200	300	400	500
Velocities (fps)	3100	2870	2651	2442	2243	2053
Energy (ft-lbs)	2347	2011	1716	1456	1228	1029
Trajectory (in.)		1.4	0	-6.3	-18.5	-37.6

Ballistic Tip SBST223SS load is 3850 fps, which compares well against the company's 22-250 Rem 55gr load with a MV of 3680 fps, the 223 Rem 55gr load with a MV of 3240 fps, and even Weatherby's 224 W'by Magnum, whose 55gr Spitzer Point runs 3650 fps at the muzzle. So it's hard to say that the 223 WSSM doesn't bring magnum performance to the party.

Likewise, the 243 WSSM beats out the standard-length cartridge with which it would compete. It delivers a 55gr round at a sizzling 4060 fps MV, besting the company's 243 Win 55gr load at 3910 fps. Likewise, at a heavier 95gr bullet weight, the WSSM develops 3250 fps MV compared to the 3100 fps MV for the 243 Win. But both fall well behind the 95gr 240 Weatherby Magnum Ballistic Tip at 3420 fps MV.

The 25 WSSM matches up well against its primary competitor, the 25-06 Rem, but doesn't exceed the former wildcat's downrange numbers. In fact, Winchester's data shows no difference between the 25 WSSM and the 25-06 at three bullet weights: 85gr, 3470 fps MV; 115gr, 3060 fps MV, 120gr, 2990 fps MV. Clearly, Winchester built the 25 WSSM not to eclipse the 25-06 in its own catalog. The comparable-diameter 257 Wby Mag load with an 87gr (not 85gr) load has a MV of 3825 fps—355 fps faster than either the WSSM or 25-06. Head to head at 115gr, the 257 W'by pushes 3400 fps MV, and at 120gr, it generates 3305 fps MV, upticks of 340 fps and 315 fps, respectively. ●

12: Overlooked 6.5s

6.5 Carcano (6.5x52mm)

6.5 Japanese Arisaka

6.5 Creedmoor

6.5mm Remington Magnum

6.5x54 Mannlicher-Schönauer

6.5x55 Swedish Mauser

260 Remington

6.5x284 Norma

6.5 Grendel

6.5x47 Lapua

264 Winchester Magnum

Introduced by Hornady in 2007, the 6.5 Creedmoor is now chambered by Ruger and DPMS in hunting rifles. Hornady is loading hunting rounds in its Superformance line with both the new 120gr GMX and the venerable 129gr SST bullets.

Many of these midrange cartridges have suffered from a lack of love recently, which is difficult to cipher—their ballistics are usually sound, and in some cases, they are superb.

When it started out, the **6.5 Carcano (6.5x52mm)** was not overlooked in any way. In fact, from 1891 to the end of WWII, it was the official Italian military cartridge used in the bolt-action Mannlicher-Carcano rifle. In the surplus rifle market, these rifles have found surprisingly wide acceptance, considering the limitations of the round. Because it doesn't develop very high pressures, the 6.5 Carcano doesn't match the ballistics of other 6.5mm cartridges, and because the Mannlicher-Carcanos use gaintwist rifling, 140gr-or-higher bullet weights are preferred. For many years, Norma has remained the sole manufacturer of cases and ammunition for the 6.5 Carcano.

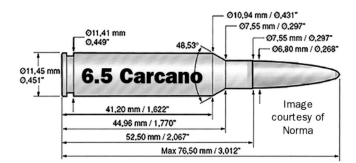

Image courtesy of Norma

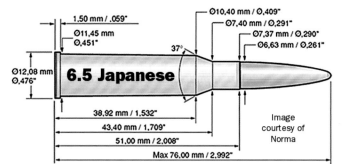

Image courtesy of Norma

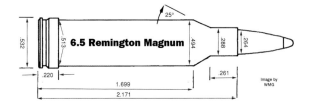

Image by WMG

Another foreign midrange 6mm that's a novelty in this country is the **6.5 Japanese Arisaka**, aka the **6.5x50mm Japanese** or the **6.5x50R.** The 6.5x50mm cartridge was introduced in 1897 and served as a Japanese military cartridge through World War II. The 1897 rifle in which it was originally chambered was unsafe, and it was replaced in 1905 with the Model 38 Arisaka and later by the Model 99 Arisaka, thus the variety of names the cartridge accrued.

The European 6.5x50R designation indicates that this is a (semi) rimmed case. It is also the shortest of the many 6.5mm military chamberings introduced at the turn of the century. The 6.5x50mm military cartridge was loaded with a 139gr bullet at 2500 fps in a 32-in. barrel. Currently, Norma is the sole producer of unprimed cases and loaded 6.5x50mm ammunition.

Hornady rolled out the **6.5 Creedmoor** for Across-the-Course, High Power shooters, 3-gun competitors in 2007. It's smaller than a 260 Rem but larger than the 6.5x47 Lapua, measuring 1.920 inch in length from base to mouth. It has a 30-degree shoulder and minimal body taper. It was the result of collaboration by Dave Emary, Hornady's senior ballistician, and Dennis DeMille, general manager of Creedmoor Sports and two-time NRA National High Power Rifle Champion. The 6.5 Creedmoor was originally built for match rifles such as the Tubb 2000 and DPMS/Panther Arms LR Series, but it's grown out to be a hunting round now as well.

Introduced in 1966, the **6.5mm Remington Magnum** (or **6.5 RemMag** and **6.5 Magnum**) was designed to produce 270 Win performance from Remington's short-action Model 600 carbine. The 6.5mm Rem Mag was formed by necking down the 350 Rem Mag belted case. It uses a standard belted case (0.532 inch rim diameter and 0.513 inch head diameter) with an 2.170-in. case length and a 25-degree shoulder angle. Factory-loaded ammunition for the 6.5mm Mag is available only from Remington, and is loaded with a 120gr Core-Lokt PSP bullet (BC .323) that runs 3210 fps at the muzzle and develops 2745 ft-lbs of energy. From 18.5- and 20-in. barrels, the 6.5 RemMag pushes a 120gr bullet to 2900 fps and a 125gr bullet to 3100 fps, but it will handle 129- to 140gr bullets.

The **6.5x54 Mannlicher-Schönauer** cartridge was a modernization of the original 6.5 Mannlicher cartridge, dating from 1892. The 6.5x54 M-S was actually developed in 1900, and it found wide and fast acceptance. Greece adopted it as a military cartridge in 1903, and English hunters used the 6.5x54 M-S as the 256 Mannlicher for wild sheep and medium-size game all the way up to elephants, as witnessed by the exploits of W. D. M. "Karamojo" Bell. He killed several hundred elephants using 160gr FMJ bullet loads in a 256 Mannlicher rifle. However, the 6.5x54 M-S 160gr roundnose is best used as a medium-size game-getter for anything up to mule deer.

The **6.5x55 Swedish Mauser** is another European-bred metric 6mm that chugs along as a specialty cartridge. Many believe it is the finest medium-capacity 6.5mm cartridge developed during the end of the 19th century. Despite the name, however, Mauser did not develop the 6.5x55; instead, it was the result of a joint Norwegian and Swedish commission to find a suitable military cartridge, and both Scandinavian countries adopted it as such in 1894. More than 115 years later, it's still the most popular hunting cartridges in Norway, Sweden and Finland because of its moderate velocity, long, heavy bullet, and deep penetration. Every year, 6.5x55 rifles firing 156gr bullets on hot charges account for tens of thousands of moose in Norway and Sweden. Smaller animals such as roe fall to the 6.5x55 Swedish Mauser's 140gr bullet, with moderate powder charges to reduce meat damage. The S-M also shoots 100- to 120gr bullets with flat trajectories, emphasizing its all-round suitability.

The **260 Remington's** name is its actual bullet designation rounded down. It shoots 6.5mm (0.264-inch) bullets out of a necked-down 308 Win case, like the 243 Win. However, it began its commercialized life in 1996 as the 6.5-08 A-Square, the company that submitted the first SAAMI-reviewed specifications. Frankly, we like the A-Square name better because it's more descriptive, though just as promotional. However, wildcat versions predated the factory load by 45 years. The 260 Rem has about 5% less usable case capacity than the 6.5x55.

Like the 6x284, the **6.5x284 Norma** is based on the 284 Win case introduced in 1963. Certainly, 6.5 wildcats likely existed as soon as the 284 case came out, because necking down the parent case produces a hunting/varminting cartridge that outclasses the 6.5x55 by about 100 yards for any given application. Also, it's a favorite for 1000-yard target shooting.

Norma standardized the 6.5x284 as a factory round in 2001, a year after marketing the first factory 6.5-284 cases for handloading. Two favorite Norma factory loads come in 120gr Nosler Ballistic Tip or 140gr Nosler Partition bullets. The 120gr round runs at 3117 fps at the muzzle and the 140gr unit slows to 2953 fps at the muzzle.

In 2002, Bill Alexander of Alexander

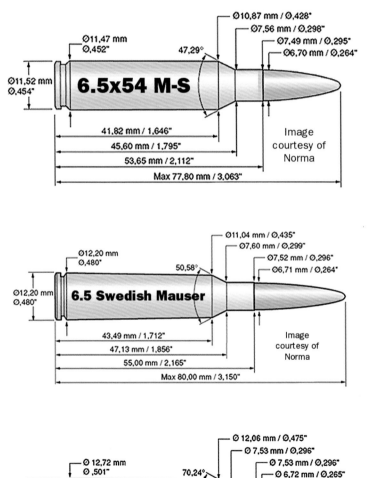

Image courtesy of Norma

Arms and Arne Brennan finished development of the **6.5 Grendel**, an improved version of the PPC cartridge family. The name "6.5 Grendel" is a trademark owned by Alexander Arms. In 1998, Brennan had begun searching for a new competition round for the AR-15 to exceed the

Several companies, including Hornady, offer factory loads for the 6.5 Grendel. This is the 123gr A-Max target round.

In its ballistic literature, Lapua includes velocities and trajectories out to 1000 yards for some bullets. One, the Scenar 123gr boattail, leaves the muzzle at 2790 fps and is still traveling 1553 fps at 800 yards and 1301 fps at 1000 yards.

This Nosler Trophy Grade 260 Rem is topped with a 125gr Partition Bullet. Energies at hunting ranges are impressive: 100 yards, 2090 ft-lbs, 300 yards, 1544 ft-lbs. Trajectories are pretty flat as well, with a MV of 2950 fps, velocity at 100 yards 2744 fps, and velocity at 300 yards, 2359 fps.

SELECTED LOADS & BALLISTICS

Norma 6.5 Carcano 156gr Alaska Roundnose

Range, Yards	Muzzle	100	200	300	400	500
Velocities (fps)	2330	2082	1849	1636		
Energy (ft-lbs)	1881	1501	1185	927		
Trajectory (in.)		2.2	0	-12.5		

Norma 6.5 Japanese 156gr Alaska Roundnose

Range, Yards	Muzzle	100	200	300	400	500
Velocities (fps)	2067	1835	1622	1431		
Energy (ft-lbs)	1480	1167	911	710		
Trajectory (in.)		1.6	0	–17.5		

Remington 6.5mm Rem Mag R65MM2
120gr Core-Lokt Pointed Soft Point

Range, Yards	Muzzle	100	200	300	400	500
Velocities (fps)	3210	2905	2621	2353	2102	1867
Energy (ft-lbs)	2745	2248	1830	1475	1177	929
Trajectory (in.)		2.7	0	-3.5	-15.6	-35.3

Lapua 6.5x55mm Swedish 123gr Scenar

Range, Yards	Muzzle	100	200	300	400	600
Velocities (fps)	2720	2548	2379	2217		1769
Energy (ft-lbs)	2028	1779	1551	1347		858
Trajectory (in.)		5	5	0		-63

Federal 6555B 6.5x55mm Swedish 140gr Soft Point

Range, Yards	Muzzle	100	200	300	400	500
Velocities (fps)	2650	2450	2260	2080	1900	1740
Energy (ft-lbs)	2185	1865	1585	1340	1120	935
Trajectory (in.)		2.2	0	-9.0	-25.9	-52.8

Lapua 6.5x47 Lapua 139gr Scenar No. 4316012

Range, Yards	Muzzle	100	200	300	400	600
Velocities (fps)	2690	2537	2387	2242		1839
Energy (ft-lbs)	2231	1985	1757	1550		1043
Trajectory (in.)		5	5	0		-61

Norma 6.5-284 140gr Nosler Partition

Range, Yards	Muzzle	100	200	300	400	500
Velocities (fps)	2953	2746	2546	2356		
Energy (ft-lbs)	2711	2342	2013	1742		
Trajectory (in.)		0.6	0	-6.0		

Hornady 6.5 Grendel 123gr A-MAX

Range, Yards	Muzzle	100	200	300	400	500
Velocities (fps)	2620	2435	2257	2087	1925	1770
Energy (ft-lbs)	1875	1619	1392	1190	1012	856
Trajectory (in.)		2.2	0	-9	-26	-52.5

Federal Premium P260B 260 Rem 120gr Nosler BT

Range, Yards	Muzzle	100	200	300	400	500
Velocities (fps)	2950	2730	2510	2310	2110	1930
Energy (ft-lbs)	2320	1980	1680	1420	1190	990
Trajectory (in.)		1.6	0	-7.1	-20.8	-42.1

Federal Prem. P260A 260 Rem 140gr Sierra GameKing BTSP

Range, Yards	Muzzle	100	200	300	400	500
Velocities (fps)	2700	2490	2280	2090	1910	1730
Energy (ft-lbs)	2265	1920	1620	1360	1130	935
Trajectory (in.)		2.1	0	-8.8	-25.3	-51.9

Remington 260 Rem RL2601 140gr Core-Lokt PSP

Range, Yards	Muzzle	100	200	300	400	500
Velocities (fps)	2360	2171	1991	1820	1660	1511
Energy (ft-lbs)	1731	1465	1232	1029	856	710
Trajectory (in.)		2.5	0	-11.7	-34.0	-68.9

Remington 264 Win Mag R264W2 140gr Core-Lokt PSP

Range, Yards	Muzzle	100	200	300	400	500
Velocities (fps)	3030	2782	2548	2326	2114	1914
Energy (ft-lbs)	2854	2406	2018	1682	1389	1139
Trajectory (in.)		1.4	0	-6.9	-20.2	-41.3

Winchester 264 Win Mag X2642 140gr Power-Point

Range, Yards	Muzzle	100	200	300	400	500
Velocities (fps)	3030	2782	2548	2326	2114	1914
Energy (ft-lbs)	2854	2406	2018	1682	1389	1139
Trajectory (in.)		1.8	0	-7.2	-20.8	-42.2

Nosler Custom 264 Win Mag 14013 100gr BT

Range, Yards	Muzzle	100	200	300	400	500
Velocities (fps)	3400	3105	2829	2569	2324	2093
Energy (ft-lbs)	2567	2141	1777	1465	1199	972
Trajectory (in.)	0	-2.12	-8.6	-20.3	-38.6	

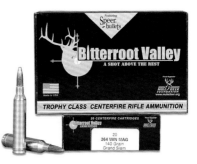

This Bitterroot Valley Ammunition, produced in Montana, uses inspected and resized once-fired brass. This 264 Win Mag load has a 140gr Grand Slam Bullet running 2790 fps at the muzzle.

speeds and high ballistic-coefficient (BC) bullets to conserve speed downrange.

In 2005, Finnish ammunition maker Nammo Lapua developed the **6.5x47 Lapua** in tandem with Swiss rifle manufacturer Grünig & Elmiger to create a serious competition target-shooting round. Accordingly, the 6.5x47's chamber dimensions are optimized for target bullets. The base diameter and overall length of the 6.5x47 Lapua are similar to the 308 Winchester, allowing it to accept the same bolt heads and fit into similar actions and magazines. The 6.5x47 Lapua brass case is also parent for a 6x47 round.

Made to compete with the 257 Weatherby Magnum, the **264 Winchester Magnum** rolled out to big fanfare in 1958, and for good reason. A 140gr spitzer—probably the best all-round bullet choice for the cartridge—can still reach 3100 fps MV in a 26-in. barrel, and its high sectional density helps it retain high energy out to 300 and 400 yards, as the accompany tables show. In a long barrel, it is the effective twin of the 270 Win. Guns with 22- or 24-in. barrels produce disappointing results. It's based on the 458 Win Mag case, introduced two years before the 264. Though the 6.5 Rem Mag was also sold as a factory load at the same time, the 264 Win Mag can be said to be the only "successful" commercial 6.5mm cartridge until the 260 Rem came along. In the field, its reputation as a flat-shooting jet firing 125gr and 129gr bullets made it a favorite of cross-canyon deer hunters. ●

performance of the 308 Winchester. In May 2003, Alexander Arms demonstrated the first prototype 6.5 Grendel weapon, and in January 2004, the new cartridge debuted with Lapua brass. In early 2007, Wolf brand 6.5 Grendel ammunition became available. The case head diameter of the Grendel is the same as that of the parent case the 220 Russian. Like the 6.8 SPC, the Grendel resembles the 280 British. The 6.5 Grendel design uses moderate starting

13: Pretenders to the 270

The *WINCHESTER* Model 54... ...ndard High-Power Bolt Action Sporting R... Calibers... W.C.F. and .30 Gov't 06.

270 Winchester

6.8mm SPC

270 WSM

270 W'by Mag

This bear is confronting the wrong cowboy in this Winchester Repeating Arms & Ammunition poster with artwork by Frank Stick. © Winfield Galleries, LLC, St. Louis, Missouri. Used with permission. To view current artwork and pricing, log on to www.WinfieldGalleries.com.

There are a handful of cartridges which account for the bulk of rounds fired every year. The 22 LR, of course, is the unchallenged leader in the clubhouse. Among centerfires, the 223/5.56mm NATO dominates the landscape. From there, picking the most popular rounds becomes a little more difficult, but the 30-30, 30-06, 308, are in the discussion. And, of course, the **270 Winchester.**

It is a historical oddity that the 270 Winchester—merely a necked-down 30-06 Springfield case that accepts a 0.277-in. bullet—overshadows its parent, especially when the parent is a former military cartridge. The 270 came about in 1925 when Winchester introduced the cartridge with the 0.277-in. bullet, unique among rifle chamberings at the time. What the company couldn't foresee was that the 270 Win would become one of the most popular hunting cartridges in the world, mainly because it offers better long-range performance than most other commercial big-game cartridges.

The basic dimensional data for the round don't suggest anything unusual. The specs for the rimless bottleneck case are a bullet diameter of .277, neck diameter, .310; shoulder diameter, .441; base diameter, .473; rim thickness, .045; case length, 2.540; cartridge length of 3.340, and a large rifle primer, all shot in a 1:10 twist barrel. But through some mojo, this arrangement of metal and powder, combined with a 130gr bullet, is deadly for deer, antelope, mule deer, sheep and practically any other critter in North America. Also, it handles 150- to 160gr bullets for elk, moose, and caribou, and lighter bullets for varmints. Yes, other cartridges shoot bigger bullets at comparable speeds, but the 270's manageable recoil and relatively flat trajectory, combined with its terminal performance, make it a great field gun for many of us, as the late gunwriter Jack O'Connor asserted.

Perhaps more humbling for wildcatters and ammo makers of this century is how good the 86-year-old round still is, and how widely it's chambered, from its introduction in the Winchester Model 54 and later available in the Model 70, and in every other action style out there. That's a high hill to climb for pretenders to the 270's dominance, but they do try.

For example, from 2002 to 2004, the **6.8mm Remington Special Purpose Cartridge** (6.8 SPC or 6.8x43mm) was developed in collaboration with individual members of US SOCOM troops from the 5th Special Forces Group and the U.S. Army Marksmanship Unit. Historically, it's ballistically similar to the 1950s-era 280 British. Based based on the 30 Remington cartridge, the 6.8 SPC was designed

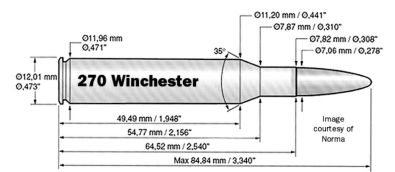

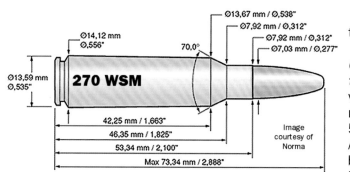

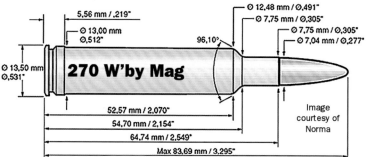

Top to bottom are the 270 Win, 270 WSM, and 270 W'by Magnum. The 270 Win continues to show amazing staying power, even against ballistically better, more modern rounds.

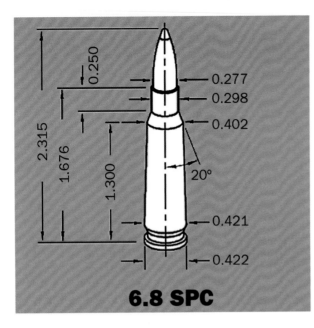

6.8 SPC

Dimensions shown: 0.250, 0.277, 0.298, 0.402, 20°, 0.421, 0.422, 2.315, 1.676, 1.300

The 6.8 SPC Remington, here in Silver State Armory's 110gr Sierra Pro Hunter Soft Point, competes with the 270 Win, 270 WSM, and 270 W'by Mag only in bullet diameter. Compared to the 270 Win, the 6.8 is smaller in areas that really count, such as rim diameter (.417 SPC, .470 270 Win); case length (1.686 SPC, 2.540 270 Win), and cartridge length (.2.260 SPC, 3.280 270 Win). That translates to much less downrange performance, but that's to be expected, since the 6.8 was designed to supply more oomph—but not too much—to battlefield rifles. This 6.8 load gins up 2500 fps MV, which with a 200-yard zero translates to ballistics of +3.5 in. at 100 yards and -12.6 in. at 300 yards.

to address the deficiencies of the terminal performance of the 5.56x45mm cartridge.

Its 6.8mm bullet translates to a .277-caliber projectile, and in its 115gr form, it has a ballistic coefficient of 0.350. Because its overall length is comparable to the 5.56 mm NATO round, it's easy to adapt to AR-15/M16 rifles. The 6.8 SPC delivers 44% greater energy than the 5.56 mm NATO (M4 configuration) at 100 to 300 meters, generating around 1759 ft-lbs of muzzle energy with a 115gr bullet compared to the 5.56x45mm round producing 1325 ft-lbs with a 62gr bullet. Newer chamber specs for the 6.8 SPC allow for higher-pressure ammo.

Hornady 6.8mm SPC 8146 110gr BTHP with Cannelure

Range, Yards	Muzzle	100	200	300	400	500
Velocities (fps)	2550	2313	2088	1877	1680	1500
Energy (ft-lbs)	1588	1306	1065	860	689	550
Trajectory (in.)		2.10	0	-10.1	-30.0	-62.4

Remington 6.8 SPC PRC68R4 Premier 115gr Core-Lokt Ultra

Range, Yards	Muzzle	100	200	300	400	500
Velocities (fps)	2625	2332	2058	1805	1574	1372
Energy (ft-lbs)	1759	1389	1082	832	633	481
Trajectory (in.)		2.5	0	-10.7	-32.2	-67.8

Hornady 270 Win 130gr GMX Superformance

Range, Yards	Muzzle	100	200	300	400	500
Velocities (fps)	3190	2976	2769	2573	2385	2202
Energy (ft-lbs)	2937	2553	2213	1911	1642	1404
Trajectory (in.)		1.2	0	-5.8	-16.8	-33.9

Hornady 270 Win 8085 150gr InterLock SP

Range, Yards	Muzzle	100	200	300	400	500
Velocities (fps)	2840	2642	2452	2270	2095	1929
Energy (ft-lbs)	2686	2324	2002	1716	1462	1239
Trajectory (in.)		1.7	0	-7.5	-21.8	-44.1

Remington Express 270 Win R270W1 100gr Pointed Soft Point

Range, Yards	Muzzle	100	200	300	400	500
Velocities (fps)	3320	2924	2561	2225	1916	1636
Energy (ft-lbs)	2448	1898	1456	1099	815	594
Trajectory (in.)		2.3	2.8	-3.6	-16.2	-38.5

Rem. Prem 270 Win PRA270WA AccuTip 130gr AccuTip BT

Range, Yards	Muzzle	100	200	300	400	500
Velocities (fps)	3060	2845	2639	2442	2254	2076
Energy (ft-lbs)	2702	2335	2009	1721	1467	1243
Trajectory (in.)		1.4	zero	-6.4	-18.6	-37.7

Winchester 270 Win X2705 130gr Power-Point

Range, Yards	Muzzle	100	200	300	400	500
Velocities (fps)	3060	2802	2559	2329	2110	1904
Energy (ft-lbs)	2702	2267	1890	1565	1285	1046
Trajectory (in.)		1.8	0	-7.1	-20.6	-42

Winchester 270 Win SXP270W 150gr XP3

Range, Yards	Muzzle	100	200	300	400	500
Velocities (fps)	2950	2763	2583	2411	2245	2086
Energy (ft-lbs)	2898	2542	2223	1936	1679	1449
Trajectory (in.)		1.5	0	-6.7	-19.5	-39.1

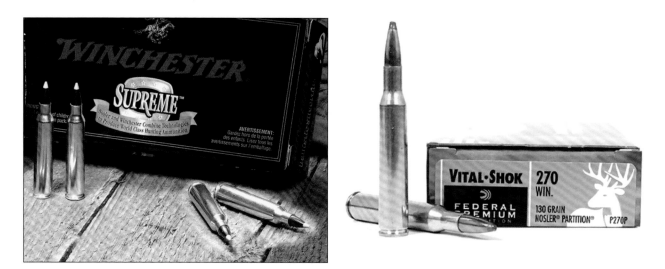

Left: At top are some of Winchester's 270 Win nickel-plated Supreme cases with Ballistic Silvertips, and below them are Federal Vital-Shok 130gr Nosler Partitions. As the accompanying tables show, the 130gr loads conform fairly closely to the Federal's specs: MV: 3060 fps; V@100 yards, 2829 fps, and V@300 yards, 2401 fps. 270 Win 150gr loads spin out at MV 2800 fps, V@100 yards, 2565 fps; V@300 yards: 2130 fps. With 150s, maximum point blank range is 236 yards with zero set at 202 yards.

Left, the red Winchester Power Max Bonded load is a 130gr 270 WSM cartridge that runs 2980 fps @ 100 yards; 2445 fps @ 300 yards, and 1969 fps @ 500 yards. This allows for a 300-yard zero with only 1.2 inches of holdunder @ 200 yards and 6 inches of hold-over at 400 yards. Right: Careful attention to case lengths and bullet concentricity can yield better-than-factory accuracy. These are Winchester cases and bullets for the 270 Win and 270 WSM.

Right: This Weatherby 270 W'hy Mag has a 130gr solid-copper Barnes Triple-Shock X Bullet, perfect for the turbo-charged version of the 270 Winchester. The case body derives from the 300 H&H Magnum, necked down to accept a .277 bullet and gave hunters a flatter shooting, harder hitting 270. Ideal for long range, medium size game. As you can see in the accompanying tables, the 270 Wby Mag has better MV, 3400 fps, than the other 270s, as well as downrange speed 3176 fps @ 100 yards and 2761 fps @ 300 yards. That translates into energies of 3338 ft-lbs at the muzzle, 2912 ft-lbs @ 100 yards, and 2201 ft-lbs @ 300 yards. All photos courtesy of the manufacturers.

Winchester's in-house challenger to the 270 Win is the **270 Winchester Short Magnum** (WSM), introduced in 2002 as a necked-down 300 WSM, which itself debuted in 2001. The short magnums are based on the 404 Jeffery. Surprisingly, the 2.100-in.-long 270 WSM case holds more powder than the 2.540-in.-long 270 Win, mainly due to the thicker case (.538 at the shoulder and .556 at the bottom of the body). This keeps the loaded rounds shorter (2.888 in.) overall, and allows them to chamber in short-action guns. But for most hunters, that alone isn't enough to trade in the long-action 270. Does the 270 WSM outperform the 270 Win? Yes, with more case capacity, 270 WSM beats the 270 Win in velocities by about 8%.

Take a fairly recent introduction of cartridges in 2009, when Winchester made its XP3 bullet (2006) available as a 130gr Supreme load, what O'Connor called the perfect weight bullet for the 270 Win. The 270 Win XP3 cartridge had a muzzle velocity of 3050 fps compared to the 270 WSM's 3275 fps MV. Correspondingly, that 270 Win load developed 2685 ft-lbs of muzzle energy, well behind the WSM's 3096 ft-lbs. Ballistically, as well the 270 Win would drop 6.5 inches at 300 yards (when sighted in at 200 yards), a little more than the 270 WSM XP3's 130gr trajectory of bullet drop of 5.5 inches at 300 yards (200-yard zero).

However, both Winchester loads take a back seat to the booming **270 Weatherby Magnum**, a .277-in.-diameter-bullet round that was the first of Roy Weatherby's line of belted magnum cartridges, circa 1943. The California genius necked down and shortened the 300 H&H case, and then fireformed it to his proprietary chamber. It has a straightish case body, with the shoulder diameter measuring .491 in. and the case base .512 in. The 270 Weatherby outperforms the 270 Win across the board, but with noticeably more recoil, and, of course, substantial expense. A box of Weatherby ammo costs two to three times what a box of 270 Win shells goes for, so we may postulate that the Weatherby's premium price and premium recoil will keep it from successfully storming the walls of goodwill the 1920s-era round has built. ●

SELECTED LOADS & BALLISTICS

Winchester 270 WSM SBST2705 130gr Ballistic Silvertip

Range, Yards	Muzzle	100	200	300	400	500
Velocities (fps)	3275	3041	2820	2609	2408	2215
Energy (ft-lbs)	3096	2669	2295	1964	1673	1416
Trajectory (in.)		1.1	0	-5.5	-16.1	-32.8

Remington Express 270 WSM R270WSM1 130gr Core-Lokt SP

Range, Yards	Muzzle	100	200	300	400	500
Velocities (fps)	3285	2986	2707	2444	2196	1963
Energy (ft-lbs)	3114	2573	2114	1724	1392	1112
Trajectory (in.)		2.1	1.9	-3.2	-14.1	-32.2

Rem. Express 270 WSM PRA270WSMB 150gr AccuTip BT

Range, Yards	Muzzle	100	200	300	400	500
Velocities (fps)	3160	2972	2792	2618	2452	2291
Energy (ft-lbs)	3325	2941	2595	2283	2002	1748
Trajectory (in.)		2.1	1.8	-3.0	-12.8	-28.5

Winchester 270 WSM S270WSMCT 140gr AccuBond CT

Range, Yards	Muzzle	100	200	300	400	500
Velocities (fps)	3200	2989	2789	2579	2413	2236
Energy (ft-lbs)	3184	2779	2418	2097	1810	1555
Trajectory (in.)		1.2	0	-5.7	-16.5	-33.3

Winchester 270 WSM SXP270S 150gr XP3

Range, Yards	Muzzle	100	200	300	400	500
Velocities (fps)	3120	2926	2740	2561	2389	2224
Energy (ft-lbs)	3242	2850	2499	2184	1901	1648
Trajectory (in.)		1.3	0	-5.9	-17.1	-34.5

Weatherby 270 W'by 100gr SP

Range, Yards	Muzzle	100	200	300	400	500
Velocities (fps)	3760	3396	3061	2751	2462	2190
Energy (ft-lbs)	3139	2560	2081	1681	1346	1065
Trajectory (in.)		2.3	3.0	0	-7.6	-21.0

Weatherby 270 W'by 130gr Barnes TSX

Range, Yards	Muzzle	100	200	300	400	500
Velocities (fps)	3400	3176	2963	2761	2567	2382
Energy (ft-lbs)	3338	2912	2536	2201	1903	1638
Trajectory (in.)		2.6	3.3	0	-7.9	-21.0

Weatherby 270 W'by 150gr Partition

Range, Yards	Muzzle	100	200	300	400	500
Velocities (fps)	3245	3029	2823	2627	2439	2259
Energy (ft-lbs)	3507	3055	2655	2298	1981	1699
Trajectory (in.)		3.0	3.7	0	-8.7	-23.2

14: Super 7mms

20 CENTER FIRE CARTRIDGES

FEDERAL

FEDERAL CARTRIDGE CORPORATION, MINNEAPOLIS, MINNESOTA

7m/m MAUSER
175 GRAIN SOFT POINT *HI-SHOK* BULLET

WARNING
KEEP OUT OF THE REACH OF CHILDREN

The 7mm Mauser, aka 7x57 Mauser, is 119 years old, being introduced in 1892 for the Mauser Model 1892 rifle. The 7x57's use in Mauser rifles led to the 30-06's development by the U.S., which sought a round to compete with the German chambering. Its success as a hunting round arises from a reasonably flat trajectory with moderate recoil. Important safety note: Old military surplus rifles in 7x57mm need to be checked by a gunsmith before firing them, and modern 7x57mm loads generally shouldn't be used in the older rifles.

7x57 Mauser

7x57R Mauser

7-30 Waters

284 Winchester

280 Remington

7x64 Brenneke

7x65R

7mm-08 Remington

7mm WSM

7mm Rem SAUM

7mm Remington Magnum

7mm Weatherby Magnum

7mm RUM

7mm STW

The 7mm cartridges encompass a lot of territory, from the soft-shooting 7-30 Waters up to the 7mm Weatherby Magnum, and everything in between. Only the 30-calibers occupy as much space in the SAAMI dimensional tables because these two midrange calibers can be loaded up and down, necked up and down, and otherwise manipulated to form many other rounds. One reason the Sevens have been so successful are good bullets weighing from 100gr to 180gr, and in many respects they are better ballistically over the larger-diameter 30-calibers. For instance, the Berger 180gr VLD has an almost unmatched 0.684 BC (see the glossary for a full explanation of ballistic coefficient). Overall, to match the BC of many 7mm bullets, 30-caliber bullets of similar profile have to weigh a lot more, which causes more recoil to generate similar trajectories.

The remarkable **7x57 Mauser,** aka **275 Rigby,** is more than 110 years old—119 to be exact. The round was introduced in 1892 for the Mauser Model 1892 rifle, a military pairing adopted by Spain and several South American countries. It was very effective against the British in the Boer War in South Africa and against U.S. troops in the Spanish-American War. In fact, the 7x57's use in Mauser rifles led to the 30-06's development by the U.S. government. And what made it successful as a conflict round also contributes to its success as a hunting round, combining a reasonably flat trajectory with moderate recoil. Still, it's odd that the 7x57mm Mauser continues to be as popular as it is, because it's too long to fit in short actions, and modern long actions handle much more powerful rounds. Important safety note: Old military surplus rifles in 7x57mm need to be checked by a gunsmith before firing them, and modern 7x57mm loads generally shouldn't be used in the older rifles (depending on age and condition). The **7x57R Mauser** is the rimmed version of the 7x57 Mauser, being developed for use in breechbreak combination guns shortly after the rimless 7x57. The 7x57R is less powerful than the rimless Mauser cartridge because easy extraction is important in the rimmed's use in break-open guns.

One of the milder cartridges in this class is the **7-30 Waters,** so named for Ken Waters, at the time technical editor of Handloader and Rifle magazines. In 1977, he took a 30-30

Hornady 7x57mm Mauser 8155 139gr InterLock Boattail Soft Point

Range, Yards	Muzzle	100	200	300	400	500
Velocities (fps)	2680	2455	2241	2038	1846	1667
Energy (ft-lbs)	2216	1860	1550	1282	1052	858
Trajectory (in.)		2.1	0	-9.1	-26.6	-54.3

Norma 7x57R 156gr Oryx

Range, Yards	Muzzle	100	200	300	400	500
Velocities (fps)	2608	2339	2090	1860		
Energy (ft-lbs)	2356	1895	1512	1198		
Trajectory (in.)		2.4	0	-10.3		

Federal 7mm Mauser 7A 175gr Power-Shok Soft Point RN

Range, Yards	Muzzle	100	200	300	400	500
Velocities (fps)	2390	2090	1812	1564	1348	1177
Energy (ft-lbs)	2219	1697	1276	950	706	538
Trajectory (in.)		3.2	0	-14.1	-42.4	-90.4

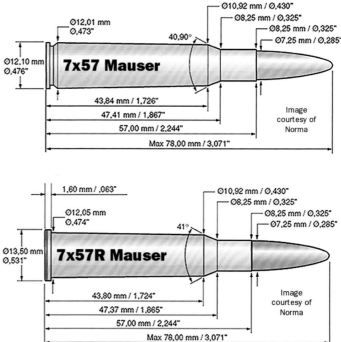

case and necked it down slightly, from an original neck diameter of .328 to a modified neck diameter of .306. The .284-in. 7mm bullet was slightly smaller than the .308-in. diameter of the 30-30. The case lengths were similar (2.03 for the 30-30 for 2.04 for the 7-30), as were the cartridge lengths (2.53 for the 30-30 for 2.550 for the 7-30). As the accompanying ballistic tables show, the 7-30 outdoes the 30-30 downrange, with a Federal Nosler 120gr flat-

Federal Premium 7-30 Waters P730A 120gr Sierra GameKing

Range, Yards	Muzzle	100	200	300	400	500
Velocities (fps)	2700	2297	1929	1603	1329	1128
Energy (ft-lbs)	1942	1405	991	685	471	339
Trajectory (in.)		2.6	0	-12.2	-38.1	-84.5

Federal's Premium Vital-Shok 7-30 Waters load is one of the few available for the round. This has a 120gr Sierra GameKing Soft Point Boat Tail with a muzzle velocity of 2700 fps and muzzle energy of 1942 ft-lbs. Photo courtesy of Midway USA.

Winchester 284 Winchester X2842 150gr Power-Point

Range, Yards	Muzzle	100	200	300	400	500
Velocities (fps)	2860	2609	2371	2145	1933	1734
Energy (ft-lbs)	2724	2266	1872	1533	1244	1001
Trajectory (in.)		1.8	0	-8.0	-23.6	-48.6

Hornady 280 Rem 81586 139gr GMX Superformance

Range, Yards	Muzzle	100	200	300	400	500
Velocities (fps)	3070	2871	2681	2499	2324	2156
Energy (ft-lbs)	2908	2544	2218	1927	1666	1434
Trajectory (in.)		1.0	0	-6.2	-18.0	-36.2

Federal 280 Rem P280TT1 160gr Trophy Bonded Tip

Range, Yards	Muzzle	100	200	300	400	500
Velocities (fps)	2800	2625	2456	2294	2138	1988
Energy (ft-lbs)	2785	2448	2143	1870	1624	1404
Trajectory (in.)		1.8	0	-7.5	-21.8	-43.6

nose bullet shooting at more than 2700 fps, compared to the lightest 30-30 bullet weight, 150gr, traveling 300 fps slower in a Winchester Super-X 150gr Power Max Bonded bullet. Like that, the Waters becomes a higher-pressure round suitable for use in modern Winchester Model 94 and Marlin Model 336 rifles, with substantially improved trajectories. Accordingly, U.S. Repeating Arms began chambering the 7-30 Waters in a Winchester Model 94 (1983), and two years later, 1986 Thompson/Center began chambering Contender barrels for the 7-30 Waters. The 7mm International Rimmed cartridge is similar to the commercial 7-30 Waters except the 7mm-IR's sharper shoulder and less body taper.

Like the Waters, the **284 Winchester** is one of the milder Sevens—and its name wins the truth-in-advertising award for accurate dimensional description. The rebated-rim bottleneck case shoots a .284-in. diameter bullet. Case length is 2.170 in., and the cartridge overall length is 2.750 in. The corresponding diameters are rim (.470 in.), neck (.312 in.), shoulder (.465 in.), and base (.495 in.). Introduced in 1963, the 284 was built to give the hunter 270 Win ballistics in autoloader and lever-action rifles, and compared to the rimless bottleneck 270 Win case,

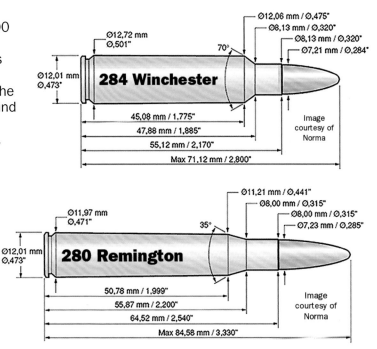

the shorter, fatter 284 does develop comparable velocities. For example, the Cor-Bon DPX Hunter 284 Winchester 140gr Barnes Triple-Shock X bullet has a muzzle velocity of 2900 fps, and a Hornady Custom 270 Win 140gr Spire Point Boat Tail has a muzzle velocity of 2940 fps. All in, the 284's OAL is the same as the 308 Win's, but the brass holds almost as much powder as the 270 Win and 280 Rem.

Speaking of the **280 Remington,** this analog of the 270 Win develops the same or better ballistics than the 270, but its use of high-quality 7mm bullets gives it an edge as a hunting round, many believe. It's also similar to the 7x64 Brenneke. The rimless bottleneck 280 case length is 2.540 in., and the cartridge overall length is 3.330 in. The 7x64mm Brenneke's case length is 2.510 in., and the cartridge overall length is 3.210 in. The important case diameters (280/7.64) are rim (.472/.468 in.), neck (.315/.305 in.), shoulder (.441/.422 in.), and base (.470/463 in.). The 280 Rem was introduced by its parent company in 1957 for the Model 740 autoloader and the next year in the Model 725 bolt action. It was also called the 7mm Rem Express (1979-1981). The 280 is nothing more than a 270 case (itself based on the 30-06) with the shoulder moved forward 0.050 in. and necked up to accommodate 7mm bullets. Fortunately, the slightly longer case

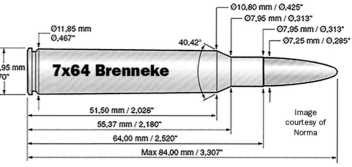
SELECTED LOADS & BALLISTICS

Hornady 7mm-08 Rem 80576 139gr GMX Superformance						
Range, Yards	Muzzle	100	200	300	400	500
Velocities (fps)	2910	2718	2534	2358	2189	2026
Energy (ft-lbs)	2613	2280	1982	1716	1478	1267
Trajectory (in.)		1.6	0	-7.0	-20.3	-40.9

Remington 7mm-08 PRA7M08RB 140gr AccuTip Boat Tail						
Range, Yards	Muzzle	100	200	300	400	500
Velocities (fps)	2860	2670	2489	2314	2146	1986
Energy (ft-lbs)	2542	2216	1925	1664	1432	1225
Trajectory (in.)		1.7	zero	-7.3	-21.1	-42.5

Federal 7mm-08 708CS 150gr Speer Hot-Cor SP						
Range, Yards	Muzzle	100	200	300	400	500
Velocities (fps)	2650	2438	2235	2043	1859	1689
Energy (ft-lbs)	2339	1979	1664	1390	1151	950
Trajectory (in.)		2.2	0	-9.2	-26.5	-54.4

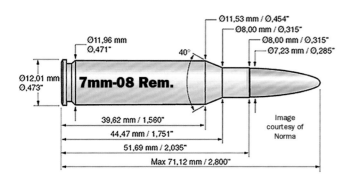

body doesn't allow 280 cartridges to chamber in 270 rifles, but 270 rounds will chamber in 280 rifles, which is just as dangerous.

The *7x64 Brenneke* (1917) is named for Wilhelm Brenneke, a German cartridge designer best known for his shotgun slugs. His cartridge designs were marked by increasing powder capacity, thus power, by increasing case lengths, with the 7x64 being a good example. Brenneke sought to win a military contract by increasing the length of the 8x57 to an 8x64, and he later necked down the 8x64 to accept a 7mm bullet. It predates the similar 280 Rem by almost 40 years, but the 7x64 Brenneke is more versatile, accepting bullets as light as 80gr up to 180gr. With similar bullets, it performs much like the 270 Win. The *7x65R* (1920) is another Brenneke innovation, a rimmed round suitable for use in Central Europe's break-open guns, which needs a rimmed cartridge to provide metal surface for extraction.

The *7mm-08 Remington* was a wildcat created for the metallic silhouette game because it has milder recoil than its parent case, the 308 Winchester, but it still developed enough downrange energy to knock over ram silhouettes at 500 meters. It is a 308 Winchester (7.62x51 NATO) necked down for 7mm bullets, but the 7mm-08's case capacity is less than the 7x57 Mauser's. Naturally, both the 7mm-08 and the 308 are rimless bottlenecks, with the 7mm-08 case length at 2.035 in., and the cartridge overall length is 2.800 in. The 308 Winchester's case length is 2.015 in., and the cartridge overall length is 2.750 in. The important case diameters (7mm-08/308) are rim (.473/.470 in.), neck (.315/.344 in.), shoulder (.454/.454 in.), and base (.470/470 in.). Remington standardized the 7mm-08 as a factory round in 1980, first appearing in the short-action Model 788 and Model 700 rifles.

In some respects, the battle for market share between the **7mm Winchester Short Magnum** and the **7mm Remington Short Action Ultra Magnum** began in 2000 when Winchester brought out the 300 Winchester Short Magnum, a short, fat magnum chambering. The 7mm Winchester Short Magnum and the 7mm Rem Short Action Ultra Magnum were both introduced in 2001 as head-to-head competitors that are shortened conventional rimless shouldered versions of the 404 Jeffery case. Both can drive big bullets at 3000+ fps, as the accompanying ballistic tables show. Currently, the WSM family far outsells Remington's Short Action Ultra Magnums, but is that a performance issue, or a matter of timing? Naturally, both the 7mm WSM and the SAUM are rimless bottlenecks, with the WSM case length at 2.100 in., and the cartridge overall length is 2.860 in. The SAUM case length is 2.035 in., and the cartridge overall length is 2.825 in. In the air, the Remington 7mm SAUM PR7SM1 140gr Core-Lokt Ultra Bonded load (BC, 0.409) cranks out 3175 fps of muzzle velocity, keeping 2086 fps of speed at 500 yards. Corresponding muzzle energies are 3133 and 1353 ft-lbs, and with a 200-yard zero, there's -2.4 in. of drop at 250 yards, -6.0 at 300, -17.7 at 400, and -36.0 at 500. A 140gr Ballistic Silvertip bullet in Winchester's 7mm WSM SBST7MMS load makes 3225 fps of muzzle velocity, keeping 2233 fps of speed at 500 yards. Corresponding muzzle energies are 3233 and 1550 ft-lbs., and with a 200-yard zero, there's -5.6 in. of drop at 300 yards, -16.4 at 400, and -33.1 at 500.

If you handload, Winchester is currently the only choice for commercial 7mm WSM cases, but many shooters use excellent Norma 270 WSM and 300 WSM brass and neck them up or down. Most prefer necking down the 300 WSM brass. The WSM case uses a magnum boltface and a conventional, large rifle primer. All in, the 7mm SAUM holds less powder (73.6

grains versus 81.0 grains) and has a slightly longer neck than the WSM. Norma now makes 300 SAUM brass that can be necked down to 7mm, which may help the SAUM compete with the WSM. Remington and Nosler also sell

SELECTED LOADS & BALLISTICS

Federal 7mm WSM P7WSMTT1 160gr Trophy Bonded Tip

Range, Yards	Muzzle	100	200	300	400	500
Velocities (fps)	3000	2817	2641	2472	2309	2153
Energy (ft-lbs)	3197	2819	2478	2171	1894	1646
Trajectory (in.)		1.5	0	-6.4	-18.5	-37.2

Winchester 7mm WSM X7MMWSM 150gr Power-Point

Range, Yards	Muzzle	100	200	300	400	500
Velocities (fps)	3200	2915	2648	2396	2157	1933
Energy (ft-lbs)	3410	2830	2335	1911	1550	1245
Trajectory (in.)		1.3	0	-6.3	-18.6	-38.5

Winchester 7mm WSM X7MMWSMBP 150gr PMax Bonded

Range, Yards	Muzzle	100	200	300	400	500
Velocities (fps)	3200	2948	2710	2484	2270	2066
Energy (ft-lbs)	3410	2894	2446	2055	1716	1421
Trajectory (in.)		1.3	0	-6	-17.6	-36.1

Remington 7mm SAUM PR7SM4 160gr Premier Core-Lokt

Range, Yards	Muzzle	100	200	300	400	500
Velocities (fps)	2960	2733	2518	2313	2117	1931
Energy (ft-lbs)	3112	2654	2252	1900	1592	1331
Trajectory (in.)		3.1	0	-3.7	-16.2	-36.5

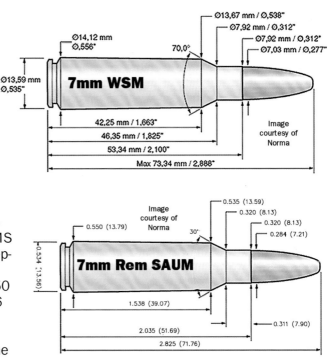

Hornady 7mm Rem Mag 80629 154gr InterBond

Range, Yards	Muzzle	100	200	300	400	500
Velocities (fps)	3035	2854	2680	2512	2351	2196
Energy (ft-lbs)	3149	2784	2455	2158	1890	1648
Trajectory (in.)		1.4	0	-6.2	-18.0	-36.0

Norma 7mm Rem Mag 140gr Nosler BST

Range, Yards	Muzzle	100	200	300	400	500
Velocities (fps)	3150	2933	2723	2520		
Energy (ft-lbs)	3085	2672	2303	1976		
Trajectory (in.)		1.2	0	-5.9		

Federal 7mm Rem Mag P7RT1 175gr TB Bear Claw

Range, Yards	Muzzle	100	200	300	400	500
Velocities (fps)	2750	2530	2320	2121	1931	1753
Energy (ft-lbs)	2938	2487	2092	1747	1448	1193
Trajectory (in.)		2.0	0	-8.5	-24.6	-50.2

SELECTED LOADS & BALLISTICS

Remington 7mm Rem Ultra Mag PR7UM1 140gr Core-Lokt

Range, Yards	Muzzle	100	250	300	400	500
Velocities (fps)	3425	3158	2907	2669	2444	2229
Energy (ft-lbs)	3646	3099	2626	2214	1856	1545
Trajectory (in.)		1.8	0	-2.7	-11.9	-27.0

Remington 7mm Rem Ultra Mag PR7UM5 175gr A-Frame PSP

Range, Yards	Muzzle	100	250	300	400	500
Velocities (fps)	3025	2831	2645	2467	2296	2212
Energy (ft-lbs)	3555	3114	2718	2364	2047	1764
Trajectory (in.)		2.4	zero	-3.4	-14.5	-32.2

Remington 7mm Rem Ultra Mag PRSC7MMB 150gr Scirocco

Range, Yards	Muzzle	100	250	300	400	500
Velocities (fps)	3110	2927	2751	2582	2419	2262
Energy (ft-lbs)	3221	2852	2520	2220	1948	1704
Trajectory (in.)		2.4	zero	-3.4	-14.5	-32.2

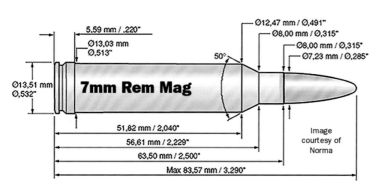

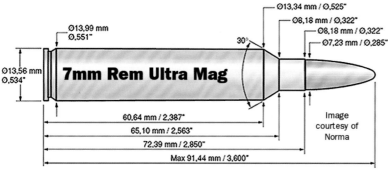

300 SAUM cases that can be necked down to 7mm.

Remington's original Big Seven is chambered in many rifles, and it shoots many bullet weights from a 140gr spitzer up to 160gr loaded to about 3000 fps for elk and moose. Except for neck diameter, the belted bottleneck **7mm Remington Magnum** is almost identical to the 264 Winchester Magnum, introduced in 1958 and predating the 7mm Rem Mag by four years. Case length for both the 264 Win

Mag and 7mm Rem Mag is 2.500 in. and their rim diameters measure .532 in. The neck diameters are .289 in. for the smaller round and .315 in. for the 7mm RM. In fact, the 7mm RM also strongly resembles the 275 H&H Magnum (1912), the latter of which has a neck diameter of .318 in. and cartridge OAL of 3.300 in., and other measurements nearly the same as the 7mm RM. Or, looked at another way, both are 458 Winchester Magnum cases necked down to accept .284-in. bullets. Several people are due some measure of credit for creating and popularizing early variations of the 7mm RM, early wildcat versions of which included the 7mm Mashburn Super Magnum, the 280 Rem Magnum, and the 275 H&H Magnum.

At one time, the **7mm Weatherby Magnum** would have been at or near the top of the 7mm food chain, but it compares poorly with some newer rounds. As noted, the 7mm W'by Mag closely resembles the 275 H&H Magnum, with case lengths of 2.500 in. and 2.550 in., respectively. Dimensionally, their cartridge overall lengths are close as well, 3.300 in. for the 275 and 3.360 in. for the 7 W'by Mag. The other important case parameters (7 W'by Mag/275) are rim diameter (.531/.532 in.),

Remington 7mm STW RS7MSTWA 140gr A-Frame PSP

Range, Yards	Muzzle	100	250	300	400	500
Velocities (fps)	3325	3020	2735	2467	2215	1978
Energy (ft-lbs)	3436	2834	2324	1892	1525	1215
Trajectory (in.)		2.0	zero	-2.9	-12.8	-28.8

Federal 7mm STW P7STWTT1 160gr Trophy Bonded Tip

Range, Yards	Muzzle	100	200	300	400	500
Velocities (fps)	3100	2913	2733	2561	2394	2235
Energy (ft-lbs)	3414	3014	2653	2329	2036	1774
Trajectory (in.)		1.3	0	-6.0	-17.2	-34.6

Norma 7x65R 170gr Vulkan

Range, Yards	Muzzle	100	200	300	400	500
Velocities (fps)	2658	2402	2162	1942		
Energy (ft-lbs)	2665	2177	1767	1425		
Trajectory (in.)		2.2	0	-9.6		

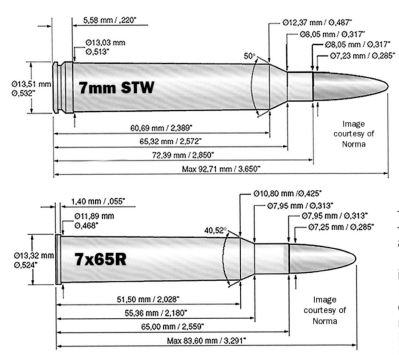

Image courtesy of Norma

RUM and .31 in. longer than the 7mm W'by Mag.

Introduced in 2001, the **7mm Remington Ultra Magnum** is a step up from the plain ol' 7mm Rem Magnum. Compared to the 7mm Rem Magnum, top 7mm Ultra loads deliver 25% more energy at 300 yards, all a result of using a full-length, non-belted case with a head diameter that is somewhat larger than belt diameter of original belted numbers. It has significantly more capacity than any conventional belted magnum. See for yourself in a head-to-head comparison. The 7mm Rem Ultra Magnum PR7UM1 140gr Premier Core-Lokt bullet has a BC of 0.409, and it shoots that pill 3425 fps at the muzzle, then 3158 fps at 100 yards, 2907 fps at 200 yards, 2669 fps at 300 yards, 2444 fps at 400 yards, and 2229 fps at 500 yards. That translates into very flat trajectories, with a 250-yard zero, the shooter will see only -2.7 inches of drop at 300 yards, -11.9 inches of drop at 400 yards, and -27.0 of drop at 500 yards. The same bullet in the 7mm Rem Mag goes 3175 fps at the muzzle, then 2934 fps at 100 yards, 2707 fps at 200 yards, 2490 fps at 300 yards, 2283 fps at 400 yards, and 2086 fps at 500 yards. That translates into very flat trajectories, with a 250-yard zero, the shooter will see only -3.0 inches of drop at 300 yards, -13.0 inches of drop at 400 yards, and -29.0 of drop at 500 yards.

A couple of cartridges introduced in 1997—the **7mm Shooting Times Westerner** and the 30-378 Weatherby and—are among the best long-range big-game rounds ever made in America. Among the 7mms, the Shooting Times Westerner eclipses the performance standards of the 7mm Rem Mag. Writer Layne Simpson created the 7mm Shooting Times Westerner cartridge in 1989 and named it for his employer, *Shooting Times* magazine. The Westerner moniker comes from its expected use as a long-range cartridge, as opposed to the less popular 7mm Shooting Times Easterner based on the 307 Winchester cartridge. The 7mm Shooting Times Westerner uses a parent case of the 8mm Rem Mag, which is necked down to 7mm and its case taper straightened somewhat. Standard factory loads feature a 140gr bul-

neck diameter (.314/.318 in.), shoulder diameter (.492/.375 in.), and base diameter (.511/513 in.). But when you line up the dimensions of the 7 W'by Mag, the 7STW, and the 7RUM, you can see how it falls into the midrange of 7mm performance. Cartridge length favors the 7 Shooting Times Westerner narrowly, with its 3.680 in. length being slightly longer than the RUM's 3.650 and the 7 W'by Mag's 3.360. Case length likewise favors the STW's 2.86 in. OAL, .01 in. more than the

Federal 7mm W'by Mag P7WBTT1 160gr Trophy Bonded Tip

Range, Yards	Muzzle	100	200	300	400	500
Velocities (fps)	3100	2913	2733	2561	2394	2235
Energy (ft-lbs)	3414	3014	2653	2329	2036	1774
Trajectory (in.)		1.3	0	-6.0	-17.2	-34.6

Hornady 7mm W'by Mag 80689 154gr InterBond

Range, Yards	Muzzle	100	200	300	400	500
Velocities (fps)	3200	3012	2832	2659	2492	2331
Energy (ft-lbs)	3501	3101	2741	2416	2123	1858
Trajectory (in.)		1.2	0	-5.5	-15.9	-32.0

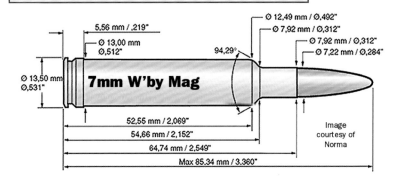

Image courtesy of Norma

let with an muzzle velocity of 3325 fps. With current factory loads, the 7mm Westerner has an 11% energy gain over the 7mm Rem Mag and a 7.1% edge over the 7mm W'by Mag at 400 yards. Using data from Remington's 7mm Rem Mag factory load, we find that the 7mm Rem Mag has a point-blank range (assuming a 6-in. zone) of 306 yards with a 262-yard zero. The 7mm Shooting Times Westerner with the same bullet has a point-blank-range of 322 yards with a 275-yard zero. At the 7mm Rem Mag's limit of point-blank-range, the 7mm STW is only about 1.5 inches low. At 400 yards the 7mm Rem Mag is 13.21 inches below the line of sight and the 7mm Shooting Times Westerner is 10.58 inches.

The 7mm Rem Mag has 2240 ft-lbs of energy at 200 yards, 1878 ft-lbs at 300 yards, 1564 ft-lbs at 400 yards and 1292 ft-lbs at 500 yards. In contrast, the 7mm STW has 2521 ft-lbs of energy at 200 yards, 2123 ft-lbs at 300 yards, 1776 ft-lbs at 400 yards, and 1475 ft-lbs at 500 yards. ●

15: The 308s

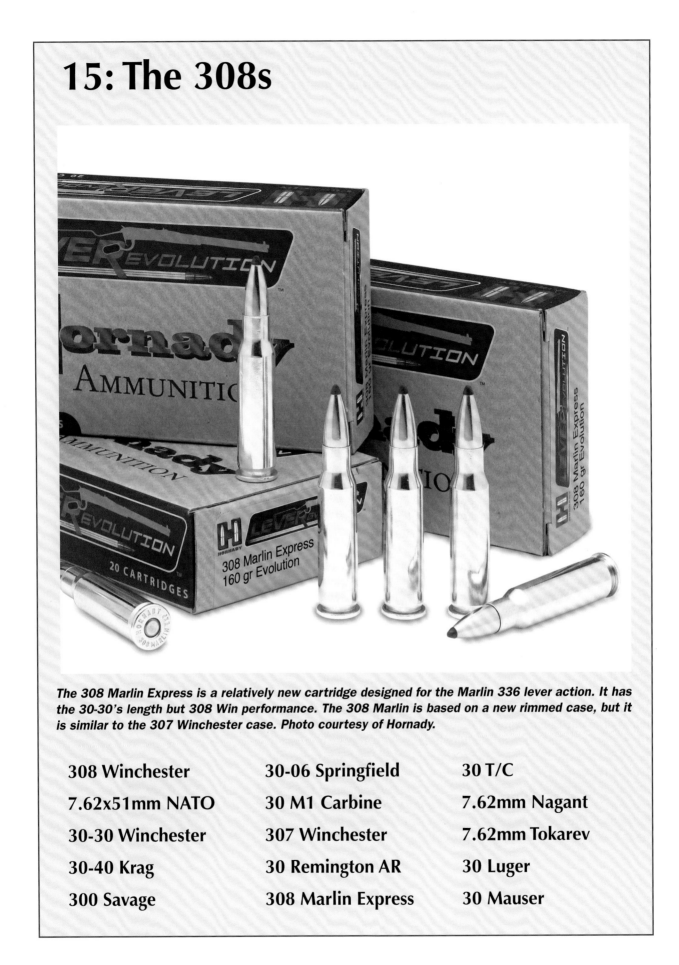

The 308 Marlin Express is a relatively new cartridge designed for the Marlin 336 lever action. It has the 30-30's length but 308 Win performance. The 308 Marlin is based on a new rimmed case, but it is similar to the 307 Winchester case. Photo courtesy of Hornady.

308 Winchester	30-06 Springfield	30 T/C
7.62x51mm NATO	30 M1 Carbine	7.62mm Nagant
30-30 Winchester	307 Winchester	7.62mm Tokarev
30-40 Krag	30 Remington AR	30 Luger
300 Savage	308 Marlin Express	30 Mauser

Like the 7mms, the 308-caliber cartridges have wide-ranging uses and histories. There are other 308s that are called something else—for example, the magnum 300s treated in the next chapter all have .308-in.-diameter bullets—but the standard 308s have amazing backgrounds and include some of the most famous cartridges ever swaged.

To start with the 308s, then, what better place to begin than with the namesake round for the group: the **308 Winchester,** aka **7.62x51mm NATO.** The 7.62x51mm itself was born of the idea to match the performance of the original 30-06 Springfield military loading in a smaller, lighter package, initially called the T-65. The 7.62mm round's adoption as a military cartridge in 1951 springboarded the creation of the 308 Win as the civilian version of the military standard the next year, though the 7.62x51mm NATO and 308 Win are not identical because of tolerances—much like the 5.56mm and the 223 Rem. Accordingly, some commercial rifles will not handle military ammunition. The 308 is an excellent and well-rounded hunting and accuracy cartridge, delivering nearly as much velocity as the 30-06 in short-action guns, and it's a particularly good choice in lever-action guns, where the 30-06's length would hamper the Springfield's utility.

Another good lever choice is the hoary **30-30 Winchester.** The name 30-30 reflects a common black-powder nomenclature wherein cartridges were often designated by caliber, charge and bullet weight, with the second "30" meaning 30 grains of smoke-

Two of the most popular cartridges appear in this chapter, the 308 Win and the 30-06 Springfield. Here are a handful of 308 and 7.62x51mm loads available from some less well known sources. Top right is the Cor-Bon 308 Win with a 168gr Barnes Solid Copper TSX bullet with muzzle velocity (MV) of 2600 fps and muzzle energy (ME) of 2522 ft-lbs. Below that is a 7.62x51mm DAG 147gr FMJBTs in a 200-round battle pack, made by DAG Mfg. of Germany. The brass case is Berdan primed with a cupro-nickel-plated steel jacket with a lead core bullet. The jacket will respond to a magnet. Below that in a plain box is Federal's Sniper Ammo 7.62mm NATO M118, with a 175gr Sierra Matchking hollowpoint boattail and case headstamped F.C 2008 through 2010. This ammo was manufactured in the USA by licensed contractors and is the same spec as the L.C Headstamped ammo. It's designed to shoot 10-in. groups at 1000 meters and has a retained velocity of 1193 fps at that distance. Bottom is the Dynamic Research Technology (DRT) 308 Win 175gr copper-jacketed frangible hollowpoint, and is informally called "Dead Right There." This copper-jacketed ammunition has a compressed powder core which is as fine as talcum powder. When it comes into contact with organic tissue, the hydrostatic shock of the soft material going into the hollow point makes the entire core projectile expand. The bullet will not pass through the target, making it suitable for home defense or close-quarter combat. The bullet has a copper jacket, just like any other lead core bullet. The core is made from compressing two or three metals into a small cylindrical core. This core is placed in the jacket and has a cap placed on top of it to contain the core when the bullet is formed. The bullet opens after about 1.5 inches of penetration. Images courtesy of CheaperThanDirt.com.

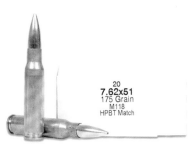

less powder. In Europe, it is known as the 7.62x51R, and it was also called the 30 Winchester Center Fire (WCF) or 30 Winchester at one time. The first small-bore smokeless-powder sporting cartridge, the 30-30 Win has probably killed more deer than any other round. It was first chambered in the Model 1894 lever-action rifle in 1895.

The **30-40 Krag** was the first smokeless cartridge available in sporting rifles, predating the 30-30 Win by at least three years. The Krag was the U.S. government's replacement for the 45-70 Government in 1892. It was chambered in the Krag-Jørgensen repeating bolt-action rifle designed by the Norwegians Ole Herman Johannes Krag and Erik Jørgensen in the late 19th century and adopted as a standard arm by Denmark, the United States of America and Norway. Ole Krag himself was a captain in the

The 30-40 Krag isn't widely loaded, despite its effectiveness for more than 100 years. Here's a BVAC 30-40 Krag load that shoots a 165gr Grand Slam load at MV 2194 fps, velocity at 100 yards, 1994 fps; and velocity at 300 yards, 1630 fps. Maximum Point Blank Range is 187 yards with zero set at 160 yards. Image courtesy of CheaperThanDirt.com.

Norwegian Army and director of Kongsberg Våpenfabrikk, the Norwegian government's weapons factory. Ballistically, the 30-40 Krag and the 300 Savage covered below are nearly identical.

The **300 Savage** was a levergun cartridge that perhaps was ahead of its time. Introduced in 1920 and chambered in the Savage Model 99 levergun, the 300 Savage offered a notable increase in performance over the popular 30-30 Winchester. In fact, it was originally loaded

The 30-30 Win has been said to be the most popular deer load of all time, and most of its current production is concentrated in two bullet weights. Top is the Barnes VOR-TX 150gr Triple-Shock X Bullet Flat Nose, which is the traditional bullet shape suitable for lever guns with tubular magazines, MV 2335 fps. Below that is a 150gr Winchester load with spitzer bullets that are better ballistic choices with lever or other actions that have detachable magazines, MV 2390 fps. Winchester also makes a roundnose Ballistic Tip suitable for tubular or box magazines. Hornady's 30-30 Win LEVERevolution load at bottom improves the 30-30's ballistics, shooting a heavier 160gr FTX at MV 2400 fps. Images courtesy of Midway USA.

The 300 Savage, like the 30-30 and the 30-40 Krag, continues to find a place in the woods. Most versions of this round currently are loaded with 150gr and 180gr bullets, such as the BVAC 150gr 300 Savage Grand Slam load, with a MV of 2534 FPS. A comparable Remington Express 150gr Core-Lokt Soft Point runs 2630 fps at the muzzle and develops 2303 ft-lbs ME. The Federal Power-Shok 300 Savage 180gr Soft Point comes in at 2350 fps MV and 2207 ft-lbs ME. Top image courtesy of Cheaper-ThanDirt.com; bottom images courtesy of Midway USA.

to 30-06 performance levels with a 150gr bullet, with the intent of duplicating the ballistics of the original U.S. Ball Cartridge, caliber .30, Model of 1906. Until the introduction of the 308 Win, the 300 Savage was the only 30-caliber cartridge suitable for use in short-action rifles. Surprisingly, the 300 Savage spurred the birth of the 308 Win cartridge in the 1950s. The modern-looking 300 Savage case has a sharp 30-degree shoulder angle and a short neck to maximize powder capacity. Current factory loads using a 150gr spitzer bullet start at 2630 fps, and with 180gr spitzers, the Savage has a 2350 fps muzzle velocity. Sadly, Savage no longer offers a rifle in 300 Savage.

Like the 30-30 Win, the **30-06 Springfield** (aka 7.62x63mm) continues to be one of the top cartridges in annual sales, and no other standard case has been used as the basis for more factory and wildcat cartridges. It got its start in 1903 (30-03) when the United States introduced what was, at the time, the most powerful military cartridge in the world fitted for a new and modern bolt-action rifle, the famous 1903 Springfield. However, both the Springfield rifle and Springfield cartridge infringed on Mauser patents, which led to the

As with the 308 Win, the 30-06 Springfield can be loaded up and down with ease to accomplish whatever shooting task the operator wishes. Here's Remington's Managed-Recoil 30-06 Springfield, which has a lightweight 125gr Core-Lokt Pointed Soft Point with half the felt recoil of normal ammunition. Accuracy isn't affected—in fact, it may be improved when the shooter isn't flinching. MV 2660 fps, ME 1964 ft-lbs. Photos courtesy of Remington.

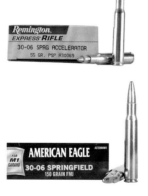

A sampling of the bullet weights and styles for the 30-06 include lighter bullets (top row, left to right), such as Remington's Express 30-06 Springfield Accelerator 55gr Pointed Soft Point, with a MV of 4080 fps; Federal Premium Vital-Shok 110gr Barnes Tipped Triple-Shock X Bullet; and the Golden Bear 145gr FMJ with brass-coated steel cases. In the second row are the Federal American Eagle 30-06 Springfield (M1 Garand) 150gr FMJ, Federal Premium Gold Medal 168gr Sierra MatchKing Hollow Point Boat Tail, and Black Hills Gold 168gr Hornady A-Max. In the third row are two bigger-game hunting bullets, Hornady's Superformance 180gr SST, which is loaded with proprietary propellants that increase velocity up to 200 fps (MV 2820 fps), and the Cor-Bon DPX Hunter 180gr Barnes Triple-Shock X Bullet. Bottom row: Norma's 200gr Oryx bullet and HSM's Trophy Gold 210gr Berger Hunting Very Low Drag (VLD) HPBT. Photos courtesy of Midway USA.

U.S. paying infringement royalties to Mauser. In 1906, the U.S. military recalled the Springfield rifles and modified them to accept a cartridge with a shorter neck, the 30-06. The reasons behind the 30-06's success are its blend of tolerable recoil, accuracy, and ballistics with bullets from 110 to 220 grains.

Yet another military cartridge in this group is the **30 M1 Carbine**, introduced in 1940 in the M1 Carbine. It was a straight-walled 30-caliber cartridge loaded with a 110gr roundnose bullet that had a muzzle velocity of 1975 fps. Its role was to make the WWII GI more deadly with a short, lightweight rifle than with a pistol. In October 1940, the M1 Carbine idea got its start in an Army Ordnance circular that suggested developing a 30-caliber cartridge similar to the "Winchester Self-loading Cartridge, Caliber .32." This led to the production of the "Caliber .30 SL, M1" cartridge directly based on the 32 Self-Loading in February 1941 and, after a design competition, adoption of the Winchester-designed M1 carbine in October 1941.

Though it may not sound like it, the **307 Winchester** does indeed chamber a 308-caliber bullet. The 307 Win is a rimmed version of the 308 Win, and it was made in 1982 for the Winchester Model 94 XTR Angle Eject Carbine. The "307" designation is intended to avoid confusion with the 308 Win, which it did so successfully that it's nearly obsolete. As the accompanying tables show, the 307 is a significant improvement over the 30-30 Win as

Factory loadings for the excellent 307 Winchester are thin. Winchester still makes the load in its Super-X line with a 180gr Power-Point bullet, which runs 2510 fps at the muzzle. Photo courtesy of Midway USA.

a hunting cartridge, but because Marlin didn't build its Model 336 in this chambering, the Model 94 was the only factory rifle ever available in 307 Win, unlike the ubiquitous thutty-thutty.

Though it may seem like the 308s are an exclusively old fraternity, there are some more modern entries in the category. For example, in 2009 Remington brought out the **30 Remington AR**, a short-case cartridge suited for the company's lightweight R-15 AR-style rifle. Remington said the 30 Rem AR (or RAR) cartridge produces ballistics similar to the venerable 308 Win with pressures suitable for the lightweight R-15 platform. Initial loadings were in the Remington Core-Lokt or Premier AccuTip lines in 125gr bullet weights and a UMC metal case practice round loaded with a 123gr bullet. The new cartridge was based on the 450 Bushmaster case, but because the pointed 30-caliber RAR bullet was longer than the blunt-nosed 45-caliber bullet in the 450 Bushmaster, the case was shortened to 1.530 inches from the original case length of 1.700 inches, which keeps its overall cartridge length compatible with the standard AR-15 magazine. The result is a short, fat rebated-rim case that has about the same case capacity as the 30-30 Winchester.

Another recent entry is an addition to the Hornady LEVERevolution ammunition line, the **308 Marlin Express.** This new cartridge was designed for use in the Marlin 336 action with a 30-30 length, and Hornady called the 308 Marlin the most advanced lever-gun cartridge ever, saying it rivals the 308 Win Hornady's LEVERevolution ammo gives lever-action chamberings such as the 30-30, 35 Remington, 444 Marlin, 450 Marlin and 45-70 Government flatter trajectories because of an elastomer tip that increases the ballistic coefficient of the bullet and eliminates the chance of accidental ignition. The 308 Marlin is based on a new rimmed case, but it is similar to the 307 Win case with the shoulder set back .0998

The M1 carbine in 30 Carbine is alive and well with a selection of factory ammos, including the Cor-Bon DPX Hunter with a 100gr Barnes Triple-Shock X Bullet, MV 2025 fps, ME 911 ft lbs, Federal's Power-Shok 110gr Round Nose Soft Point, MV 1990 fps, ME 967 ft-lbs, and the Sellier & Bellot 110gr Full Metal Jacket, MV 2024 fps, ME 1001 ft-lbs. Photos courtesy of Midway USA.

Remington made its 30 Remington AR round to offer 308 Win-class ballistics in the AR-15 form. This is the UMC 30 Remington AR with a 123gr Full Metal Jacket, MV 2800 fps, ME 2141 ft-lbs. Left photo courtesy of Remington. Right photo courtesy of Midway USA.

inch. The 308 Marlin Express cartridge has the same neck and case shoulders as the 307, but on the 308 Marlin, the case is shortened by .115 inch, the shoulders are moved back, and the cartridge case has more taper to aid in extraction. But the LEVERevolution 160gr flex-tip spitzer bullet is the big advance over the 307's flat-tip-bullet loads, with the spitzer's longer ogive and a ballistic coefficient of .400. It develops a MV of 2660 fps and is still clocking along at 1836 fps at 400 yards, and it only drops -23.5 inches at that distance. Marlin and Hornady have discovered that a 1:10 barrel twist with a 160gr bullet shoots slightly flatter and prints tighter groups.

Another 2009 entry is the **30 T/C (or 30 TC),** a short-action (308 length) rimless rifle cartridge that was developed for Thompson/Center's Icon bolt rifle by Hornady. It is similar to the rimmed 308 Marlin Express, except that

rather than being a step behind the 308 Win in performance, the 30 TC with a Hornady-loaded 150gr bullet exceeds the muzzle velocity of the 308 Win. by 180 fps. Amazingly, the 30 TC runs faster than the 308 Win, but the TC has a smaller case capacity—about 20 percent less powder. Hornady ballistics (see accompanying tables) for the 30 TC show that a 150gr SST InterLock bullet exits the muzzle at 3000 fps and retains high velocities and flat trajectories as it reaches 100 yards (2772 fps, -1.5 in.), 200 yards (2555 fps, zero range), and 300 yards (2348 fps, -6.9 in.). For the company's 165gr SST InterLock load, those readings are 2850 fps at the muzzle; 2644 fps at 100 yards; 2447 fps at 200 yards; and 2258 fps at 300 yards, with trajectories of +1.7 inches at 100 yards; zero at 200 yards; and −7.6 inches

Hornady built the 30 TC for the Thompson/Center Icon bolt-action rifle, and the company loads it in a Superformance 150gr InterLock Super Shock Tip (SST) bullet. It has a sharp, pointed polymer tip and a Muzzle Velocity of 3000 fps and Muzzle Energy of 2997 ft. lbs. The 165gr load has a Muzzle Velocity of 2850 fps and Muzzle Energy of 2975 ft-lbs. The three-bullet photo shows the scale of the (left to right) 308 Win, 30 TC, and 30-06 Springfield.

Introduced in 2006, Hornady's LEVERevolution ammunition produces up to 40% more energy than traditional flat-point loads and travels up to 250 fps faster. The soft polymer flex tip won't dent the primer of the round in front of it. This Hornady 308 Marlin Express 160gr FTX develops muzzle velocity of 2660 fps and muzzle energy of 2513 ft-lbs. The Remington Express 308 Marlin Express has a 150gr Core-Lokt Soft Point with a MV of 2725 fps and ME of 2473 ft-lbs. Photos courtesy of Midway USA.

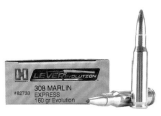

Top photo courtesy of Hornady, other photos courtesy of Midway USA.

at 300 yards.

By their names, it would seem that two handgun rounds fit in this size class, but their designations are misleading. The **7.62mm Nagant (Russian)** cartridge was specifically

designed for use with the gas seal system and of the Russian Nagant M1895 revolver. The slightly bottlenecked case completely encloses the bullet, resembling a blank cartridge, but the round fires a 97gr flat-nosed lead bullet

SELECTED LOADS & BALLISTICS

Hornady 308 Win 80938 150gr InterBond Superformance

Range, Yards	Muzzle	100	200	300	400	500
Velocities (fps)	3000	2772	2555	2348	2151	1963
Energy (ft-lbs)	2997	2558	2173	1836	1540	1282
Trajectory (in.)		1.5	0	-6.9	-20.0	-40.7

Hornady 308 Win 80926 155gr BTHP Steel Match

Range, Yards	Muzzle	100	200	300	400	500
Velocities (fps)	2610	2396	2191	1997	1816	1642
Energy (ft-lbs)	2344	1975	1652	1372	1134	928
Trajectory (in.)		2.3	0	-9.5	-27.2	-56.7

Hornady 30-30 Win 82731 140gr MonoFlex LEVERevolution

Range, Yards	Muzzle	100	200	300	400	500
Velocities (fps)	2500	2201	1922	1668		
Energy (ft-lbs)	1943	1505	1149	865		
Trajectory (in.)		3.0	0.4	-11.8		

Hornady 30-30 Win 8085 170gr InterLock

Range, Yards	Muzzle	100	200	300	400	500
Velocities (fps)	2200	1796	1450	1186		
Energy (ft-lbs)	1827	1218	793	530		
Trajectory (in.)		0	-9.4	-35.7		

Remington Express 30-30 Win Accelerator R3030A 55gr SP

Range, Yards	Muzzle	100	200	300	400	500
Velocities (fps)	3400	2693	2085	1570	1187	986
Energy (ft-lbs)	1412	886	521	301	172	119
Trajectory (in.)		1.7	1.6	-9.9	-34.3	-83.3

Remington 30-40 Krag R30402 180gr Core-Lokt PSP

Range, Yards	Muzzle	100	200	300	400	500
Velocities (fps)	2430	2213	2007	1813	1632	1468
Energy (ft-lbs)	2360	1957	1610	1314	1064	861
Trajectory (in.)		1.2	-3.2	-16.2	-39.9	-76.7

Winchester 300 Savage X3001 150gr Power-Point

Range, Yards	Muzzle	100	200	300	400	500
Velocities (fps)	2630	2336	2061	1810	1575	1372
Energy (ft-lbs)	2303	1817	1415	1091	826	627
Trajectory (in.)		2.5	0	-10.0	-32.1	-67.6

Hornady 30-06 S'fld 81188 180gr InterBond Superformance

Range, Yards	Muzzle	100	200	300	400	500
Velocities (fps)	2820	2764	2447	2272	2104	1944
Energy (ft-lbs)	3178	2764	2393	2063	1769	1509
Trajectory (in.)		1.8	0	-7.6	-21.9	-44.1

SELECTED LOADS & BALLISTICS

Remington 30-06 S'fld Accelerator R30069 55gr PSP

Range, Yards	Muzzle	100	200	300	400	500
Velocities (fps)	4080	3484	2964	2499	2080	1706
Energy (ft-lbs)	2033	1482	1073	763	528	355
Trajectory (in.)		1.4	1.4	-2.6	-12.2	-30.0

Winchester 30 Carbine X30M1 110gr Hollow Soft Point

Range, Yards	Muzzle	100	200	300	400	500
Velocities (fps)	1990	1567	1236	1035	923	842
Energy (ft-lbs)	967	599	373	262	208	173
Trajectory (in.)		6.5	0	-29.3	-90.9	

Winchester 307 Winchester X3076 180gr Power-Point

Range, Yards	Muzzle	100	200	300	400	500
Velocities (fps)	2510	2179	1874	1599	1363	1177
Energy (ft-lbs)	2518	1897	1403	1022	742	554
Trajectory (in.)		2.9	0	-12.9	-39.6	-85.1

Remington 30 Rem AR PRA30RAR1 125gr AccuTip Boat Tail

Range, Yards	Muzzle	100	200	300	400	500
Velocities (fps)	2800	2531	2278	2039	1816	1610
Energy (ft-lbs)	2176	1778	1440	1153	915	719
Trajectory (in.)		2.0	0	-8.7	-25.8	-53.5

Hornady 308 Marlin 82734 140gr Monoflex LEVERevolution

Range, Yards	Muzzle	100	200	300	400	500
Velocities (fps)	2800	2531	2278	2039	1817	1610
Energy (ft-lbs)	2437	1991	1612	1292	1026	806
Trajectory (in.)		3.0	2.1	-5.6	-21.3	-48.3

Hornady 308 Marlin 82733 160gr FTX LEVERevolution

Range, Yards	Muzzle	100	200	300	400	500
Velocities (fps)	2660	2438	2226	2026	1836	1659
Energy (ft-lbs)	2513	2111	1761	1457	1197	978
Trajectory (in.)		3.0	1.7	-6.7	-23.5	-50.7

Hornady 30 TC 81004 150gr SST Superformance

Range, Yards	Muzzle	100	200	300	400	500
Velocities (fps)	3000	2772	2555	2348	2151	1963
Energy (ft-lbs)	2997	2558	2173	1836	1540	1283
Trajectory (in.)		1.5	0	-6.9	-20.0	-40.7

Hornady 30 TC 81014 165gr SST Superformance

Range, Yards	Muzzle	100	200	300	400	500
Velocities (fps)	2850	2645	2448	2261	2081	1910
Energy (ft-lbs)	2975	2562	2196	1872	1586	1336
Trajectory (in.)		1.7	0	-7.5	-21.9	-44.0

"The 30 Did It" is the name of this Winchester calendar artwork by A.B. Frost (circa 1898). We're not sure which round the guide is referring to, but it could have been at least a couple of rounds in this chapter. The 30-40 Krag is a reasonable guess, since it was one of the earliest chamberings of the Model 1895 lever action shown in the hunter's hand. Amazingly, this scene could be recreated today with a 2010-production-year rifle because Winchester Repeating Arms offered the Model 1895 in 30-40 Krag. The catalog number of the rifle is 534070115, and it has a 24-inch barrel with a 42-inch overall length. MSRP, $1179. Poster artwork © Winfield Galleries, LLC, St. Louis, Missouri. Used with permission. To view current artwork and pricing, log on to www.WinfieldGalleries.com.

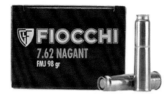

Since 1928, Prvi Partizan has been producing custom ammunition in Serbia. This 7.62mm Russian Nagant has a 98gr full-metal-jacket flat point enclosed in the case body—the gas seal design. It amasses a MV of 738 fps and ME of 118 ft-lbs. The Fiocchi is a 97gr FMJ making 785 fps MV and 250 ft-lbs ME. Photos courtesy of Midway USA.

at 1080 fps, comparable to the 32 Magnum revolver cartridge. The gun was designed by Henri-Leon Nagant, a Belgian gunmaker, under contract to Tsar Nicholas II. After the Russian Revolution of 1917, it was said that a Nagant was used to murder the Tsar and his family. In battle, the M1895 saw action in the Russo-Japanese War, World War I, and the Russian and Spanish civil wars, to name a few. The "gas seal" system operated by cocking the hammer, either manually or in the double action mode, which then pushed the gun's cylinder forward so that the recessed mouth of the chamber entered the tapered rear end of the barrel. This prevented the escape of gas from the gap between the cylinder and barrel. The cartridge, aka the 7.62x38mmR and 7.62 mm Nagant and Cartridge, Type R) has its projectile seated below the mouth of the cartridge, with the cartridge crimp sitting just above the bullet. When fired in the Nagant revolver, the crimp expands into the forcing cone, completing the gas-seal. One advantage of the round, if proper brass can be found, is that it leaves the chambers totally clean, and there is no need to scrape out lead and powder residue. The rimmed case accepts a 7.493mm (.2950 in.) diameter bullet, not 7.62mm, as the name implies. The neck diameter is .286 in., base diameter 0.352 in., and the case has a .388-in. rim. The next two measurements describe the odd nature of the round, with its case length and overall length of 38.86mm, or 1.530 in.

Another Russian round, the **7.62mm Tokarev,** goes by a number of other names, such as 7.62 Soviet pistol, 7.62 Russian, and 7.62mm TT. It started out as the 7.63mm Mauser automatic-pistol cartridge chambered for the

Prvi Partizan 7.62 mm Nagant 98gr FPJ A-470

Range, Yards	Muzzle	25	50	100
Velocities (fps)	740	725	705	690
Energy (ft-lbs)	119	114	109	104
Trajectory (in.)		0	-3.2	-2.3

Prvi Partizan 7.62 mm Tokarev 85gr JHP A-174

Range, Yards	Muzzle	25	50	100
Velocities (fps)	1675	1535	1405	1275
Energy (ft-lbs)	529	444	373	307
Trajectory (in.)		0	-0.5	-8.4

Prvi Partizan 7.62 mm Tokarev 85gr FMJ A-147

Range, Yards	Muzzle	25	50	100
Velocities (fps)	1720	1575	1445	1315
Energy (ft-lbs)	558	469	393	326
Trajectory (in.)		0	-0.5	-8.2

Winchester 7.62x25 Tokarev 85gr FMJ MC762TOK

Range, Yards	Muzzle	50
Velocities (fps)	1645	1311
Energy (ft-lbs)	511	323

Winchester 30 Luger (7.65mm) X30LP 93gr FMJ

Range, Yards	Muzzle	100	200
Velocities (fps)	1220	1110	1040
Energy (ft-lbs)	305	255	225

Prvi Partizan 7.65mm Parabellum 93gr FMJ A-549

Range, Yards	Muzzle	25	50	100
Velocities (fps)	1280	1185	1105	1050
Energy (ft-lbs)	339	290	253	228
Trajectory (in.)		0	-0.7	-10.9

Winchester 30 Carbine X30M1 110gr Hollow Soft Point

Range, Yards	Muzzle	50	100
Velocities (fps)	1790	1601	1430
Energy (ft-lbs)	783	626	500

Note: The 30 Carbine's history is covered under the rifle section, and rifle ballistics are included there. These ballistics are for a single-shot handgun, such as the Thompson/Center, with a 10-in. barrel.

Prvi Partizan 30 Mauser 85gr FMJ

Range, Yards	Muzzle	25	50	100
Velocities (fps)	1510	1385	1275	1165
Energy (ft-lbs)	430	362	306	256
Trajectory (in.)		0	-0.6	-9.2

Fiocchi 30 Mauser 88gr FMJ

Range, Yards	Muzzle	25	50	100
Velocities (fps)	1425			
Energy (ft-lbs)	390			

Mauser C96 pistol. The 7.63×25 ammunition was used by Russian forces in the early 1920s, and the pistol remained popular with the Bolsheviks. In the late 1920s when the Tokarev automatic pistol was developed, it was designed around the Mauser cartridge. For manufacturing convenience, the barrel of the Tokarev was 7.62mm, thus the 7.62mm Tokarev was born. The Soviet round and the original Mauser cartridge are similar, so much so that Mauser rounds can usually be fired in Tokarev pistols, but not Tokarevs in Mauser pistols. The differences are the size of the extractor groove and a different primer size. The Tokarev shoots a .307-in.-diameter bullet (7.8mm), with a cartridge neck diameter of 0.33 in and a shoulder diameter of 0.37 in. The base has a diameter of .38 in., with a rim diameter of 0.39 in. Case length is 0.98 in., and overall length is 1.35 in.

In 1898, German arms manufacturer Deutsche Waffen und Munitions Fabriken (DWM) built the **7.65x21mm Parabellum** (aka 30 Luger, 7.65mm Luger), employing work from firearms designers Georg Luger and Hugo Borchardt, who shortened the round from the earlier 7.65x25mm Borchardt. Called the 7.65mm Parabellum in most European countries, the 30 Luger was introduced in 1900 in the then-new Luger semiautomatic pistol,

and served as the standard pistol cartridge of the Swiss Army (1940s). It's been chambered in several pistols, including the Benelli B80, Browning Hi-Power, Astra A-80, Beretta 92, and Ruger P94, as well as some submachine guns, such as the SIG Bergmann (1920), the Swiss M/Neuhausen MKMS, and the Austrian MP34. The 9x19mm Parabellum cartridge is an expanded bottleneck version of the 7.65mm Luger, with the two having almost identical case widths, rim widths, and overall lengths.

The **30 Mauser (aka 7.63 Mauser, 7.63x25mm, 30 Borchardt)** is a copy of the earlier (1893) Borchardt round and was amped up for the stronger 1896 Mauser pistol. The pistol that accepts the 30 Mauser (7.63mm) is the 1896 Mauser, designed in 1895 by the Feederle brothers, one of whom (Fidel) was

Fiocchi is one of the few manufacturers who produce modern ammunition for classic handguns, and in some calibers, it is the exclusive manufacturer. They load these classic cartridges in accordance with original specifications. Fiocchi utilizes fully reloadable brass cases, non-corrosive boxer primers and selected smokeless powders. This Fiocchi Pistol Classic 30 Luger holds a 93gr FMJ bullet, with a MV of 1200 fps. Photo courtesy of Cheaper-ThanDirt.com.

At the left is the 30 Mauser round, whose 85gr bullet makes 1060 fps, paired up with a 9mm with a 147gr FMJ.

in charge of the experimental division of the Mauser factory. Ultimately over a million of these were made. The "Broomhandle" Mauser pistol shown adjacent was as fine an example of the design as most shooters would ever want. In it, Prvi Partizan 85gr ammunition produced a prominent muzzle flash along with a loud blast. Original loads were specified to make 1400 fps, but the Prvi loads got only 1065 fps in this gun. Accuracy for this collectible was around 2.5 inches for five shots at 15 yards.

As noted earlier, the 7.62x25mm Russian Tokarev has essentially the same dimensions as the Mauser round, but the newer Tokarev round meant for various pistols is loaded hotter than the Mauser offering, making it dangerous to fire in a Broomhandle 30 Mauser pistol. Although reloading specs call for .308-diameter bullets, many 30 Mauser guns need .312-in.-diameter slugs to prevent keyholing. The safest bet is to slug your bore prior to determine the best bullet diameter. If an older gun requires .312-diameter bullets, they are the same size as bullets suitable for 32 autos and revolvers and are in wide supply. ●

16: Magnum 308s

A step above the 308-class rounds in powder capacity are the 300 Magnums, with both short- and long-action versions: 300 Holland & Holland Magnum, 300 Winchester Magnum, 300 Weatherby Magnum, 30-378 Weatherby Magnum, 300 Remington SAUM, 300 Remington Ultra Magnum, 300 Ruger Compact Magnum, 300 Winchester Short Magnum, and 308 Norma Magnum. All in, these rounds kick a lot more and cost a lot more per shell than the 308 Win and 30-06 Springfield, but they might not deliver as much ballistics as the shooter might expect for the trade-off in pain and coin. While it is true that a 300 Mag of various formulations do add distance to the maximum point-blank range calculations above the '06—which in simple terms means they shoot flatter with the same bullet weight—they have to burn a lot of powder to do it.

The granddaddy of the group is the ***300 Holland & Holland Magnum,*** introduced as Holland's Super 30 in 1925. It was also called the 300 Magnum, 300 Belted Rimless Magnum, and H&H Super 30. The "Super .30" was first offered in the U.S. by the Western Cartridge Company, though no American commercial rifles were chambered for it until 12 years after its introduction. Its elevation into as a premier US hunting cartridge began in 1935,

The 300 H&H Magnum's genesis began in 1912, when the British firm of Holland & Holland created a new belted-Mag African cartridge called the 375 H&H. The "lighter" 300 H&H was a 375 H&H case necked down to accept .308-in. bullets, but otherwise retains the 2.850-in. case, with considerable body taper, sloping shoulder and long neck.

when a shooter named Ben Comfort won the 1000-yard Wimbledon Cup Match at Camp Perry with it. Within two years, Winchester had chambered its new Model 70 for the 300 H&H, followed by Remington with the 721 and 700 rifles. When loaded to its SAAMI Maximum Average Pressure of 54,000 C.U.P. in a rifle of suitable barrel length (26 inches), the 300 H&H's performance was once exceeded only by the 300 Weatherby Magnum.

Whether the 300 H&H continues to be chambered in many domestic rifles is beside

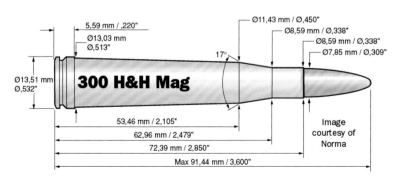

300 H&H Mag

Ø13,51 mm / Ø,532"
5,59 mm / ,220"
Ø13,03 mm / Ø,513"
Ø11,43 mm / Ø,450"
Ø8,59 mm / Ø,338"
Ø8,59 mm / Ø,338"
Ø7,85 mm / Ø,309"
17°
53,46 mm / 2,105"
62,96 mm / 2,479"
72,39 mm / 2,850"
Max 91,44 mm / 3,600"

Image courtesy of Norma

the point, at least in one sense. It will live on as being the basis for most magnum-cartridge designs since. The traditional British factory load drove a 180gr bullet at 2750 fps MV with 3020 ft-lbs ME, and the standard 300 H&H factory load in the US was a 180gr bullet at 2920 fps MV. As the accompanying ballistic tables show, the 300 H&H can hold its own with any other 300-mag out there. But it uses a full-length magnum action, which puts it at a disadvantage because of the heavier gun weight.

The H&H's next two challengers came along courtesy of Roy Weatherby, who created the **300 Weatherby Magnum** in 1944, itself (and the 1962-era 340 Weatherby Magnum)based on the original H&H belted case. Many see the 300 W'by Mag as a 300 H&H Improved, and the shooter can fire 300 H&H cases in a 300 W'by Mag chamber to make fire-formed brass. In addition to Weatherby's rifles, the Ruger No. 1, Remington M700, and Winchester M70 are available in 300 W'by Mag. One note: Most handloaders know that much of the published

The 300 W'by uses a full-length case and must be loaded into a long action. It remains one of the largest commercial 30-caliber cases, which produces impressive results, especially in a 26-in. barrel. Photo courtesy of Weatherby.

300 Weatherby Mag load data was developed in freebore-chambered Weatherby Mark V rifles, so some of those loads generate excessive pressure if used in rifles with shorter chamber throats.

The next Weatherby big 30-caliber was the **30-378 Weatherby Magnum,** based on the 378 W'by Mag case. In 1959, the US Army asked Weatherby to neck-down the 378 to 30-caliber and load specially-designed Speer 30gr bullets so the military could test armor plating's resistance to high-speed projectiles. Result: MVs of 5000 fps then 6000 fps with dense, slow-burning propellants. But the 30-378 W'by Mag wasn't just rich, it was also pretty. In July 1967, York, Pennsylvania, benchrest shooter Earl Chronister (now deceased) became the first 1,000-yard shooter to record a 10-shot groups in the 4s, when he put 250gr Sierra MatchKing bullets fired from a 30-378 Mag into 4.375 in., a record that stood until 1993.

Weatherby loadings include a 130gr Barnes TTSX (BC .350), 165gr Nosler Ballistic Tip (BC .475) and Barnes TSX (BC .398); 180gr Barnes TSX (BC .453), Nosler AccuBond (BC .507), and Nosler Ballistic Tip (BC .507); and 200gr Nosler Partition (BC .481). Trajectories are impressive. With 300-yard zeros, the 130gr Barnes TTSX drops only -19.61 inches at 500 yards, bettered only slightly by the 165gr Barnes TSX (-19.60 in.) and 165gr Nosler Ballistic Tip (-19.50 in.), and followed by the 180gr Barnes TSX (-21.77 in), Nosler AccuBond and Nosler Ballistic Tip (-20.00 in.), and 200gr Nosler Partition (-24.30 in.). Though it's hard to endorse the practice, the 30-378 W'by Mag

SELECTED LOADS & BALLISTICS

Weatherby 30-378 W'by Mag 130 Barnes TTSX

Range, Yards	Muzzle	100	200	300	400	500
Velocities (fps)	3740	3417	3118	2839	2577	2329
Energy (ft-lbs)	4039	3372	2807	2327	1917	1567
Trajectory (in.)		2.1	2.9	0	-7.2	-19.6

Weatherby 30-378 W'by Mag 165gr Ballistic Silvertip

Range, Yards	Muzzle	100	200	300	400	500
Velocities (fps)	3500	3275	3062	2859	2665	2480
Energy (ft-lbs)	4488	3930	3435	2995	2603	2253
Trajectory (in.)		2.4	3.0	0	-7.4	-19.5

Weatherby 30-378 W'by Mag 200gr Partition

Range, Yards	Muzzle	100	200	300	400	500
Velocities (fps)	3160	2955	2759	2572	2392	2220
Energy (ft-lbs)	4434	3877	3381	2938	2541	2188
Trajectory (in.)		3.2	3.9	0	-9.1	-24.3

Norma 308 Norma Mag 180gr Oryx

Range, Yards	Muzzle	100	200	300	400	500
Velocities (fps)	2953	2622	2313	2031		
Energy (ft-lbs)	3486	2745	2138	1649		
Trajectory (in.)		1.7	0	-8.2		

The baddest mamma-jamma on the planet? May be. This is the 30-378 W'by Mag shown full size, with an overall length of 3.75 inches. Photo courtesy of Weatherby.

"Deer Camp Surprise" was a Winchester Western rifle cartridge pro- motional poster around 1954, with artwork by Dwyer. As in most deer camps of the time, there's a selec- tion of bolt guns and lever actions the hunters are scrambling to put into play. © Winfield Galleries, LLC, St. Louis, Mis- souri. Used with permission. To view current art- work and pricing, log on to www. WinfieldGalleries. com.

is capable of taking elk and similar species beyond 600 yards cleanly and with one shot. The shooter pays for that privilege by having to endure fierce recoil and muzzle blast.

In 1960 Norma's **308 Norma Magnum** debuted, beating Winchester and Remington in standardizing a standard-length 30-caliber magnum. However, the 300 Win Mag (see below), introduced three years later, has similar ballistics and is now one of the most popular chamberings for the 300 mags. This is unusual because the latter-appearing round usually is at a competitive disadvantage. The 308 Norma Mag has a longer case neck, which many believe is a better all-around design, and Norma notes that the 308NM develops unusually consistent pressures and velocities, particularly in loads using 180gr and heavier bullets. If the need arises, 308 Norma Mag cases can be made by necking up a 7mm Rem Mag case or necking down 338 Win Mag cases, though they will be short in overall length.

The de facto leader in the 300 magnum class came with the 1963 debut of the **300 Winchester Magnum,** which replaced the 300 H&H in the Model 70 bolt action. The 300 Win Mag's short case, short neck, and straight case give it a powder capacity of 79.5 grains of water to the 300 H&H's 72.2 grains, but the 300 Win Mag's shorter, fatter case makes it more efficient, thus its slightly better ballistics. In contrast, the 300 W'by Mag, basically a blown-out 300 H&H with the taper removed, holds nearly 85 grains. Of all the varmint and big-game cartridges developed and introduced by Winchester, the 1963-vintage 300 Winchester Mag is the fifth most successful. Only the 243, 270, 30-30, and 308 Winchester cartridges are more popular. Among the magnums available to American hunters, only the 7mm Rem Mag is more popular than the 300 Win Mag.

The 300 Win Mag was based on the 338 Win Mag by moving the 338's shoulder forward .156 in. and lengthening the case .120 in. It differs from earlier Winchester short magnums in having a slightly longer case, perhaps a result of the 308 Norma Magnum, which probably preempted Winchester from developing a 30-caliber short magnum based on the wildcat 30-338. A common barrel twist rate is 1:10 with a bore groove diameter of .307 in. Maximum case length is 2.620 in., with a trimmed case length of 2.610 in.

Remington introduced its upgraded counterpart to the 300 Win Mag in 1999 in the form

SELECTED LOADS & BALLISTICS

Federal 300 Win Mag 300WGS 150gr Speer Hot-Cor SP

Range, Yards	Muzzle	100	200	300	400	500
Velocities (fps)	3150	2898	2661	2435	2221	2017
Energy (ft-lbs)	3305	2798	2358	1975	1643	1355
Trajectory (in.)		1.3	0	-6.2	-18.3	-37.5

Hornady 300 Win Mag 82012 150gr GMX Superformance

Range, Yards	Muzzle	100	200	300	400	500
Velocities (fps)	3400	3150	2914	2690	2477	2273
Energy (ft-lbs)	3850	3304	2827	2409	2043	1721
Trajectory (in.)		1.0	0	-5.10	-15.0	-30.6

Winchester 300 Win Mag X300WM1BP 150gr Power Max

Range, Yards	Muzzle	100	200	300	400	500
Velocities (fps)		2981	2693	2422	2168	1929
Energy (ft-lbs)	3605	2959	2415	1954	1565	1239
Trajectory (in.)			1.2	0	-6.0	-18.0

Hornady 300 Win Mag 82028 165gr InterBond Superformance

Range, Yards	Muzzle	100	200	300	400	500
Velocities (fps)	3260	3035	2821	2617	2422	2235
Energy (ft-lbs)	3893	3373	2915	2505	2148	1830
Trajectory (in.)		1.1	0	-5.5	-16.1	-32.7

Hornady 300 Win Mag 82198 180gr InterBond Superformance

Range, Yards	Muzzle	100	200	300	400	500
Velocities (fps)	3130	2927	2732	2546	2366	2195
Energy (ft-lbs)	3917	3424	2983	2589	2238	1925
Trajectory (in.)		1.3	0	-5.9	-17.3	-34.8

Remington Premier 300 Win Mag RS300WA 200gr A-Frame

Range, Yards	Muzzle	100	200	300	400	500
Velocities (fps)	2825	2595	2377	2169	1971	1786
Energy (ft-lbs)	3544	2990	2508	2088	1726	1416
Trajectory (in.)		1.8	0	-8.0	-23.4	-47.8

of the **300 Remington Ultra Mag,** whose parent case is the 404 Jeffery. It significantly ups the ante over the 300 Win Mag and 300 W'by Mag, with 20% and 13% more powder capacity than those rounds, respectively. Said another way, in this class it is second only to the 30-378 W'by Mag in case capacity; however, it is more efficient than the 30-378 because it can produce nearly as much velocity with 10% less powder. The round, aka the 300 Ultra Mag or 300 RUM, shoots a 7.62mm (.308 in.) bullet out of its beltless, rebated-rim case, which gives the 300 UM the same base diameter (.532 in.) as belted magnums, so it functions in common actions. Other members of the Ultra Mag family include the 7mm RUM, 338 RUM, and 375 RUM.

Remington Express RUM R300UM1-P1 Power Level I
150gr PSP Core-Lokt

Range, Yards	Muzzle	100	200	300	400	500
Velocities (fps)	2910	2617	2342	2083	1843	1622
Energy (ft-lbs)	2820	2281	1827	1445	1131	876
Trajectory (in.)		1.8	0	-8.2	-24.4	-50.9

Remington Premier RUM PR300UM3-P2 Power Level II
180gr Swift Scirocco Bonded

Range, Yards	Muzzle	100	200	300	400	500
Velocities (fps)	2980	2793	2614	2442	2276	2116
Energy (ft-lbs)	3549	3118	2730	2382	2070	1790
Trajectory (in.)		1.5	0	-6.6	-19.0	-38.1

Remington Premier RUM PR300UM3-P3 Power Level III
180gr Swift Scirocco Bonded

Range, Yards	Muzzle	100	200	300	400	500
Velocities (fps)	3250	3048	2856	2672	2495	2325
Energy (ft-lbs)	4221	3714	3260	2853	2487	2160
Trajectory (in.)		2.0	1.7	-2.8	-12.3	-27.3

Federal Vital-Shok 300 RUM P300RUMC 200gr Nosler Partition

Range, Yards	Muzzle	100	200	300	400	500
Velocities (fps)	3070	2869	2676	2492	2315	2146
Energy (ft-lbs)	4185	3654	3181	2758	2380	2044
Trajectory (in.)		1.4	0	-6.2	-18.0	-36.4

Remington's eight factory loads include 150-, 180-, and 200gr bullet weights in three different power levels. Power Level I cartridges are similar to the 30-06. Power Level II mimics the 300 Win Mag, and PLIII fodder is full-on loads in 150-, 180-, and 200gr bullets. MV is 3450 fps for the 150gr Swift Scirocco Bonded bullet, 3250 fps for a 180gr Core-Lokt pill, and 3032 fps for the 200gr Premier A-Frame. To put everything in scale, a typical 200gr load in the 300 RUM develops 3032 fps MV and 4083 ft-lbs ME, compared to the 300 RSAUM (2790 fps/3458 ft-lbs), 300 WSM (2822 fps/3538 ft-lbs), 300 Win Mag (2822 fps/3538 ft-lbs), 300 W'by Mag (2987 fps/3963 ft-lbs), and 30-378 W'by Mag (3160 fps/4434 ft-lbs).

The appearance of the Winchester's *300 Winchester Short Magnum* (perhaps the line should be called the Winchester Short Fat Magnums, since that's how the cases are always described) shouldn't surprise shooters since Winchester has a distinguished history of making short-bolt-action big-game hunting rifles in the 308-case family of cartridges dating back to the 1950s, including the 308 Win, 243 Win, and 358 Win, or in the 1960s in the form of the 284 Win. Also, the 300 WSM joins a distinguished group of 30-caliber loads in the family: the 30-30 Win (1895), the 308 Win (1952), and the 300 Win Mag (1963).

The 300 Winchester Short Magnum came out in 2000, a year ahead of *Remington's 300 Short Action Ultra Magnum (SAUM)* design. Both designs are loosely based upon shortened 404 Jeffery cases and are conventional rimless shouldered shapes. The WSM cartridge is 2.860 in overall length, and the case length is 2.100 in. It's easy to see a mild taper in the WSM's case, moving from the top measurements (neck diameter, .344 in.; shoulder diameter, .538 in.) to the bottom (base diameter, .555 in.), and that base diameter gives the shooter an idea of how fat the WSM really is, compared to the rounds above. The WSM's bottleneck case has a 35-degree shoulder. In the field, the short 300 WSM round mirrors the belted-magnum 300 Win Mag, which is based on a modified 375 H&H case, but the WSM lives in an action that saves about a half-inch of bolt throw.

The latest entries in the 300 magnum class likewise follow the WSM's design cues. The 2001 introduction of the 300 Remington Short Action Ultra Mag (RSAUM) cartridge was a year behind the WSM, and it looks like the RSAUM is headed for the dust bin of history courtesy of the 300 WSM. In one respect this is surprising, since the 300 RSAUM's ballistics cited above and in the accompanying tables are similar to 300 Win Mag and 300 WSM. The 300 RSAUM's 2.015-inch-long beltless case is based on the 300 RUM, retaining the 30-degree shoulder angle of the parent case with a short neck in an OAL of 2.825 in., allowing it to work in the Model 7 short-action rifle.

Remington currently produces four loads with a range of bullet weights for the RSAUM: a Premier 150gr Core-Lokt Ultra Bonded cartridge, an Express 165gr Pointed Soft Point Core-Lokt, a Premier Core-Lokt Ultra 180gr Bonded, and an Express 190gr Boat Tail Hollow Point Match round. Big Green produces three 300 WSM loads with 150- and 180gr, whereas Winchester doesn't load the RSAUM at all. Also, a check of major ammo retailers Midway USA and Cheaper Than Dirt show them selling two brands of 300 RSAUM (Remington and Nosler) and 11 brands of 300 WSM (Remington, Nosler, Winchester, Federal, HSM, Barnes, Norma, DoubleTap, Black Hills, BVAC, and Cor-Bon). Only one Remington rifle was

Federal Vital-Shok 300 WSM P300WSMK 130gr Barnes Tipped Triple-Shock X Bullet

Range, Yards	Muzzle	100	200	300	400	500
Velocities (fps)	3500	3204	2927	2667	2421	2189
Energy (ft-lbs)	3536	2963	2473	2053	1692	1383
Trajectory (in.)		0.9	0	-5.0	-14.9	-30.8

Winchester 300 WSM S300WSMCT 180gr AccuBond CT

Range, Yards	Muzzle	100	200	300	400	500
Velocities (fps)	3010	2822	2643	2470	2304	2144
Energy (ft-lbs)	3622	3185	2792	2439	2121	1837
Trajectory (in.)		1.4	0	-6.4	-18.5	-37.2

Remington Premier 300 WSM PRA300WSMB 180gr AccuTip Boat Tail

Range, Yards	Muzzle	100	200	300	400	500
Velocities (fps)	3010	2812	2622	2440	2265	2097
Energy (ft-lbs)	3621	3159	2746	2378	2050	1757
Trajectory (in.)		2.5	2.1	-3.4	-14.8	-32.9

Remington Express 300 RSAUM RM300SM7 190gr Boattail Hollowpoint Match

Range, Yards	Muzzle	100	200	300	400	500
Velocities (fps)	2900	2725	2557	2395	2239	2089
Energy (ft-lbs)	3547	3133	2758	2420	2115	1840
Trajectory (in.)		1.6	0	-6.9	-19.9	-39.8

Remington Premier 300 RSAUM PR300SM1 150gr Core-Lokt Ultra Bonded

Range, Yards	Muzzle	100	200	300	400	500
Velocities (fps)	3200	2901	2622	2359	2112	1880
Energy (ft-lbs)	3410	2803	2290	1854	1485	1177
Trajectory (in.)		1.3	0	-6.4	-19.1	-39.6

Hornady 300 RCM 82230 150gr GMX Superformance (20-in. barrel)

Range, Yards	Muzzle	100	200	300	400	500
Velocities (fps)	3175	2935	2707	2491	2284	2088
Energy (ft-lbs)	3357	2868	2440	2066	1738	1451
Trajectory (in.)		1.2	0	-5.6	-16.5	-33.6

Hornady 300 RCM 82228 180gr InterBond Superformance

Range, Yards	Muzzle	100	200	300	400	500
Velocities (fps)	3040	2840	2649	2466	2290	2121
Energy (ft-lbs)	3693	3223	2804	2430	2096	1789
Trajectory (in.)		1.40	0	-6.4	-18.5	-37.2

being chambered for the 300 RSAUM in 2010, the Model Seven CDL. More ominously for the RSAUM, there were eight Remingtons chambered for the 300 WSM in 2010 (M700 CDL SF, M700 SPS, M700 SPS Stainless, M700 XCR, M700 Alaskan Ti, M700 XCR II, and the Model Seven CDL and XCR Camos.)

Introduced in 2008, the most recent 308-caliber magnum cartridge is the **300 Ruger Compact Magnum** (RCM), developed by Hornady for Ruger. It is based on a shortened 375 Ruger case, being a beltless bottleneck case with a rim and head diameter of .532 in., the same dimension as the belted magnums. The 300 RCM's case length is 2.100 inches, the same length as the WSM cartridges. Case capacity is 72.7 grains of water. Overall cartridge length is 2.825 inches.

So what's the *raison d'être* behind the RCM? Because the RCM case is not a rebated-rim design, it offers improved feeding compared to the WSM and RSAUMs. Hornady's sales

angle on the RCMs (there's also a 338 RCM covered in a later chapter) are that they match 300 and 338 Win Mag performance in quick-handling rifles like the Ruger M77 Hawkeye, which features a 20-in. barrel and weight just over 6.5 pounds. Hornady points out that the 300 Win Mag requires a 24- or 26-in. barrel to get its work done to full effectiveness.

Hornady offers 300 RCM factory loads with 150-, 165-, and 180gr bullets, and the accompanying tables show the performance of the 300 RCM compares to, but does not exceed, other 300 magnums. Hornady's advertised MVs out of a 20-in. barrel are, by bullet weight, 150gr SST, 3170 fps; 165gr SST, 3030 fps; and 180gr SST, 2900 fps. ●

17: The Mice That Roar

The latest round in this class, the 327 Federal Magnum was introduced in November 2007 by Federal Cartridge, and Ruger chambered a 6-shot version of the SP101 for the new round. The 327 FM uses the .312-in. diameter bullets found in the 32 H&R Magnum, 32 S&W, 32 S&W Long, and 32-20 Winchester. The 327, in essence, is a 32-20 with a slightly smaller case. Or, the 327 is a 32 H&R Magnum case lengthened by one-eighth inch and thickened internally to take twice the pressure.

32 Auto (32 ACP)

32 Smith & Wesson

32 Smith & Wesson Long

32 H&R Magnum

327 Federal Magnum

32-20 WCF

Three 32 ACPs with different nose treatments include the 60gr Winchester Silvertip HP, left, the 71gr American Eagle full metal jacket, center, and the 60gr Speer Gold Dot hollowpoint, right. They're a perfect fit for the lightweight Kel-Tec P32PK. Nearly every manufacturer of autoloading handguns in the world have built millions of small pocket autoloaders in 32 ACP, so it must be doing something right.

Generally speaking, the 32-caliber class of handguns gets the brush-off from many CCW shooters, who want to "stop" someone with a "big" round, not a popgun. However, when a fellow shooter asks, "Is there a good self-defense gun out there with limited recoil?", the **32 Auto (32 ACP)** comes to mind. Most readers would wonder about the 32's power, and that's a legitimate worry: in most cases, it produces less than 100 foot-pounds of muzzle energy. Still, even though many other cartridges enjoy far greater publicity, it is thought that more handguns have been chambered for the 32 ACP than for any other. It is estimated that during the first 10 years of the 32 ACPs existence, Fabrique Nationale (FN) alone produced more than 500,000 pistols in this caliber.

In guns like the Kel-Tec P32PK, the Walther USA PPK, and the Taurus PT132SSP, for example, the trade-off between always-easy-to-carry gun size and last-ditch power may be enough for many concealed carriers to try a 32 (which in the case of the 32 ACP, is actually a .309-in.-diameter bullet). Under 7 yards, guns like these chambered for the 32 ACP can print sub-1-inch groups, and they don't weigh much. Amazingly, the 7.65mm Browning cartridge, as it was known when introduced by the Belgium firm FN in 1899, was John Browning's first successful semiautomatic pistol, and similarly-sized guns continue the tradition. The locked-breech semiautomatic Kel-Tec P32PK, for example, tips the scales at just 7 ounces loaded with 7 rounds of American Eagle 71gr TMJs, 60gr Winchester Silvertip HPs, or Speer Gold Dot 60gr GDHP rounds. In 1903, Colt introduced its first Browning-designed autoloader, the Pocket Model, chambered for the same cartridge, but renamed it the 32 Automatic Colt Pistol, or 32 ACP for short. The semi-rimmed design pushed a 71gr FMJ bullet at a MV just above 900 fps, or about 130 foot pounds of kinetic energy. Shot out of real guns, some current loads don't get there.

For example, Speer's Gold Dot 32 ACP 60gr GDHP makes 841 fps MV in a PPK, for an ME of 94 ft-lbs. Federal's American Eagle 32 ACP 71gr TMJ AE32AP, will do a little better, 789 fps and 98 ft-lbs. But Winchester's 60gr Silvertip HP X32ASHP shot in a Taurus PT132SS generates 878 fps at the muzzle, translating to 103 ft-lbs ME.

Three cartridges, the **32 Smith & Wesson, 32 Smith & Wesson Long (32 Colt New Police),** and the **32 H&R Magnum** represent three generations of the same cartridge thinking.

The grandpappy of the group is the 1870s-vintage 32 Smith & Wesson, which was originally a blackpowder cartridge pushing an 85gr bullet around 705 fps. As a smokeless offering from Remington, Winchester, and others, the 32 S&W is currently loaded with .312-in.-diameter 85gr and 88gr bullets, mainly because thousands of antique, but still functioning, revolvers were chambered for it. For instance, Winchester's 32 Smith & Wesson X32SWP load uses an 85gr Lead Round Nose pushed at 680 fps MV to generate 90 ft-lbs of energy.

The stretched version of the 32 S&W is called, unsurprisingly, the 32 Smith & Wesson Long. Perhaps "Longer" would have been more syntactically correct, but it was introduced in either the Smith & Wesson Model 1896 Hand Ejector revolver, or in 1903. Either way, for many years wheelguns spinning the 32 S&W Long were popular among detectives and plainclothes officers, eventually losing out to the 38 Smith & Wesson Special. At that time, the 32 S&W Long was about a third more powerful than the 32 S&W. Now, the Remington Express 32 S&W Long R32SWL 98gr Lead Round Nose

"FRESH MEAT FOR THE OUTFIT."

A.B. FROST.

WINCHESTER
REPEATING ARMS CO.
NEW HAVEN, CONN.

"Fresh Meat for the Outfit," Winchester calendar artwork by A.B. Frost (circa 1901) doesn't delineate what round put the antelope in the pot, but the 32-20 Winchester is a pretty good guess. It was introduced by Winchester in 1882 for the Model 73 lever-action rifle, and earned its chops as a medium-power cartridge in both rifle and revolver. It's appropriate for small and medium game out to 100 yards and won't destroy a lot of meat. Calendar artwork © Winfield Galleries, LLC, St. Louis, Missouri. Used with permission. To view current artwork and pricing, log on to www.WinfieldGalleries.com.

The 32 S&W Magtech Sport 85gr LRN 32SWA generates 680 fps MV and 87 ft-lbs ME. The Sellier & Bellot 32 S&W Long 100gr LRN #V311312U specs are MV 886 fps; and ME 174 ft-lbs. Photos courtesy of Midway USA.

makes 705 fps at the muzzle and 115 ft-lbs ME, or 28% more energy. Surprisingly, the 32 SWL has pretty good ballistics at 50 yards, dropping only -2.3 in.

If the 32 S&W Long could have been called the Longer, then the 32 H&R Magnum could as easily have been called the 32 Smith & Wesson Longest, since this joint creation of Harrington & Richardson and the Federal Cartridge Company is nothing more than a lengthened version of the 32 SWL, having been introduced in a 5-shot revolver in 1984. Happily, all three cartridges with .312-in. bullet diameters can be fired in revolvers chambered for the 32 HRM. But the Magnum has substantially more pop than Dad and Grandpap, making around 230 ft-lbs of energy at the muzzle, slightly better than a 158gr 38 Special.

In fact, the pairing of the 32 H&R Magnum and a Ruger SP101 SP-3231X makes a potent defense rig, and training with 32 S&W makes even recoil-shy shooters smile. Firing the H&R Magnum ammunition, it's easy to see why this caliber hangs on. The recoil is pleasant, and accuracy does not depend largely on recoil control, a characteristic common to snub-nosed revolvers of more powerful calibers. And on the receiving end, 85gr JHPs make 1100 fps and produce about 211 ft-lbs of energy. Or, 32 H&R Mag 50gr MagSafe Defender frangible ammunition produces 1700 fps and 321 ft-lbs muzzle energy.

Like a 32 H&R Magnum gun will chamber and safely fire the 32 S&W and 32 S&W Long, or likewise, a 357 Magnum revolver will also shoot 38 Special, a **327 Federal Magnum** revolver fires 32 H&R Magnum ammunition. The

327 Mag was introduced in November 2007 by Federal Cartridge, and Ruger chambered a 6-shot version of the SP101 for the new round. The 327 FM uses the .312-in. diameter bullets found in the 32 H&R Magnum, 32 S&W, 32 S&W Long, and 32-20 Winchester (1882). The 327, in essence, is a 32-20 with a slightly smaller case. Or, the 327 is a 32 H&R Magnum case lengthened by one-eighth inch and thickened internally to take twice the pressure. The design idea was to take a slightly larger 32 H&R Magnum case, pour in better powder, and get 357 Magnum terminal performance without the bigger gun's recoil. But as the accompanying tables show, the 327 FM delivers energies more in line with the 9mm Luger, or between 334 ft-lbs and 435 ft-lbs. However, we have shot American Eagle 100gr slugs that zoomed along at 1410 fps, making the resulting 442 ft-lbs of muzzle energy approach the

The 327 Federal Magnum, left, is an 85gr Federal Hydra Shok hollowpoint load. Second from left is a 100gr American Eagle JSP 327 round, then a 32 H&R Magnum 85gr Federal Personal Defense hollowpoint, and a 95gr Federal Champion Lead Semi-Wadcutter with grayish dry lubricant. Pairing either one with a Ruger SP101 SP-3231X, below, makes a potent defense rig.

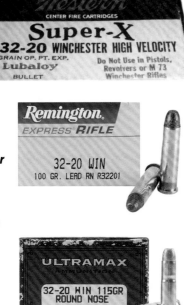

Don't doubt the 32-20's longevity. Here's an early box of Western Super-X 32-20 Winchester. This high-velocity 80gr load was too hot for handguns and M73 Winchester rifles, as the warning makes clear. Like Winchester, Remington catalogs its 32-20 as a rifle load, but in modern revolvers, it's safe to shoot it. This R32201 Remington Express 100gr Lead RN pops out the muzzle (rifle) at 1210 fps, generating 325 ft-lbs energy. Ballistics are sound, too, with a 50-yard zero, it only drops -5.9 in. at 100 yards. Ultramax loads a 115gr version.

459 ft-lbs of a 125gr 357 Mag load shot from a 3-in.-barrel Smith & Wesson 386SC. An appealing option would be an eight-shot model based on a medium-sized frame like Ruger's GP100.

One of the issues with the round has been the gun's sensitivity to fouling. We've seen that after just 20 rounds of 100gr JSP ammunition, one chamber fouled badly, requiring too much force (in our view) to push fresh rounds into place. We should note that 85gr Hydra-Shok rounds left less debris. Overall, we noticed that keeping the barrel and chambers of the 327 model clean made a bigger difference in terms of accuracy and operation than it did in a 32 H&R Magnum SP101 revolver.

Because of the 327 FM's appearance, it's worth touching on the overlooked **32-20 WCF,** aka **32 Winchester.** Designed as a rifle cartridge (Winchester introduced it in 1882 for the Model 73 lever action), the 32-20 has appeared in lever, slide, bolt-action, and single-shot rifles. Several companies still make boutique loads for it, including Remington (100gr Lead Flat Nose, #28410), Ultramax (115gr #CB32201), and Black Hills (115gr

LFN #DCB3220N1), among others. Interestingly, long before the 327 FM, the 32-20 was the parent case of the 25-20 and the 218 Bee. ●

SELECTED LOADS & BALLISTICS

Winchester 32 Automatic X32ASHP 60gr Silvertip Hollow Point

Range, Yards	Muzzle	50	100
Velocities (fps)	970	895	835
Energy (ft.-lbs.)	125	107	93
Trajectory (in.)		NA	NA

Winchester 32 S&W X32SWP 85gr Lead RN

Range, Yards	Muzzle	50	100
Velocities (fps)	680	645	610
Energy (ft.-lbs.)	90	81	73
Trajectory (in.)		NA	NA

Winchester 32 S&W X32SWP 85gr Lead RN

Range, Yards	Muzzle	50	100
Velocities (fps)	680	645	610
Energy (ft.-lbs.)	90	81	73
Trajectory (in.)		NA	NA

Remington Express 32 S&W Long R32SWL 98gr Lead RN

Range, Yards	Muzzle	50	100
Velocities (fps)	705	670	635
Energy (ft.-lbs.)	115	98	88
Trajectory (in.)	0	−2.3	−10.5

Federal 32 H&R Magnum 85gr JHP PD C32HRB

Range, Yards	Muzzle	25	50	75	100
Velocities (fps)	1120	1067	1023	986	953
Energy (ft.-lbs.)	237	215	197	183	171
Trajectory (in.)	0	-1.0	-4.1	-9.4	

Federal Premium 327 Fed Mag 85gr Hydra-Shok JHP PD PD327HS1 H

Range, Yards	Muzzle	25	50	75	100
Velocities (fps)	1400	1306	1221	1150	1091
Energy (ft.-lbs.)	370	322	281	250	225
Trajectory (in.)	0	-0.4	-2.2	-5.7	

Winchester 32-20 Win X32201 100gr Lead (Rifle Ballistics)

Range, Yards	Muzzle	100	200	300
Velocities (fps)	1210	1021	914	835
Energy (ft.-lbs.)	325	232	185	155
Trajectory (in.)		15.9	0	-57.5

18: Martial Cartridges

The 30-06 Springfield, 308 Win and many others could fit in this chapter of cartridges which were created for martial purposes, but these offbeat rounds have maintained their military bearing more so than others that have been domesticated for other uses.

The **7.5x55 Swiss,** also known as the **7.5x55 Schmidt-Rubin,** was adopted in 1911 for the Schmidt-Rubin rifle as yet another 308 bore. Development for the round started 22 years earlier, however, when it was adopted for the Schmidt-Rubin straightpull bolt-action rifle, which was plagued by gas leaks, which limited safe working pressure. The 1911 version of the rifle could withstand 45,500 psi, realizing the potential of the 7.5x55 case. At this higher pressure, the 7.5 essentially duplicates the performance of the 308 Win. It stayed the primary Swiss round until the end of Schmidt-Rubin rifle service life, but it was also adapted to the Model 57 assault rifle. Its bullet diameter is .308, which is confusing since the original loading used a bullet near 7.5mm in diameter (0.299-inch), but it was paper-patched to work in a 30-caliber bore. Other specifications include a neck diameter of .334 in, shoulder diameter of .452 in, base diameter of .494 in, and a case length of 2.18 in and a cartridge length of 3.05 in. Norma 7.5x55 factory loads show a 180gr soft-point bullet developing 2651 fps MV (see accompanying tables for additional ballistics), which also readily compares to the British 303. Note: Higher pressure loads with larger bullets cannot be used in the original Model 1889 rifle.

The **303 British** predates the Swiss as an official military cartridge by a year. It was adopted by the Brits in 1888 and remained as a martial round until it was supplanted by the 7.62x51mm NATO in the 1950s. Around 1897, it began being loaded in the U.S. The original loading combined a 215gr roundnose bullet with a compressed charge of blackpowder. Around 1892, the blackpowder load was replaced with a Cordite propellant that generated more velocity but less pressure. A later loading using a lighter, pointed bullet for the military, which in turn spawned many wildcats designed for bolt-action rifles. Ballistically, the 303 British betters the 30-40 Krag covered in

SELECTED LOADS & BALLISTICS

Norma 7.5x55 Swiss 180gr Oryx

Range, Yards	Muzzle	100	200	300	400	500
Velocities (fps)	2494	2195	1926	1680		
Energy (ft-lbs)	2484	1928	1480	1127		
Trajectory (in.)		2.8	0	-12.2		

Norma's 7.5mm Schmidt-Rubin (7.5x55 Swiss) load has a 180gr Oryx Protected Point bullet running at MV 2494 fps and producing ME of 2484 ft-lbs. This ammunition is not intended to be fired in a Model 1889 Schmidt-Ruben rifle. This ammunition creates an unsafe pressure that the Model 1889 action was not designed to handle. Photos this chapter courtesy of Midway USA.

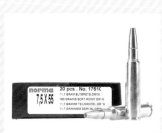

SELECTED LOADS & BALLISTICS

Winchester 303 British X303B1 180gr Power-Point

Range, Yards	Muzzle	100	200	300	400	500
Velocities (fps)	2460	2233	2018	1817	1629	1459
Energy (ft-lbs)	2418	1993	1628	1320	1060	851
Trajectory (in.)		2.7	0	-11.0	-33.2	68.3

Hornady 303 British 8225 150gr SP

Range, Yards	Muzzle	100	200	300	400	500
Velocities (fps)	2685	2441	2210	1992	1787	1598
Energy (ft-lbs)	2401	1984	1627	1321	1064	851
Trajectory (in.)		2.2	0.	-9.3	-27.4	-56.5

Remington UMC 303 British L303B1 174gr Metal Case

Range, Yards	Muzzle	100	200	300	400	500
Velocities (fps)	2475	2209	1960			
Energy (ft-lbs)	2366	1885	1484			
Trajectory (in.)		0	-5.9	-21.4		

an earlier chapter with a long .311-in. bullet. Sierra, Speer, and Hornady offer .311-in. bullets of various weights.

The **7.7 Japanese,** also known as the **7.7x58mm Japanese Arisaka,** took over for

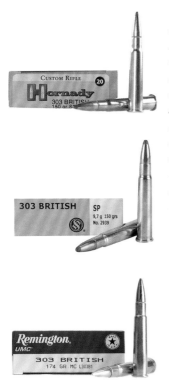

This Hornady Custom 303 British load has a 150gr Spire Point loaded with non-corrosive Boxer primed reloadable brass cases. Muzzle Velocity: 2685 fps. Muzzle Energy: 2401 ft-lbs. The Sellier & Bellot 150gr Soft Point runs a little slower, developing 2654 fps MV and 2347 ft-lbs ME. Remington's UMC brand has a 174gr FMJ flying at MV 2475 fps and hitting with ME of 2366 ft-lbs.

the weak 6.5 Japanese Arisaka (covered earlier) as a Japanese army round in 1939. Because both rounds were in the field during the changeover, this caused confusion in the Japanese ranks, hindering the country's war effort. Norma has produced cases and loaded ammunition with the proper head size for use in the many surplus and souvenir rifles that made their way to the U.S. after WWII. Ballistically, the 7.7 falls between the 300 Savage and 308 Win, using .311-in. diameter bullets like the 303 British.

Another early military round was the **7.65 Argentine,** which Mauser designed for the 1889 Belgian-pattern rifle as the 7.65x53 Mauser. Actual bullet diameter is supposed to be 0.313 inch, but 0.311-inch and 0.312-inch bullets are also common in rifles used in Argentina, Bolivia, Columbia, Ecuador, Peru, and Turkey. Before WWII, both Remington and Winchester chambered factory rifles for this round and offered sporting ammunition. Today, Norma is the sole supplier of cases. Compare the 7.65 to the 308 Win in modern guns and the observant shooter won't see much difference. Original military loads used a 211gr round-nose bullet, but most modern hunting rounds use 150- and 180gr pointed bullets.

The **7.62x39mm** round has a lot of aliases, including the **7.62mm Soviet, 7.62mm Warsaw Pact (or WP),** or **7.62 mm ComBloc,** and **30**

Short Russian, the Short distinguishing it from the older 30 Russian (7.62x54mmR, covered below). Developed for the Soviet RPD machine gun in 1943, the 7.62x39mm is the world's most popular cartridge for assault rifles. It is better known for being chambered postwar in SKS and AK-47 rifles, by both militaries and civilians. Thirty to fifty million Kalashnikov rifles have been chambered for 7.62x39mm, and about 55 minor and major nations use it as their military standard. In the 1970s, the 7.62x39mm was replaced by the 5.45x39mm cartridge used in the AK-74. Standard groove diameter of foreign military rifles in 7.62x39mm is .311 inch, and most factory ammunition is loaded with those diameter bullets.

The 7.62x39mm is about as powerful as the 30-30 Win, which may explain some of its popularity, but the Russian has been chambered in more action styles than the lever standard. Examples: AR-15s by Olympic Arms, Del-Ton Inc, and others; Ruger's Mini-30, Remington's

SELECTED LOADS & BALLISTICS

Norma 7.65 Argentine 174gr Soft Point

Range, Yards	Muzzle	100	200	300	400	500
Velocities (fps)	2494	2169	1873	1611		
Energy (ft-lbs)	2401	1816	1356	1003		
Trajectory (in.)		2.9	0	-12.9		

Norma 7.7 Japanese 174gr Soft Point

Range, Yards	Muzzle	100	200	300	400	500
Velocities (fps)	2494	2169	1873	1611		
Energy (ft-lbs)	2401	1816	1356	1003		
Trajectory (in.)		2.9	0	-12.9		

Norma loads a full range of older metric rounds, such as the 7.65mm Argentine Mauser and 7.7mm Japanese in 174gr round nose and spitzer bullets.

SELECTED LOADS & BALLISTICS

Fiocchi Shooting Dynamics 7.62x39 762SOVA 124gr FMJ

Range, Yards	Muzzle	100	200	300	400	500
Velocities (fps)	2375	2100	1844	1611	1405	1234
Energy (ft-lbs)	1552	1214	936	715	544	419
Trajectory (in.)		0	-6.4	–23.1		

Winchester 7.62x39mm Russian X76239 123gr Soft Point

Range, Yards	Muzzle	100	200	300	400	500
Velocities (fps)	2365	2033	1731	1465	1248	1093
Energy (ft-lbs)	1527	1129	818	586	425	327
Trajectory (in.)		3.1	0	-15.4	-46.3	-98.4

Federal GM76254RM 7.62x54R 175gr Gold Medal

Range, Yards	Muzzle	100	200	300	400	500
Velocities (fps)	2610	2434	2264	2102	1946	1797
Energy (ft-lbs)	2647	2301	1992	1716	1471	1255
Trajectory (in.)		2.2	0	-9.0	-25.7	-51.8

Winchester 7.62x54R MC54RSP 180gr Soft Point

Range, Yards	Muzzle	100	200	300	400	500
Velocities (fps)	2625	2302	2003	1729	1485	1281
Energy (ft-lbs)	2751	2117	1603	1195	882	655
Trajectory (in.)		2.9	0	-11.6	-34.9	-74.1

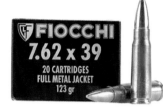

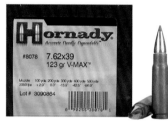

There are dozens of loads for the ubiquitous 7.62x39mm Russian, including the Wolf Military Classic 124gr Full Metal (Bi-Metal) Jacket Steel Case load. It features berdan-primed steel cases that have been polymer-coated. Each round is loaded with copper-washed steel jacket (bi-metal) bullets. Cases are not reloadable. Muzzle Velocity, 2330 fps. The Fiocchi Shooting Dynamics 7.62x39mm Russian has a 123gr FMJ that has a lead core with a copper jacket. The Hornady ammunition has a 123gr V-Max bullet loaded in lacquer-coated steel cases with non-corrosive berdan primers. The V-Max bullet features a polymer tip that raises (improves) the ballistic coefficient. Muzzle Velocity, 2350 fps.

Compact Model 799 Mini Mauser bolt-action rifle (2006) and others. The standard military load for the 7.62x39 fires a 123gr FMJ bullet at a MV of 2350 fps. One Remington factory load shoots a 125gr PSP bullet at 2365 fps. As noted in earlier chapters, the 7.62x39mm is the parent cartridge of the 220 Russian, 22 PPC, and 6mm PPC cartridges.

The big brother of the 7.62x39mm Short Russian was the **7.62x54R (Russian),** chambered in the Mosin-Nagant bolt-action rifle in 1891. Amazingly, it was used until the end of WWII by Russia, Finland, and China. All military loads use Berdan primers. Norma offers superior-quality cases designed to use Boxer primers, so the handloader can load for and enjoy this still-viable 19th century design. Nominal groove diameter is supposed to be somewhat larger than standard 30-caliber rifles. Bullets of 0.309- to 0.311-inch are supposed to be correct; however, rifles with abnormally oversize bores are common.

The **8mm Mauser (7.92 Mauser, 8x57 JS, 8x57mm Mauser),** a performance counterpart to the 30-06 Springfield, was adopted by the Germany military in 1888 and followed by other countries, including Czechoslovakia, Poland, and China. According to Norma sources, the moniker "Mauser" is a misnomer because this

The Winchester USA 762x54mm rimmed Russian round uses a 180gr jacketed soft point. The Silver Bear employs a 174gr FMJ, MV 2495 fps. The Silver Bear ammunition is loaded to military specifications into non-reloadable zinc-coated steel cases.

cartridge was developed by a German military commission at Spandau Arsenal, for chambering in the forerunner of the now famous M-98 Mauser bolt-action rifle. The "J" in the name is a misreading of the original "I" letter, which

There are plenty of choices in 8x57mm Mauser (8mm Mauser), in both foreign and domestic production. Some are the Prvi Partizan 196gr Soft Point, Muzzle Velocity, 2181 fps; Muzzle Energy, 2072 ft-lbs., the Federal Power-Shok 170gr Soft Point, Muzzle Velocity, 2360 fps; Muzzle Energy, 2012 ft-lbs; and Nosler Custom's 200gr AccuBond Spitzer, Muzzle Velocity, 2475 fps; Muzzle Energy, 2720 ft-lbs.

SELECTED LOADS & BALLISTICS

Norma 8x57 JRS 196gr Alaska

Range, Yards	Muzzle	100	200	300	400	500
Velocities (fps)	2395	2113	1857	1624		
Energy (ft-lbs)	2497	1945	1500	1149		
Trajectory (in.)		3.1	0	-13.2		

Norma 8x57 JS 196gr Alaska

Range, Yards	Muzzle	100	200	300	400	500
Velocities (fps)	2526	2241	1982	1742		
Energy (ft-lbs)	2777	2188	1709	1322		
Trajectory (in.)		2.6	0	-11.5		

Winchester 8mm Mauser (8x57) X8MM 170gr Power-Point

Range, Yards	Muzzle	100	200	300	400	500
Velocities (fps)	2360	1970	1623	1333	1123	997
Energy (ft-lbs)	2102	1464	994	671	476	375
Trajectory (in.)		3.8	0	-17.2	-54.1	

Remington Express 8mm Mauser R8MSR 170gr Core-Lokt

Range, Yards	Muzzle	100	200	300	400	500
Velocities (fps)	2360	1969	1622	1333	1123	997
Energy (ft-lbs)	2102	1463	993	671	476	375
Trajectory (in.)		1.6	-4.4	-23.7	-62.8	-129

stood for "Infanterie" in German. In 1905, Germany increased working pressure of this cartridge and switched from a 226gr 0.318-inch roundnose bullet (2095 fps) to a 154gr 0.323-inch spitzer bullet (2880 fps). The "S" in the designation stands for "Spitzer" and also indicates that the bore was either originally made for, or was altered for, 0.323-inch bullets. Of course, .323-inch bullets must not be used in Model 89 rifles with .318-inch bores.

The 8x57 JRS is a rimmed version of that case, specifically for use in double rifles and combination guns. Originally, these two cartridges differed only in rim design. The accompanying tables show the comparison in more detail, but, generally, a 30-30 Win 170gr round will shoot make 2200 fps MV, and an 8mm Mauser 170gr makes 2360 fps MV. A 308 Win 150gr runs at 2820 fps MV, and 8mm 150gr load will go 2880 fps MV. ●

19: Thumpers on Both Ends

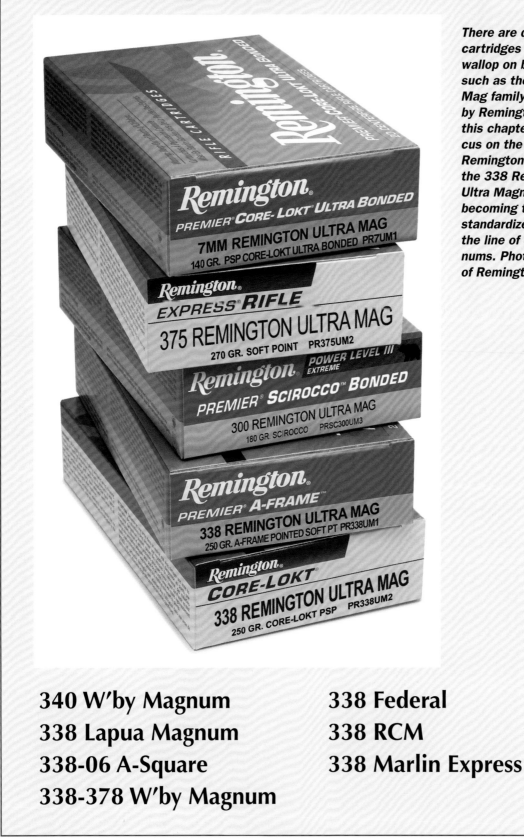

There are quite a few cartridges that pack a wallop on both ends, such as the entire Ultra Mag family designed by Remington. For this chapter, we focus on the 338 RUM. Remington introduced the 338 Remington Ultra Magnum In 2000, becoming the second standardized member of the line of Ultra Magnums. Photo courtesy of Remington.

340 W'by Magnum

338 Lapua Magnum

338-06 A-Square

338-378 W'by Magnum

338 Federal

338 RCM

338 Marlin Express

The 338 family of cartridges are meant for the biggest North American game and many African animals. They are a decided step up from the 7mms or 308-caliber magnums, but not quite elephant or water-buffalo class like the 416 Rigby and the 458 Win Mag.

The eldest of the group is the **338 Winchester Magnum,** introduced in 1958 along with the 264 Win Mag (covered earlier) and two years after the 458 Win Mag. Many believe it is one of the better, if not best, elk, moose, and grizzly cartridge with 250gr bullets running about 2650 fps, but it will handle bullets as light as 200 grains for deer. According to the Hodgdon Data Manual, 26th Edition, a single 338 Win Mag load for all big game, including the dangerous variety, would consist of the Nosler 250gr Partition pushed along at 2700 to 2800 fps by H4350, H414, IMR-4350, or IMR-4831. Its overall length is 3.34 in, with a maximum case length of 2.50 in.

Factory loads for the 338 Win Mag offer bullet weights of 180, 200, 210, 225, and 250 grains. Winchester's 200gr Ballistic Silvertip bullet cranks out a MV of 2950 fps. Remington's 225gr Core-Lokt spitzer bullet travels 2780 fps MV. Federal's Premium Safari Rifle load pushes a 250gr Nosler Partition to 2660 fps MV.

The **340 Weatherby Magnum** debuted in 1962 as a response to the 338 Win Mag. It uses the same case as the 300 W'by Mag, and will handle bullets ranging from 200 to 300 grains. It holds a lot more powder than the 338 Win Mag, pushing 250gr bullets between 200 and 300 fps more MV than the 338 Win Mag. Another way to look at it, the Weatherby cartridge delivers as much punch at 400 yards as the 338 Win Mag does at 300. And, despite its name, the 340 W'by Mag uses .338-in. bullets, same as the 338 Magnum.

Another thumper of more recent vintage, the **338 Lapua Magnum (8.6x70)** was birthed in 1987 by Lapua of Finland. It was originally intended for use in military and police sniper-type rifles, and is based on the 416 Rigby case, shortened and necked down, to accept the smaller .338-in.-diameter bullet. The 338 Lapua has about 14% greater case capacity

SELECTED LOADS & BALLISTICS

Federal Prem 338 Win Mag P338A3 180gr Nosler AccuBond

Range, Yards	Muzzle	100	200	300	400	500
Velocities (fps)	3120	2860	2610	2380	2160	1950
Energy (ft-lbs)	3890	3265	2730	2265	1865	1520
Trajectory (in.)		1.4	0	-6.4	-19.1	-39.2

Hornady Superformance 338 Win Mag 185gr GMX 82226

Range, Yards	Muzzle	100	200	300	400	500
Velocities (fps)	3080	2850	2632	2424	2226	2036
Energy (ft-lbs)	3896	3337	2845	2413	2034	1703
Trajectory (in.)		1.4	0	-6.4	-18.8	-38.2

Winchester 338 Win Mag SBST338 200gr Ballistic Silvertip

Range, Yards	Muzzle	100	200	300	400	500
Velocities (fps)	2950	2724	2509	2303	2108	1922
Energy (ft-lbs)	3864	3294	2794	2355	1972	1640
Trajectory (in.)		1.6	0	-7.1	-20.8	-42.3

Federal Premium 338 Win Mag P338A2 210gr Nosler Partition

Range, Yards	Muzzle	100	200	300	400	500
Velocities (fps)	2830	2600	2380	2180	1980	1790
Energy (ft-lbs)	3735	3155	2650	2210	1825	1500
Trajectory (in.)		1.8	0	-8.0	-23.3	-47.5

Hornady Custom 338 Win Mag 225gr SST 82234

Range, Yards	Muzzle	100	200	300	400	500
Velocities (fps)	2785	2575	2375	2184	2001	1828
Energy (ft-lbs)	3875	3313	2818	2382	2000	1670
Trajectory (in.)		1.9	0	-8.0	-23.4	-47.4

Hornady Superformance 338 Win Mag 225gr SST 82233

Range, Yards	Muzzle	100	200	300	400	500
Velocities (fps)	2840	2758	2582	2414	2252	2096
Energy (ft-lbs)	4318	3798	3331	2911	2533	2194
Trajectory (in.)		1.5	0	-6.8	-19.5	-39.1

The problem most shooters have with the 338 Win Mag is the stiff recoil, about 30 ft-lbs in a 9-pound gun.

Weatherby 340 W'by Mag 200gr SP H340200SP

Range, Yards	Muzzle	100	200	300	400	500
Velocities (fps)	3221	2946	2688	2444	2213	1995
Energy (ft-lbs)	4607	3854	3208	2652	2174	1767
Trajectory (in.)		3.3	4.0	0	-9.9	-27.0

Weatherby 340 W'by Mag 225 SP H340225SP

Range, Yards	Muzzle	100	200	300	400	500
Velocities (fps)	3066	2824	2595	2377	2170	1973
Energy (ft-lbs)	4696	3984	3364	2822	2352	1944
Trajectory (in.)		3.6	4.4	0	-10.7	-28.6

Weatherby 340 W'by Mag 250gr Partition N340250PT

Range, Yards	Muzzle	100	200	300	400	500
Velocities (fps)	2941	2743	2553	2371	2197	2029
Energy (ft-lbs)	4801	4176	3618	3120	2678	2286
Trajectory (in.)		3.9	4.6	0	-10.9	-28.9

Hornady Match 338 Lapua 250gr BTHP 8230

Range, Yards	Muzzle	100	200	300	400	500
Velocities (fps)	2900	2760	2625	2494	2366	2242
Energy (ft-lbs)	4668	4229	3825	3452	3108	2791
Trajectory (in.)		1.5	0	-6.6	-18.8	-37.1

Remington 338 Lapua Mag RM338LMR1 250gr Scenar

Range, Yards	Muzzle	100	200	300	400	500
Velocities (fps)	2960	2820	2683	2551	2423	2299
Energy (ft-lbs)	4863	4412	3996	3613	3259	2932
Trajectory (in.)		1.4	0	-6.3	-17.9	-35.4

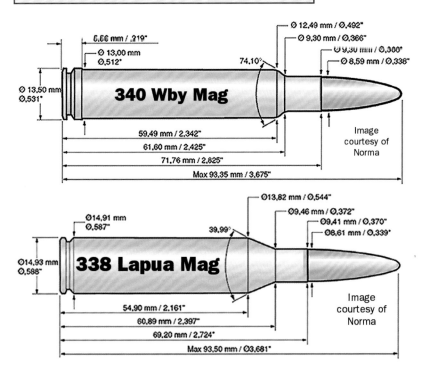

Image courtesy of Norma

sas, was asked by the United States Marine forces to develop a long-range rifle for sniper applications. RAI was a relatively small company, owned by late Jerry Haskins, operating mainly in the field of defense technology projects. Officially, the project was to develop a target rifle for 1000 yards. Haskins developed a prototype for an extremely simplified target rifle, the concept of which is widely called the Haskins rifle. Haskins designed the model 500 for the 50 BMG cartridge and the model 300 for the 300 Win Mag cartridge, but the 300 Win Mag cartridge did not fulfill the army penetration requirements.

The search for a new RAI 300 caliber with better ballistic properties started with the 378 W'by Mag case, necked down to .338 in., but the case shape caused poor feeding. The next parent case was a rimless 416 Rigby, necked down to accept a .338 bullet. This new caliber, known as the 338/416 or 8.58x71, prompted the search for a new .338-caliber FMJ bullet, which Lapua eventually solved. The resulting 338 Lapua Magnum held a powder load of almost 6 grams of slow-burning powder; thus, it needs a large rifle magnum primer.

Remington introduced the **338 Remington Ultra Magnum** in 2000, becoming the second standardized member of the line of Ultra Magnums. Based on the 404 Jeffery, the 338 RUM is a full-length case with moderate body taper and a relatively sharp shoulder. The maximum

than the 340 Weatherby Magnum, but the Lapua has the advantage of using a conventional case that feeds from a box magazine more easily. Its popularity as a sniper cartridge continues to grow, and Lapua assesses that demand as somewhere between the 300 Win Mag and 50 BMG. Sako, Mauser, and Accuracy International among others produce complete sniper rifles in this chambering.

However, the birth of the 338 LM dates back to 1982, when an American company Research Armament Industries of Rogers, Arkan-

Federal Premium 338 RUM P338RUMA 210gr Nosler Partition

Range, Yards	Muzzle	100	200	300	400	500
Velocities (fps)	3050	2810	2580	2370	2160	1970
Energy (ft-lbs)	4335	3685	3115	2615	2180	1805
Trajectory (in.)		1.5	0	-6.6	-19.6	-39.8

Federal Premium P338RUMA1 338 RUM 225gr AccuBond

Range, Yards	Muzzle	100	200	300	400	500
Velocities (fps)	3020	2850	2680	2520	2360	2210
Energy (ft-lbs)	4555	4045	3585	3165	2785	2445
Trajectory (in.)		1.4	0	–6.2	-17.9	-36.0

Remington 338 RUM PR338UM2 250gr Core-Lokt PSP

Range, Yards	Muzzle	100	200	300	400	500
Velocities (fps)	2860	2647	2443	2249	2064	1887
Energy (ft-lbs)	4540	3888	3314	2807	2363	1977
Trajectory (in.)		1.7	0	-7.6	-22.0	-44.7

A-Square 338-06 A-Square 200gr Nosler Ballistic Tip

Range, Yards	Muzzle	100	200	300	400	500
Velocities (fps)	2750	2553	2364	2184	2011	
Energy (ft-lbs)	3358	2894	2482	2118	1796	
Trajectory (in.)		1.90	0	-8.22	-23.63	

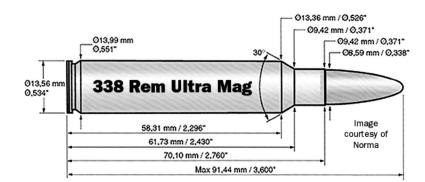

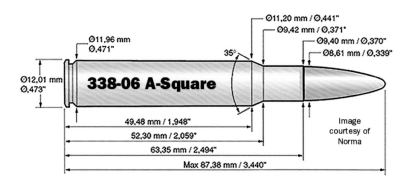

overall length is 3.675 in with a maximum case length of 2.825 in. Muzzle energy exceeds the 338 Win Mag by about 25%, making the 338 RUM very similar to the 340 W'by Mag ballistically. Like Weatherby, Remington equips its 338 RUM rifles with 26-in. barrels to get every fps from those huge charges of slow-burning powder.

The ***338-06 A-Square*** was a wildcat made by necking up the 30-06 case to accept 0.338-in. bullets, and it was made a factory load by A-Square in 1998. The wildcat's history began, however, shortly after the end of WWII, according to Norma, when Charles O'Neil, Elmer Keith, and Don Hopkins invented a similar wildcat using the old 33 Winchester bullet (0.333-in.). It took better spitzer bullets popularized by the 338 Win Mag and the 340 W'by Mag for the 338-06 to show better performance than the 30-06 and the similar 35 Whelen. Since it uses far less powder and generates somewhat less velocity, the 338-06 produces far less recoil than the 338 Win Mag. Weatherby now produces factory-made rifles for the cartridge.

Based on the 378 Weatherby Magnum case, the ***338-378 Weatherby Magnum*** was another cartridge developed by Weatherby in the 1960s. However, until newer, slower propellants became available, the 338-378 W'by Mag would not improve significantly upon the 340 W'by Mag's performance, despite a big case-capacity advantage. With the advent of superior propellant choices, Weatherby asked Norma to begin loading ammunition in 1998, and now the 338-378 W'by Mag can launch 250gr bullets faster than 3000 fps. However, using far less powder, the 340 W'by Mag launches the same bullet at 2850 fps.

In 2006, the ***338 Federal*** became the first sporting rifle cartridge to carry Federal Cartridge Co.'s name. It is the 308 Win case necked up to .338 in, but with increased velocity over the 308 cartridge. Of course, the Federal has the ability to work with heavier bullet weights. It produces muzzle energy that is greater than a 30-06 and comparable to the 7mm Rem Mag. Three 338 Federal loads describe its appeal. It shoots a 180gr Nosler AccuBond bullet at 2840 fps MV and 3223 ft-lbs MV, about 200 fps faster than a standard 180gr 308 Win load. A 185gr Barnes Triple-Shock bullet is rated at 2760 fps MV and 3129 ft-lbs ME, and a 210gr Nosler Partition flies at 2630 fps MV and 3225 ft-lbs energy. Because it is based on the 308 Win, the 338 Federal can be chambered in short-action rifles without heavy recoil.

Hornady's **338 Ruger Compact Magnum** was designed to compete with the 325 WSM in a 20-in. barrel, 4 inches shorter than what the short magnums typically require for best performance. Hornady ballistician Dave Emary, who pioneered Hornady's LEVERevolution rounds, says the company used proprietary propellants to gain that edge in the Ruger Compact Magnum, both the 300 and 338 RCM. Both are derived from the 2.580-in.-long 375 Ruger case, and all three have a .532-in. head and base diameter. In contrast, the rebated-rim WSM series has a .535 head and a maximum body diameter of .555 in. The Hornady 338 case measures 2.015 in., base to mouth, slightly shorter than the 300 RCM's 2.100-in. case. Shoulder angle is 30 degrees. Both are loaded to an OAL of 2.840 in., like the WSMs. The bigger RCM case is shorter (about the 308 Win's length) to accept current cannelured bullets designed for the 338 Win Mag. All in, the 338 RCM holds about as much powder as a 338-06. Or, looked at another way, the 338 RCM is a more powerful version of the 338 Federal and a close match to the

SELECTED LOADS & BALLISTICS

Federal P338FA1 338 Federal 180gr Nosler AccuBond

Range, Yards	Muzzle	100	200	300	400	500
Velocities (fps)	2830	2590	2350	2130	1930	1730
Energy (ft-lbs)	3200	2670	2215	1820	1480	1200
Trajectory (in.)		1.8	0	-8.2	-23.9	-49.3

Federal Vital-Shok P338FC 338 Federal 185-gr Barnes Triple-Shock X-Bullet

Range, Yards	Muzzle	100	200	300	400	500
Velocities (fps)	2750	2500	2260	2030	1820	1620
Energy (ft-lbs)	3105	2560	2090	1695	1355	1080
Trajectory (in.)		2.0	0	-8.9	-26.2	-54.4

Federal Vital-Shok P338FTT2 338 Federal 200-gr Trophy Bonded Tip

Range, Yards	Muzzle	100	200	300	400	500
Velocities (fps)	2630	2430	2240	2060	1890	1730
Energy (ft-lbs)	3070	2625	2230	1885	1580	1320
Trajectory (in.)		2.2	0	-9.2	-26.3	-53.6

Federal Vital-Shok P338FB 338 Federal 210gr Nosler Partition

Range, Yards	Muzzle	100	200	300	400	500
Velocities (fps)	2630	2410	2200	2010	1820	1650
Energy (ft-lbs)	3225	2710	2265	1880	1545	1265
Trajectory (in.)		2.3	0	-9.4	-27.3	-56.3

325 WSM. The RCM's advantage is that four rounds will fit in a magazine instead of three 325s.

The **338 Marlin Express** is another Emary brainchild and a larger version of the 308 Marlin Express. After the introduction in 2007 of the high-performance lever-action 308 Marlin Express cartridge, which approximated 308 Win performance from a tubular magazine-fed lever-action rifle, the 338 Marlin's design goal in 2009 was to match the 30-06 and draw near the 338 Federal's ballistics when shot from a lever action, such as Marlin's Model 338 MXLR and 338 MX. Those lever-action rifles have been relegated to short-range work in the past, because the rounds they used employed ballistically inferior flat- or round-nose projectiles to prevent an accidental discharge due to a primer strike during recoil. That changed somewhat in 2006, when Hornady unveiled its FTX bullet loaded in the company's LEVERevolution ammunition line. The FTX featured a red elastomeric polymer spitzer tip that allowed these cartridges to be used safely in tubular magazines. The FTX first appeared in traditional lever-action cartridges such as 30-30 Win,

SELECTED LOADS & BALLISTICS

Weatherby 338-378 W'by Mag 200gr Accubond N333200ACB

Range, Yards	Muzzle	100	200	300	400	500
Velocities (fps)	3380	3130	2894	2670	2457	2254
Energy (ft-lbs)	5075	4351	3720	3166	2681	2256
Trajectory (in.)		2.7	3.4	0	-8.3	-22.4

Weatherby 338-378 W'by Mag 225 Barnes TSX B333225TSX

Range, Yards	Muzzle	100	200	300	400	500
Velocities (fps)	3180	2974	2778	2591	2410	2238
Energy (ft-lbs)	5052	4420	3856	3353	2902	2501
Trajectory (in.)		3.1	3.8	0.0	-8.9	-24

Weatherby 338-378 W'by Mag 250gr Partition N333250PT

Range, Yards	Muzzle	100	200	300	400	500
Velocities (fps)	3060	2856	2662	2475	2297	2125
Energy (ft-lbs)	5197	4528	3933	3401	2927	2507
Trajectory (in.)		3.5	4.2	0.0	-9.8	-26.4

Hornady Superformance 338 RCM 185gr GMX 82238

Range, Yards	Muzzle	100	200	300	400	500
Velocities (fps)	2980	2755	2542	2338	2143	1958
Energy (ft-lbs)	3647	3118	2653	2242	1887	1575
Trajectory (in.)		1.5	0	-6.9	-20.3	-41.2

Hornady Superformance 338 RCM 200gr SST 82237

Range, Yards	Muzzle	100	200	300	400	500
Velocities (fps)	2950	2744	2547	2358	2177	2004
Energy (ft-lbs)	3846	3342	2879	2468	2104	1784
Trajectory (in.)		1.6	0	-6.9	-20.1	-40.7

Hornady Superformance 338 RCM 225gr SST 82236

Range, Yards	Muzzle	100	200	300	400	500
Velocities (fps)	2750	2575	2407	2245	2089	1940
Energy (ft-lbs)	3778	3313	2894	2518	2180	1880
Trajectory (in.)		1.9	0	-7.9	-22.7	-45.4

Hornady LEVERevolution 338 Marlin Exp 200gr FTX 82240

Range, Yards	Muzzle	100	200	300	400	500
Velocities (fps)	2565	2365	2174	1992	1820	1658
Energy (ft-lbs)	2922	2484	2099	1762	1471	1221
Trajectory (in.)		3.0	1.2	-7.9	-25.9	-54.3

Remington 338 Marlin Express R338ME1 250gr Soft Point

Range, Yards	Muzzle	100	200	300	400	500
Velocities (fps)	2189	1922	1676	1458	1273	1132
Energy (ft-lbs)	2659	2049	1560	1180	900	711
Trajectory (in.)		2.0	-4.7	-23.7	-59.2	-116

35 Rem, 444 Marlin, 45-70 Government and 450 Marlin, then later in 308 Marlin Express (see earlier chapter), 32 Special, 460 S&W Mag, 500 S&W Mag, and 450 Bushmaster.

Still, the 338 Marlin Express case is not based the 308 Marlin Express. Instead, Hornady designed a new case with a base diameter (.507 in.) based on the 376 Steyr (0.506 in. base). It also had a .553-in.-wide and .050-in.-thick rim, and the case shoulder was 25 degrees. Case length is 1.890 in., slightly shorter than the 308 ME, with a maximum cartridge overall length

The Federal Premium 338 Federal Vital-Shok Ammunition powers a 185gr Barnes Triple-Shock X Bullet to a MV of 2750 fps and ME of 3106 ft-lbs In terms of recoil, it's one of the gentler choices in this 338 class. Photo courtesy of Federal.

of 2.600 in. Case capacity is 59.4 grains of water, compared to the 30-06 (65.7gr/H_2O) and the 338 Federal (53.3 Gr/H_2O). As far as firearms that chamber the 338 ME, Marlin has said relatively minor modifications were needed to make the 338 MX and 338 MXL platforms (based on the 1895M/450 Marlin receiver) function properly. Mainly, changes to the internal geometry, building a new breech bolt with a 0.553-in. rim diameter, and removing the bulged profile in the 1895 and 444 Big Bore rifle tubular magazines. ●

20: Underappreciated 35s

What is it about .35-caliber rifle cartridges that get them no love? Domestically, the 35 Remington, 356 Winchester, 358 Winchester, 35 Whelen, 350 Remington Magnum, and 358 Norma Magnum haven't produced a hit rifle or a high-profile cartridge near the popularity of the 270 Win, 7mm Rem Mag, 30-06, 300 Win Mag, or several others. When the most popular guy at your party is the 35 Remington, then your group has a credibility problem.

The **35 Remington,** introduced in 1906 but not chambered in the Remington Model 8 autoloading rifle until 1908, is second only to the 30-30 among deer hunters who prefer a lever-action carbine. At one point or another, Remington chambered the 35 Rem in the Model 81 Woodsmaster autoloader, Model 14 pump (1921-1935), Model 141 slide action (1936-1940), Model 720 bolt action (1941-1942), Model 600 bolt-action carbine (1964-1967), Model 760 Gamemaster (1952-1980), and until recently, the Model Seven. And Winchester, Mossberg and Savage have chambered the 35 Rem. As of December 2010, the 35 Rem was still available in the Marlin Model 336 lever action 60 years after the two were originally paired. The 35 Rem has a rimless case and a small shoulder. It's squatty and usually loaded with a 200gr RN bullet running about 2100 fps, but a 180gr Speer is a favorite handloader's bullet or H4895 or H335 powders. According to the Accurate Arms loading manual, 39.0 grains of 2520 develops only 27,800 psi peak pressure with suitable 35 Rem bullets. The maximum allowable length is 2.525 inches.

Of the **35 Whelen's** birth, the Hodgdon Manual says, "Back in 1922, government employees Townsend Whelen and James V. Howe of Springfield Armory developed the 400 Whelen, a wildcat formed by 30-06 configuration. During that same year, while Whelen was away on a hunting trip, Howe decided to neck the 400 on down to 35 caliber and thus created what he decided to call the 35 Whelen," which accepted a .358-in. 250gr to 275gr bullet. The

Previous page: "Yukon Trouble," a Remington promotional poster painted by Lynn Bogue Hunt (circa 1909), touts the 35 Rem along with the company's 25, 32, and 30-30 Rem rounds. © Winfield Galleries, LLC, St. Louis, Missouri. Used with permission. To view current artwork and pricing, log on to www. WinfieldGalleries.com.

A number of companies load the 35 Whelen in a variety of bullet weights and styles. For instance, Midway USA stocks the Hornady Superformance 35 Whelen 200gr Soft Point, DoubleTap's 200gr Barnes Triple-Shock X Bullet, and the Remington Express 200gr Pointed Soft Point. In the 225gr load, Nosler and DoubleTap use a Nosler AccuBond Spitzer, Federal in its Premium Vital-Shok line a Trophy Bonded Bear Claw. Nosler also loads a Nosler Partition Spitzer. Up a step, Nosler makes a 250gr Partition Spitzer in its Custom line; DoubleTap loads a jacketed soft point, and Remington employs a pointed soft point. At the top of the heap sits DoubleTap's 310gr Woodleigh Weldcore. DoubleTap Woodleigh photo courtesy of the manufacturer, other photo courtesy of Midway USA.

case was loaded with enough powder to drive a bullet at about 2400 fps. The Whelen runs on par with the 9.3x62mm Mauser, developed by German Otto Bock in 1905 and the 350 Rigby Magnum, developed by John Rigby of London in 1908. It's also the ballistic twin of the short, belted 350 Rem Mag, introduced in 1965. Interestingly, the Whelen can take on rounds in the next weight class up, such as the 375 Holland & Holland Magnum. With similar ballis-

SELECTED LOADS & BALLISTICS						

Remington Express 35 Rem R35R1 150gr PSP Core-Lokt

Range, Yards	Muzzle	100	200	300	400	500
Velocities (fps)	2300	1874	1506	1218	1039	934
Energy (ft-lbs)	1762	1169	755	494	359	291
Trajectory (in.)		1.8	-4.9	-27.1	-72.5	-150

Remington Express 35 Rem R35R2 200gr SP Core-Lokt

Range, Yards	Muzzle	100	200	300	400	500
Velocities (fps)	2080	1698	1376	1140	1001	911
Energy (ft-lbs)	1921	1280	841	577	445	369
Trajectory (in.)		2.3	-6.1	-33.0	-86.6	-174

DoubleTap 35 Whelen 200gr Barnes TSX Lead Free

Range, Yards	Muzzle	100	200	300	400	500
Velocities (fps)	2850	2628	2418	2218	2028	1847
Energy (ft-lbs)		3607	2596	2185	1826	1515
Trajectory (in.)		1.8	0	-7.7	-22.5	-45.8

Federal Vital-Shok 35 Whelen P35WT1 225gr Trophy Bonded Bear Claw

Range, Yards	Muzzle	100	200	300	400	500
Velocities (fps)	2600	2351	2116	1895	1690	1503
Energy (ft-lbs)	3377	2761	2238	1793	1428	1128
Trajectory (in.)		2.4	0	-10.1	-30.2	-62.2

Remington Express 35 Whelen R35WH3 250gr PSP

Range, Yards	Muzzle	100	200	300	400	500
Velocities (fps)	2400	2197	2005	1823	1652	1496
Energy (ft-lbs)	3197	2680	2230	1844	1515	1242
Trajectory (in.)		1.3	-3.2	-16.6	-40.0	-76.3

DoubleTap 35 Whelen 310gr Woodleigh Weldcore JSP

Range, Yards	Muzzle	100	200	300	400	500
Velocities (fps)	2300	2130	1966	1810		
Energy (ft-lbs)	3641	3122	2884	2661		
Trajectory (in.)		1.4	-3.4	-17.2		

DoubleTap 358 Win 225gr Nosler Accubond

Range, Yards	Muzzle	100	200	300	400	500
Velocities (fps)	2520	2362	2211	2064	1923	1789
Energy (ft-lbs)	3173	2788	2441	2129	1848	1598
Trajectory (in.)		2.4	0	-9.5	-27.2	-54.3

Winchester 356 Win X3561 200gr Power-Point

Range, Yards	Muzzle	100	200	300	400	500
Velocities (fps)	2460	2114	1797	1517	1284	1113
Energy (ft-lbs)	2688	1985	1434	1022	732	550
Trajectory (in.)		3.2	0	-14.1	-43.4	-93.9

Winchester 348 Win X3483 200gr Silvertip

Range, Yards	Muzzle	100	200	300	400	500
Velocities (fps)	2520	2215	1931	1672	1443	1293
Energy (ft-lbs)	2820	2178	1656	1241	925	697
Trajectory (in.)		2.8	0	-11.9	-35.8	-75.7

tics, the Whelen gains an edge because it fits a standard-length Mauser action, whereas the long, belted 375 requires a bigger bullet slot. Remington added the 35 Whelen to its list of factory cartridges in 1988 with 200gr and 250gr loads in Remington limited edition rifles.

Several decades later, Winchester took the same path as did Whelen by necking up the case of an existing, plentiful military round—the 308 Win—to take a .358-in. bullet. This happened in 1955, and the resulting round was called the **358 Winchester** and initially chambered in both the Winchester Model 88 lever action and the bolt-action Model 70 Featherweight. The company intended to replace the older tube-fed Model 71 lever-action in 348 Win with the 358 Win in the rotary-bolt box-magazine Model 88.

Hornady's LEVERevolution ammunition does quite a bit better at the muzzle than Remington's 35 Rem loads (see table), producing 2225 fps MV and 1721 ft-lbs ME. Photo courtesy Midway USA.

This Buffalo Bore 348 Win 250gr Jacketed Flat Nose Bonded Core is loaded up to maximum SAAMI specifications, so this ammunition is not intended for older guns. It is safe to use in any Winchester or Browning 71 in good condition. Chamber pressures are 33,000 CUP, with 2250 fps MV and 2810 ft-lbs ME. The Winchester 356 Win uses a 200gr Power-Point running 2640 fps at the muzzle. DoubleTap's 358 Win 310gr Woodleigh Weldcore JSP load packs a wallop with 2075 fps MV and 2965 ft-lbs ME. Buffalo Bore and Winchester photos courtesy of Midway USA; DoubleTap photo courtesy of the manufacturer.

While not technically a 35, the **348 Winchester** plays in the same sandbox. It was developed by Winchester and introduced in the Model 71 lever action rifle in 1936. Oddly, no standard production rifle has been available in 348 Win since the excellent Model 71 rifle

DoubleTap 358 Norma Magnum 250gr Nosler Partition						
Range, Yards	Muzzle	100	200	300	400	500
Velocities (fps)	2850	2682	2520	2365	2216	2071
Energy (ft-lbs)	4510	3992	3525	3105	2725	2382
Trajectory (in.)		1.7	0	–7.2	–20.5	–41.0

Remington Exp 350 Rem Mag R350M1 200gr PSP Core-Lokt						
Range, Yards	Muzzle	100	200	300	400	500
Velocities (fps)	2775	2471	2186	1921	1678	1461
Energy (ft-lbs)	3419	2711	2122	1639	1250	947
Trajectory (in.)		2.1	0	–9.4	–28.3	-59.7

was discontinued in 1958. Note: If you own a 71 chambered for 348 Win, buy as much factory ammo, cases, and bullets as you can, because the 348 case is not easily formed from any other case, and .348-in. bullets are scarce.

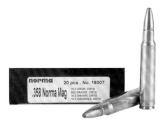

The **356 Winchester** was developed in parallel with the 307 Win, both being based on the 308 Win case with a rim added to allow it to function properly in leverguns. The 356 Win is much better on big game than the 30-30 Win and 35 Rem and compares favorably to the 348 Win and 358 Win. When it was introduced in 1982, the 356 Winchester was chambered in the Model 94 XTR, a beefed-up version of the Model 94 Winchester, as well as Marlin's 336ER. In 1987, only five years after its introduction, U.S. Repeating Arms stopped making Model 94 carbines in 356 Win but brought it back in 1988. Hornady's 35-caliber 200gr FTX bullet vastly improves the 356 Win's downrange ballistics, and the company recommends H 4895 powder. Hornady cautions, however, that FTX bullets require specialized loading techniques for the round. To achieve a high ballistic coefficient, the company had to lengthen the ogive, or nose, of the bullet, which means the case may need to be trimmed shorter than the suggested .010 in. under SAAMI maximum length that Hornady recommends for conventional bullets.

The 358 Win was followed four years later by the 1959 introduction of the most powerful of the factory standardized 35s, the **358 Norma Magnum.** Credit for its development goes to Nils Kvale of Norma, and it became the first commercially loaded .35-caliber magnum available to the domestic market since the 35 Newton (1915). The performance of the 358 Norma Magnum is on par with the 338 Win Mag, except that with most loads, the 338 shoots a bit flatter but the 358 delivers slightly

Exclusive to Midway, this Nosler Custom 350 Rem Mag has a 225gr Partition Spitzer at 2550 fps MV.

more energy. Said another way, with the right bullet the 358 Norma will do anything that the longer 375 H&H will do but using a standard-length action. According to Norma, one of the few guns factory-chambered for the 358 Norma Magnum Model 97 take-down made by Schultz & Larsen. Also, in the U.S., Ultra Light Arms once chambered the 358 Norma Magnum in its Model 28 Short rifle.

The latest entrant into this field is the 2002-reintroduced **350 Remington Magnum,** a 308 Win-length short magnum cartridge. It was first introduced in 1965 in the Model 600 carbine, and as such it was most powerful factory-loaded cartridge available in a short-action rifle. Besides the Models 600 and 660, the 350 Mag also saw its way into the Remington Model 700 BDL, Ruger Model 77, and Remington Model 700 Classic rifles. Some have called the 350 Rem Mag a 35 Whelen in a compact package. The 350 Rem Mag has a short, fat belted case that is larger in diameter than the 30-06/35 Whelen but about a half-inch shorter. Also, it's not as big around as the WSM cases. What may have hurt the 350 Rem Mag's acceptance wasn't its ballistics, but rather the Model 600 carbine's cosmetics. That gun had an 18-in. barrel, vent rib, and high-gloss two-tone laminated stock. It thumped on both ends, because the stout 350 cartridge punished the shooter in this lightweight package. The Model 660 came out in 1968 without the 600's ventilated rib and with a 20-in. barrel, but it, too, was discontinued. The latest iteration of a 350 Rem Mag-chambered gun was the Model 673 rifle, a variation of the Model Seven bolt action, which lasted from 2003 to 2004. ●

21: Historic 9mms

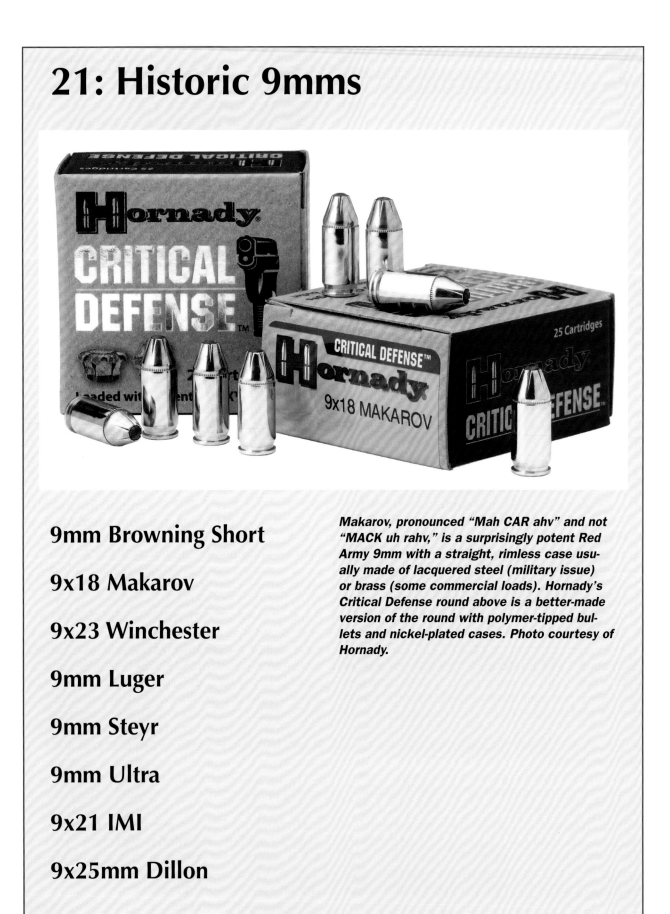

9mm Browning Short

9x18 Makarov

9x23 Winchester

9mm Luger

9mm Steyr

9mm Ultra

9x21 IMI

9x25mm Dillon

Makarov, pronounced "Mah CAR ahv" and not "MACK uh rahv," is a surprisingly potent Red Army 9mm with a straight, rimless case usually made of lacquered steel (military issue) or brass (some commercial loads). Hornady's Critical Defense round above is a better-made version of the round with polymer-tipped bullets and nickel-plated cases. Photo courtesy of Hornady.

The 9mm cartridges encompass a lot of history, geography, and range of performance. Also, some similar designations and inaccurate cartridge names can confuse even the most attentive shooter. Among some of the 9mms rounds are the 9mm Kurz (Short), 9mm Makarov, 9x18 M, 9x19, 9mm Parabellum, and 9mm Long. The 9x17mm (1908) is also called the 9mm Kurz, 9mm Short, and 380 ACP, with a bullet diameter of .356 in. Used in some Walther pistols, the 9x18mm Ultra is also called the 9mm Police, and it has a bullet diameter of .355 in. Likewise, the 9x19, also called the 9mm Parabellum and 9mm Luger, shoots bullets of .355 in. diameter. So do the 9mm Steyr, 9x21mm, 9x23mm Winchester, and 9x25 Dillon: .355 in.-diameter bullets. The outlier in the 9mm family is the 9mm Makarov, which has a bullet diameter of .364 in.

In more detail, the **380 ACP,** or as it's better known in Europe, the **9mm Browning Short** or 9x17mm, was introduced in 1908 in the Colt M1908 pistol. The "Short" part of the name distinguishes it from the 9mm Browning "Long" introduced in the FN Browning 1903 pistol. In Europe it came out four years later in the John Browning-designed FN Model 1910 pistol. Known variously as the 9mm Browning *Kurz* or 9mm Browning *Corto,* depending on whether the shooter spoke German or Italian, the 380 Auto has been chambered by nearly every manufacturer of semi-automatic pistols. Like the 32 ACP, the 380 continues to be an extremely popular choice for self defense, and it is vastly better at that task than either the 25 or the 32 Autos. It takes a slightly larger-diameter bullet, .356 in., than the .355-in.-diameter bullets specified for most of the 9mms treated below. Despite its relegation as a "pocket pistol" round, the 9mm Kurz found favor among many military and police organizations, and it was even adopted as a standard military pistol load in Czechoslovakia, Italy, and Yugoslavia. The more powerful 9x19 eventually obsoleted it for NATO military units. The .68-in.-long straight-wall case is usually brass, but aluminum and steel cases do appear, and the round's OAL length is just a hair under an inch, .98 in. Many loads, such as the 380 ACP Hornady Critical Defense 90gr FTX, come in at or slightly below 200 ft-lbs energy when shot from a 4-in. barrel.

First things first on the **9x18 Makarov,** or simply the **9mm Makarov.** How to pronounce "Makarov?" The correct pronunciation of Makarov is, "Mah CAR ahv," and not "MACK uh rahv." The Red Army fought the Great Patriotic War of 1941-45 with both the semi-automatic Tokarev TT pistols and the obsolete Nagant M1895 revolvers, but after the war, the GAU (in English, the General Artillery Department of General Staff) issued a new set of requirements for a military and police pistol. Boiled down, those requirements were for a compact double-action like the Walther PP. Three calibers were offered, the 7.65x17SR Browning, 9x17 Browning, and a new 9x18, the last a product of the designer Syomin inspired by the German 9x18 Ultra. A major difference was that the 9x18 Soviet had a bullet diameter of 9.2mm, the Western 9mm round was 9.02mm in diameter. Trials for a new pistol started in 1947, and in 1948, the Makarov pistol in 9x18 was selected as the next military sidearm for Soviet armed forces, but it took three more years of refinement before the "9mm Pistolet

SELECTED LOADS & BALLISTICS

Hornady Critical Defense 380 ACP 90gr FTX
(4-in. test barrel)

Range, Yards	Muzzle	50	100
Velocities (fps)	1000	910	841
Energy (ft-lbs)	200	165	141
Trajectory (in.)		NA	NA

Remington GS380B Golden Saber 102gr Brass-Jacketed HP
(4-in. test barrel)

Range, Yards	Muzzle	50	100
Velocities (fps)	940	901	866
Energy (ft-lbs)	200	184	170
Trajectory (in.)		-1.2	-5.1

Hornady's Critical Defense 90gr FTX is designed to expand at low muzzle velocity, 1000 fps. The Golden Saber 102gr Brass Jacketed Hollow Point #29410 features primer and mouth waterproofing, nickel-plated cases, and treated powders for low muzzle flash. Photos courtesy of Midway USA.

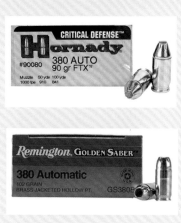

The 9mm Steyr is a centerfire pistol cartridge originally developed for the Steyr M1912 military pistol and was the

service ammunition for Austria-Hungary during World War I and remained the service ammunition for Austria and Romania between the World Wars. It is dimensionally similar to, but not interchangeable with the 9x23mm Largo. Fiocchi makes this 9mm Steyr (#9SA) with a 115gr FMJ that generates MV of 1080 fps and ME of 300 ft-lbs.

The 9mm Ultra got its start during 1930s as an experimental joint development of the GECO and Carl Walther compa-

nies, both from Germany, but it wasn't until the early 1970s that it was revived as the 9mm Police to supply German police with weapons more effective than the 7.65mm Browning and 9mm Kurz. Eventually, the 9x19 Luger put the 9x18 Police almost fully in retirement. However, Fiocchi loads a 100gr FMJ 9x18mm Ultra #FMJTC that makes 1065 fps MV and 250 ft-lbs ME. The 9x18 Police and Ultra rounds are similar except for headstamps; both have straight, rimmed cases and usually are loaded with a jacketed bullet of truncated cone shape. It is not interchangeable with the 9x18 Makarov.

Developed during 1980s, the 9x21 IMI cartridge is a virtual copy of the 9x19 Luger, except for the 2mm-longer

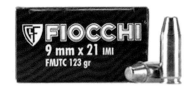

case, which in U.S. measurement translates to .830 in. for the 9x21 and .754 in. for the Luger. But the overall cartridge lengths for both are 1.16 in. Its purpose is to avoid restrictions on civilian use of military-caliber cartridges in countries like Italy and France. It should not be confused with a Russian armor-piercing bullet with hardened steel core, the 9x21 7N29. This 9x21mm load uses a 123gr FMJ Truncated Cone to make 1200 fps MV and 410 ft-lbs ME. Photos courtesy of Midway USA.

The 9x25mm Dillon, also known as the 9x25 Dillon, is a pistol wildcat cartridge developed by employ-

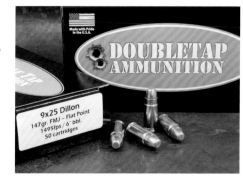

ees working at Dillon Precision for use in USPSA/IPSC Open guns. The cartridge is made by necking down a 10mm Auto case to 9mm. With a cartridge-case capacity of 24.9 grains, the short-necked and steep-shouldered 9x25mm Dillon holds twice the powder of a 38 Super case. Only DoubleTap makes a factory load for the 9x25 Dillon, and it's stout. The DT load pushes a 125gr FMJ-FP Match bullet to 1495 fps when shot from a Lone Wolf 6-in. barrel. Photo courtesy of DoubleTap.

Makarova" was made official.

The 9mm Makarov or 9mm PM has a straight, rimless case usually made of lacquered steel (military issue) or brass (some commercial loads). The standard Soviet military/police load used a round-nosed jacketed bullet with a composite core, made partly of lead and partly of mild steel (as a less expensive alternative to lead). Other loads include a frangible SP-8 (1980) to be used on aircraft. Surplus ammo is typically Berdan primed and often steel cased. Berdan primers use an anvil that is in the case. There are special tools for removing Berdan primers, but the primers themselves are hard to find. Also, steel-case ammo may ruin your reloading dies. So after you shoot them, toss the Berdan and steel cases.

The **9x23 Winchester** (1996) is a pistol cartridge developed by Winchester to replace the 38 Super in IPSC, USPSA, and IDPA competition. Its unique design facet was the use of a strengthened case that allows the 9x23mm Win to operate around 40,000 CUP compared to the 38 Super's max around 30,000 CUP. In mid-1994, shooter John Ricco had actually designed and had reamers for a "9x23 Super," a huge improvement over the 38 Super. Winchester tapered the case a bit and decide to market it themselves, which Ricco thought infringed on his Super patent. Lawsuits were filed and two years later, settled. Almost four years went by without a reliable source for the 9x23mm brass. That supply problem, coupled

The Silver Bear #A918RHPN 9mm Makarov load employs a 94gr HP in non-reloadable zinc-coated steel cases. Muzzle Velocity: 1000 fps.

Loaded by Cor-Bon, the Pow'Rball round is a controlled expansion copper-jacketed compressed

lead core hollow point bullet capped with a polymer ball, giving the bullet an FMJ profile. It is designed for enhanced feeding in semi-automatics. The brass cases are reloadable. Muzzle Velocity: 1250 fps, Muzzle Energy: 242 ft-lbs.

Loaded with copper Barnes X Bullets, the 9x23mm Win Cor-Bon DPX 125gr Barnes XPB Hollow Point load makes 1350 fps

MV and 506 ft-lbs MV. Cor-Bon will occasionally use popular industry branded brass, depending on availability. Photos courtesy of Midway USA.

with USPSA reducing the power factor necessary to make Major-level loads from 175 to 165, doomed the 9x23 Win because then 38 Super guns were able to make Major power factor at lower pressures. Still, some fans of the round believe it is a better fit for a 1911 than the venerable 45 ACP. Reasons: It makes a 1911 a 10+1 gun with factory magazines while duplicating the prowess of the 125gr 357 Magnum load. Also, the smaller diameter of the 9x23 cartridge makes it sit higher in the magazine, which improves feeding, along with a slight case taper.

The **9mm Luger** is the most widely used centerfire autoloader cartridge in the United States. On a global scale, nearly twice as many 9mm Luger cartridges are manufactured each year than any other single cartridge caliber. The popularity of the 9mm Luger (9x19mm) has been constant in Europe since World War I in both pistols and submachine

SELECTED LOADS & BALLISTICS

Winchester MC918M 9x18 Makarov 95gr FMJ

Range, Yards	Muzzle	50	100
Velocities (fps)	1017	925	
Energy (ft-lbs)	212	180	
Trajectory (in.)		NA	NA

Federal American Eagle 9mm Makarov (9x18mm Makarov) AE9MK 95gr FMJ

Range, Yards	Muzzle	25	50	75	100
Velocities (fps)	1000	957	921	888	858
Energy (ft-lbs)	211	193	179	166	155
Trajectory (in.)	0	-1.5	-5.5		-12.3

Federal Personal Defense 9mm Luger PD9CSP2H 105gr Expanding Full Metal Jacket (EFMJ)

Range, Yards	Muzzle	25	50	75	100
Velocities (fps)	1230	1140	1069	1014	969
Energy (ft-lbs)	353	303	266	240	219
Trajectory (in.)	0	-0.8	-3.4		-8.2

Federal American Eagle 9mm Luger (9x19mm Para) AE9DP 115gr FMJ

Range, Yards	Muzzle	25	50	75	100
Velocities (fps)	1180	1106	1048	1001	961
Energy (ft-lbs)	356	312	280	256	236
Trajectory (in.)	0	-0.9	-3.7		-8.7

Federal 9mm Luger (9x19mm Parabellum) P9HS1 124gr Hydra-Shok JHP Premium Personal Defense

Range, Yards	Muzzle	25	50	75	100
Velocities (fps)	1120	1070	1028	993	961
Energy (ft-lbs)	345	315	291	271	255
Trajectory (in.)	0	-1.0	-4.0		-9.3

Federal 9mm Luger (9x19mm Parabellum) AE9FP 147gr FMJ Flat Point American Eagle

Range, Yards	Muzzle	25	50	75	100
Velocities (fps)	1000	976	953	933	914
Energy (ft-lbs)	326	311	297	284	273
Trajectory (in.)	0	-1.4	-5.2		-11.5

Winchester X923W 9x23 Win 125gr Silvertip Hollow Point

Range, Yards	Muzzle	50	100
Velocities (fps)	1450	1249	1103
Energy (ft-lbs)	583	433	338
Trajectory (in.)		NA	NA

Most self-defense shooters will posit that the 9mm Luger 124gr and 147gr weight loads are "standards" for the caliber. Some prefer the lighter 115gr bullet, however. At right, top, is the Hornady Critical Defense Ammunition 115gr FTX #90250. Unlike most other hollowpoint bullets, the Flex Tip bullet has a soft polymer insert that allows for consistent and reliable expansion. Nickel-plated cases are nice. Muzzle velocity, 1140 fps; muzzle energy, 332 ft-lbs.

At the right is the 9mm Luger +P Speer Gold Dot Short Barrel 124gr JHP #23611 load. The Short Barrel ammunition develops a strong muzzle velocity of 1150 fps and 364 ft-lbs of energy.

The Federal American Eagle Ammunition 147gr FMJ #AE9FP is a load designed specifically for target shooting, training and practice. It's loaded to the same specifications as Federal's Premium loads, but at a more practical price for plinking. Load specs are 960 fps MV and 301 ft-lbs ME.

The loads above are standard fodder, but the 9mm Luger +P Glaser Pow'RBall #PB09100/20 has a 100gr copper-jacketed compressed lead core hollow point bullet capped with a polymer ball. Muzzle velocity is impressive at 1450 fps, with a correspondingly high ME of 467 ft-lbs.

Right, another high-energy load is the Black Hills 115gr EXP (Extra Power) JHP #M9N6, which develops 400 ft-lbs ME on a MV of 1250 fps. Photos courtesy of Midway USA.

guns. It provides better ballistics than contemporary rounds such as the 7.63mm (.30) Mauser, and 7.65mm (.30) Luger/Parabellum. Also called the 9mm Parabellum (German, "for war"), it was introduced in 1902 in the Luger automatic pistol, and in 1904 became the official military cartridge of the German navy and was later adopted by the German army. The list of variants springing from the 9mm Parabellum is impressive, including the 9mm Browning Long (1903), the 9mm Mauser (1908), the 380 Auto, and 9mm Steyr (1912), the 9x18mm Makarov, the 9mm Winchester Magnum (1977), the 9mm Federal, and 9x23mm Winchester. Ballistically, it sits about halfway between the 38 Special and 357 Magnum cartridges. Ammunition for the 9mm is loaded by virtually every manufacturer in the world, and within the U.S. there are at least 35 different loads produced by more than a dozen companies in bullet weights from 88 to 147 grains. Most authorities would probably agree that the 124gr FMJ and 115gr JHP are the "standard" defensive loads. ●

22: The 'Unknown' 36s

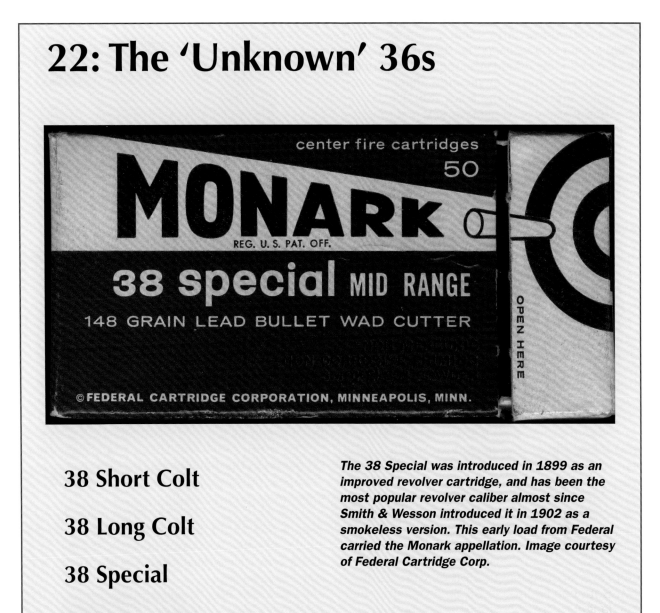

center fire cartridges
50

MONARK
REG. U. S. PAT. OFF.

38 special MID RANGE
148 GRAIN LEAD BULLET WAD CUTTER

© FEDERAL CARTRIDGE CORPORATION, MINNEAPOLIS, MINN.

OPEN HERE

38 Short Colt

38 Long Colt

38 Special

38 Super Auto

357 SIG

357 S&W Magnum

The 38 Special was introduced in 1899 as an improved revolver cartridge, and has been the most popular revolver caliber almost since Smith & Wesson introduced it in 1902 as a smokeless version. This early load from Federal carried the Monark appellation. Image courtesy of Federal Cartridge Corp.

So, you wonder after reading the chapter header on the previous page, what 36-caliber handgun loads do I not know about? Some long-ago-forgotten obscure French load, fired once and left on the field? Actually, no. The 36s are simply the best-selling midrange rounds of all time. They're just called 38s.

Why are 38s actually closer to .36 bore diameter—.357 to be more exact? In the 19th century, stuffing a .36-caliber lead ball into a self-contained metallic cartridge meant the resulting round fit a bored-through .38-caliber cap-and-ball revolver cylinders. So the "38" describes the chamber diameter rather than the bore diameter, as has loosely become our naming convention.

The **38 Short Colt** and **38 Long Colt** are the beginning of the main part of the 38 line. The Short Colt was a heeled cartridge intended for conversions of the .36-cal cap-and-ball revolvers from the Civil War. It originally took an inside-lubricated bullet around 125gr to 135gr, which is reflected in the only widely available current factory load, the Remington Express 125gr LRN #28368, a lead roundnose cartridge that has a MV of 730 fps and ME of 150 ft-lbs. The SC's dimensions are the same as the LC's except for overall case length and overall cartridge length. The heeled SC shot a .357-in. bullet out of a .357 neck diameter case, with a base diameter of .378, a rim diameter of .433, and a rim thickness of .055 in. Naturally, the Short Colt (overall case length .76 in., OAL 1.1 in.) is shorter than the Long Colt (overall case length 1.03 in., OAL 1.32 in.). Both can be fired in 38 Sp revolvers, but it's dangerous to shoot Specials in SC and LC guns, and should not be attempted.

As long as people keep buying 38 Special ammo, manufacturers will continue to build new guns for it. Here's the Ruger LCR No. 5401 38 Special, $525. The LCR featured an aluminum upper and a glass-filled polymer lower.

At the muzzle, the 38 Long Colt fired a 150gr lead bullet at 770 fps/195 ft-lbs, and in 1889 the revolver and cartridge were accepted for use by the U.S. Navy and then in 1892, the Army, giving rise to the New Army and New Navy model names. Improvements to the wheelguns led to the Models 1892, 1894, 1895, 1896, 1901 and 1903. Trouble for the LC began in the Philippines in 1905, when an escaping prisoner, Antonio Caspi, was shot four times at close range by a 38 Colt revolver,

There's thin factory loadings for the Short Colt and Long Colt loads. Remington makes a 38 Short Colt 125gr Lead Round Nose #R38SC with 730 fps MV and 150 ft-lbs ME. The Black Hills 38 Long Colt 158gr LRN #DCB38CLTN1 is made for Cowboy Action Shooting. All loads use new brass and come in period-correct boxes. Muzzle Velocity: 650 fps. Goex's Black Dawge Black Powder 145gr LFN #1067 is a 38 Long Colt Loaded with blackpowder. The bullets are cast from a soft alloy and pre-lubed with SPG Lube. Muzzle Velocity: 710 fps. Photos courtesy of Midway USA.

SELECTED LOADS & BALLISTICS

Remington Express 38 Short Colt 125gr LRN R38SC
(6-in. barrel)

Range, Yards	Muzzle	50	100
Velocities (fps)	730	685	645
Energy (ft-lbs)	150	130	115
Trajectory (in.)		-2.2	-9.4

Black Hills Cowboy Action 38 Long Colt 158gr LRN

Range, Yards	Muzzle	50	100
Velocities (fps)	650		
Energy (ft-lbs)			
Trajectory (in.)			

but was still resisting. He was eventually subdued by a knock on the head from the butt of a Springfield carbine. Three bullets had entered Caspi's chest. Situations like that led to many servicemen preferring the 45 Colt Single Action, and the LC's lack of stopping power eventually gave rise to the 38 Special.

The **38 Special** was introduced in 1899 as an improved revolver cartridge, and has been the most popular revolver caliber almost since Smith & Wesson introduced it in 1902 as a smokeless version. It differs a little from the LC at the bottom, having these case dimensions: .357-in. bullet diameter, .379-in. neck

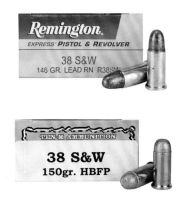

The 38 Special is sometimes confused with the 38 Smith & Wesson, since S&W introduced both rounds. However, the 38 Smith & Wesson, aka 38 Super Police or 38 Colt New Police, isn't the same round as the Special. The 38 S&W was designed by Smith & Wesson and introduced during the late 1870s, and was chambered a number of pocket revolvers made by Harrington & Richardson, Smith & Wesson, Colt, and Iver Johnson. Remington makes a 38 S&W Express 146gr round, #22276 with a lead roundnose bullet, that produces MV of 685 fps and ME of 150 ft-lbs. Ten-X makes a cowboy action version of the 38 S&W with a 150gr lead hollow base flat point bullet, load #38000148, running 600 fps at the muzzle. Photos courtesy of Midway USA.

SELECTED LOADS & BALLISTICS

Remington Express 38 Special 110gr Semi-Jacketed Hollow Point +P R38S10 (4-in. barrel)

Range, Yards	Muzzle	50	100
Velocities (fps)	995	926	871
Energy (ft-lbs)	242	210	185
Trajectory (in.)		-1.2	-5.1

Remington Golden Saber 38 Special 125gr Brass-Jacketed Hollow Point +P GS38SB (4-in. barrel)

Range, Yards	Muzzle	50	100
Velocities (fps)	975	929	885
Energy (ft-lbs)	264	238	218
Trajectory (in.)		-1.0	-5.2

Remington UMC 38 Special 158gr Lead Round Nose L38S5 (4-in. barrel)

Range, Yards	Muzzle	50	100
Velocities (fps)	755	723	692
Energy (ft-lbs)	200	183	168
Trajectory (in.)		-2.0	-8.3

diameter, with a base diameter of .379, a rim diameter of .440, and a rim thickness of .054 in., with an overall case length of 1.16 in. and OAL 1.55 in.

In the 1930s, bigger, stronger guns lead to higher-pressure loads, and you couldn't be sure of which pressure-rated load you were buying until 1974, when SAAMI instituted the (+P) higher rating. The current SAAMI maximum pressures for the round are: standard 38 Sp, 17,000 psi; .8 (+P), 18,500 psi; and 357 Magnum, 35,000 psi. At 17k psi, the standard 38 Sp 158gr lead load will garner about 900 fps, and at 20,000 psi, a +P load makes 158gr lead bullet rated at 1000 fps. Like almost all pistol cartridges called "38," the 38 Sp actually takes .357-in.-diameter bullets.

The issue most shooters worry about is putting +P-rated ammo in a given revolver, especially an older one. In modern guns, even the lightweight pocket guns can be +P rated. Using +P ammo in a standard gun does not present a safety hazard, it's just that the backstrap will stretch and the gun will generally loosen if too many +P loads are fired. It's probably not possible to fire enough actual self-defense +P loads to hurt a standard revolver. Older models are another issue, and the best rule of thumb is to get a vintage gun checked out by a gunsmith before stuffing it with a selection of higher-powered 38s. If the gun is chambered

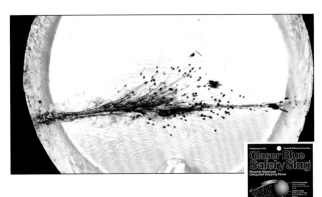

This 9-in. cylinder of ordnance gelatin shows the penetration of a 38 Sp +P Glaser Blue Tip Safety Slug with a prefragmented tip. Reduces wall shoot-throughs.

The 38 Special was introduced in 1902, and for many years, was a classic sidearm for lawmen.

High-capacity autoloaders chambered in 9mm Luger have largely displaced it in LE use, but +P loadings of the 38 Special arguably make it a better self-defense cartridge for than the 9mm Parabellum. The loads adjacent represent the range of the 38 Special's frequent bullet weights. The Federal Premium Personal Defense Reduced Recoil has a 110gr Hydra-Shok JHP clocking right along at 1000 fps MV and developing 244 ft-lbs ME. The +P

CCI Blazer 125gr JHP #3514 uses a non-reloadable aluminum case. MV, 940 fps; ME, 245 ft-lbs. Speer's Gold Dot Short Barrel 135gr JHP #23921 is a 38 Special +P load with 860 fps MV and 222 ft-lbs ME. The Buffalo Bore 158gr Lead SWHPGC #20A has a Lead Semi-Wadcutter

Hollow Point Gas Check bullet loaded to SAAMI maximum pressure 38 Special +P, developing 1000 fps MV and 351 ft-lbs MV. Photos courtesy of Midway USA.

for 357 Mag, then obviously it will handle all ranges of 38 Sp pressures. Like most other handgun rounds, the 38/357's main reason to be is for self defense, or "others" defense, depending on the situation.

Toward that end, I have shot or supervised the shooting of hundreds of 38/357 rounds into ballistic gelatin, and it is a special kind of drudgery that produces interesting images, but which is a soul-killing activity. The purpose of shooting into gelatin is to see how a bullet transfers its kinetic energy to vital organs of the target, which when described honestly, is a human attacker. This description of "terminal" performance is the third leg of ballistics, which from the time of firing are interior ballistics, exterior ballistics, then terminal, or ending,

ballistics. The purpose of such testing is, when boiled down to its essence, "Will a given bullet save the shooter's ass in a time of dire need?" The answer is unknowable, of course, because of so many variables. But the 38/357 is as good an answer to the question as there is, because its performance has been wrung out at every bullet weight. And the 38/357 offers both bullet expansion and penetration that is better than most, and outdone by just a few other handgun cartridges.

But what can the shooter who's interested in cartridges take away from an in-depth look at 38 Special hollowpoint loads? Answer: A deep appreciation for a round built around the turn of the last century. Looking at 110gr and 125gr self-defense loads, the author used a stock Smith & Wesson Model 686-2 with a 4-in. barrel and Winchester's 110gr Silvertip hollowpoints, Federal's Premium Personal Defense 110gr Hydra-Shoks, Remington's 110gr Semi-JHP. At a heavier weight, there was Cor-Bon's 125gr JHP +P, the Remington 125gr Semi-JKTD HP +P, the 125gr Golden Saber +P, Speer's 125gr Gold Dot +P, the Federal 129gr Hydra-Shok +P and 125gr Classic +P rounds, and Winchester's 125gr STHP SX +P cartridge.

Firing these rounds into an 18-in. block of Kind and Knox Ordnance Gelatin, then measuring and recording the penetration and expansion of each bullet finds that all penetrated at least 13 inches, with 12 inches generally considered the acceptable minimum penetration for defense loads. Certainly, there are some bad loads out there, but there are plenty to choose from that will balance all the issues most shooters care about: recoil, accuracy, dependability, and stopping power.

The other rounds in this chapter are made for revolvers, but the **38 Super Auto,** or **38 Super** as it's usually known, and the **357 SIG** are substantial but notable variations on the theme. First, the straight-case Super fires a .358-in.-diameter bullet, up 0.001 in. from the .357-caliber bullets in the 38 revolvers side and the bottleneck 357 SIG case. Elsewhere, too, the Super and the SIG diverge in many significant ways. The Super has these case dimensions (.382-in. neck diameter, base diameter of .383, a rim diameter of .405, and a rim thickness of .045 in., with a case length of 0.9 in. and OAL of 1.28 in.), compared to the 357 SIG (.381-in. neck diameter, a base diameter of .425, a rim diameter of .424, a case length

Wilson Combat's 38 Super 124gr Hornady XTP Jacketed Hollow Point #A38SU-124-XTP is available exclusively at Mid-wayUSA and Wilson Combat. It uses low flash powder, which preserves night vision. Features a taper crimp that enhances feed reliability and extraction. MV is rated at 1335 fps, but every lot is chronographed, so resulting velocity may vary and will be listed on each box. This Cor-Bon 125gr JHP #SD38X125 38 Super +P uses

skived bullets with scored jackets that expand quickly. MV 1350 fps, ME 487 ft-lbs. Photos courtesy of Midway USA.

of 0.865 in. and OAL of 1.14 in.). The SIG also has shoulder, with a diameter of .424.

The Super was introduced by Colt in the Government Model pistol (1929) as a better version of the vintage 1900 38 Colt Automatic Cartridge. Ninety-four years later, Swiss firearms manufacturer SIG Sauer and Federal Cartridge collaborated on making the 357 SIG cartridge by necking down a 40 S&W case to accept .355-in. bullets. The intent was to duplicate the performance of 125gr 357 Mag load (when fired from a 4-in. revolver). As such, the 357 SIG became the first modern bottleneck commercial handgun cartridge introduction since 1961, when Remington introduced the unsuccessful 22 Remington Jet. It is interesting to compare the ballistics of the 357 SIG, 38 Super, 357 Mag, and 38 Special +P (see next chapter for full ballistics), and the 9mm Luger (see previous chapter for full ballistics) when loaded with bullets of similar weights. Remington is one company that loads all five rounds with bullet weights separated by only a few grains. Big Green loads three 357 SIG units, one of which is the Express R357S11 125gr JHP, that when shot from a 4-in. barrel, makes a MV of 1350 fps and ME of 506 ft-lbs. Remington lists 10 357 Mag loads, four of which contain 125gr bullets. Three of them share the same ballistics, an example of which is the R357M1 Remington Express 125gr Semi-Jacketed Hollow Point, which develops a MV of 1450 fps and ME of 583 ft-lbs. The same configuration in 38 Special +P, the

R38S2 Remington Express 125gr Semi-Jacketed Hollow Point, makes a MV of 945 fps and ME of 248 ft-lbs. The 38 Super only comes in one Remington load, the L38SUP UMC 130gr Metal Case unit, which has a MV of 1215 fps and ME of 426 ft-lbs. While the others don't quite measure up, clearly the SIG is in the ballpark with the 357 Mag, but not quite on the basepaths with the revolver round.

Though the **357 S&W Magnum** is certainly the top centerfire revolver cartridge of the 20th century, it came along well into that

SELECTED LOADS & BALLISTICS

Remington 38 Super UMC 130gr L38SUP (4-in. barrel)

Range, Yards	Muzzle	50	100
Velocities (fps)	1215	1099	1017
Energy (ft-lbs)	426	348	298
Trajectory (in.)		-0.8	-3.6

Remington Express 357 Mag 110GR Semi-Jacketed Hollow Point R357M7 (4-in. barrel)

Range, Yards	Muzzle	50	100
Velocities (fps)	1295	1094	975
Energy (ft-lbs)	410	292	232
Trajectory (in.)		-0.8	-3.5

Remington UMC 357 Mag 125gr Jacketed Soft Point L357M12 (4-in. barrel)

Range, Yards	Muzzle	50	100
Velocities (fps)	1450	1240	1090
Energy (ft-lbs)	583	427	330
Trajectory (in.)		-0.6	-2.8

Remington Express 357 Mag 158gr Semi-Wadcutter R357M5 (4-in. barrel)

Range, Yards	Muzzle	50	100
Velocities (fps)	1235	1104	1015
Energy (ft-lbs)	535	428	361
Trajectory (in.)		-0.8	-3.5

Remington Core-Lokt Hunting 357 Mag 165gr JHP RH357MA (8.3-In. barrel)

Range, Yards	Muzzle	50	100
Velocities (fps)	1290	1189	1108
Energy (ft-lbs)	610	518	450
Trajectory (in.)		-0.7	-3.1

Remington Express 357 Mag 180gr Semi-Jacketed Hollow Point R357M10 (8.3-in. barrel)

Range, Yards	Muzzle	50	100
Velocities (fps)	1145	1053	985
Energy (ft-lbs)	524	443	388
Trajectory (in.)		-0.9	-3.9

In addition to the handgun loads listed at left, the 357 Magnum is a capable rifle round, too. This Hornady LEVERevolution 140gr FTX #92755 is safe to shoot in tubular magazines. Muzzle Velocity, 1440 fps; Muzzle Energy, 644 ft-lbs. Another common bullet weight for the 357 Magnum is a 125gr JHP, like that found in the Federal Premium Personal Defense #C357B. Muzzle Velocity, 1450 fps; Muzzle Energy, 584 ft-lbs. Photos courtesy of Midway USA.

Here's one 357 SIG load that produces 357 Mag energy. This Buffalo Bore 125gr JHP #25A creates 1433 fps MV and 575 ft-lbs ME. DoubleTap's 147gr FMJ #357 is no slouch at 1255 fps MV and 514 ft-lbs ME. Photos courtesy of Midway USA.

The Smith & Wesson 619 357 Magnum No. 164301 has a traditional profile, but with modern upgrades. The 619 has a round-butt stainless-steel medium-large L- frame with a full-length ejector rod. It's a 7-shooter, too.

Remington introduced the 357 Maximum cartridge in 1983, but it's no longer listed in the company's factory loads on www.remington.com. It was intended for handgun silhouette competition and hunting. Grizzly Cartridge Co. still makes a 357 Maximum load, #GC357MX200 with a 200gr Lead Wide Flat

Nose Gas Check cast bullet. It is powerful, with a muzzle velocity of 1675 fps and muzzle energy of 1283 ft-lbs.

100-year period, in April 1935, when Smith & Wesson presented the gun/ammo combo to FBI Director J. Edgar Hoover. It was the first American cartridge to be labeled "Magnum," and until eclipsed by the 44 Magnum, it was the most powerful handgun cartridge produced in the world. Like so many other cartridges, the 357 was a response to a need, this time for a revolver cartridge that could be a gangster-getter. (Surprisingly, lawman Frank Hamer used a 38 Super during the fatal apprehension of Bonnie and Clyde.) In 1930, S&W introduced the 38/44 Heavy Duty 38 Special revolver built on the company's 44-size N-Frame, but that round's 30% performance

uptick over the Special wasn't enough. Next, Philip B. Sharpe and S&W's Major Douglas Wesson lengthened the 38 Special case one-eighth inch, and in 1934 Winchester's 357 Magnum drove a 158gr lead bullet to 1515 fps, or nearly twice the velocity of the Special firing a 158gr bullet. The name was a combination of the bullet's actual diameter and Wesson's taste for champagne. Oenophiles know a "magnum" bottle is larger than a standard bottle. Obviously, the concept works with cartridges, too. ●

23: The Everything Rounds

The 375s have probably accounted for more dangerous game, from bears up to and including Cape buffalo and elephants, than any other large-caliber cartridge, yet in some loadings, they can be used quite ably on deer, elk, and moose. When loaded with a spitzer bullet, a 375-class round in a lighter weight will shoot flat beyond 300 yards and deliver energy matched by few other cartridges. Most shooters believe, however, that most of the 375s are too powerful for anything but moose and dangerous bears in North America, thus strongly tying the class to Africa, where it is ideal for most species.

The standard against which all the .375-caliber rounds compete is the estimable **375 Holland & Holland Magnum,** which originated in 1912 with a 0.375-in.-diameter bullet, as the name suggests. "Holland & Holland's 375 Belted Rimless Magnum Express" soon became the most popular choice for all-round African hunting. One of the striking facets of the 375 H&H's ballistics are its similarity downrange to the 30-06, albeit with heavier bullets in the 375. If, for example, the shoot-

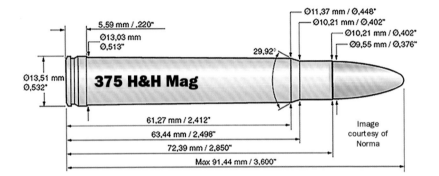

Because the 375 H&H Mag's case has a narrow shoulder, it needed a belt to ensure proper headspacing, and it's long—so much so that magnum-length actions had to be created by removing steel from behind the lower locking lug recess in the front of standard-length Mauser actions.

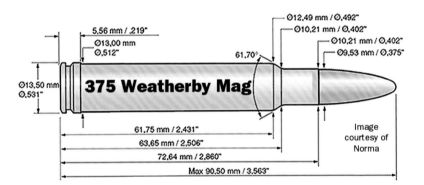

As the accompanying tables show, the 375 W'by generates pushes a 300gr Nosler Partition bullet to 2800 fps MV compared to the Federal 375 H&H Magnum P375SA 300gr Swift A-Frame Cape-Shok's 2450 fps MV. This didn't impress shooters.

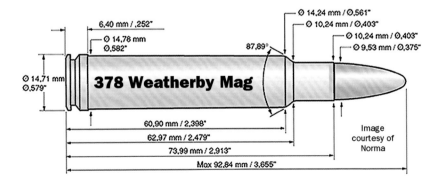

Among American-designed big-game rounds, only the 416 and 460 W'by Mags, cartridges identical to the 378 W'by Mag except for caliber, burn more powder.

Federal 375 H&H Mag P375T4 250gr Trophy Bonded BC

Range, Yards	Muzzle	100	200	300	400	500
Velocities (fps)	2670	2412	2169	1940	1728	1534
Energy (ft-lbs)	3957	3230	2612	2089	1657	1305
Trajectory (in.)		2.3	0	-9.6	-28.6	-59.4

Federal 375 H&H Mag 375A 270gr Soft Point Power-Shok

Range, Yards	Muzzle	100	200	300	400	500
Velocities (fps)	2690	2418	2162	1922	1700	1500
Energy (ft-lbs)	4338	3505	2803	2214	1733	1348
Trajectory (in.)	2.3	0	-9.6	-28.9	–60.3	

Federal 375 H&H Mag P375SA 300gr Swift A-Frame

Range, Yards	Muzzle	100	200	300	400	500
Velocities (fps)	2450	2194	1953	1730	1527	1349
Energy (ft-lbs)	3998	3206	2541	1994	1553	1213
Trajectory (in.)		2.9	0	-12.1	-35.8	-74.8

Weatherby 375 W'by Mag 300gr Partition N375300PT

Range, Yards	Muzzle	100	200	300	400	500
Velocities (fps)	2800	2572	2366	2140	1963	1760
Energy (ft-lbs)	5224	4408	3696	3076	2541	2084
Trajectory (in.)		1.9	0	-8.2	-23.9	-48.7

Weatherby 378 W'by Mag 270gr SP H378270SP

Range, Yards	Muzzle	100	200	300	400	500
Velocities (fps)	3180	2921	2677	2445	2225	2017
Energy (ft-lbs)	6062	5115	4295	3583	2968	2438
Trajectory (in.)		1.3	0	-6.1	-18.1	-37.1

Winchester 375 Win X375W 200gr Power-Point

Range, Yards	Muzzle	100	200	300	400	500
Velocities (fps)	2200	1841	1526	1268	1089	980
Energy (ft-lbs)	2150	1506	1034	714	527	427
Trajectory (in.)	4.4	0	-19.5	-60.8		

Remington Express 375 RUM PR375UM2 270gr Soft Point

Range, Yards	Muzzle	100	200	300	400	500
Velocities (fps)	2900	2558	2241	1947	1678	1442
Energy (ft-lbs)	5041	3922	3010	2272	1689	1246
Trajectory (in.)		1.0	0	–8.9	-27.0	-57.6

Remington Premier 375 RUM PR375UM3 300gr A-Frame PSP

Range, Yards	Muzzle	100	200	300	400	500
Velocities (fps)	2760	2505	2263	2035	1822	1624
Energy (ft-lbs)	5073	4178	3412	2759	2210	1757
Trajectory (in.)		1.8	0	-3.5	-26.1	-53.9

Hornady 376 Steyr 8234 225gr InterLock SP

Range, Yards	Muzzle	100	200	300	400	500
Velocities (fps)	2600	2331	2078	1842	1625	1431
Energy (ft-lbs)	3377	2714	2157	1694	1319	1023
Trajectory (in.)	2.5	0	-10.6	-31.4	-65.5	

Hornady 376 Steyr 8237 270gr InterLock SP-RP

Range, Yards	Muzzle	100	200	300	400	500
Velocities (fps)	2600	2372	2156	1951	1759	1582
Energy (ft-lbs)	4052	3373	2787	2283	1855	1500
Trajectory (in.)	2.3	0	-9.9	-28.9	-59.2	

Hornady 375 Ruger 8231 270gr SP-RP Superformance

Range, Yards	Muzzle	100	200	300	400	500
Velocities (fps)	2840	2600	2372	2156	1951	1759
Energy (ft-lbs)	4835	4052	3373	2786	2283	1855
Trajectory (in.)		1.8	0	–8.0	-23.6	-48.2

Hornady 375 Ruger 300gr DGS Superformance

Range, Yards	Muzzle	100	200	300	400	500
Velocities (fps)	2660	2344	2050	1780	1536	1328
Energy (ft-lbs)	4713	3660	2800	2110	1572	1174
Trajectory (in.)		2.4	0	-10.8	-32.6	-69.2

er compares a 270gr Soft Point Power-Shok 375 H&H and a similar 180gr 30-06 load in an earlier chapter, he'll see the 375 bullet starts at 2690 fps to the 30-06's 2700 fps, which translates into a -9 in. drop at 300 yards for the '06 and -9.6 for the H&H, or a point-blank hold to about 300 yards, like the Springfield.

Bullets are crucial in maximizing the 375 H&H Magnum's effectiveness, and there are a selection of great controlled expansion projectiles, including the Nosler Partition, and Sierra's 300gr spitzer boattail and Speer's 250gr Grand Slam. For maximum penetration on elephants and Cape buffalo, there are 300gr solids from Speer, Hornady, Barnes, and A-Square, among others. A quick look at one company's 375 H&H Mag loadings will attest to its popu-

larity. Federal, for instance, has 11 375 H&H offerings ranging from as light as 250 grains up to 300 grains in its 2010 catalog.

The 375 H&H Magnum owned this class until the 1945 introduction of the **375 Weatherby Magnum,** which Roy Weatherby created by "improving" the 375 H&H Magnum case by reducing body taper, applying his patent "double-radius" shoulder, and adding 10% more case capacity, according to Norma documents. As the accompanying tables show, the 375 Weatherby generates 350 fps more muzzle velocity than a comparable Federal load. In particular, the 375 W'by Mag pushes a 300gr Nosler Partition bullet to 2800 fps MV/5224 ft-lbs ME compared to the Federal 375 H&H Magnum P375SA 300gr Swift A-Frame Cape-

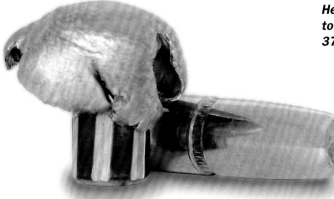

Here's what a dangerous-game round is supposed to do: Penetrate deeply, hang together. This is a 375 H&H Mag slug, courtesy of Norma.

Shok's 2450 fps MV/3998 5224 ft-lbs ME. Oddly, this significant ballistic upgrade didn't impress shooters at the time, because Weatherby didn't sell many 375 W'by rifles.

So, in 1953, Weatherby stepped up the performance margin even more with its powerful **378 Weatherby Magnum.** The 378 W'by Mag, a belted version of the 416 Rigby case, has an inside diameter that's about 15% larger than the H&H's capacity, making its powder capacity about 33% more. That capacity is an important historical note because, to assure ignition of powder charges exceeding 100 grains, Weatherby asked Federal to develop a new primer, the result of which was the Federal 215 Magnum primer. The company still loads both the 375 W'by Mag in a 300gr Partition and the 378 W'by Mag 300gr in a FMJ and a roundnose round. As noted above, the 300gr Partition rates 2800 fps at the muzzle and an awesome 5224 ft-lbs of muzzle energy. It only drops -8.2 in. at 300 yards. But the 378 W'by Mag 300gr FMJ is even awesomer at 2925 fps

The 375 Ruger was a joint project between Hornady and Ruger, and it became the first big-game rifle cartridge to bear the Ruger name. The 375 Ruger uses a unique case designed by Hornady and Ruger. The case is a rimless design, with the base diameter of .532 in, which is the same diameter of the belt on belted magnum cases based on the .300 H&H Magnum and 375 H&H Magnum. As Ruger intended the cartridge to be chambered in standard length bolt action rifles the case length was kept to 2.580 in. The max cartridge OAL is 3.340 in. Image courtesy of Hornady.

mv and 5699 ft-lbs muzzle energy. It drops 0.4-in. more at 300 yards than the 375 W'by Mag load, or -8.6 in.

It was 25 more years before there was another 375 entry, and that round was the little-known **375 Winchester,** which barely hangs on with a few factory chamberings for lever guns. The 375 Win, loaded to a maximum working pressure of 50,000 CUP, was introduced in the Winchester Model 94 (1978), a rifle with strengthened receiver walls. The round later became available in the Marlin M336 and Savage M99. Winchester discontinued the 250gr factory load in the 1980s, leaving just the 200gr version in Winchester's catalog.

One explanation of the 375 Win's failure is that it is too similar to the 35 Rem and inferior to the 444 Marlin and 45-70 Government. The 375 has better numbers than at least the 35 Rem. In Winchester's 200gr Power-Point the 375 Win generates 2200 fps MV/2150 ft-lbs ME, compared to the same bullet in the 35 Rem., 2020 fps MV/1812 ft-lbs ME.

The **375 Remington Ultra Magnum** was introduced in 2001 and is the largest RUM. With very little taper in the case body and a sharp shoulder, the 375 RUM is a stretched 404 Jeffery case with about 25% more case capacity than the 375 H&H. That capacity, added to the use of higher working pressures, gives the 375 RUM a big ballistic advantage over most other rounds in this chapter. Remington, DoubleTap, Nosler, and Cor-Bon offer factory loads. In Remington's Express 270gr Soft Point comes in well behind the Weatherby 378 W'by Mag 270gr SP, with 2900 fps MV/5041 ft-lbs ME for the RUM and 3180 fps MV/6062 ft-lbs ME. The margin narrows a bit with 300gr loads, with the RUM's 300gr A-Frame PSP at 2760 fps MV/5073 ft-lbs ME, the 375 W'by Mag 300gr Partition developing 2800 fps MV/5224 ft-lbs ME, and the 378 W'by Mag 300gr FMJ at 2925 fps MV/5699 ft-lbs muzzle energy.

The appearance of the 375 RUM and the longtime availability of the 378 W'by Mag may explain why the **376 Steyr** cartridge, officially unveiled in 1999 in the Scout rifle, languishes. That's a fair description, because the Scout chambering was dropped in January 2009,

The 375 RUM and the 378 W'by Mag may have made the 376 Steyr cartridge effectively extinct. The Steyr was officially unveiled in 1999 in the Scout rifle, above, but was dropped from the gun's cartridge list in January 2009. It has been available in Steyr's Pro Hunter series, but may be discontinued in that line as well. The 376 Steyr is based on the 9.3x64mm Brenneke, although the Steyr is about 4mm shorter.

and was available in Steyr's Pro Hunter series, but may be discontinued in that gun as well. The 376 Steyr (9.55x60mm) was originally specified for a 0.358-in-diameter bullet in Jeff Cooper's original "Lion Scout" big bore rifle, but it made sense to make it a .375-in bullet to make sure it met many African countries' minimum bullet size of .375 caliber for certain game. The 376 Steyr is based on the 9.3x64mm Brenneke, although the Steyr case is about 4mm shorter. Size-wise, that makes it fit between the 350 Rem Mag and the 375 H&H Mag. Various names were proposed, with Cooper favoring the 376 Dragoon. The 376 case holds around 80 grains of water, while the 375 H&H holds around 90 grains water, and both cartridges can be loaded to 62,000 psi. Only Hornady currently produces 376 ammunition in the U.S., in 225gr and 270gr choices.

Opening the aperture a bit, the 376 falls below the top 35-caliber offerings and the H&H, if you compare muzzle energies across various bullet weights. For example, the 376 Steyr makes 3900 ft-lbs ME with a 270gr bullet, less than a 358 Norma Mag 250gr at 4500 ft-lbs ME; a 375 H&H 270gr at 4310 ft-lbs ME; and a 9.3x64mm Brenneke 247gr at 4180 ft-lbs ME. However, to its credit, the 376 Scout's barrel is only 19 inches in length. Recoil energy for the 376 is 25.4 ft-lbs with a 225gr round @ 2350 fps, and 34 ft-lbs with a 270gr bullet @ 2420 fps. For scale, 308 Win 150gr bullet @ 2835 fps makes 16.6 ft-lbs of recoil.

The relatively new **375 Ruger**, introduced in 2006, uses the same .532-in. rim diameter as the 375 H&H, but Ruger's belt is fatter. The Ruger has slightly more case capacity, even though at 2.500 inches case length, it's .3-in. shorter than the H&H. The straight, unbelted case was designed to equal the 375 H&H's performance in a standard-length 30-06 action and fit existing belted-magnum bolt faces. However, because of its more efficient case, the 375 Ruger beats 375 H&H velocities in all bullet weights in 22- or 23-in. barrels, as the accompanying tables show. ●

Right: The Weatherby's, Inc. rifle ad at right was for the new "378" cartridge, along with Weatherby's rifles and Imperial Scope. The full-page two-color advertisement was for magazines and was labeled #1260. It was prepared by Motti & Siteman Advertising Agency in Los Angeles.

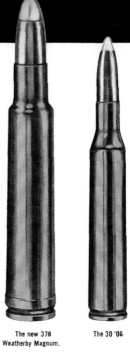

Weatherby
WORLD'S MOST POWERFUL RIFLES & SCOPES

▲
FOR THE SHAH OF IRAN
Custom 300 Weatherby Magnum
with 4X Weatherby Imperial Scope.

A Weatherby Magnum bullet traveling at ultra-high velocity kills with one shot—even though no vital spot is hit! See the fabulous new "378" cartridge for the world's largest game—now in stock. Or choose your favorite from a 257-270-7MM-300 and 375 Weatherby Magnum at $250.00. Standard calibers at $230.00.

Dominate the field with a new Weatherby Imperial Scope—2¾X, 4X, 6X, or the NEW Variable 2¾ to 10X—for the world's greatest combination of killing power and accuracy. Prices start at $69.50.

See your nearest dealer or write for free information to
WEATHERBY'S INC., 2779 Firestone Boulevard, South Gate, California

The new 378
Weatherby Magnum.

The 30 '06

24: Chasing the 38-40 Win.

Ranchmen protecting Stock from Wolves.

The 38-40 Winchester was introduced in 1874 for the company's lever-action rifles, but current loadings are intended for revolvers. Several single-action revolvers have recently been chambered for this cartridge, including the Ruger Vaquero. Derived from the 44-40 Winchester, it is actually a 40-caliber cartridge shooting .401-caliber bullets. © Winfield Galleries, LLC, St. Louis, Missouri. Used with permission. To view current artwork and pricing, log on to www.WinfieldGalleries.com.

41 Remington Magnum   40 Smith & Wesson

10mm Auto

Among the cartridge families, this powerful trio of factory-available rounds is remarkable for their modern design, power across the board, and accuracy of their diameter nomenclature. Just that last fact alone is enough to like them. The 40s include the 40 S&W, 41 Remington Magnum, and 10mm Auto, whose respective bullet diameters are .400, .410, and .400, or 10.2mm.

There aren't any halfway loads here, either. Today, the **41 Remington Magnum** for example develops more than 700 ft-lbs of energy in its most common bullets weights of 180gr and 210gr. That fits into its design concept from 1964, when Smith & Wesson chambered it in the Model 57 revolver as a cartridge suited for law enforcement that split the power zone between the 357 Mag and the 44 Mag. Even though it has a modern chambering date, the 41 Mag's roots trace back to 1873 and the 38-40 Winchester (which shot 200gr .403-diameter lead flatnose bullets to around 1000 fps), the underpowered 41 Long Colt (1877), and the 400 Eimer, made by Joplin, Missouri gunsmith "Pop" Eimer in 1924. However, the 41 Mag faltered at its inception, due to competition from other concepts (Bill Jordan preferred the Model 19 357 Mag, and Elmer Keith rooted for the Model 29 44 Mag) and that the 41 Mag's performance was simply too much for most LE shooters to handle comfortably—two initial 41 Magnum 210gr loads were released at 1500 fps and 1150 fps. Also, the Model 58 and Model 57 revolvers turned out to be too big to be carried comfortably by police.

The **10mm Auto** was introduced in 1983 in the Bren Ten autoloading pistol, the brainchild of ballistician Whit Collins and in consultation with Jeff Cooper. However, like the 41 Rem Mag, the concept of a powerful mid-bore cartridge dates back almost 140 years to the 38-40 Winchester (38 WCF) round introduced in the Winchester Model 1873 lever-action rifle. Cooper's notion of pushing a 200gr .400-in. diameter bullet to 1,000 fps in the 1970s prompted Collins to look for existing rifle cases that had the proper casehead dimensions and could be trimmed down to proper length to fit in a 9mm Browning Hi-Power magazine. In 1972, the resulting 40 G&A (Guns & Ammo magazine supplied some research help) had a 180gr bullet moving at 1,050 fps out of a 5-in. Hi-Power barrel. Then in 1973, Cooper and Collins looked at a .40-cal round with a longer case for 1911 semi-autos. The Bren Ten semiautomatic 40 Super cartridge, which

If the reader wants to take a walk on the wild side, borrow or rent a used Taurus M415Ti chambered for 41 Mag. The Taurus's lightweight titanium frame coupled with 210gr loads like the Federal Classic Hi-Shok JHP or a 175gr Silvertip Hollow Point from Winchester make the recoil-reduction porting and Ribber grips seem totally inadequate. This Winchester Supreme high-performance Platinum Tip is marketed as handgun hunting ammunition with a notched lead core and two-part hollow point cavity. The 240gr bullet is housed in nickel-plated brass and has a MV of 1250 fps and a big ME 833 ft. lbs. Bottom photo courtesy of Midway USA.

SELECTED LOADS & BALLISTICS

Winchester 38-40 Win X3840 180gr Soft Point
(partial rifle ballistics)

Range, Yards	Muzzle	50	100	200
Velocities (fps)	1160	999	901	827
Energy (ft.-lbs.)	538	399	324	273
Trajectory (in.)		3.4	0	-33.8

The 40-cal pistol cartridges have a tough competitor to measure up to: The circa-1873 38-40 Win, which generates ballistics on par with the more modern rounds. Photo courtesy of Midway USA.

is now called the 10mm Auto, was the result. A 1984 Bren Ten catalog called the Norma factory-loaded 10mm Auto cartridge a centerfire, rimless, straight-walled cartridge that measures 1.250 inches in overall length with a

Federal Vital-Shok 41 Rem Mag 180gr Barnes Expander P41XB1

Range, Yards	Muzzle	25	50	75	100
Velocities (fps)	1340	1262	1193	1134	1084
Energy (ft.-lbs.)	718	636	569	514	470
Trajectory (in.)		0	-0.5	-2.5	-6.1

Federal Vital-Shok 41 Rem Mag 210gr Swift A-Frame P41SA

Range, Yards	Muzzle	25	50	75	100
Velocities (fps)	1270	1207	1152	1105	1065
Energy (ft.-lbs.)	752	680	619	570	529
Trajectory (in.)		0	-0.6	-2.8	-6.8

Remington Express 41 Rem Mag 210gr Soft Point R41MG1 (4-in. barrel)

Range, Yards	Muzzle	50	100
Velocities (fps)	1300	1162	1062
Energy (ft.-lbs.)	788	630	526
Trajectory (in.)		-0.7	–3.2

Federal Premium Personal Defense 10mm Auto 180gr Hydra-Shok JHP P10HS1

Range, Yards	Muzzle	25	50	75	100
Velocities (fps)	1030	998	970	945	921
Energy (ft.-lbs.)	424	398	376	357	339
Trajectory (in.)		0	-1.3	-4.9	-10.9

Remington UMC 10mm Auto 180gr Metal Case L10MM6 (5-in. barrel)

Range, Yards	Muzzle	50	100
Velocities (fps)	1150	1063	998
Energy (ft.-lbs.)	529	452	398
Trajectory (in.)		-0.9	–3.7

Federal Premium Personal Defense 40 S&W 165gr Hydra-Shok JHP P40HS3

Range, Yards	Muzzle	25	50	75	100
Velocities (fps)	980	950	924	899	876
Energy (ft.-lbs.)	352	331	312	296	281
Trajectory (in.)		0	-1.5	-5.6	-12.3

Remington Golden Saber 180gr Brass-JHP GS40SWB (5-in. barrel)

Range, Yards	Muzzle	50	100
Velocities (fps)	1015	960	914
Energy (ft.-lbs.)	412	3	68	334
Trajectory (in.)		–1.3	–4.5

Though built for an autoloader like the Colt Delta Elite at right, the 10mm Auto also shows up in a wheelgun. Perhaps the best-known revolver that adapts auto-rimmed ammunition for use in a revolver is the Smith & Wesson Model 625 chambered for 45 ACP. But another big-bore revolver from S&W that loads its rounds in a moon clip is the 10mm Auto 610. The 40 S&W and 10mm Auto rounds use straight-walled cases that feature an extractor groove just in front of the case head, the profile of which remains even with the diameter of the case. Moon clips that grab each round by the extractor groove and bridges across the rear of the cylinder are necessary to hold the rounds in position. The 610 revolver was built on the "N" frame, which until the arrival of the Model 500 Magnum was the largest revolver platform available from Smith & Wesson. The 610 is all stainless steel, and with its full-lug barrel and non-fluted cylinder. This 10mm Auto round is Hornady's Custom 155Gr XTP JHP #9122, with a Muzzle Velocity of 1265 fps and Muzzle Energy of 551 ft-lbs. Photo courtesy of Midway USA.

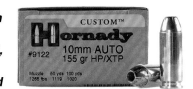

37,000 CUP, resulting in energy at the muzzle of 640 ft-lbs.

Despite these eye-popping performance figures, the round languished, being chambered only in the Bren Ten until Colt chambered the 10mm in a 1911 Government Model, the Colt Delta Elite. In that big frame, the round got a boost when the FBI selected it as the agency's standard service cartridge, declaring the 10mm Auto to be "the best law enforcement cartridge available." However, when the agency touted the 10mm, it did so with an "FBI Lite" load that pushed a Sierra 180gr JHP 10mm bullet to 950 fps. Coincidentally, that same power level could also be reached by a

10.16mm-diameter (.40 cal.) bullet. It used a standard .210-in.-diameter large-pistol primer with a truncated cone 200gr bullet. Out of a Norma 5-in. test barrel, MV was 1200 fps at

CHAPTER 24: CHASING THE 38-40 Win.

At bottom is the Smith & Wesson M&P40 No. 209200 in 40 S&W is a good example of a gun built to fit the round—it's basically the same size as the company's M&P9 9mm polymer gun. This Smith & Wesson M&P40 gets a lot of things right. The beavertail, sights, and slide cuts were excellent, and the gun had a roomy accessory rail and a reversible magazine release. The Remington UMC 40 S&W 180gr JHP #23694 at right has a MV of 1015 fps and ME of 412 ft-lbs. Ammo photo courtesy of Midway USA.

.40/10mm-caliber cartridge with a shorter case, and such a "10mm Auto Short" would fit in 9mm pistol frames instead of a full-size 45 ACP frame. Then, in January 1989, Winchester and S&W jointly introduced the new 40 S&W cartridge—essentially a 10mm Short—for the S&W Model 4006, that matched the FBI's performance specifications for the 10mm Auto. The 40 Smith & Wesson became so popular that it has pushed the 10mm Auto into obscurity. The FBI later switched to Glocks chambered for the 40 S&W.

So, the 10mm Auto spawned not only its replacement, but also a field of other good cartridges. The 41 Action Express (designed by Evan Whildin in 1986) is a near-ballistic-twin of the 40 S&W. The 10mm Magnum was a proprietary cartridge of AMT/iAi, and it was nearly identical in dimensions to a standard 10mm Auto, except that the case was lengthened from .99 to 1.25 in. In the Biblical tradition of Jesse begat David who begat Nathan, the 10mm Auto begat the 40 S&W which begat the 357 SIG—basically a 40 S&W case necked down to accept a 9mm bullet. The 9x25mm Dillon is a 10mm Auto cartridge necked down to accept 9mm (.355-in.) bullets. The 400 Cor-Bon is a 45 ACP case necked down to accept a 10mm bullet, which provides near-10mm Auto performance with a bottleneck case at lower pressures. And the 10mm Express, produced by the Texas Ammunition Company, is a standard 10mm Auto cartridge dimensionally, but loaded to higher velocities, such as a 200gr JHP with 1250 fps/694 ft-lbs muzzle specs. Essentially, the Texas Ammunition Company's 10mm Express loads bring the 10mm back to its original levels.

As noted above, the **40 Smith & Wesson** (or metrically, the 10x22mm Smith & Wesson) is a rimless pistol cartridge developed jointly by Winchester and Smith & Wesson that duplicates the performance of the FBI's reduced-velocity 10mm cartridge, and which could be retrofitted into medium-frame semiautomatics. Twenty or so years ago, the 40's development at Winchester was a secret—it even had the code name of "Swordfish."

What gun manufacturers learned in the early days of the 40's youth was that to get the desired performance (a 180gr bullet running near 1,000 fps) required more than slapping a 40 barrel in a 9mm handgun. Interestingly, the 10mm Auto crowd didn't readily accept the 40 S&W, calling it the "40 short and weak," which in comparison to full-throat 10mm loads, it is. Still, if the 40 S&W hangs around as long as the highly regarded 38-40 Win from the 1870s—and whose ballistics it mirrors—then the 10mm Short will be called an unqualified success. ●

25: The Top End

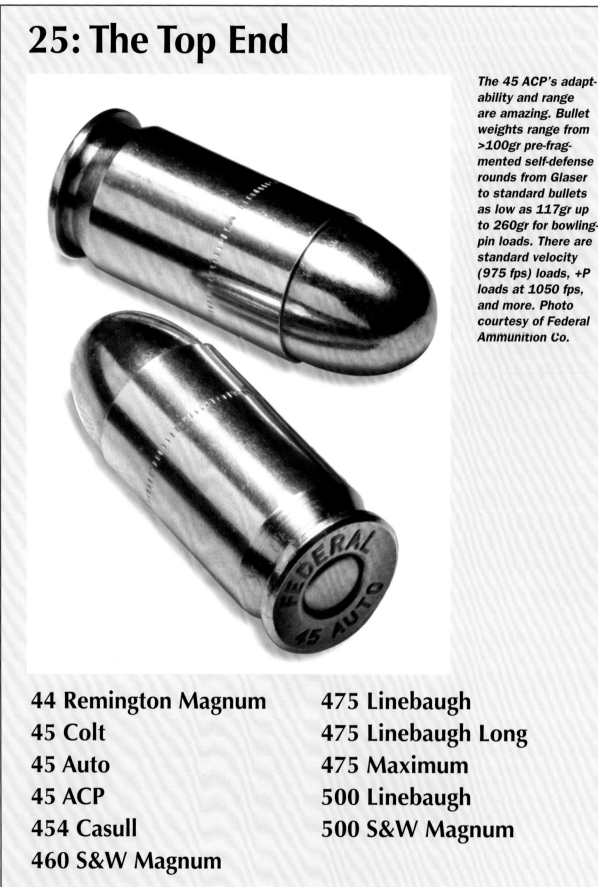

The 45 ACP's adaptability and range are amazing. Bullet weights range from >100gr pre-fragmented self-defense rounds from Glaser to standard bullets as low as 117gr up to 260gr for bowling-pin loads. There are standard velocity (975 fps) loads, +P loads at 1050 fps, and more. Photo courtesy of Federal Ammunition Co.

44 Remington Magnum
45 Colt
45 Auto
45 ACP
454 Casull
460 S&W Magnum

475 Linebaugh
475 Linebaugh Long
475 Maximum
500 Linebaugh
500 S&W Magnum

The top end of the handgun spectrum is populated by some of the biggest names in ammunition history, and many of these loads have been around in some form for more than 100 years. The older rounds have paved the way for hotter, more powerful loads that, for the moment, seem to have reach the apex of what is controllable in a repeating handgun.

For example, there's the Linebaugh line, which includes the **475 Linebaugh** and the **500 Linebaugh.** John Linebaugh began experimenting with the 45 Colt in the early 1980s, making guns such as a 10-inch-barrel 45 Colt built on a 44 Magnum El Dorado frame and cylinder. That round would shoot 1700 fps with 260gr bullets. The next step was to go big with his 500 Linebaugh, using 348 Win brass trimmed to 1.410, inside neck reamed, and loaded with .511-in. bullets. It would launch a 440gr bullet at 1250 fps. With the 475, he split the difference picked the parent 45-70 brass and trimmed to 1.410 in., then loaded it with .476-in. bullets.

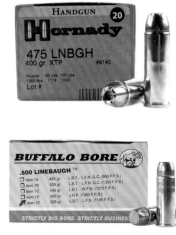

Linebaugh, a custom revolver maker, had been using 348 Win brass to make cases for his 500 Linebaugh custom revolvers, so when he found out that 348 Win brass would be discontinued, he developed the 475 Linebaugh on 45-70 brass. Tim Sundles, who founded Buffalo Bore Ammunition Co., contracted with Starline to produce several million rounds of brass bearing 475 and 500 Linebaugh headstamps and worked with Hodgdon Powder Co. to produce standardized loads utilizing lead and jacketed bullets.

John Linebaugh's eponymous 475 Linebaugh, chambered in a Freedom Arms Model 757 production revolver, may still be the most powerful repeating handgun ever offered as an over-the-counter firearm. The Freedom five-shot revolver throws a 475 Linebaugh 420gr bullet at 1350 fps, just over 1700 ft-lbs. In contrast, the 44 Magnum propels a 250gr bullet at 1250 fps/800 ft-lbs of muzzle energy. The obsolete 475 Wildey Magnum uses cut-off 284 Win brass that can be handloaded with either 250gr or 300gr bullets to get over 1600

Hornady 475 Linebaugh 400gr XTP #9140 (7.5-in. barrel))			
Range, Yards	Muzzle	50	100
Velocities (fps)	1300	1177	1084
Energy (ft-lbs)	1501	1231	1043

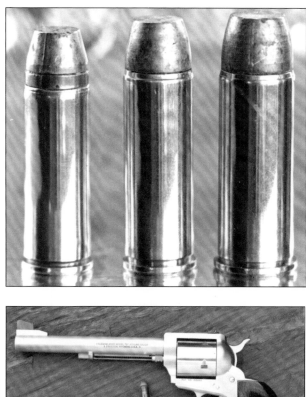

Top, from the left are a heavily loaded 45 Long Colt with a 350gr bullet, next to the 475 Linebaugh lead flat-nose load by Buffalo Bore. In the Hornady load top left, the 475's 400gr slug leaves the gun at 1300 fps. Beside it is the massive 500 Linebaugh, formerly a custom cartridge, but now loaded by BB in 400gr, 435gr, and 525gr formulations. Bottom left is the 500 Linebaugh load from Buffalo Bore, 1410 ft-lbs ME. Above, the Freedom Arms Field Grade Model chambered in 475 Linebaugh comes with 4.75-, 6-, or 7.5-in. barrels.

fps/>1700 ft-lbs, but the ammo is not commercially loaded. The 429 Super Bower pushes a 365gr .429-in.-diameter bullet at 1990 fps/3200 ft-lbs, but it requires a single-shot handgun, not a repeater. The 500 Linebaugh beats the 475 for bullet weight, but the 475 wins for velocity, and the two calibers are very close in power to each other. For example, a 475 Linebaugh Hornady Custom 400gr XTP JHP #9140 goes at a 1300 fps MV and 1501 ft-lbs ME, compared to the 500 Linebaugh Buffalo Bore 525gr Lead Long Flat Nose #1E/20 at 1100 fps MV and 1410 ft-lbs ME. In factory loads, the 50 AE shoots a 325gr bullet around 1400 fps/1400 ft-lbs. The 454 Casull can get 1600 fps out of a 300gr bullet, putting it right up there with the Linebaugh, depending on the exact load. But the 454 Casull can't handle bullets over 300 grains without deep-seating them, which can jack up pressures.

Newer loads for custom guns include the **475 Linebaugh Long,** aka **475 Maximum.** But stretching the 475 Linebaugh to 1.610 in. requires converting a Ruger 357 Maximum revolver to the new bore size. The 500 Linebaugh Long is a 1.610-in.-length .50-caliber cartridge made from 348 Win brass, and it will max out with a 440gr bullet at 1550 fps.

The **454 Casull** came along in the mid-1950's and lived as a wildcat for many years. The product of gunsmith Dick Casull and Jack Fullmer has been a production revolver manufactured by Freedom Arms since 1983. Because conventional six-shot cylinders were not strong enough to handle the pressures, Casull initially used (1954) a Colt Single Action fitted with a five-shot 45 Colt cylinder to make his load produce 1550 fps with a 250gr bullet. To improve safety, in 1957 Casull built his own single-action frame that would withstand a 300gr bullet moving at 1700 fps. As far as muzzle energy, the 454 Casull produces about 50% more punch than the 44 Rem Mag, producing about the same amount of recoil as a 338 Win Mag in a 10-pound shoulder-fired rifle. For reduced-velocity loads, the 45 Colt can be loaded in modern 45 Colt cases and fired in the Casull revolver. The 454 Casull's brass is purposely made longer than 45 Colt brass to prevent someone dropping a 454 load into a 45 Colt.

Smith & Wesson's two biggest magnums are the **460 S&W Magnum** and **500 S&W Magnum.** The 460 has a bullet diameter of .454, rim diameter of .520, case diameter of .478, an overall case length of 1.800, and a cartridge overall length of 2.300 in. The 460 cartridge is a lengthened version of the 454 Casull, which is a longer 45 Colt, so both can be fired in a revolver chambered for the 460 Magnum. As an

SELECTED LOADS & BALLISTICS					
Federal Vital-Shok 454 Casull 250gr Barnes Expander P454XB1					
Range, Yards	Muzzle	25	50	75	100
Velocities (fps)	1530	1423	1326	1239	1165
Energy (ft-lbs)	1299	1123	976	852	753
Trajectory (in.)		0	-0.2	-1.6	-4.4

Winchester's 454 Casull Supreme 260gr Partition #SPG454 has a heavy rear lead core and a fully tapered jacket that ruptures at the thin jacket mouth, curling the jacket uniformly outward at high or low velocities. The enclosed rear core retains more than half of the original bullet weight for deep penetration. MV 1800 fps, ME 1871 ft-lbs. Photo courtesy of Midway USA.

The Ruger Alaskan can fire either for 45 Colt or 454 Casull, as the barrel markings indicate. It shot standard-pressure 45 Colts with 2.3-in. accuracy and the hottest loads are controllable enough.

example of what the 460 can do, look at the Federal Premium Vital-Shok 275gr Barnes XPB #P460XB1 load, which pushes the XPB Hollow Point Lead Free bullet to 1840 fps MV/2067 ft-lbs ME. The 460 Mag generates 35% more recoil than the 44 Mag but only 6% more than the 454 Casull.

For those who want the largest pistol on the block, the 500 S&W Magnum is your caliber. According to the Bureau of Alcohol Tobacco, Firearms, and Explosives (BATFE) regulations, rifle and handgun bores are limited to one-half inch, unless the firearm is registered as a destructive device and a Federal $200 tax is paid and all other requirements are met. Some other manufacturer could make a longer cartridge, but the overall length on the 500 S&W is already more than 2 inches long, and it accommodates bullet weights from light 275gr hollowpoints to heavy 400gr platinum-coated bullets. To compare, the cartridge overall length (COL) of the 44 Mag is 1.6 inches, whereas the COL of the 500 S&W is 2.085 in. The muzzle energy is substantially different. A potent Winchester load for the 44 Mag is a 250gr platinum-tip hollowpoint which has a listed velocity of 1250 fps and muzzle energy of 867 foot-pounds. Winchester's 500 S&W 400gr platinum-tip hollowpoint has a listed muzzle velocity of 1800 fps and muzzle energy of 2877 ft-lbs — more than three times the energy of the 44 Magnum out of revolvers with 8-in. barrels. A handloaded Barnes X 275gr XPB with the lightest powder charge recom-

Another top-end round is the 45 G.A.P. (short for Glock Automatic Pistol) cartridge, designed by Ernest Durham, an engineer with CCI/Speer, at the request of firearms manufacturer Glock to provide a cartridge that would equal the power of the 45 ACP but was shorter to fit in a more compact handgun, and with a stronger case head to reduce the possibility of case neck blowouts. It fits into pistols like the Glock 38, above, a midsize pistol that carries 8+1 rounds of 45 GAP. The 45 GAP is the first commercially-introduced cartridge that carries the Glock name. The 45 GAP has the same diameter as the 45 ACP, but is slightly shorter, and uses a small-pistol primer instead of the large-pistol primer most commonly used in 45 ACP. Remington UMC box is filled with 230gr FMJs. The Federal American Eagle's are 185gr TMJs.

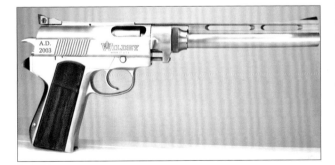

Left, the 44 Auto Mag Pistol (AMP) cartridge was introduced in 1971 as a rimless, straight-wall case originally formed by trimming a 308 Win or 30-06 case to 1.30 in. length. The 44 AMP was designed to shoot .429-in. bullets at about the same velocity as the 44 Magnum. Left to right in the ammo photos, the two assembled rounds are Cor-Bon's 240gr 44 Mag and Cor-Bon's 240gr 44 Auto-Mag round. Note how the rim of the 44 Mag differs from the rim of the 44 Auto-Mags.

The Cor-Bon Hunter 44 Automag 240gr JHP has a MV of 1450 fps and ME of 1120 ft-lbs. Photo courtesy of Midway.

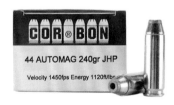

The Wildey 44-10 Survivor was chambered for 44 Auto-Mag Available barrel lengths ranged from 5 inches to 18 inches. This gun was gas operated, and there was a ribbed collar where the barrel joins with the frame that can be turned to adjust gas flow. In 1983 the Auto Mag pistol was featured in the fourth Dirty Harry movie, Sudden Impact. Clint Eastwood's character Harry Callahan uses his 44 Auto Mag pistol to kill Mick the Rapist after Harry loses his Smith & Wesson Model 29 revolver in a fist fight. In 1987 the Eddie Murphy movie Beverly Hills Cop II featured the 44 Auto Mag and the spent cartridge cases were used as a plot device to locate the alphabet bandit. Used Auto Mag pistols now sell for around $2000.

mended (11.0 grains of Hodgdon Titegroup) produced a velocity of 1000 fps (400 fps less than a factory Cor-Bon load) and a muzzle energy of 600 ft-lbs (half the power of Cor-Bon's 1200 ft-lbs). This is a comfortable and easily controlled load in the big X-frame revolvers, even for recoil-sensitive shooters.

Importantly, the guns' cylinders are long enough to handle cartridges loaded with pointed bullets, including the 454 Casull in the 460 Mag Switching to more streamlined projectiles flattens the trajectories of both cartridges to make 225-yard shots feasible for the handgun hunter.

Introduced in 1955 in the Model 29 revolver, the **44 Remington Magnum** was inspired by heavy loadings of the 44 Special by Elmer Keith. Remington and Smith & Wesson teamed up to produce the round and the accompanying revolver, soon followed by Ruger's Super Blackhawk, conversions of the old Winchester Model 92 lever action, factory .44-cal. long rifles like Ruger's autoloading carbine, the current Marlin 1894 lever gun, and others. One of the classic hunting loads for the 44 Magnum uses a 240gr bullet at about 1800 fps, and if the 44 Mag has a strike against it as a deer cartridge, it's the curved trajectory beyond 100 yards. The 44 Magnum is well-known as a revolver round, but it also finds its way into autoloaders such as the Desert Eagle. The Magnum Research Desert Eagle is a big black pistol with a 6-in. barrel and standard black finish. Although this gun is built on a U.S. patent registered in 1986, it is actually a product of Israeli Military Industries, LTD. or, I.M.I. The Desert Eagle 44 Magnum is a gas-operated semi-automatic pistol fed from an eight-round single-column magazine. Fed with good 44 fodder, it is capable of printing five-shot groups

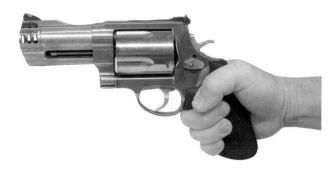

The Smith & Wesson 500 S&W Magnum No. 163504 revolver has a satin-stainless finish, Hogue Sorbothane Recoil Absorbing Grips with deep finger grooves, and a muzzle compensator.

The 500 S&W Magnum Winchester 400gr platinum tips (left cartridge) shot 1.5-in. groups at 25 yards, a performance duplicated by a 275gr Barnes handload (standing right, and front).

DoubleTap's 500 S&W Magnum 275gr Barnes XPB Hollow Point generates 1990 fps out of an 8.375-in. barrel.

Federal's 460 S&W Premium Vital-Shok 275gr Barnes XPB Hollow Point Lead-Free #P460XB1 pops out the muzzle at 1840 fps and generates 2067 ft-lbs ME. Ammo photos courtesy of Midway USA.

SELECTED LOADS & BALLISTICS

Federal Vital-Shok 460 S&W 275gr Barnes Expander P460XB1

Range, Yards	Muzzle	25	50	75	100
Velocities (fps)	1840	1759	1681	1606	1533
Energy (ft-lbs)	2067	1890	1726	1575	1434
Trajectory (in.)		0	0.2	-0.4	-1.8

Federal Vital-Shok 500 S&W 325gr Swift A-Frame P500SA

Range, Yards	Muzzle	25	50	75	100
Velocities (fps)	1800	1677	1559	1449	1350
Energy (ft-lbs)	2338	2028	1754	1515	1315
Trajectory (in.)		0	0.1	-0.6	-2.4

Though the 44 Magnum is certainly known for its performance in revolvers like the Ruger, top, it also performs well in semi-autos like the Desert Eagle.

In rifles, the round's ballistics can be improved by using Hornady LEVERevolution FTX bullets, which improve aerodynamics. Muzzle Velocity: 1410 fps; Muzzle Energy: 993 ft-lbs. One of the stouter loads out there for the 44 Mag is Buffalo Bore's +P+ 340gr Lead Flat Nose Gas Check unit, which pushes the big bullet to 1478 fps MV and develops a big 1649 ft-lbs ME. Ammo photos courtesy of Midway USA.

measuring less than 3 inches on average at 25 yards. In one test, PMC 180gr and 240gr JHPs averaged 2.5 and 2.9 inches respectively. Likewise, Cor-Bon 240gr JHPs shot average

The 44 Smith & Wesson Special, or better known as the 44 Special, is a lengthened 44 Russian case. The 44 Rem Mag case was created by adding length to the 44 Special case. Introduced around 1907, the 44 Special was once far more popular than it is today, being eclipsed now by the 44 Magnum. Even though the 44 Special is not as powerful as the 44 Mag, it is still a great choice in the modern carry revolver. Two loads for the cartridge are the Winchester Super-X 246gr LRN, which produces a MV of 755 fps and ME 310 ft-lbs. Blackpowder fans might like the characteristics of Goex's Black Dawge Black Powder 205gr Lead Flat Point, which uses blackpowder to generate a MV of 751 fps. Photos courtesy of Midway USA.

SELECTED LOADS & BALLISTICS

Federal Power-Shok 44 Rem Mag 240gr JHP C44A

Range, Yards	Muzzle	25	50	75	100
Velocities (fps)	1230	1169	1117	1073	1035
Energy (ft-lbs)	806	729	665	613	571
Trajectory (in.)		0	-0.7	-3.1	-7.4

Federal Champion 44 Special 200gr Semi-Wadcutter HP C44SA

Range, Yards	Muzzle	25	50	75	100
Velocities (fps)	870	848	826	806	787
Energy (ft-lbs)	336	319	303	289	275
Trajectory (in.)		0	-2.1	-7.4	-16.0

groups measured at 2.5 in. The Cor-Bon round produced a remarkable 1198 ft-lbs of muzzle energy, but when the round is fired from the big Desert Eagle, the shooter isn't taxed. In fact, the Desert Eagle 44 Magnum is capable of shooting very accurately out to 75 yards with the right scope and careful choice of ammunition.

When we speak of big-bore handguns, the **45 Colt** cartridge is among the most respected. The 45 Colt was introduced in 1873, and it is among the oldest centerfire handgun cartridges still in common use. Originally designed as a martial cartridge, the 45 Colt was often used at longer ranges than we might try today.

The 45 ACP +P Glaser Pow'RBall 165gr #PB45165 is a controlled expansion copper-jacketed compressed lead core hollow point bullet capped with a polymer ball. MV 1225 fps, ME 550 ft-lbs.

From left to right are four 45 Colt loads: Winchester's 225gr Silvertip, the Cor-Bon 200gr jacketed hollowpoint, the all-copper 225gr Cor-Bon DPX, and Speer's 250gr Gold Dot. The Winchester and Speer rounds are standard pressure. The two Cor-Bons were +P. When shooting the +Ps, be prepared for about 20% more recoil than a 45 ACP +P loading and 50% more recoil than the standard-pressure Silvertip loading.

Want to go back to the beginning of the 45 ACP's history? You could do worse than shooting 200gr loads in a Colt Black Army 1918, right.

SELECTED LOADS & BALLISTICS

Federal American Eagle 45 Colt 225gr JSP AE45LC

Range, Yards	Muzzle	25	50	75	100
Velocities (fps)	860	844	828	813	799
Energy (ft-lbs)	369	356	343	330	319
Trajectory (in.)		0	-2.2	-7.5	-16.1

Many shooters forget that the 45 ACP is also available in a revolver, S&W's 625, above right. Moon clips make shooting the Auto-style hull possible in a wheelgun, below right.

SELECTED LOADS & BALLISTICS

Federal Premium Personal Defense 45 Auto 185gr JHP C45C

Range, Yards	Muzzle	25	50	75	100
Velocities (fps)	950	923	899	876	855
Energy (ft-lbs)	371	350	332	315	300
Trajectory (in.)		0	-1.7	-6.0	-13.1

Federal Premium Personal Defense 45 Auto 230gr Hydra-Shok JHP P45HS1

Range, Yards	Muzzle	25	50	75	100
Velocities (fps)	900	882	865	848	832
Energy (ft-lbs)	414	397	382	367	354
Trajectory (in.)		0	-1.9	-6.7	-14.6

Hornady 45 ACP +P 200gr HP XTP TAP FPD

Range, Yards	Muzzle	50	100
Velocities (fps)	1055	982	926
Energy (ft-lbs)	494	428	380
Trajectory (in.)			

Many production guns stand testament to the 45's pushing development of firearms. One is the Springfield Armory TRP Light Rail Model PC9105LP. Consumers demand this level of firearms sophistication to highlight the round's capabilities.

It was reputed to be capable of taking down an Indian war pony at 100 yards. The Army and Marine Corps, the Texas Rangers, the Royal Canadian Mounted Police and the New York State Patrol were just a few agencies to carry the 45 Colt on duty. Currently, there are three or four power levels loaded in the 45 Colt. One is ultra-hot loads designed for hunting revolvers such as Ruger Blackhawk and the Freedom Arms 454 Casull. Another are Cowboy loads that use a 250gr or 255gr bullet running between 650 fps and 800 fps. A third level are loads suitable for use in the Taurus Judge, Smith & Wesson double-action revolvers, and the strong US Fire Arms (USFA) single-action revolvers and the Ruger Vaquero. The +P 45 Colt full-power loads push a 250gr semi-wadcutter at about 1000 fps.

In this group, it is certainly possible for the most popular centerfire round in history to be at the bottom in terms of power, but that, in itself, is instructive. The **45 Auto,** or **45 ACP** for Automatic Colt Pistol, is a round that predates the gun that made it famous by seven years. In Colt Automatic Pistols, Donald B. Bady wrote, "Colt's developed a .45 inch caliber automatic pistol because of the demand for that bullet diameter. When U.S. Government field trials with small quantities of .38 automatic pistols demonstrated that caliber was insufficient, the importance of preparing a .45 was increased. Work started on this project in 1904, presumably arising from the .41 inch caliber program just concluded. By early 1905, Colt's had successfully fired a .45 bullet from an enlarged version of the Military Model 1902 style pistol. By mid-1905, the Colt .45 automatic pistol was in limited production." However, the load that participated in those Thompson-LaGarde military tests was a 200gr bullet running at 900 fps, not a 230gr bullet making 850 fps.

If the reader wishes to recreate some of the conditions of those military tests, he can grab up a vintage collectible from the period—not recommended, they're too valuable to shoot— or a current-production Colt Black Army 1918 No. 01018 45 ACP and stuff it with comparable loads used in the test. The Colt Black Army is a close copy of the original as it was manufactured in 1918, though its dust cover and lockwork are 1911A1. The Black Army does not have the finger grooves, improved hammer and short trigger of the later 1911A1. In short, it comes very close to being a true 1911. It's not hard to imagine the awesome impression the 45 must have made on men who cut their martial teeth on underpowered revolvers.

Despite 45 ACP and the Colt Government Model pistol being retired from military duty in 1985 by the older and less powerful 9mm Luger, civilian shooters still prefer it over many latecomer rounds. The United States Practical Shooting Association (USPSA) has said that more than 70 percent of its members use the 45 ACP in competition. The 45's adaptability and range are amazing. 45 ACP bullet weights range from >100gr pre-fragmented self-defense rounds from Glaser to standard bullets as low as 117gr up to 260gr for bowling-pin loads. There are plenty of standard velocity units (975 fps), +P loads running at 1050 fps, and more.

There are dozens, if not hundreds, of 1911-style pistol variants now, plus another polymer category that shoots the 45 cartridge. Picking a pistol that exhibits all the refinements found in the launching pad over the last century would be easy—many handgun manufacturers have 45-chambered high-end guns. If you want to handle one that exhibits many of the choices in a production gun, try the Springfield Armory TRP Light Rail Model PC9105LP 45 ACP. The gun has a Teflon Armory Kote black finish, accessory rail, textured gray G10 grips relieved area to help access the magazine-release button, and a stainless match-grade bull barrel that extends from the slide. There are also ambidextrous safety levers, an extended beavertail safety, 20-lpi checkering on both the frontstrap and mainspring housing, front rear and rear cocking serrations in the slide, an adjustable Bo-Mar style rear sight with tritium inserts, a matching low-profile tritium front sight, and many other features.

Shooting the venerable 45 ACP in a gun like the Springfield brings home an unmistakable point: Consumers demanded this level of firearms sophistication because they believe in the round. That will probably be as true in 2111 as it is in 2010. ●

26: The Big Boys

The artist for "Cowboy with Elk," a Western Cartridge Co. promotional poster, is unknown. Plenty of the big-boy cartridges in this chapter have been chambered in lever actions and killed quite a few elk. © Winfield Galleries, LLC, St. Louis, Missouri. Used with permission. To view current artwork and pricing, log on to www.WinfieldGalleries.com.

416 Rigby

416 Rem Mag

416 W'by Mag

404 Jeffery

444 Marlin

450 Bushmaster

45-70 Government

450 Marlin

458 Win Mag

460 W'by Mag

470 Nitro Express

500 Nitro Express

50 BMG

The top end of the cartridge power spectrum is populated with some of the best-known names from history, and these Big Boy rounds have led to the development of dozens, if not hundreds, of smaller cartridges that have been chopped and swaged and necked down to propel smaller pills at massive velocities. Still, most of the rounds in this group are made for serious game, such as bears and buffalo.

Starting with the smallest bullet diameter and working our way up, there are three 416-caliber rounds that develop some of the most useful power on the planet. The **416 Rigby, 416 Remington Magnum,** and **416 Weatherby Magnum** were all built to fill niches in the hunting-cartridge lineup that shooters wanted. John Rigby's namesake number was introduced in 1911, for use in bolt-action Mauser rifles, which John Rigby & Co. imported into Britain. John Rigby & Co. had the exclusive distributorship from 1898 to 1912 for the U.K. market of Mauser rifles and components that were manufactured by the Mauser firm. The rimless bottleneck design took .416-in.-diameter bullets in a .4461-in. neck. Shoulder diameter was .5402 in., and the base diameter .589 in. The rim measured .586 in. diameter. The case was 2.9 in. long, and the overall cartridge ran 3.75 inches in length. This made it suitable for "magnum-length" actions, which in turn allowed Rigby to stuff the cartridge full of Kynoch-manufactured Cordite, an early smokeless propellant. Because Cordite's performance could vary in hot temperatures, the round was loaded to just over 38,000 psi, which pushed a 400gr bullet to 2375 fps MV. With a properly zeroed rifle, this allows a point-blank hold up to about 250 yards.

The **416 Remington Magnum,** introduced in 1988, sought to shoot as flat as the 375 H&H Mag and hit harder than the 458 Win Mag. The 416 Rem Mag's belted bottleneck case accepts a .416-in.-diameter bullet in a .447-in. neck. The shoulder is 0.487 in., with a 0.509-in. base diameter and .530-in. rim diameter.

SELECTED LOADS & BALLISTICS

Federal 416 Rigby P416SA 400gr Swift A-Frame Cape-Shok

Range, Yards	Muzzle	100	200	300	400	500
Velocities (fps)	2350	2128	1917	1722	1542	1381
Energy (ft-lbs)	4905	4021	3264	2633	2111	1693
Trajectory (in.)		3.1	0	-12.7	-37.2	-76.3

Norma 416 Rigby 450gr Soft Nose

Range, Yards	Muzzle	50	100	150	200
Velocities (fps)	2150	2040	1933	1830	1731
Energy (ft-lbs)	4620	4158	3735	3347	2996
Trajectory (in.)	-1.6	0.3	0	-2.6	-7.7

Winchester 416 Rigby S416RSLS 400gr Nosler Solid

Range, Yards	Muzzle	100	200	300	400	500
Velocities (fps)	2370	2061	1778	1524	1309	1145
Energy (ft-lbs)	4988	3774	2807	2064	1522	1163
Trajectory (in.)		3.4	0	-14.5	-44.0	

This Hornady Dangerous Game Ammunition 416 Rigby has a 400gr DGX Flat Nose Expanding bullet. The DGX bullet expands while Hornady's DGS loads are a non-expanding, homogenous style bullet designed for deeper penetration. This one runs 2415 fps at the muzzle. Kynamco Limited has revived the Kynoch ammunition brand, the originator of the classic British Nitro Express cartridges. Over the last 10 years Kynamco has made extensive developments in modernizing many well known British proprietary cartridges, such as blending modern powders and using modern boxer primers. These changes have yielded identical internal and external ballistics while lowering breech pressures, producing cooler burning temperatures and reducing lead erosion when compared to the original ammunition. This Kynoch 416 Rigby hurls a 410gr Woodleigh Weldcore Soft Point at 2300 fps MV and 4702 ft-lbs ME. Norma's African PH cartridges optimize ballistic criteria such as bullet momentum, sectional density and penetration. They have heavy-for-caliber bullets have good sectional densities and better KO values. Photos courtesy of Midway USA.

The case alone is 2.85 inches long, and the whole shebang measures 3.6 inches in length. If those numbers sound familiar, they should. The 416 Rem Mag is an 8mm Rem Mag case necked up, as the 8mm Rem Mag's line (all in inches) shows: bullet diameter .323, neck diameter .341, shoulder diameter .4868, base diameter .5126, rim diameter .530, case length 2.85, cartridge length 3.6. Like Rigby's 416, the Rem 416 is loaded to around 2400 fps with a 400gr bullet. But the Remington cartridge will work in shorter actions, such as the Remington M700, Winchester M70, and other rifles with actions of similar length.

The **416 Weatherby Magnum,** introduced a year after the 416 Rem Mag, eclipses the latter in case capacity and downrange fps. The belted bottleneck 416 W'by Mag's line in inches (bullet diameter .416, neck diameter .444, shoulder diameter .561, base diameter .582, rim diameter .580, case length 2.915, cartridge length 3.75) compares to the 378 W'by Mag's, which Weatherby just necked up to accept the larger bullet (base diameter 0.584, rim diameter 0.580, case length 2.920, cartridge length 3.690). Interestingly, Weatherby had created the 378 W'by Mag case by swaging a belt onto the original 416 Rigby.

Next in line is the **404 Jeffery (10.75x73),** named for William Jackman Jeffery, who introduced this cartridge in 1905 as a rimless version of the popular 400 Jeffery. However, the "404" is misleading, because the round uses a .423-in.-diameter bullet. Aka the 404 Rimless Nitro Express, after 1912 W.J. Jeffery built 404 rifles on standard-length 98 Mausers with only magazine and bolt-face modifications. Other early 404 RNE firms included Vickers, Cogswell & Harrison, Waffenfabrik Mauser, and others, and at one point, European manufacturer RWS loaded this round. Norma now offers 404 cases for handloading and wildcatting, and the company loads the round, but it's almost as powerful as the 416 Rigby. This defeats the purpose of the 404 Jeffery, whose recoil is mild compared to the 416s.

Though a decided step down in power from the 416s and 404 Jeffery, the **444 Marlin** (intr. 1964) is still cataloged by its namesake, Marlin Firearms, as bear and moose lever-action choices in the Model 444XLR and Model 444. The round develops nearly 1.5 tons of muzzle energy in

SELECTED LOADS & BALLISTICS

Norma African PH 416 Rem Mag 450gr Woodleigh Solid FMJ

Range, Yards	Muzzle	50	100	150	200
Velocities (fps)	2150	2037	1928	1823	1722
Energy (ft-lbs)	4620	4148	3715	3321	2963
Trajectory (in.)		-1.6	0.3	0	-2.6	-7.8

Federal Premium 416 Rem Mag P416RT2 400gr Speer Trophy Bonded Sledgehammer

Range, Yards	Muzzle	100	200	300	400	500
Velocities (fps)	2400	2100	1823	1574	1357	1185
Energy (ft-lbs)	5115	3918	2951	2200	1636	1246
Trajectory (in.)		3.2	0	-13.9	-41.9	-89.2

DoubleTap 416 Rem Mag 350gr Barnes TSX Lead Free

Range, Yards	Muzzle	100	200	300	400	500
Velocities (fps)	2725	2515	2316	2127	1946	1774
Energy (ft-lbs)	5771	4917	4169	3515	2942	2447
Trajectory (in.)		2.0	0	-8.5	-24.7	50.1

Federal Premium 416 Rem Mag P416RT2 400gr Cape-Shok ammunition uses the well-named Speer Trophy Bonded Sledgehammer bullet. It produces 2400 fps MV and 5115 ft-lbs ME. The PH in Norma's African PH line stands for "professional hunter," and rounds like this 416 Rem Mag 450gr Woodleigh Solid FMJ are sold specifically for hunting dangerous game. MV: 2150 fps, ME: 4620 ft-lbs. The 416 Rem Mag was the first American-made 416 (1988) because of growing interest in the 416 caliber for hunting in Africa. The 416 Rem Mag has the advantage of fitting into many common actions that can take the 375 H&H, yet it delivers more or less the same ballistics and energy as the old 416 Rigby. This DoubleTap line uses a 350gr Barnes TSX copper bullet making 2725 fps/5771 ft-lbs at the muzzle. Bottom photo courtesy of DoubleTap. Top photos courtesy of Midway USA

Weatherby 416 W'by B416350TSX 350gr Barnes TSX

Range, Yards	Muzzle	100	200	300	400	500
Velocities (fps)	2880	2702	2530	2365	2207	2054
Energy (ft-lbs)	6448	5674	4977	4349	3785	3279
Trajectory (in.)		1.6	0	-7.0	-20.4	-40.8

Weatherby 416 W'by H416400RN 400gr Rn-Ex

Range, Yards	Muzzle	100	200	300	400	500
Velocities (fps)	2700	2417	2152	1903	1676	1470
Energy (ft-lbs)	6474	5189	4113	3216	2493	1918
Trajectory (in.)		2.3	0	-9.7	-29.3	-61.2

Kynoch 404 Rimless Nitro Express 404gr

Range, Yards	Muzzle	50	100
Velocities (fps)	2125	1996	1872
Energy (ft-lbs)	4010	3540	3115
Trajectory (in.)			

Norma African PH Ammunition 404 Jeffery 450gr Woodleigh Weldcore Soft Nose

Range, Yards	Muzzle	50	100	150	200
Velocities (fps)	2150	2048	1949	1853	1760
Energy (ft-lbs)	4620	4191	3795	3430	3096
Trajectory (in.)	1.6	0.2	0	-2.5	-7.6

Hornady 404 Jeffery 400gr DGS 8239

Range, Yards	Muzzle	100	200	300
Velocities (fps)	2300	2046	1809	1592
Energy (ft-lbs)	4698	3717	2906	2251
Trajectory (in.)		0	-6.9	-24.4

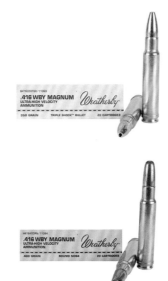

These two Weatherby 416 W'by Mag loads use Norma brass. This 350gr load uses a Barnes Triple-Shock X (TSX) bullet at MV 2880 fps and ME a whopping 6448 ft-lbs. The 400gr roundnose load's stats are 2700 fps/6474 ft-lbs. Photos courtesy Midway USA.

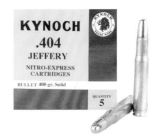

Kynoch's 404 Rimless Nitro Express was introduced by Jeffery for their bolt-action rifles around 1910. It was designed to replicate the ballistics of the popular 450/400 and rifles were made by various well known makers at the time, which included Jeffery, Cogswell & Harrison, and Westley Richards. The 404 Rimless NE Jeffery (10.75x73), introduced in 1909 and chambered in Mauser actions, became the workhorse of several African Game Departments. It wasn't as famous as other cartridges for African big game, but was much more widely used. Photos courtesy of Midway USA.

these 22- and 24-inch-barrel guns. Creating the round was a joint effort between Marlin and Remington to fill a lever-action power gap created in 1958 when Winchester discontinued the Model 71 in 348 Win, leaving the 35 Rem as the top of the lever heap. Notable in its line is the bullet diameter @ .429 in., the same diameter bullets as the 44 Rem Mag revolver cartridge. The rimmed straightwall case has a case length of 2.225 inches and a maximum cartridge length of 2.57 inches. It later begat the 450 Marlin.

Bushmaster's newest rifle—the **450 Bushmaster**—was built to house the 450 Bushmaster cartridge, a Hornady effort to wring every last ounce of performance from the AR-15 platform for bears, moose, and hogs out to 200 yards. The 450 Bushmaster fires Hornady's 0.452-in. 250gr SST FTX bullet, and its overall cartridge length matches the 223 Rem at 2.260 in. The cartridge was adapted from a 6.5mm–284 case (a la the 45 Professional)

with the neck cut off to accommodate the .452-caliber bullet. AR-type magazine boxes contain the Bushmaster 450s, with the modifi-

Cor-Bon 444 Marlin 225gr DPX Hunter DPX444225-20

Range, Yards	Muzzle	100	200	300	400
Velocities (fps)	2200	1842	1522	1256	
Energy (ft-lbs)	2418	1695	1157	787	
Trajectory (in.)		4.4	0	-19.6	

Remington Express 444 Marlin R444M 240gr Soft Point

Range, Yards	Muzzle	100	200	300	400	500
Velocities (fps)	2350	1815	1377	1087	941	846
Energy (ft-lbs)	2942	1755	1010	630	472	381
Trajectory (in.)		2.2	-5.4	-31.4	-86.7	-180

Hornady 444 Marlin 82744 265gr FTX LEVERevolution

Range, Yards	Muzzle	100	200	300	400	500
Velocities (fps)	2325	1971	1652	1380		
Energy (ft-lbs)	3180	2285	1606	1120		
Trajectory (in.)		3	-1.4	-18.6		

Remington 450 Bushmaster PRA450B1 250g Soft Point

Range, Yards	Muzzle	100	200	300	400	500
Velocities (fps)	2200	1831	1508	148	1073	967
Energy (ft-lbs)	2686	1860	1262	864	639	519
Trajectory (in.)		0	-5.1	-14.0	-72.6	-147

Hornady 450 Bushmaster 250gr FTX LEVERevolution

Range, Yards	Muzzle	100	200	300	400	500
Velocities (fps)	2200	1840	1524	1268		
Energy (ft-lbs)	2686	1879	1289	893		
Trajectory (in.)		2.5	-3.4	-24.5		

Cor-Bon began as a custom bullet-making company. The Penetrator and Hard Cast loads are designed for very large, tough-skinned and heavy-boned animals. The Penetrator loads use a heavy, full jacket with a hard linotype core. MV, 2100 fps; ME 2988 ft-lbs. Photo courtesy of Midway USA.

The 450 Bushmaster debuted on the Remington R-15 platform. One load, the 450 Bushmaster PRA450B1 260gr AccuTip shown at right and below, has a Power Port on top of a .45-caliber 260gr AccuTip. Photos courtesy of Remington.

cation of a blue single-stack follower installed to accommodate the diameter of the cartridge. Magazine capacities heavily cut compared to the 223 Rem; e.g., a 30-round magazine of 223 Rem will top out at nine 450 Bushies. The 16- and 20-in. barrels are cut for 1:24 right-hand twists. The guns themselves are fitted with larger bolt faces (.475 in.) than a standard AR to handle the rim diameter of .473 in. The 450 Bushmaster case measures .499 in. at the case head and tapers to .478 in. at the case mouth. Capacity is 55.1 grains H_2O. Its rebated rim measures .473 in. Hornady figures show the maximum average operating pressure to be 38,500 psi, propelling the 250gr FTX bullet at 2200 fps from a 20-in. barrel. In a 16-in. barrel, velocity drops about 100 fps.

The **45-70 Government's** (intr. 1873) original designation was the 45-70-500 (caliber/powder charge/bullet weight), a nomenclature that deserves to be resurrected. It was the second military cartridge standardized by the

U.S. Army (the 50-70 Gov't predates it by four years) and was designed for use in the single-shot Trapdoor Springfield rifle. It served the Army for 19 years until the Krag-Jørgensen rifle in 30 Army (aka 30-40 Krag) took over in 1892. As a hunting cartridge, it was chambered in the Winchester Model 1886 lever action until 1935, then discontinued until Marlin offered it again in the 1970s in the Model 1895 levergun. The 45-70 is the oldest centerfire cartridge still being chambered in modern rifles, and factory loads are available from Hornady, Goex, Black Hills, Buffalo Bore, Ultramax, DoubleTap, Winchester, Remington, Cor-Bon, Federal, and others. Because of the 45-70's blackpowder history, it's important to recognize that older guns chambered for the round will not handle modern cartridge pressures. Factory loads or handloads for old blackpowder rifles and replicas should top out at no more than 29,000 psi. For new Marlin lever actions and Ruger falling block rifles, stay between 29,000 psi to 43,500 psi. The top-end 58,000-psi loads are intended only for use in Ruger falling block rifles.

Hornady 45-70 Gov't 82747 325gr FTX LEVERevolution

Range, Yards	Muzzle	100	200	300	400	500
Velocities (fps)	2050	1729	1450	1225		
Energy (ft-lbs)	3032	2158	1516	1083		
Trajectory (in.)		3.0	-4.1	-27.8		

Remington Express 45-70 Gov't R4570G 405gr Soft Point

Range, Yards	Muzzle	100	200	300	400	500
Velocities (fps)	1330	1168	1055	977	918	869
Energy (ft-lbs)	1590	1227	1001	858	758	679
Trajectory (in.)		0	-24.0	-78.6		

Federal 45-70 Gov't 4570AS 300gr Speer Hot-Cor HP

Range, Yards	Muzzle	100	200	300	400	500
Velocities (fps)	1850	1612	1400	1226	1097	1010
Energy (ft-lbs)	2280	1730	1305	1001	802	679
Trajectory (in.)		5.9	0	–23.9	-71.0	-146

The 45-70 Government is a rimmed straightwall round with a 2.105-in. case and a 2.550-in. OAL. The Cor-Bon DPX Hunter load shoots a 300gr bullet to 1900 fps MV and 2405 ft-lbs ME out of an 18.5-in. test barrel. Photos courtesy of Midway USA and Cor-Bon.

Mitch Mittelstaedt of Hornady spearheaded the development of the ***450 Marlin*** (intr. 2000), which was designed to update, modernize, and replace the 45-70 after 130 years. The 450 Marlin is the smallest .458-in. commercial rifle cartridge introduced in the last century. The 450 Marlin has the same bore diameter and uses the same bullets as the 45-70, and they have similar case capacities (53.2 grains H_2O for the 450 versus the 45-70's 56.2 grains. Externally, the 450 Marlin is a rimless, belted cartridge, unlike the rimmed 45-70 cartridge. Some people refer to the 450 Marlin as a shortened 458 Winchester, and that's accurate, but it's also true for all belted magnums. However, the 450 cartridge

Hornady 450 Marlin 82750 325gr FTX LEVERevolution

Range, Yards	Muzzle	100	200	300	400	500
Velocities (fps)	2225	1887	1585	1331		
Energy (ft-lbs)	3572	2569	1813	1278		
Trajectory (in.)		3.0	-2.2	-21.3		

Hornady 450 Marlin 8250 350gr InterLock FP

Range, Yards	Muzzle	100	200	300	400	500
Velocities (fps)	2100	1720	1397	1156		
Energy (ft-lbs)	3427	2298	1516	1039		
Trajectory (in.)		0	-10.4	-38.9		

Hornady's two loads feature a 325gr FTX, top, and a 350gr flat-point. Photos courtesy of Hornady.

was given an extra-wide belt to prevent it from chambering in other firearms. In the field, the 450 comes in substantially below a modern 45/70's velocities, as the adjacent ballistic tables show.

Winchester rescued Africa's dangerous-game and professional hunters in 1956 when the company created the ***458 Winchester Magnum*** for elephant and other "heavies" hunting in Africa. After World War II ended, Kynoch stopped production of its Cordite-based cartridges, leaving a void as prewar stocks of double-rifle rounds such as the 450 Nitro Express shrank. Winchester's introduction of an "African" version of the Model 70 rifle 458 Win Mag was an affordable, modern bolt-action rifle shooting a smaller and shorter case loaded at significantly higher pressure. Winchester attempted to duplicate performance of the well proven and respected 450 Nitro Express, by launching a 500gr 0.458-inch bullet at about 2150 fps. With modern propellants and tested handloads, the 458 Win Mag can match the ballistics of original 450 NE loads in a standard-length bolt action. But beyond the 458's performance on dangerous game, the case also spawned the development of magnum cartridges that fit 30-06-length actions. Examples are the 338

Winchester 458 Win Mag S458WSLSP 500gr Nosler Partition

Range, Yards	Muzzle	100	200	300	400	500
Velocities (fps)	2240	2000	1776	1572	1390	1237
Energy (ft-lbs)	5570	4440	3503	2742	2145	1699
Trajectory (in.)		3.6	0	-14.7	-43.5	

Federal Prem 458 Win Mag P458T1 400gr Trophy Bonded BC

Range, Yards	Muzzle	100	200	300	400	500
Velocities (fps)	2250	2025	1813	1619	1442	1290
Energy (ft-lbs)	4496	3641	2919	2327	1846	1478
Trajectory (in.)		3.5	0	–14.3	-41.6	-86.3

Weatherby 460 W'by B460450TSX 450gr Barnes TSX

Range, Yards	Muzzle	100	200	300	400	500
Velocities (fps)	2660	2422	2197	1983	1783	1598
Energy (ft-lbs)	7072	5864	4823	3932	3178	2553
Trajectory (in.)		2.2	0.0	-9.5	-27.8	-57.1

Weatherby 460 W'by H460500RN 500gr Rn-Ex

Range, Yards	Muzzle	100	200	300	400	500
Velocities (fps)	2600	2301	2022	1764	1533	1333
Energy (ft-lbs)	7504	5877	4539	3456	2608	1972
Trajectory (in.)		2.6	0.0	-11.1	-33.5	-71.1

Norma's 458 Win Mag Hunting load features a 500gr Barnes Banded solid copper-zinc bullet. MV is 2007 fps, and ME is 4745 ft-lbs. Photo courtesy of Cheaper Than Dirt.

The 460 W'by Mag can do everything in Africa, using lighter bullets for zebra, eland, and other non-dangerous game and 500gr solids for everything else. Photo courtesy of Weatherby.

Win Mag, 264 Win Mag, and the 7mm Rem Mag.

The **460 Weatherby Magnum** was the most powerful factory cartridge from its 1958 introduction (when it displaced the 600 Nitro Express), until the introduction of H&H's 700 Nitro express in 1988. Weatherby built the 460 by necking up the 378 W'by Mag to accept .458-caliber bullets. All in, no other cartridge can match the 460's 8000 ft-lbs pounds of muzzle energy, but that kind of energy punishes the shooter with fierce recoil. Accordingly, all Weatherby 460s use a muzzle brake.

Joseph Lang is credited with creating the **470 Nitro Express** in 1900 to take elephant, rhino, buffalo, and hippos. It has likely become the most popular of the British big-game chamberings—gaining much of that goodwill after 1907, when the Brits banned .45-caliber cartridges in India and Sudan to prevent rebels from obtaining ammunition for stolen military rifles. The 470 NE launches a 500gr bullet at about 2150 fps MV, generating around 5000 ft-lbs ME. Kynoch ceased production of 470 NE ammunition in the 1960s. In 1989, Federal began producing 470 NE ammunition, and now several firms offer it as a factory load, including Kynoch Ltd.

The **500 Nitro Express** was derived from the 500 Black Powder Express (circa 1880s), and like most other black-powder-to-smokeless conversions that used big cases, the resulting modern cartridge is a beast, pushing a 570gr bullet to 2150 fps. The rimmed 500 NE case resembles the 50-140 Sharps in dimensions that Sharps hulls can be fashioned from 500s. The 500 gains an edge over smaller Nitros (450 NE, 470 NE, and 475 NE) because it can shoot larger bullets at the same velocities as maximum bullets in the smaller chamberings. The 500 NE comes in 3- and 3.250-in. versions, with domestic factory chamberings being exclusively 3 inches. Many hunters who use double rifles say the 500 Nitro Express is the top end of shootable power in a rifle weighing 10 to 11 pounds.

It is amazing to contemplate the current status of the **50 Browning Machine Gun (BMG)** cartridge. Unlike some of the other Boomers in this chapter, the shooter activity using the massive 50 BMG continues to expand. John

Federal 470 NE P470C 500gr Barnes Triple-Shock X Bullet

Range, Yards	Muzzle	100	200	300	400	500
Velocities (fps)	2150	1936	1737	1554	1389	1249
Energy (ft-lbs)	5132	4160	3349	2680	2142	1732
Trajectory (in.)		3.9	0	-15.5	-45.4	-93.6

Norma African PH 470 Nitro Express 500gr Soft Nose

Range, Yards	Muzzle	50	100	150	200
Velocities (fps)	2100	2002	1906	1814	1725
Energy (ft-lbs)	4897	4449	4035	3654	3304
Trajectory (in.)		0.3	0	-2.7	-8.0

Hornady 470 Nitro Express 500gr DGS

Range, Yards	Muzzle	100	200	300	400	500
Velocities (fps)	2150	1885		1429		
Energy (ft-lbs)	5132	3946		2267		
Trajectory (in.)		0	-8.9	-30.9		

Norma 500 Nitro Express 3-in. 570gr Soft Nose

Range, Yards	Muzzle	50	100	150	200
Velocities (fps)	2100	2000	1903	1809	1719
Energy (ft-lbs)	5583	5064	4585	4145	3364
Trajectory (in.)		0.3	0	-2.7	-8.0

Norma 500 Nitro Express 3-in. 570gr FMJ

Range, Yards	Muzzle	50	100	150	200
Velocities (fps)	2100	2000	1903	1809	1719
Energy (ft-lbs)	5583	5039	4538	4081	3664
Trajectory (in.)		0.3	0	-2.7	-8.1

Hornady 500 Nitro Express 8268 3-in. 570gr DGX

Range, Yards	Muzzle	100	200	300	400	500
Velocities (fps)	2150	1881	1635	1419		
Energy (ft-lbs)	5850	4477	3384	2547		
Trajectory (in.)		0	-9.0	-31.1		

Cor-Bon 500 Nitro Express 570gr FPBS EH500N570FPBS-10

Range, Yards	Muzzle	100	200	300	400	500
Velocities (fps)	2150	1837	1556	1320		
Energy (ft-lbs)	5849	4271	3065	2205		
Trajectory (in.)		0	-8.9	-32.2		

Norma's African PH 470 Nitro Express comes in a 500gr Soft Nose, shown here, and an FMJ load. Both put around 4900 ft-lbs of energy on the target at the muzzle, which the hunter likely hopes he won't need. At more suitable shooting distances, it makes about 4500 ft-lbs of energy at 50 yards, 4035 at 100 yards, and 3304 at 200 yards. Image courtesy of Norma.

Moses Browning invented the round in 1918 and it was adopted for machine-gun use by the US military in 1923, making it the longest-serving cartridge in military history. Known metrically as the 12.7x99mm cartridge, the American dimensions for the BMG are shocking when compared to other rounds, The rimless bottleneck's line (in inches) is: bullet diameter .510, neck diameter .560, shoulder diameter .714, base diameter .804, rim diameter .804, case length 3.910, cartridge length 5.545. Bullet weights, likewise, are massive. There's the US M33 Ball projectile, which weighs 647 grains and has a 0.670 ballistic coefficient. The US M8 API bullet goes 622.5 grains with a BC of 0.650. The light-

If you want a 500 Nitro Express in a double rifle, makers such as Krieghoff, Merkel, Searcy, Westley Richards, Sig, Rigby, Holland & Holland, and others have made them recently. Heym and Hambrusch are well-know bolt-action rifles chambered for 500 Nitro Express. Image courtesy of Hornady.

weight US M20 APIT pill weighs 619 grains with a BC of 0.650. Then there's Hornady A-Max big boy, a 750gr bullet with an astounding 1.050 BC. The US M33 .50 BMG military load uses a 668gr FMJ-BT bullet at 2910 fps MV, producing 12550 ft-lbs ME. Used by the military to destroy equipment, it's also employed by military snipers as a super-long-distance anti-personnel choice. Recreational shooters, such as those in the 50 Caliber Shooters Association, compete with the 50 BMG in 1000-meter matches, which happens to be the same distance at which Marine snip-

SELECTED LOADS & BALLISTICS

Hornady 50 BMG 750gr A-MAX Match

Range, Yards	Muzzle	100	200	300	400	500
Velocities (fps)	2820	2728	2637	2549	2462	2376
Energy (ft-lbs)	13241	12388	11580	10815	10090	9403
Trajectory (in.)		1.5	0	-6.5	-18.3	-35.8

PMC 50 Caliber 50A 660gr FMJ-BT

Range, Yards	Muzzle	100	200	300	400	500
Velocities (fps)	3080	2854	2639	2444	2248	2061
Energy (ft-lbs)	13688	11753	10049	8619	7292	6129
Trajectory (in.)		3.1	3.9	4.7	2.8	0

Barrett 50 BMG M33 661gr Ball

Range, Yards	Muzzle Velocity	Energy ft-lbs	Trajectory in.
0	2750		
100	2601	9934	0
200	2458	8870	-2.1
300	2319	7897	-10
400	2185	7009	-24
500	2055	6201	-46
1000	1483	3230	-302
1500	1102	1782	-967

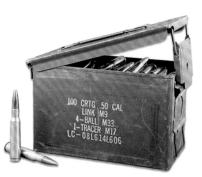

For those who like their 50 BMG in bulk, there's the BVAC FMJ Ball 690gr rounds sold in the handy 150-round can.

The Magtech Sport Shooting 50 BMG load is a 625gr FMJ boattail bullet. Photos courtesy of Cheaper Than Dirt.

ers are expected to engage a man-sized target with a 308 Win. While it is true that the 50 BMG will reach out to extended distances, only the best shooters can hit targets at 1500 to 1700 yards. The accompanying ballistics from Barrett show what the round actually does out to 1500 yards. The Barrett 50 BMG

This Hornady 50 BMG 750gr A-MAX Match bullet is a beast, developing huge energies, 13241 ft.-lbs. at 100 yards and still 9403 ft.-lbs. at 500 yards. There's only -36 inches of drop at 500 yards.

M33 Ball ammunition is loaded with a 661gr projectile with a BC of 0.62. Shot out of a Model 82A1 Barrett 50 BMG with a 29-in. barrel, the 100-yard velocity is 2602 fps, making 9935 ft-lbs ME. With a 100-yard zero, stats @ 200 yards are 2459 fps, 8871 ft-lbs, -2.1 in. drop. At 500 yards, the line is 2056 fps, 6201 ft-lbs, and -46 in. drop. At 1000 yards, the 50 BMG develops 1484 fps, 3231 ft-lbs, and −303 in. drop. Then, in the next county at 1500 yards, it's still going 1102 fps, making 1782 ft-lbs energy, and dropping -967 in. ●

27: Wildcat & Proprietary Cartridges

What better way to introduce this listing of wildcat and proprietary cartridges than to recognize the company that has probably turned more wildcats into proprietary rounds? The history of Weatherby began in the mid-1940s when a young cartridge "wildcatter" named

TOMORROW'S RIFLES TODAY

Many years of study and research have been expended to bring you these scientifically designed cartridge conversions. We have covered the field from the long range varmint shooter to the man who wishes to safely hunt the largest and most dangerous animals the world over.

Over 4000 ft. per second M.V. can be obtained from any of our conversions. The .220 "Rocket", .257, .270 and .300 Weatherby

Magnums. We can convert your present bolt-action rifle or install a new type graphite steel barrel. We manufacture .220, .257, .270 and .300 caliber ultra speed bullets designed to give maximum accuracy. $5.00 per hundred.

Write for our booklet "Tomorrow's Rifles Today," fully explaining our conversions, as well as other ballistical information. (Please send 50¢ to cover mailing and handling charges.)

WEATHERBY'S RIFLE CONVERSIONS — 8823 Long Beach Blvd. — South Gate, California

Roy Weatherby set out to change the world of firearm performance. Roy believed that lightweight bullets traveling at super-high speeds provided the best combination for one-shot kills. Based upon that philosophy, he spent the next decade developing the high-powered Weatherby Magnum cartridges for which the company is known today (.224, .240, .257, .270, 7mm, .300, .30-378, .340, .338-378, .375, .378, .416 and .460). Throughout that period, Roy was also producing or re-chambering rifles designed specifically to accommodate his super-charged ammunition, as the ad at right from the October 1945 issue of American Rifle magazine shows. At that time, he was producing his rifles on FN Mauser and French Brevex Magnum Mauser actions. However in 1957, Roy would again catch the attention of the shooting and hunting world with a proprietary action called the Mark V. The foundation for the Mark V was the need for a stronger, safer action, able to withstand tremendous pressure, and the possibility of blown primers and ruptured case heads due to the unpredictability of early handloaded and wildcat cartridges. Images and history courtesy of Weatherby.

Today's wildcat round is tomorrow's hot new factory load, or a proprietary round catches fire among a larger audience, and it gets selected for wider chambering. Here a compilation of various cartridges in development by individuals or companies, or shooting groups.

10 Eichelberger Long Rifle
10 Eichelberger Squirrel
10 Eichelberger Pup
12 Eichelberger Long Rifle
12 Eichelberger WRM
12 Cooper CCM
12 Eichelberger Carbine
14 Eichelberger Long Rifle
14 Eichelberger WRM
14 Eichelberger Dart
14 Eichelberger Flea
14 Cooper (CCM)
14 Eichelberger H&R Mag
14 Eichelberger Carbine
14 Squirrel
14 Eichelberger Hornet
14 Walker Hornet
14 Jet Junior
14 Eichelberger Bee
14/221 Eichelberger
14/221 Walker
14/222 Eichelberger
14/222 Eichelberger Mag
14-221
14-222
14 Walker Hornet
17 Squirrel
17 Hornet
17 Flickertail
17 GSG
17 Ackley Bee
17 Pewee
17 Landis Woodsman
17/221
17 Javelina
17/222
17/222 Rimmed
17 Mijet
17-40 Jet
17-40 Jet Rimless
17-32 Jet
17-223
17-06
17 CCM
17 Hornet (Ackley)
17 PMC/Aguila

17 Mach IV (now commercialized as 17 Remington Fireball)
17 PPC
17-222
17-223
17/23 SMC
17-357 RG (.172" Wildcat based on the 357 SIG)
191 (4.85mm SAA)
19 Calhoon Hornet
19 Badger
19-223

20-06
20 VarTarg
20 Tactical
218 Mashburn Bee
219 Donaldson Wasp
22 K-Hornet
R-2 Lovell
22 Super Jet
22 Cheetah
22 Waldog
22 BR Remington
22 Eargesplitten Loudenboomer
22-06
22/30-30 Improved
22-303
220 Wotkyns-Wilson Arrow
220 Weatherby Rocket
22-243 Middlested
224 Clark
22 Newton
222 Rem. Rimmed
22/303
22-243 Middlestead
223 AI
224 Harvey Kay-Chuk
224 R-C Maxi
228 Ackley Magnum
240 Apex (240 Belted Nitro Express and 240 Magnum Flanged)
25/303
25 Ugalde (25 TCU)
25 Krag
25 Ackley Krag
25-303
250-3000 Ackley Improved
257 Ackley Improved
25-284
25/303
264 LBC-AR
264 Warrior Mag (6.5x40 mm)
270 REN
270 IHMSA

270 Savage
275 H&H Magnum

30 BR
30 USA

Winchester produced seven different cartridge boards before the turn of the century in the following years. This one is the Winchester 1879 Cartridge Board. These boards were made by the factory and given to dealers to display all of the various cartridges and shotgun shells offered by Winchester at the time. © Winfield Galleries, LLC, St. Louis, Missouri. Used with permission. To view current artwork and pricing, log on to www.WinfieldGalleries.com.

30 Kurz
308x1.5" Barnes
30 Herrett
30-30 Ackley Improved
30 IHMSA
30 Walker
30-03
309 Bull
300 Dakota
300 ICL Grizzly
300 Lapua Magnum
300 Remington American
   Magnum
300 Whisper
300-221
303-06
30-06 Ackley Improved
30-338 Winchester Magnum
30-378 Weatherby
30 Cody Express
330 Dakota
333 OKH
333 Jeffery Flanged
334 OKH
338-223 Straight
338-378 KT (338-378
   Weatherby)
338-50 Talbot
338-06 A-Square
338 Whisper (Series 1)
338 Whisper (Series 2)
338 Voschol
338x57 O'Connor
38-45 Auto (38-45 Auto Pistol,
   38-45 Clarke)
357 Auto Mag
357-44 Bain & Davis
35-30/30 (35-30)
35 Samba (Also 35 WSM)
357/44 B & D (Bain and Davis)
357 Herrett
35 Ackley Magnum
375 Dakota
375 Whisper (Series 2)
375 Whelen (35 Whelen
   Improved)

401 Herter Powermag
400 Whelen
40-65 Winchester
40-70 Sharps
408 Chey Tac
416 Barnes
416 Barrett
416 Taylor
416 Whisper (Series 2)

425 Westley Richards
44 Henry
445 Super Magnum
458x1.5" Barnes
45 Silhouette
452x2" (458x2" American)
450 Alaskan (45-348 Winchester
   Improved)
450 Howell
450 Watts Magnum
451 Detonics
45-90 Sharps
45-110 Sharps
45-120 Sharps
450 Watts Magnum
458 SOCOM
470 Capstick
475 OKH
475 Ackley
475 Wildey Magnum
475 Linebaugh
475 Ackley Magnum (475 OKH
   Magnum)

500 Phantom
500 Linebaugh
510 Nitro Express
50-70 Government
50-90 Sharps
50-110 Winchester
50-140 Sharps
50 Alaskan
50 Beowulf
50 BMG
50 Peacekeeper
500 Black Powder Express
500 Jeffrey Nitro Express
500 No 2 Express
500 Nitro Express 3"
500 Nitro Express for
   blackpowder 3"
500/450 Nitro Express
500/465 Nitro Express
505 Gibbs
505 Jeffery
510 DTC Europ
510 Fat Mac
510 Whisper
550 Magnum
550 Nitro Express
577 Nitro Express
577 Tyrannosaur (577 T-Rex)
577 Snider
577/450 Martini-Henry
577/500 Magnum Nitro Express
585 Nyati

600 Nitro Express
600/577 REWA
600 Overkill

700 AHR
700 Hubel Express
700 Nitro Express

Metrics
4.5mm MKR
5mm Craig
5mm/35 SMC
MMJ 5.7mm

6x45mm (6mm-223 Rem)
6mm TCU
6x47mm (6mm-222 Rem Mag)
6mm-250 (6mm International)
6mm/30-30 Improved
6mm-284
6-06
6-284
6mmAR
6mm BRX
6mm Dasher
6mm XC
6x45 mm
6x47 Swiss Match (6mm/222
   Mag)
6.5 Grendel
6.5x47 Lapua
6.5x55 Swedish Mauser
6.5mm TCU
6.5mm-06 (256-06)
6.5mm-06 Ackley Improved
6.5x57mm
6.5 CSS
7.62 Jonson
6.5 PPCX
6.5 BPC
6.5x40mm (264 Warrior Mag)
6.5 Jonson
6.5 Wby Mag

7mm Dakota
7mm TCU
7mm International Rimmed
7mm IHMSA
285 OKH (7mm-06 Mashburn,
   7mm-06)
7mm Shooting Times Easterner
   (7mm STE)
7mm Gradle Express
7x54mm Fournier

8mm-06

9mm Action Express
9x25mm Dillon

10.4x38 Vetterli   (US: "41 Swiss")
10.4x47 Italian Vetterli

12.7mm British No. 2
12.7x99mm NATO (Multi-Purpose)
12.7x108mm
14.5x114mm
15.2 mm Steyr Armor Piercing Fin Stabilized Discarding Sabot (APFSDS)
20mm caliber
30x165mm
30x173mm

Bores

10 bore
8 bore
6 bore
4 bore - approx. 25mm
2 bore - 33.6mm

JD Jones Proprietary Line

226 JDJ
6mm JDJ
257 JDJ
25-06 JDJ
6.5mm JDJ
6.5mm JDJx30
6.5 Mini Dreadnaught by JDJ
6.5mm JDJ No.2
6.5/270 JDJ
270 JDJ
270 JDJ No.2
7mm Whisper by JDJ
7mm JDJ
7mm-30 JDJ
7mm JDJ No.2
280 JDJ
7.62 Micro-Whisper by JDJ
7.63 Mini-Whisper by JDJ
300 Whisper by JDJ
309 JDJ
30-06 JDJ
8mm JDJ
338 Whisper by JDJ
338 JDJ
338-06 JDJ
358 JDJ
35-06 JDJ
9.3mm JDJ
375 Whisper by JDJ
375 JDJ
375-06 JDJ
40-44 Woodswalker by JDJ

40-454 JDJ
411 JDJ
416 JDJ
416-06 JDJ
458 Whisper by JDJ
475 JDJ
50 American Eagle by JDJ
500 Whisper by JDJ
50 Peacekeeper by JDJ
510 Whisper by JDJ
600/577 JDJ
700 JDJ
950 JDJ
14.5 mm JDJ

Lazzeroni Proprietary Line

6.53 (.257) Scramjet
7.21 (.284) Firebird
7.21 (.284) Tomahawk
7.82 (.308) Warbird
7.82 (.308) Patriot
8.59 (.338) Titan
8.59 (.338) Galaxy
10.57 (.416) Meteor
10.57 (.416) Maverick ●

28: Obsolete Cartridges

The Winchester 401 WSL was a great fit in the 1910 Rifle, but is obsolete now. This Winchester Rifles & Ammunition poster was painted (circa 1909) by Phillip R. Goodwin. © Winfield Galleries, LLC, St. Louis, Missouri. Used with permission. To view current artwork and pricing, log on to www.WinfieldGalleries.com.

Today's hot new factory load is tomorrow's forgotten cartridge. Here is a compilation of various cartridges that have existed at one time or another domestically. Next year, some might move off this list and be chambered by a factory again; or, current rounds that have some acceptance might be de-cataloged.

Obsolete Rifle Cartridges

22 Extra Long Centerfire
22 Maynard
22 Newton
22 Savage High-Power
22 High-Power
22 Winchester Centerfire
22 WCF
22-15-60 Stevens
22-15 Stevens
218 Bee
219 Zipper
219 Donaldson Wasp
220 Russian
222 Rimmed
225 Winchester
22 Savage Hi-Power
236 Navy
6mm Lee Navy
244 Remington
25 Remington
25-20 Marlin
25-20 Single Shot
25-21 Stevens
25-25 Stevens
25-35 WCF
25-35 Winchester
25-36 Marlin
256 Newton
256 Winchester Magnum
260 Remington
28-30-120 Stevens
28-30 Stevens
280 Rimless
280 Ross
30 Newton
30 Adolph Express
30 Remington
30-03 Springfield
30-03 Government
30-30 Wesson
303 Savage
301 Savage

308 Norma Magnum
32 Ballard Extra Long
32 Extra Long
32 Ideal
32 Long Centerfire
32 Long
32 Remington
32 Winchester Self Loading
32 Winchester SL
32 WSL
32 Winchester Special
32 WCF
32-20 Marlin
32-30 Remington
32-35 Stevens & Maynard
32-40 Bullard
32-40 Winchester
32-40 Ballard
32-40 WCF
32-40 Remington
33 Winchester
33 WCF
35 Newton
35 Winchester
35 WCF
35 Winchester Self Loading
35 Winchester SL
35 WSL
35-30 Maynard
35-40 Maynard
35-45 Maynard
350 Griffin & Howe Magnum
350 Holland & Holland Magnum
351 Winchester Self Loading
351 Winchester SL
351 WSL
356 Winchester
358 Norma Magnum
358 Winchester
375 Weatherby Magnum
38 Ballard Extra Long
38 Long Centerfire
38 Long
38-40 Remington-Hepburn
38-45 Bullard
38-45 Stevens
38-45 Stevens Everlasting
38-50 Ballard
38-50 Maynard
38-50 Remington-Hepburn
38-55 Stevens
38-55 Stevens Everlasting
38-56 Winchester
38-56 WCF
38-70 Winchester

38-70 WCF
38-72 Winchester
38-72 WCF
38-90 Winchester Express
38 Express
40-40 Maynard
40-50 Sharps Necked
40-1¹¹⁄₁₆-in. Sharps
40-50 Sharps Straight
40-1⅞-in. Sharps
40-60 Marlin
40-65 WCF
40-60 Maynard
40-60 Winchester
40-60 WCF
40-63 Ballard
40-70 Ballard
40-65 Ballard Everlasting
40-65 Ballard
40-65 Winchester
40-65 WCF
40-60 Marlin
40-70 Ballard
40-63 Ballard
40-70 Peabody "What Cheer"
40-70 Peabody
40-70 Remington
40-70 Sharps Necked
40-2¼-in. Sharps
40-70 Sharps Straight
40-2½-in. Sharps
40-70 Winchester
40-70 WCF
40-72 Winchester
40-72 WCF
40-75 Bullard
40-82 Winchester
40-82 WCF
40-85 Ballard
40-90 Ballard
40-90 Bullard
40-90 Peabody "What Cheer"
40-90 Peabody
40-90 Sharps Necked
40-2⅝-in. Sharps
40-90 Sharps Straight
40-3¼-in. Sharps
40-110 Winchester Express
40 Express
401 Winchester Self Loading
401 Winchester SL
401 WSL
405 Winchester
405 WCF
41 Swiss M69/81

Source: Stars & Stripes Ammunition

10.4x38Rmm Swiss Vetterli
    M69/81
10.4mm Swiss Vetterli M69/81
43 Beaumont
43 Dutch Beaumont M71/78
43 Neatherlands Beaumont
    M71/78
11x52Rmm Dutch Beaumont
43 Egyptian
11.43x50Rmm
43 Mauser
11.15x60Rmm
43 Spanish
11.15x58Rmm
44 Evans Long
44 Evans Short
44 Extra Long Ballard
44 Extra Long
44 Game Getter
44-40 Marlin
44 Colt Lightning
44 Henry Centerfire Flat
44 Long Centerfire Ballard
44 Ballard Long Centerfire
44 Wesson Extra Long
44-40 Extra Long
44-40 Marlin
44-60 Sharps & Remington
44-60 Winchester
44-60 Peabody "Creedmoor"
44-70 Maynard
44-75 Ballard Everlasting
44-75 Ballard
44-75-2½-in.
44-77 Sharps & Remington
44-2¼-in. Sharps
44-85 Wesson
44-90 Remington Special
44-90 Remington Necked
44-90 Sharps Necked
44-100 Sharps 2⅝-in.
44-105 Sharps Necked
44-95 Peabody "What Cheer"
44-95 Peabody
44-100 Ballard
44-100 Remington "Creedmoor"
44-100 Remington Straight
44-100 Wesson
45-50 Peabody Sporting
45-90 Peabody
45-60 Winchester
45-60 WCF
45-70 Van Choate
45-75 Sharps Straight
45-70 Sharps

45-2.10 Sharps
45-75 Winchester
45-75 WCF
45-90 Sharps Straight
45-100 Sharps Straight
45-110 Sharps Straight
45 Sharps Special
2.4-in., 2.6-in. 2.75-in. and 2⅞-in.
    cases
45-90 Winchester
45-82 Winchester
45-85 Winchester
45-90 WCF
45-100 Ballard
45-100 Remington Necked
45-2¼-in. Remington
45-120 Sharps 3¼-in.
45-125 Sharps 3¼-in.
45-125 Winchester
45 Express
450 Ackley
50 Spotter
50 U.S. Carbine
50-Carbine
50-50 Maynard
50-70 Government
50-70 Musket
50 Government
50-90 Sharps
50-100 Sharps
50-110 Sharps
50-2.5-in. Sharps
50-95 Winchester
50-95 Winchester Express
50 Express
50-110 Winchester
50-100 Winchester
50-105 Winchester
50-115 Bullard
50-140 Sharps
50-140 Winchester Express
55-100 Maynard
58 Berdan Carbine
58 Carbine
58 Berdan U.S. Musket
58 Berdan Musket
58 Musket
70-150 Winchester
500 Linebaugh
510 Nitro Express
585 Nyati

**Obsolete British
Rifle Cartridges**
240 Belted Rimless Nitro/

Holland's 240 Apex
240 Flanged Nitro
242 Rimless Nitro Express
244 H&H Magnum
246 Purdey
255 Jeffery Rook
256 Gibbs
256 Mannlicher
26 BSA/26 Rimless Belted Nitro
    Express
275 Holland & Holland
    Magnum/7mm H&H/
    275 Belted Magnum
275 H&H Magnum Rimmed/7mm
    Holland & Holland
    Rimmed/275 Flanged Magnum
275 No. 2 Magnum/7mm Rigby
    Magnum Flanged
275 Rigby
276 Enfield
280 British
280 Flanged/280 Lancaster
280 Jeffery
33/280 Jeffery
280 Rimless/280 Ross
297-230 Morris Short, Long,
    Extra Long, Lancaster Sporting
297/250 Rook
30 Super Flanged
300 Rook/295 Rook
300 Sherwood
301 Savage/303 Savage
303 British Mk I
303 British Mk VI
303 Magnum
310 Cadet/310 Greener
318 Rimless Nitro Express/318
    Westley Richards/318 Accel-
    erated Express
33 BSA/33 Belted Rimless/
    330 BSA
333 Jeffery Flanged
333 Jeffery Rimless
350 Griffin & Howe Magnum
350 No. 2 Rigby
350 Rigby Magnum
360 Express/360 Nitro for Black
360 Nitro Express
360 No. 2 Nitro Express
360 No. 5 Rook
369 Nitro Express
375 Flanged Magnum
375 Flanged Nitro Express 2½-
    in./370 Flanged
375 Rimless Nitro Express

Source: Stars & Stripes Ammunition

2¼-in./9.5x57mm Mannlicher
375-303 Westley Richards/375-303 Axite
380 Long Rifle
380 Short Rifle
400 Jeffery Nitro Express/450-400 3-in.
400 Purdey Light Express 3-in./400 Straight 3-in.
400/350 Rigby
400/360 Purdey Nitro Express
400-360 Westley Richards Nitro/400-360 Fraser/400-360 Evans
400/375 Belted Nitro Express
425 Westley Richards Magnum
425 W-R Semi Rimmed Magnum
450 3¼-in. BP Express
450 3¼-in. Nitro Express
450 No. 2 Nitro Express 3½-in.
450-400 BP Express 2⅜-in./450-400 Nitro for Black 2⅜-in.
450-400 Nitro Express 2⅜-in.
450-400 BP Express 3¼-in./450-400 Nitro for Black 3¼-in.
450/400 Nitro Express 3¼-in.
475 3¼-in. Nitro Express
475 No. 2 Jeffery
475 No. 2 Nitro Express
476 Nitro Express/476 Westley Richards
500 Express/500 Nitro for Black
500 Jeffery
500 Nitro Express 3-in.
500 Nitro Express 3¼-in.
505 Gibbs/505 Rimless
500/450 Caliber, all variants
500-450 3¼-in. Magnum Express/Black Powder Express
500/450 3¼-in. Nitro Express
500/465 Nitro Express
577 BP Express (All Lengths; 2½-in. to 3¼-in.)
577 Nitro Express (All Lengths; 2¼-in., 3-in., 3¼-in.)
577 Snider
577/450 Martini Henry
577/500 No. 2 BP Express
577/500 3⅛-in. Nitro Express
600 Nitro Express

Obsolete Metric Rifle Cartridges

5.6x33mm Rook
5.6x33Rmm Rook
5.6x35Rmm/22 Hornet
5.6x35Rmm Vierling/22 WCF
5.6x52Rmm (22 Savage Hi-Power)
5.6x61mm Vom Hofe Super Express
5.6x61Rmm Vom Hofe Super Express
6mm Lee Navy/236 Navy
6x29.5Rmm Stahl
6x57mm Mauser
6x58mm Forster
6x58Rmm Forster
244 Halger Magnum
6.3x53Rmm Finnish
6.5mm Remington Magnum
6.5x27Rmm
6.5x40Rmm
6.5x48Rmm Sauer
6.5x50Rmm Japanese Arisaka
6.5mm Jap
6.5x52mm Carcano/6.5x52Rmm/25-35 Winchester
6.5x53Rmm Mannlicher
6.5mm Dutch/Romanian/6.5x53Rmm Russian
6.5x53.5Rmm Daudeteau
6.5x54mm Mannlicher-Schoenauer
6.5x54Rmm Mannlicher-Schoenauer
6.5x54mm Mauser
6.5x57mm Mauser
6.5x57Rmm Mauser
6.5x58mm Portuguese
6.5x58Rmm Krag-Jorgenson
6.5x58Rmm Sauer
6.5x61mm Mauser
6.5x61Rmm Mauser
6.5x68mm Schuler
7x33mm Sako
7x54mm Finnish
7x61mm Sharpe & Hart Super/7x61mm S&H Super
7x64mm Brenneke
7x65Rmm Brenneke
7x72Rmm
7x73mm Vom Hofe
7.35x51mm Carcano
7.5x54mm French MAS
7.5x55mm Schmidt-Rubin
7.62x45mm Czech
308 Norma Magnum
7.65x53.5mm Belgian Mauser
7.7x58mm Arisaka/7.7mm Jap/31 Jap
7.92x33mm Kurz
8x42Rmm
8x48Rmm Sauer
8x50Rmm Austrian Mannlicher
8x50Rmm Lebel
8x50Rmm Siamese Mauser T45
8x51mm Mauser
8x51Rmm Mauser
8x52Rmm Siamese Mauser T66
8x53Rmm Japanese Murata/Meiji 20-8mm
8x54mm Krag-Jorgensen
8x56Rmm Hungarian Mannlicher/8mm Hungarian M31
8x56mm Mannlicher-Schoenauer
8x57Jmm Mauser/8x57Imm Mauser/8mm Mauser 0.318-in. bore

Next page: This is the famous "Double W" cartridge board, showing a historical selection of cartridges from the Civil War to the turn of the 20th Century. It has early cartridges from Winchester, Sharps, Remington, Marlin, Savage, S&W, Colt, Stevens, and several martial calibers set on a forest hunting scene at top, with insets of a mallard duck and a bull moose head on the sides. There are 161 large rifle cartridges, 39 pistol cartridges, 39 rimfire cartridges, 15 early large caliber bullets, 11 paper shotshells, 9 brass shotshell cases up to #4 gauge, and 9 boxes of primers or percussion caps. Cartridge calibers extend from the 58 to the 22. Some have 550-grain bullets. The Winchester Repeating Arms Cartridge Board from the turn of the century is a handy way to see what rounds have survived, and what rounds have gone away. © Winfield Galleries, LLC, St. Louis, Missouri. Used with permission. To view current artwork, log on to www.WinfieldGalleries.com.

Source: Stars & Stripes Ammunition

8x57JRmm
8x57Rmm 360
8x58Rmm Danish Krag
8x58Rmm Sauer
8x59mm Breda
8x60Rmm Guedes/8x60Rmm
    Kropatschek
8x56Rmm Guedes/8x56Rmm
    Kropatschek
8x63mm Swedish
8x64mm Brenneke
8x65Rmm Brenneke
8x71mm Peterlongo
8x72Rmm Sauer
8x75mm
8x75Rmm
8.15x46Rmm
8.2x53Rmm Finnish
9x56mm Mannlicher-Schoenauer
9x57mm Mauser
9x57Rmm Mauser
9x63mm
9x70Rmm Mauser/
    400-360 Westley Richards
    Nitro Express
9x71mm Peterlongo
358 Norma Magnum
9.1x40Rmm
9.3x48Rmm
9.3x53Rmm Finnish
9.3x53mm Swiss
9.3x53Rmm Swiss
9.3x57Rmm
9.3x57mm Mauser
9.3x65Rmm Collath
9.3x70Rmm
9.3x72Rmm
9.3x72Rmm Sauer
9.3x80Rmm
9.3x82Rmm
9.5x47Rmm
9.5x57mm Mannlicher-
    Schoenauer
9.5x56mm Mannlicher-
    Schoenauer/9.5x56.7mm
    Mannlicher-Schoenauer
9.5mm Mannlicher-Schoenauer
375 Nitro Express Rimless
9.5x60Rmm Turkish Mauser
9.5x73mm Miller-Greiss Magnum
10.15x61Rmm Jarmann
10.15x63Rmm Serbian Mauser
10.25x69Rmm Hunting-Express
10.3x65Rmm Baenziger
10.4x38Rmm Swiss Vetterli M69-

81/10.4x38Rmm Vetterli M69-
    81/10.4mm Swiss/41 Swiss
10.4x47Rmm Italian Vetterli
10.5x47Rmm
10.75x57mm Mannlicher
10.75x58Rmm Russina Berdan
10.75x63mm Mauser
10.75x65Rmm Collath
10.75x73mm/404 Rimless Nitro
    Express/404 Jeffery
10.8x47Rmm Martini
11x50Rmm Belgian Albini
11x52Rmm Dutch Beaumont
    M71-78/11x52Rmm Nether-
    lands Beaumont M71-78
43 Beaumont/43 Dutch Beau-
    mont M71/78/43 Neather-
    lands Beaumont M71/78
11x53Rmm Belgian Comblain
11x59Rmm French Gras
11x59Rmm Vickers
11x60Rmm Japanese Murata/
    Meiji 13-11mm
11.15x58Rmm Spanish Rem./
    43 Spanish
11.15x58Rmm Werndl
11.15x60Rmm Mauser/43
    Mauser
11.2x60mm Schuler/11.2x60mm
    Mauser/11.15x59.8mm
    Schuler
11.2x72mm Schuler/11.2x72mm
    Mauser
11.3x50Rmm Beaumont
11.4x50Rmm Austrian Werndl
11.4x50Rmm Brazilian Comblain
11.43x50Rmm Egyptian
    Rem./43 Egyptian
11.43x55Rmm Turkish
11.5x57Rmm Spanish
11.7x51Rmm Danish Remington
12.17x44Rmm Remington M67
12.5x70mm Schuler/500 Jeffery

**Obsolete American
Handgun Cartridges**
22 Remington Jet
22 Centerfire Magnum
221 Remington Fireball
256 Winchester Magnum
30 Luger
7.65x21mm Luger
30 Mauser
7.63x25mm Mauser
32 French

7.65mm MAS
32 Colt
32 Long Colt
32 Short Colt
32 Smith & Wesson
32 Smith & Wesson Gallery
32 Smith & Wesson Long
32 Colt New Police
32-44 Target
320 Revolver
35 Smith & Wesson Auto
35 Automatic
357 Auto Magnum
357 Auto Mag
357 AMP
38 ACP
38 Auto
38 Automatic
38 Auto Colt Pistol
38 Long Colt
38 Short Colt
38 Smith & Wesson
38 Colt New Police
380/200
380 Long Revolver
380 Short Revolver
41 Action Express
41 AE
41 Long Colt
41 Short Colt
44 Auto Magnum
44 Auto Mag
44 AMP
44 Bull Dog
44 Colt
44 Colt Conversion
44 Smith & Wesson American
44 Smith & Wesson Russian
44 Webley
442 RIC
442 Kurz
10.5x17Rmm
44 Webley "Bull Dog"
45 ACP Short
45 Webley
45 Smith & Wesson Schofield
45 Schofield
450 Revolver
450 Adams
455 Revolver Mk I
455 Enfield
455 Colt
455 Revolver Mk II
455 Webley Revolver Mk II
455 Webley Automatic

Source: Stars & Stripes Ammunition

"At Home On The Range" was a UMC-Remington promotional poster painted by Phillip R. Goodwin. © Winfield Galleries, LLC, St. Louis, Missouri. Used with permission. To view current artwork and pricing, log on to www.WinfieldGalleries.com.

Source: Stars & Stripes Ammunition

476 Eley
476 Enfield Mk III
50 Remington
M71 Army
50 Remington Navy

Obsolete Metric Handgun Cartridges

5mm Bergmann
5mm Clement Auto
5.45x18mm Soviet
5.5mm Velo Dog Revolver
6.5mm Bergmann
7mm Nambu
7mm Baby Nambu
7.5mm Swedish Nagant
7.5mm Swiss Army Revolver
7.62mm Russian Nagant Revolver
7.62mm Russian Nagant
7.5mm Russian Nagant
7.62x38Rmm
7.62x25mm Tokarev
7.62mm Tokarev
7.63mm Mannlicher

7.65mm Mannlicher
7.63x25mm Mauser
30 Mauser
7.65mm Borchardt
30 Borchardt
7.65mm MAS
32 French Long
7.65mm Roth-Sauer
7.65x21mm Luger
30 Luger
8mm Lebel Revolver
8mm Nambu
8mm Rast-Gasser
8mm Roth-Steyr
9mm Browning Long
9mm Federal
9mm Glisenti
9mm Largo
9mm Bayard Long
9mm Bergman-Bayard
9x23mm Largo
9mm Mauser
9mm Steyr
9mm Ultra
9x18mm Police

9mm Winchester Magnum
9x21mm
9x21mm IMI
9.8mm Automatic Colt
9.65mm Browning Automatic Colt
10.4mm Italian Revolver
10.35mm Italian Revolver
10.35mm Glisenti
11mm French Ordnance Revolver
11mm French Revolver
11mm German Service Revolver
10.6mm German Service Revolver
10.6mm German Ordnance Revolver
10.8mm German Service Revolver
10.8mm German Ordnance Revolver
11.75mm Montenegrin Revolver
11mm Austrian Gasser
11.25x36mm Montenegrin ●

Source: Stars & Stripes Ammunition

CHAPTER 28: OBSOLETE CARTRIDGES

29: Cartridge Dimensions

Cartridge	Case Type	Bullet Dia.	Neck Dia.	Shoulder Dia.	Base Dia.	Rim Dia.	Case Length	Ctge OAL
2.7mm Kolibri	Rimless Straightwall	0.107	0.139		0.140	0.140	0.370	0.430
3mm Kolibri	Rimless Straightwall	0.120	0.150		0.150	0.150	0.320	0.430
4.25mm Lilput	Rimless Straightwall	0.167	0.198		0.198	0.198	0.410	0.560
14-222	Rimless Bottleneck	0.144	0.165	0.356	0.375	0.375	1.700	1.920
17-222	Rimless Bottleneck	0.172	0.199	0.355	0.375	0.375	1.690	1.820
17 Ackley Bee	Rimmed Bottleneck	0.172	0.201	0.341	0.350	0.408	1.350	1.780
17 Ackley Hornet	Rimmed Bottleneck	0.172	0.195	0.290	0.295	0.345	1.390	1.470
17 Remington	Rimless Bottleneck	0.172	0.198	0.355	0.374	0.377	1.790	1.860
4.85 British	Rimless Bottleneck	0.197	0.220	0.353	0.375	0.376	1.925	2.455
5mm Clement Automatic	Rimless Bottleneck	0.202	0.223	0.277	0.281	0.281	0.710	1.010
218 Mashburn Bee	Rimmed Bottleneck	0.224	0.241	0.340	0.349	0.408	1.340	1.750
5mm Bergmann	Rimless Straightwall	0.203	0.230		0.273	0.274	0.590	0.960
5.45x18mm Soviet	Rimless Bottleneck	0.210	0.220		0.300	0.300	0.700	0.980
5.7x28mm FN	Rimless Bottleneck	0.220	0.249	0.309	0.310	0.310	1.130	1.710
5.45mm Soviet	Rimless Bottleneck	0.221	0.246	0.387	0.395	0.394	1.560	2.220
5.6x33mm Rook	Rimless Bottleneck	0.222	0.248	0.318	0.325	0.326	1.310	1.620
5.6x33Rmm Rook	Rimmed Bottleneck	0.222	0.248	0.318	0.325	0.366	1.310	1.640
5.6x35Rmm Vierling	Rimmed Bottleneck	0.222	0.241	0.278	0.300	0.297	1.400	1.620
297/230 Morris Extra Long	Rimmed Bottleneck	0.223	0.240	0.274	0.296	0.248	1.125	1.450
22 Remington Jet	Rimmed Bottleneck	0.223	0.247	0.350	0.376	0.440	1.288	1.580
222 Rimmed	Rimmed Bottleneck	0.223	0.349	0.352	0.374	0.462	1.682	2.144
22 Super Jet	Rimmed Bottleneck	0.224	0.248	0.372	0.379	0.440	1.266	1.750
5.7mm MMJ	Rimless Bottleneck	0.224	0.253	0.332	0.353	0.356	1.290	1.650
Cartridge	Case Type	Bullet Dia.	Neck Dia.	Shoulder Dia.	Base Dia.	Rim Dia.	Case Length	Ctge OAL

Cartridge	Case Type	Bullet Dia.	Neck Dia.	Shoulder Dia.	Base Dia.	Rim Dia.	Case Length	Ctge OAL
224 Harvey Kay-Chuk	Rimmed Bottleneck	0.224	0.243	0.293	0.294	0.347	1.350	1.600
218 Harvey Bee	Rimmed Bottleneck	0.224	0.241	0.331	0.349	0.408	1.350	1.680
22 Waldog	Rimless Bottleneck	0.224	0.245	0.431	0.440	0.441	1.375	1.820
22 Kilbourn Hornet	Rimmed Bottleneck	0.224	0.242	0.286	0.294	0.345	1.390	1.700
22 Hornet	Rimmed Bottleneck	0.224	0.242	0.274	0.294	0.345	1.400	1.720
221 Remington Fireball	Rimless Bottleneck	0.224	0.251	0.355	0.375	0.375	1.400	1.820
22 BR Remington	Rimless Bottleneck	0.224	0.245	0.450	0.466	0.468	1.502	2.000
22 PPC	Rimless Bottleneck	0.224	0.245	0.430	0.440	0.441	1.520	1.960
224 R-C Maxi	Rimmed Bottleneck	0.224	0.252	0.354	0.375	0.431	1.576	2.048
2R Lovell	Rimmed Bottleneck	0.224	0.246	0.295	0.315	0.382	1.630	1.800
222 Remington Mag	Rimless Bottleneck	0.224	0.253	0.355	0.375	0.375	1.850	2.210
222 Remington	Rimless Bottleneck	0.224	0.253	0.355	0.375	0.375	1.700	2.150
219 Donaldson Wasp	Rimmed Bottleneck	0.224	0.251	0.402	0.418	0.497	1.813	2.100
223 Remington	Rimless Bottleneck	0.224	0.249	0.349	0.373	0.375	1.760	2.100
5.56x45mm NATO	Rimless Bottleneck	0.224	0.249	0.349	0.373	0.375	1.760	2.260
22-250 Remington	Rimless Bottleneck	0.224	0.254	0.412	0.466	0.470	1.910	2.330
224 Weatherby Mag	Belted Bottleneck	0.224	0.247	0.405	0.413	0.425	1.920	2.440
225 Winchester	Rimmed Bottleneck	0.224	0.260	0.406	0.422	0.473	1.930	2.500
226 JDJ	Rimmed Bottleneck	0.224	0.256	0.410	0.419	0.473	1.930	
5.6x50mm Mag	Rimless Bottleneck	0.224	0.254	0.355	0.375	0.376	1.968	2.210
5.6x50Rmm	Rimmed Bottleneck	0.224	0.254	0.355	0.375	NA	1.970	2.210
22 Cheetah	Rimless Bottleneck	0.224	0.250	0.451	0.466	0.470	2.000	2.360
22-30-30 Improved	Rimmed Bottleneck	0.224	0.253	0.391	0.422	0.502	2.030	2.480
22-303	Rimmed Bottleneck	0.224	0.254	0.408	0.455	0.540	2.031	2.480
22-243	Rimless Bottleneck	0.224	0.260	0.454	0.471	0.471	2.045	
Cartridge	Case Type	Bullet Dia.	Neck Dia.	Shoulder Dia.	Base Dia.	Rim Dia.	Case Length	Ctge OAL

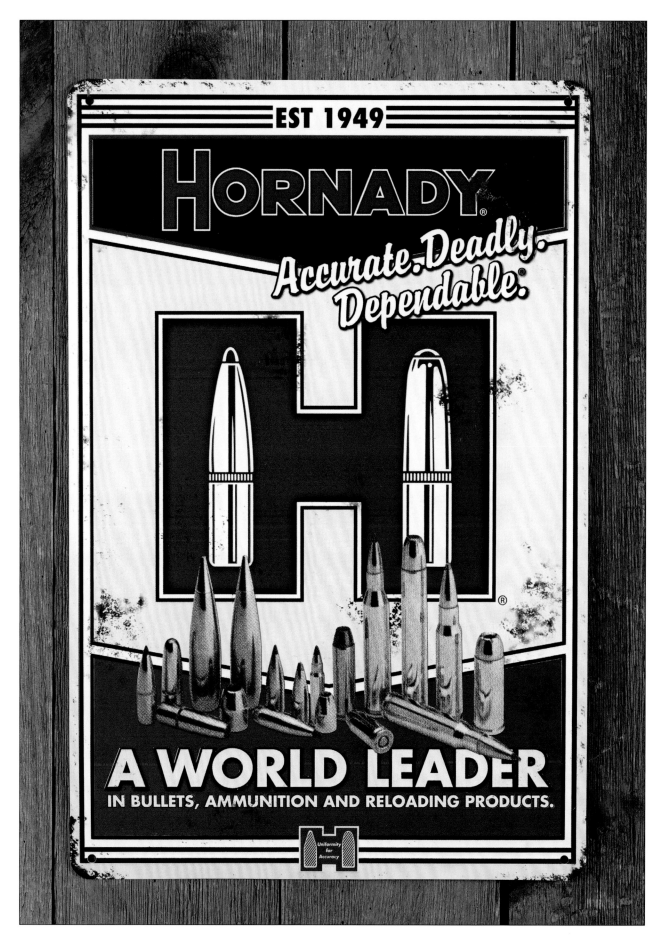

Cartridge	Case Type	Bullet Dia.	Neck Dia.	Shoulder Dia.	Base Dia.	Rim Dia.	Case Length	Ctge OAL
220 Swift	Semi-Rimmed Bottleneck	0.224	0.260	0.402	0.443	0.472	2.200	2.680
220 Wotkyns-Wilson Arrow	Semi-Rimmed Bottleneck	0.224	0.261	0.402	0.443	0.472	2.205	2.700
220 Weatherby Rocket	Semi-Rimmed Bottleneck	0.224	0.260	0.430	0.443	0.472	2.210	2.680
5.6x57mm RWS	Rimless Bottleneck	0.224	0.281	0.436	0.469	0.470	2.240	2.540
5.6x57Rmm RWS	Rimmed Bottleneck	0.224	0.281	0.436	0.469	NA	2.240	2.540
297/230 Morris Short	Rimmed Bottleneck	0.225	0.240	0.274	0.294	0.347	0.580	0.830
297/230 Morris Long	Rimmed Bottleneck	0.225	0.240	0.274	0.295	0.345	0.800	1.010
5.5mm Velo Dog	Rimmed Straightwall	0.225	0.248		0.253	0.308	1.120	1.350
224 Clark	Rimless Bottleneck	0.225	0.275	0.455	0.471	0.470	2.237	3.075
22-15-60 Stevens	Rimmed Straightwall	0.226	0.243		0.265	0.342	2.010	2.260
5.6x61mm Vom Hofe (SE)	Rimless Bottleneck	0.227	0.259	0.468	0.476	0.480	2.390	3.130
5.6x61Rmm Von Hofe	Rimmed Bottleneck	0.227	0.260	0.470	0.479	0.533	2.390	3.130
22 Extra Long (Maynard)	Rimmed Straightwall	0.228	0.252		0.252	0.310	1.170	1.410
22 WCF	Rimmed Bottleneck	0.228	0.241	0.278	0.295	0.342	1.390	1.610

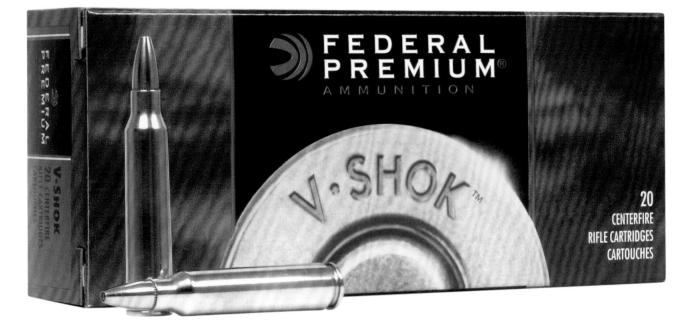

Cartridge	Case Type	Bullet Dia.	Neck Dia.	Shoulder Dia.	Base Dia.	Rim Dia.	Case Length	Ctge OAL

Cartridge	Case Type	Bullet Dia.	Neck Dia.	Shoulder Dia.	Base Dia.	Rim Dia.	Case Length	Ctge OAL
5.6x52Rmm	Rimmed Bottleneck	0.228	0.252	0.360	0.416	0.500	2.050	2.510
22 Savage High Power	Rimmed Bottleneck	0.228	0.252	0.360	0.416	0.500	2.050	2.510
22 Newton	Rimless Bottleneck	0.228	0.356	0.420	0.471	0.474	2.230	2.850
228 Ackley Mag	Rimless Bottleneck	0.228	0.265	0.445	0.470	0.473	2.250	2.550
5.6x29.5Rmm Stahl	Rimmed Bottleneck	0.243	0.262	0.301	0.320	0.370	1.160	1.440
6mm PPC	Rimless Bottleneck	0.243	0.260	0.450	0.441	0.442	1.500	2.120
6mm Bench Rest Remington	Rimless Bottleneck	0.243	0.263	0.457	0.466	0.468	1.520	2.190
6mm TCU	Rimless Bottleneck	0.243	0.265	0.354	0.376	0.378	1.740	2.250
6mm-223	Rimless Bottleneck	0.243	0.266	0.354	0.376	0.378	1.760	2.260
6mm SAW	Rimless Bottleneck	0.243	0.273	0.382	0.410	0.410	1.779	2.580
6mm-47mm	Rimless Bottleneck	0.243	0.267	0.348	0.372	0.373	1.810	2.310
6mm-222 Mag	Rimless Bottleneck	0.243	0.267	0.348	0.372	0.373	1.810	2.310
6mm JDJ	Rimmed Bottleneck	0.243	0.272	0.415	0.421	0.470	1.905	2.650
6mm-250 Walker	Rimless Bottleneck	0.243	0.274	0.420	0.468	0.470	1.910	2.210
6mm-30-30 Improved	Rimmed Bottleneck	0.243	0.275	0.392	0.422	0.502	2.030	2.550
243 Winchester	Rimless Bottleneck	0.243	0.276	0.454	0.470	0.470	2.045	2.710
6mm Remington	Rimless Bottleneck	0.243	0.276	0.429	0.471	0.473	2.233	2.73-2.825
244 Remington	Rimless Bottleneck	0.243	0.276	0.429	0.470	0.472	2.230	2.825
6x57mm Mauser	Rimless Bottleneck	0.243	0.284	0.420	0.475	0.476	2.230	2.950
244 (6mm) Halger Mag	Rimmed Bottleneck	0.243	0.287	0.435	0.467	0.519	2.250	3.040
6x58MM Forster	Rimless Bottleneck	0.243	0.285	0.437	0.470	0.468	2.260	3.080
6x58Rmm Forster	Rimmed Bottleneck	0.243	0.284	0.437	0.471	0.532	2.260	3.060
6x62mm Freres	Rimless Bottleneck	0.243	0.271	0.451	0.474	0.470	2.420	3.130
6x62Rmm Freres	Rimmed Bottleneck	0.243	0.271	0.451	0.474	NA	2.420	3.130
240 Weatherby Mag	Belted Bottleneck	0.243	0.271	0.432	0.453	0.473	2.500	3.060
Cartridge	Case Type	Bullet Dia.	Neck Dia.	Shoulder Dia.	Base Dia.	Rim Dia.	Case Length	Ctge OAL

Cartridge	Case Type	Bullet Dia.	Neck Dia.	Shoulder Dia.	Base Dia.	Rim Dia.	Case Length	Ctge OAL
6mm Navy	Rimless Bottleneck	0.244	0.278	0.402	0.445	0.448	2.350	3.110
244 Holland & Holland Mag	Belted Bottleneck	0.244	0.263	0.445	0.508	0.532	2.780	3.550
240 Mag Rimless	Belted Bottleneck	0.245	0.274	0.403	0.450	0.467	2.490	3.210
240 Mag Flanged	Rimmed Bottleneck	0.245	NA	0.402	0.448	0.513	2.500	3.250
242 Rimless Nitro Express	Rimless Bottleneck	0.249	0.281	0.405	0.465	0.465	2.380	3.200
297/250 Rook Rifle	Rimmed Bottleneck	0.250	0.267	0.294	0.295	0.343	0.820	1.060
6.5x40Rmm	Rimmed Straightwall	0.250	0.290		0.396	0.451	1.580	2.070
25 Automatic (ACP)	Rimless Straightwall	0.251	0.276		0.277	0.298	0.615	0.910
246 Purdey Flanged	Rimmed Bottleneck	0.253	0.283	0.401	0.474	0.544	2.240	2.980
242 Rimless	Rimless Bottleneck	0.253	0.281	0.405	0.465	0.465	2.380	3.200
255 Rook	Rimmed Bottleneck	0.255	0.274	0.328	0.344	0.401	1.150	1.430
25 Ackley Krag Short	Rimmed Bottleneck	0.257	0.293	0.415	0.457	0.540	2.240	Varies
25 Ackley Krag Long	Rimmed Bottleneck	0.257	0.293	0.415	0.457	0.540	2.310	Varies

Cartridge	Case Type	Bullet Dia.	Neck Dia.	Shoulder Dia.	Base Dia.	Rim Dia.	Case Length	Ctge OAL
6.5x27Rmm	Rimmed Bottleneck	0.257	0.284	0.348	0.379	0.428	1.060	1.540
256 Winchester Mag	Rimmed Bottleneck	0.257	0.283	0.370	0.378	0.440	1.281	1.530
25-20 Winchester	Rimmed Bottleneck	0.257	0.274	0.329	0.349	0.405	1.330	1.600
25-20 Single Shot	Rimmed Bottleneck	0.257	0.275	0.296	0.315	0.378	1.630	1.900
25 Uglade	Rimless Bottleneck	0.257	0.275	0.368	0.373	0.375	1.760	2.270
257 JDJ	Rimmed Bottleneck	0.257	0.288	0.415	0.421	0.500	1.905	2.810
257-3000 Improved	Rimless Bottleneck	0.257	0.284	0.445	0.467	0.473	1.910	2.520
250 Savage	Rimless Bottleneck	0.257	0.286	0.413	0.468	0.470	1.912	2.515
25 Remington	Rimless Bottleneck	0.257	0.280	0.355	0.420	0.421	2.040	2.540
6.5x52Rmm (25-35 Win.)	Rimmed Bottleneck	0.257	0.280	0.355	0.420	0.506	2.040	2.530
25-21 Stevens	Rimmed Straightwall	0.257	0.280		0.300	0.376	2.050	2.300
6.3x53Rmm Finnish	Rimmed Bottleneck	0.257	0.286	0.463	0.486	0.565	2.090	2.510
25-35 Marlin	Rimmed Bottleneck	0.257	0.281	0.358	0.416	0.499	2.120	2.500
25-303	Rimmed Bottleneck	0.257	0.294	0.400	0.455	0.541	2.220	3.050
257 Roberts (+P)	Rimless Bottleneck	0.257	0.290	0.430	0.468	0.473	2.233	2.740
257 Improved	Rimless Bottleneck	0.257	0.288	0.457	0.471	0.473	2.230	2.780
25-25 Stevens	Rimmed Straightwall	0.257	0.282		0.323	0.376	2.370	2.630
25-06 Remington	Rimless Bottleneck	0.257	0.287	0.441	0.470	0.471	2.494	3.00
257 Weatherby Mag	Belted Bottleneck	0.257	0.285	0.490	0.511	0.530	2.550	3.250
6.5x48Rmm Sauer	Rimmed Straightwall	0.260	0.284		0.433	0.495	1.880	2.430
6.5mm Arisaka	Semi-Rimmed Bottleneck	0.263	0.293	0.425	0.455	0.471	2.000	2.980
6.5x54mm MS	Rimless Bottleneck	0.263	0.287	0.424	0.447	0.450	2.090	3.020
6.5x54Rmm MS	Rimmed Bottleneck	0.263	0.287	0.424	0.447	NA	2.090	3.020
6.5x53.5mm Daudeteau	Semi-Rimmed Bottleneck	0.263	0.298	0.466	0.490	0.524	2.090	3.020
6.5mm Dutch & Romanian	Rimmed Bottleneck	0.263	0.297	0.423	0.450	0.526	2.100	3.030
Cartridge	Case Type	Bullet Dia.	Neck Dia.	Shoulder Dia.	Base Dia.	Rim Dia.	Case Length	Ctge OAL

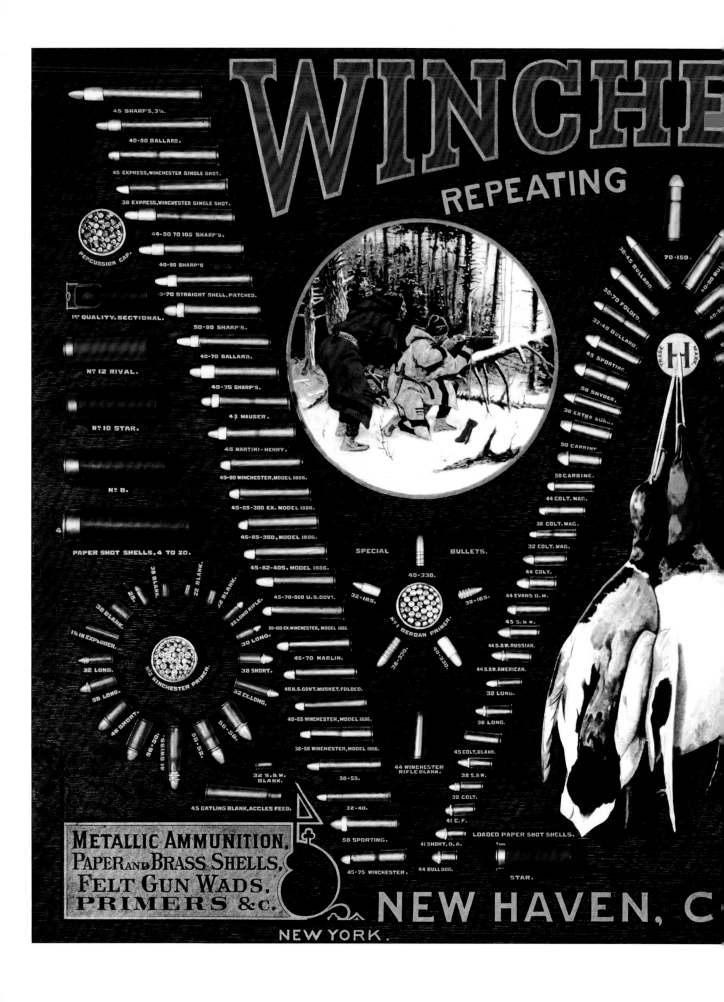

This Winchester Model 1890 "Single W" cartridge board depicts a Remington-style cowboy shooting. The board on left-hand side depicts two trappers. The center board depicts hanging mallard and canvasback. The original size is about 33 inches tall by 46 inches long. © Winfield Galleries, LLC, St. Louis, Missouri. Used with permission. To view current artwork and pricing, log on to www.WinfieldGalleries.com.

Cartridge	Case Type	Bullet Dia.	Neck Dia.	Shoulder Dia.	Base Dia.	Rim Dia.	Case Length	Ctge OAL
6.5mm Remington Mag	Belted Bottleneck	0.263	0.300	0.493	0.511	0.532	2.170	2.800
6.5x55mm Swedish	Rimless Bottleneck	0.264	0.2972	0.435	0.477	0.479	2.165	3.025
6.5mm Bergmann	Rimless Bottleneck	0.264	0.289	0.325	0.367	0.370	0.870	1.230
6.5mm Whisper	Rimless Bottleneck	0.264	0.286	0.357	0.372	0.375	1.360	Varies
6.5mm JDJ	Rimmed Bottleneck	0.264	0.293	0.410	0.419	0.467	1.930	Varies
6.5mm JDJ #2	Rimmed Bottleneck	0.264	0.292	0.450	0.466	0.502	2.000	Varies
6.5mm JDJx30	Rimmed Bottleneck	0.264	0.285	0.409	0.419	0.497	2.030	Varies
6.5x54mm Mauser	Rimless Bottleneck	0.264	0.289	0.432	0.468	0.463	2.120	2.670
6.5mm Remington Mag	Belted Bottleneck	0.264	0.300	0.490	0.571	0.582	2.170	2.74-2.80
6.5x57mm Mauser	Rimless Bottleneck	0.264	0.292	0.430	0.471	0.474	2.230	3.160
6.5x57Rmm Mauser	Rimmed Bottleneck	0.264	0.292	0.430	0.470	0.521	2.240	3.160
6.5x58mm Portuguese	Rimless Bottleneck	0.264	0.293	0.426	0.468	0.465	2.280	3.220
6.5x58mm Mauser	Rimless Bottleneck	0.264	0.293	0.426	0.468	0.465	2.280	3.220
6.5x58Rmm Krag-Jorgensen	Rimmed Bottleneck	0.264	0.300	0.460	0.500	0.575	2.290	3.250
6.5x58Rmm Sauer	Rimmed Straightwall	0.264	0.291		0.433	0.501	2.300	3.080
6.5x61mm Mauser	Rimless Bottleneck	0.264	0.297	0.452	0.477	0.479	2.400	3.550
6.5x61Rmm Mauser	Rimmed Bottleneck	0.264	0.296	0.452	0.477	0.532	2.400	3.550
256 (6.5mm) Newton	Rimless Bottleneck	0.264	0.290	0.430	0.469	0.473	2.440	3.400
6.5-06 (256/06)	Rimless Bottleneck	0.264	0.300	0.439	0.471	0.473	2.500	2.800
264 Winchester Mag	Belted Bottleneck	0.264	0.289	0.490	0.515	0.532	2.500	3.290
6.5x65mm RWS	Rimless Bottleneck	0.264	0.296	0.430	0.474	0.470	2.560	3.150
6.5x65Rmm RWS	Rimmed Bottleneck	0.264	0.296	0.430	0.475	0.531	2.560	3.150
6.5mm Carcano	Rimless Bottleneck	0.265	0.295	0.430	0.445	0.448	2.050	3.020
256 Gibbs Mag	Belted Bottleneck	0.265	0.298	0.427	0.473	0.476	2.170	3.050
6.5x68mm Schuler	Rimless Bottleneck	0.265	0.295	0.481	0.520	0.510	2.660	3.270

Cartridge	Case Type	Bullet Dia.	Neck Dia.	Shoulder Dia.	Base Dia.	Rim Dia.	Case Length	Ctge OAL

Cartridge	Case Type	Bullet Dia.	Neck Dia.	Shoulder Dia.	Base Dia.	Rim Dia.	Case Length	Ctge OAL
6.5x68Rmm Schuler	Rimmed Bottleneck	0.265	0.295	0.481	0.520	NA	2.660	3.270
26 Rimless	Rimless Bottleneck	0.267	0.306	0.445	0.513	0.530	2.390	3.130
270 Savage	Rimless Bottleneck	0.277	0.038	0.450	0.470	0.470	1.880	2.620
270 JDJ	Rimmed Bottleneck	0.277	0.305	0.415	0.421	0.467	1.905	2.875
270 Winchester	Rimless Bottleneck	0.277	0.307	0.440	0.468	0.470	2.540	3.280
270 Weatherby Mag	Belted Bottleneck	0.277	0.305	0.490	0.511	0.530	2.550	3.250
7mm Nambu	Rimless Bottleneck	0.280	0.296	0.337	0.351	0.359	0.780	1.060
280 British	Rimless Bottleneck	0.283	0.313	0.448	0.470	0.473	1.710	2.540
7x33mm Finnish SAKO	Rimless Bottleneck	0.284	0.307	0.365	0.388	0.390	1.300	1.730
7mm Whisper	Rimless Bottleneck	0.284	0.306	0.357	0.372	0.375	1.360	Varies
7mm Bench Rest Remington	Rimless Bottleneck	0.284	0.308	0.459	0.470	0.473	1.520	NA
7mm TCU	Rimless Bottleneck	0.284	0.302	0.350	0.373	0.375	1.740	2.280
7mm JDJ	Rimmed Bottleneck	0.284	0.312	0.415	0.421	0.473	1.905	2.735
7mm JDJ #2	Rimmed Bottleneck	0.284	0.313	0.450	0.466	0.502	2.000	Varies
7mm-30 JDJ	Rimmed Bottleneck	0.284	0.306	0.409	0.419	0.497	2.030	Varies
7mm-08 Remington	Rimless Bottleneck	0.284	0.315	0.454	0.470	0.473	2.035	2.800
7-30 Waters	Rimmed Bottleneck	0.284	0.306	0.399	0.4125	0.506	2.040	2.520
7mm International Rimmed	Rimmed Bottleneck	0.284	0.311	0.402	0.422	0.502	2.040	2.520
7mm ST Easterner	Rimmed Bottleneck	0.284	0.315	0.353	0.467	0.502	2.100	2.540
284 Winchester	Rebated Bottleneck	0.284	0.312	0.465	0.495	0.470	2.170	2.750
7x57mm Mauser	Rimless Bottleneck	0.284	0.320	0.4294	0.4711	0.473	2.235	3.065
7x57mmR	Rimmed Bottleneck	0.284	0.320	0.4294	0.470	0.521	2.235	3.070
275 Rigby	Rimless Bottleneck	0.284	0.324	0.428	0.474	0.475	2.240	3.070
276 Enfield	Rimless Bottleneck	0.284	0.321	0.460	0.528	0.521	2.350	3.250
7x61mm Sharpe & Hart Super	Belted Bottleneck	0.284	0.320	0.478	0.515	0.532	2.400	3.270
Cartridge	Case Type	Bullet Dia.	Neck Dia.	Shoulder Dia.	Base Dia.	Rim Dia.	Case Length	Ctge OAL

LAFLIN & RAND
POWDER COMPANY

Cartridge	Case Type	Bullet Dia.	Neck Dia.	Shoulder Dia.	Base Dia.	Rim Dia.	Case Length	Ctge OAL
275 #2 Mag (7mm Rigby Mag)	Rimmed Bottleneck	0.284	0.315	0.406	0.456	0.524	2.490	3.240
7mm Remington Mag	Belted Bottleneck	0.284	0.315	0.491	0.513	0.532	2.500	3.290
7mm WSM	Rimless Bottleneck	0.284	0.321	0.538	. 555	0.535	2.100	2.860
7mm Remington SAUM	Rimless Bottleneck	0.284	..320	0.534	0.555	0.534	2.035	2.825
7mm Remington Ultra Mag	Belted Bottleneck	0.284	0.550	0.525	0.550	0.534	2.85	3.650
275 Holland & Holland Mag	Belted Bottleneck	0.284	0.318	0.375	0.513	0.532	2.500	3.300
275 Flanged Mag	Rimmed Bottleneck	0.284	0.318	0.450	0.510	0.582	2.500	3.260
275 Belted Mag	Belted Bottleneck	0.284	0.325	0.454	0.513	0.523	2.500	3.300
7mm Dakota	Rimless Bottleneck	0.284	0.314	0.531	0.545	0.544	2.500	3.330
7x64mm Brenneke	Rimless Bottleneck	0.284	0.305	0.422	0.463	0.468	2.510	3.210
7x65Rmm Brenneke	Rimmed Bottleneck	0.284	0.308	0.422	0.463	0.521	2.530	3.210
7mm JRD	Rimless Bottleneck	0.284	0.312	0.454	0.470	NA	2.525	3.455
280 Remington	Rimless Bottleneck	0.284	0.315	0.441	0.470	0.472	2.540	3.330
285 OKH	Rimless Bottleneck	0.284	0.315	0.442	0.470	0.472	2.550	3.350
7mm Weatherby Mag	Belted Bottleneck	0.284	0.314	0.492	0.511	0.531	2.550	3.360
7x66mm Vom Hofe (SE)	Rimless Bottleneck	0.284	0.316	0.485	0.543	0.510	2.580	3.250
7mm Canadian Mag	Rebated Bottleneck	0.284	0.322	0.530	0.544	0.532	2.830	3.600
7x72Rmm	Rimmed Straightwall	0.284	0.311		0.425	0.482	2.840	3.480
7mm ST Westerner	Belted Bottleneck	0.284	0.315	0.487	0.508	0.530	2.860	3.680
7x73mm Vom Hofe Belted	Belted Bottleneck	0.284	0.315	0.483	0.527	0.533	2.870	3.880
7x75Rmm Vom Hofe (SE)	Rimmed Bottleneck	0.284	0.318	0.416	0.468	0.519	2.950	3.680
276 Pederson	Rimless Bottleneck	0.284	0.314	0.389	0.449	0.451	2.020	2.850
28-30-120 Stevens	Rimmed Straightwall	0.285	0.309		0.357	0.412	2.510	2.820
280 Flanged	Rimmed Bottleneck	0.287	0.316	0.423	0.535	0.607	2.410	3.620
7mm Rigby Mag	Rimmed Bottleneck	0.287	0.315	0.406	0.470	0.528	2.490	3.250
Cartridge	Case Type	Bullet Dia.	Neck Dia.	Shoulder Dia.	Base Dia.	Rim Dia.	Case Length	Ctge OAL

Cartridge	Case Type	Bullet Dia.	Neck Dia.	Shoulder Dia.	Base Dia.	Rim Dia.	Case Length	Ctge OAL
280 Ross	Semi-Rimmed Bottleneck	0.287	0.317	0.404	0.534	0.556	2.590	3.500
280 Jeffery	Rimless Bottleneck	0.288	0.317	0.504	0.542	0.538	2.460	3.380
7.62mm Nagant (Russian)	Rimmed Straightwall	0.295	0.286		0.335	0.388	1.530	1.530
7.35mm Carcano	Rimless Bottleneck	0.298	0.323	0.420	0.445	0.449	2.010	2.980
300 (295) Rook Rifle	Rimmed Straightwall	0.300	0.317		0.319	0.369	1.170	1.380
300 Sherwood	Rimmed Straightwall	0.300	0.318		0.320	0.370	1.540	2.020
7.65mm Roth-Sauer	Rimless Straightwall	0.301	0.332		0.335	0.335	0.510	0.840
7x60Rmm	Rimmed Bottleneck	0.304	0.336	0.507	0.517	0.607	2.490	3.200
7.62mm Russian Tokarev	Rimless Bottleneck	0.307	0.330	0.370	0.380	0.390	0.970	1.350
30 Borchardt	Rimless Bottleneck	0.307	0.331	0.370	0.385	0.390	0.990	1.340/B
30 (7.65mm) Luger	Rimless Bottleneck	0.308	0.322	0.374	0.388	0.391	0.850	1.150/B
7.63mm (7.65mm) Mannlicher	Rimless Straightwall	0.308	0.331		0.332	0.334	0.840	1.120
7.62mm Micro Whisper SP	Rimless Bottleneck	0.308	0.328	0.382	0.389	0.392	0.846	Varies/
7.63 Mini-Whisper SR	Rimless Bottleneck	0.308	0.329	0.375	0.381	0.385	0.985	Varies/
30 (7.63mm) Mauser	Rimless Bottleneck	0.308	0.332	0.370	0.381	0.390	0.990	1.360/
30 M1 Carbine	Rimless Straightwall	0.308	0.335		0.355	0.360	1.290	1.650
30 Kurz	Rimless Bottleneck	0.308	0.334	0.443	0.470	0.473	1.290	1.650
300 Whisper	Rimless Bottleneck	0.308	0.330	0.369	0.375	0.375	1.500	2.575
308x1 Barnes	Rimless Bottleneck	0.308	0.338	0.450	0.466	0.470	1.500	2.050
30 Herrett	Rimmed Bottleneck	0.308	0.329	0.405	0.421	0.505	1.610	2.010
30-30 Wesson	Rimmed Bottleneck	0.308	0.329	0.330	0.380	0.440	1.660	2.500
300 Savage	Rimless Bottleneck	0.308	0.339	0.4466	0.470	0.470	1.871	2.620
7.62x51mm NATO	Rimless Bottleneck	0.308	0.344	0.454	0.470	0.470	2.015	2.750x
308 Winchester	Rimless Bottleneck	0.308	0.344	0.454	0.470	0.470	2.015	2.750

Cartridge	Case Type	Bullet Dia.	Neck Dia.	Shoulder Dia.	Base Dia.	Rim Dia.	Case Length	Ctge OAL

Cartridge	Case Type	Bullet Dia.	Neck Dia.	Shoulder Dia.	Base Dia.	Rim Dia.	Case Length	Ctge OAL
307 Winchester	Semi-Rimmed Bottleneck	0.308	0.344	0.454	0.470	0.506	2.015	2.560
30 Remington	Rimless Bottleneck	0.308	0.328	0.402	0.420	0.421	2.030	2.540
30 American	Rimmed Bottleneck	0.308	0.328	0.402	0.4215	0.502	2.030	2.530
7.62x51Rmm	Rimmed Bottleneck	0.308	0.328	0.402	0.4215	0.502	2.039	2.530
30-30 Winchester	Rimmed Bottleneck	0.308	0.328	0.402	0.4215	0.502	2.039	2.530
30-30 Ackley Improved	Rimmed Bottleneck	0.308	0.328	0.419	0.4215	0.502	2.040	2.540
8.15x46Rmm	Rimmed Bottleneck	0.316	0.346	0.378	0.421	0.484	1.820	2.280
7.5mm French MAS	Rimless Bottleneck	0.308	0.340	0.411	0.480	0.482	2.110	2.990
7.5mm Schmidt-Rubin	Rimless Bottleneck	0.308	0.334	0.452	0.494	0.496	2.180	3.050
309 JDJ	Rimmed Bottleneck	0.308	0.335	0.453	0.470	0.514	2.200	3.160
30-40 Krag	Rimmed Bottleneck	0.308	0.338	0.419	0.4577	0.540	2.314	3.089
30 Flanged Nitro (Purdey)	Rimmed Bottleneck	0.308	0.338	0.415	0.457	0.545	2.360	2.970
30-06 Improved	Rimless Bottleneck	0.308	0.340	0.454	0.470	0.473	2.490	3.350
7.62x63mm U.S.	Rimless Bottleneck	0.308	0.340	0.441	0.470	0.473	2.490	3.340
30-06 Springfield	Rimless Bottleneck	0.308	0.340	0.441	0.470	0.473	2.494	3.340
30 Newton	Rimless Bottleneck	0.308	0.340	0.491	0.523	0.525	2.520	3.350
300 Dakota	Rimless Bottleneck	0.308	0.338	0.531	0.545	NA	2.550	3.330
308 Norma Mag	Belted Bottleneck	0.308	0.340	0.489	0.514	0.529	2.560	3.300
300 Winchester Mag	Belted Bottleneck	0.308	0.334	0.4891	0.5126	0.530	2.620	3.300
30R Blaser	Rimmed Bottleneck	0.308	0.343	0.411	0.480	0.531	2.680	3.800
300 Weatherby Mag	Belted Bottleneck	0.308	0.337	0.495	0.5117	0.530	2.825	3.560
300 Canadian Mag	Rebated Bottleneck	0.308	0.342	0.530	0.544	0.532	2.830	3.600
300 Holland & Holland Mag	Belted Bottleneck	0.308	0.338	0.447	0.513	0.530	2.850	3.600
30 Cody	Rimless Bottleneck	0.308	0.340	0.544	0.590	0.586	2.875	3.670
30 Flanged Mag (H & H)	Rimmed Bottleneck	0.308	0.338	0.450	0.517	0.572	2.940	3.690
Cartridge	Case Type	Bullet Dia.	Neck Dia.	Shoulder Dia.	Base Dia.	Rim Dia.	Case Length	Ctge OAL

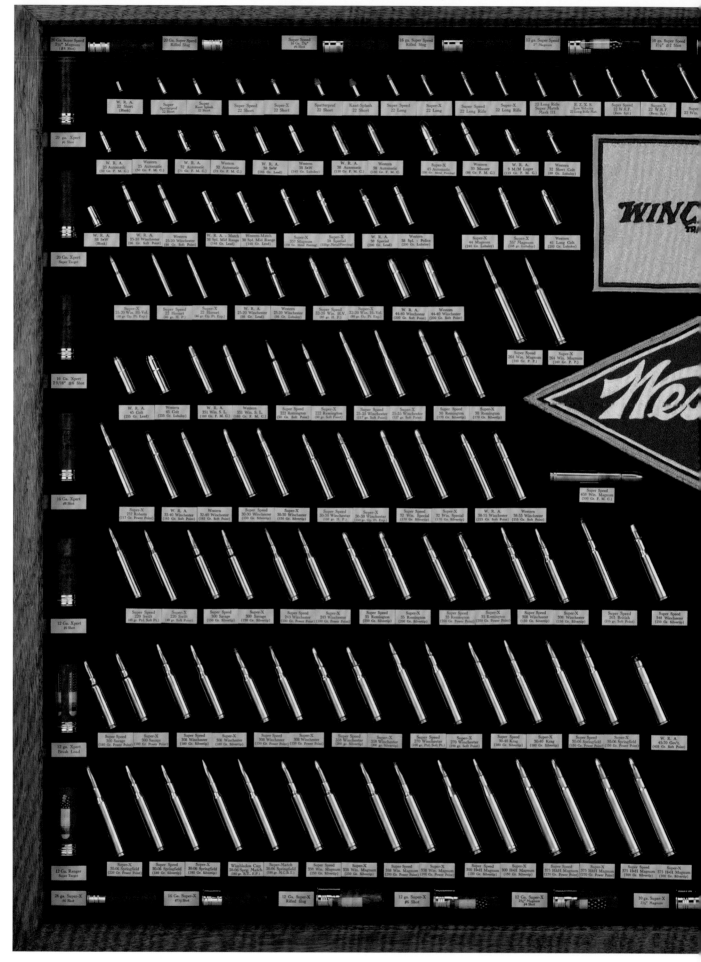

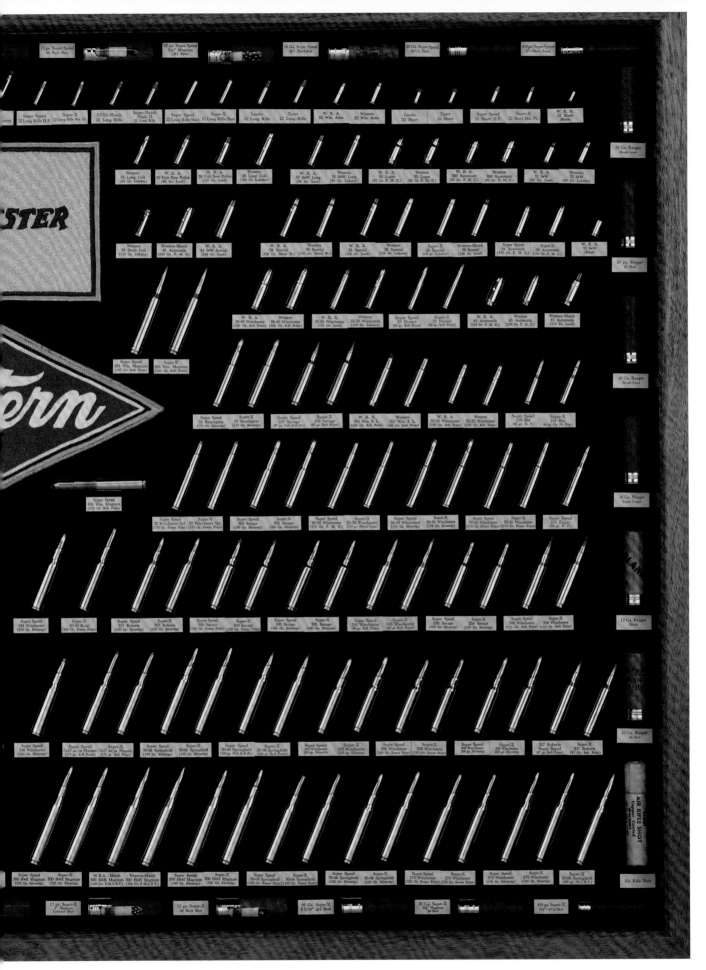

Cartridge	Case Type	Bullet Dia.	Neck Dia.	Shoulder Dia.	Base Dia.	Rim Dia.	Case Length	Ctge OAL
300 Pegasus	Rimless Bottleneck	0.308	0.339	0.566	0.580	0.580	2.990	3.750
300 Remington Ultra Mag	Rimless Bottleneck	0.308	0.344	0.525	0.550	0.534	2.850	3.600
30-378 Weatherby Mag	Belted Bottleneck	0.308	0.337	0.561	0.582	0.579	2.913	3.648
35 S&W Automatic	Rimless Straightwall	0.309	0.345		0.346	0.348	0.670	0.970
32 Automatic (ACP)	Semi-Rimmed Straightwall	0.309	0.336		0.336	0.354	0.680	1.030
7.65mm French MAS	Rimless Straightwall	0.309	0.336		0.337	0.337	0.780	1.190
7.62x45mm Czech M52	Rimless Bottleneck	0.309	0.334	0.412	0.441	0.440	1.770	2.360
32-40 Remington	Rimmed Bottleneck	0.309	0.330	0.358	0.453	0.535	2.130	3.250
7.62mm (M-43) Russian	Rimless Bottleneck	0.310	0.340	0.394	0.443	0.445	1.520	2.200
7.62x39mm	Rimless Bottleneck	0.310	0.340	0.394	0.443	0.445	1.520	2.200
7.62mm Nagant	Rimmed Bottleneck	0.310	0.332	0.453	0.484	0.564	2.110	3.020
7.62x53Rmm Russian	Rimmed Bottleneck	0.310	0.332	0.453	0.484	0.564	2.110	3.020
303 Savage	Rimmed Bottleneck	308/311	0.3322	0.4135	0.439	0.501	2.150	2.520
303 British	Rimmed Bottleneck	0.311	0.337	0.402	0.458	0.530	2.222	3.050
7.7mm Arisaka	Rimless Bottleneck	0.311	0.338	0.431	0.472	0.474	2.280	3.130
375/303 Westley Richards	Rimmed Bottleneck	0.311	0.343	0.390	0.457	0.505	2.500	3.360
32 Smith & Wesson	Rimmed Straightwall	0.312	0.334		0.335	0.375	0.610	0.920
32 Smith & Wesson Long	Rimmed Straightwall	0.312	0.335		0.335	0.375	0.920	1.270
32 H&R Mag	Rimmed Straightwall	0.312	0.333		0.333	0.371	1.075	1.350
32-20 Winchester	Rimmed Bottleneck	0.312	0.326	0.3424	0.353	0.405	1.315	1.590
32-30 Remington	Rimmed Bottleneck	0.312	0.332	0.357	0.378	0.437	1.640	2.010
32-25 Stevens & Maynard	Rimmed Straightwall	0.312	0.339		0.402	0.503	1.880	2.290
303 Mag	Rimless Bottleneck	0.312	0.345	0.462	0.530	0.557	2.340	3.250
32 Short & Long Colt	Rimmed Straightwall	0.313	0.313		0.318	0.374	0.920	1.260
7.65x53mm Mauser	Rimless Bottleneck	0.313	0.338	0.429	0.468	0.470	2.090	2.950

Cartridge	Case Type	Bullet Dia.	Neck Dia.	Shoulder Dia.	Base Dia.	Rim Dia.	Case Length	Ctge OAL

Cartridge	Case Type	Bullet Dia.	Neck Dia.	Shoulder Dia.	Base Dia.	Rim Dia.	Case Length	Ctge OAL
32-40 Bullard	Rimmed Bottleneck	0.315	0.332	0.413	0.453	0.510	1.850	2.260
310 Cadet Rifle	Rimmed Straightwall	0.316	0.320		0.353	0.405	1.020	1.590
8x48Rmm Sauer	Rimmed Straightwall	0.316	0.344		0.432	0.500	1.880	2.580
8x51mm Mauser	Rimless Bottleneck	0.316	0.344	0.436	0.467	0.467	1.980	2.670
8x51Rmm Mauser	Rimmed Bottleneck	0.316	0.344	0.436	0.467	0.515	1.980	2.880
320 Revolver	Rimmed Straightwall	0.317	0.320		0.322	0.350	0.620	0.900
32 Long, Centerfire *	Rimmed Straightwall	0.317	0.318		0.321	0.369	0.820	1.350
7.5mm Swiss Army	Rimmed Straightwall	0.317	0.335		0.345	0.407	0.890	1.290
32 Extra Long Ballard	Rimmed Straightwall	0.317	0.318		0.321	0.369	1.240	1.800
8x42Rmm M/88	Rimmed Bottleneck	0.318	0.347	0.423	0.468	0.525	1.660	2.280
8x57Rmm 360	Rimmed Bottleneck	0.318	0.333	0.375	0.427	0.485	2.240	2.960
8x71mm Peterlongo	Rimless Bottleneck	0.318	0.349	0.422	0.462	0.468	2.800	3.280
8x57mm	Rimless Bottleneck	0.318	0.345	0.411	0.466	0.467	2.940	3.500
8x75Rmm	Rimmed Bottleneck	0.318	0.345	0.411	0.466	0.522	2.940	3.510
8mm Nambu	Semi-Rimmed Bottleneck	0.320	0.338	0.388	0.408	0.413	0.860	1.250
8mm Rast-Gasser	Rimmed Straightwall	0.320	0.332		0.334	0.376	1.037	1.391
32 Winchester Self Loading	Semi-Rimmed Straightwall	0.320	0.343		0.346	0.388	1.280	1.880
32 Remington	Rimless Bottleneck	0.320	0.344	0.396	0.420	0.421	2.040	2.570
32-40 Ballard & Winchester	Rimmed Straightwall	0.320	0.338		0.424	0.506	2.130	2.590
8x50Rmm Siamese	Rimmed Bottleneck	0.321	0.347	0.450	0.480	0.550	1.980	2.970
32 Winchester Special	Rimmed Bottleneck	0.321	0.343	0.4014	0.4219	0.506	2.040	2.565
8x52Rmm Siamese	Rimmed Bottleneck	0.321	0.347	0.460	0.500	0.550	2.040	2.960
8x58Rmm Sauer	Rimmed Straightwall	0.322	0.345		0.438	0.499	2.280	3.000
8mm Danish Krag	Rimmed Bottleneck	0.322	0.355	0.460	0.500	0.575	2.280	3.200
8mm Lebel Revolver	Rimmed Straightwall	0.323	0.350		0.384	0.400	1.070	1.440
Cartridge	Case Type	Bullet Dia.	Neck Dia.	Shoulder Dia.	Base Dia.	Rim Dia.	Case Length	Ctge OAL

Cartridge	Case Type	Bullet Dia.	Neck Dia.	Shoulder Dia.	Base Dia.	Rim Dia.	Case Length	Ctge OAL
7.92mm Kurz	Rimless Bottleneck	0.323	0.352	0.440	0.470	0.470	1.300	1.880
32 Ideal	Rimmed Straightwall	0.323	0.344		0.348	0.411	1.770	2.250
8mm Austrian	Rimmed Bottleneck	0.323	0.351	0.462	0.501	0.553	1.770	3.00
8mm Lebel	Rimmed Bottleneck	0.323	0.347	0.483	0.536	0.621	1.980	2.750
8x54mm Krag Jorgensen	Rimless Bottleneck	0.323	0.351	0.435	0.478	0.478	2.120	2.850
8x56mm Mannlicher-Schoenauer	Rimless Bottleneck	0.323	0.347	0.424	0.465	0.470	2.210	3.040
8mm JDJ	Rimmed Bottleneck	0.323	0.356	0.455	0.465	0.506	2.220	Varies
8x57mm Mauser	Rimless Bottleneck	0.323	0.3493	0.431	0.469	0.473	2.240	3.250
7.9x57JSmm	Rimless Bottleneck	0.323	0.349	0.431	0.469	0.473	2.240	3.250
8x57JR3mm	Rimmed Bottleneck	0.323	0.349	0.431	0.469	0.526	2.240	3.550
8x60Smm Mauser	Rimless Bottleneck	0.323	0.350	0.431	0.470	0.468	2.340	3.110
8x60JRmm Mauser	Rimmed Bottleneck	0.323	0.345	0.432	0.468	0.524	2.360	3.200
8mm-06	Rimless Bottleneck	0.323	0.351	0.441	0.470	0.473	2.470	3.250
8x63mm Swedish	Rimless Bottleneck	0.323	0.356	0.456	0.488	0.479	2.480	3.360
8x64Smm Brenneke	Rimless Bottleneck	0.323	0.348	0.424	0.468	0.469	2.510	3.320
8x65RSmm Brenneke	Rimmed Bottleneck	0.323	0.348	0.421	0.464	0.520	2.560	3.650
8x68Smm Mag	Rimless Bottleneck	0.323	0.354	0.473	0.522	0.510	2.650	3.380
8mm Remington Mag	Belted Bottleneck	0.323	0.341	0.4868	0.5126	0.530	2.850	3.600
310 Cadet	Rimmed Straightwall	0.324	0.320		0.353	0.405	1.120	1.720
8x72Rmm Sauer	Rimmed Straightwall	0.324	0.344		0.429	0.483	2.840	3.400
7.5mm Nagant (Swedish)	Rimmed Straightwall	0.325	0.328		0.350	0.406	0.890	1.350
8x59mm Breda	Rimless Bottleneck	0.326	0.357	0.433	0.491	0.469	2.330	3.170
8mm Guedes M-85	Rimmed Bottleneck	0.326	0.354	0.490	0.543	0.620	2.340	3.250
8mm Roth-Sauer	Rimless Straightwall	0.329	0.353		0.355	0.356	0.740	1.140
Cartridge	Case Type	Bullet Dia.	Neck Dia.	Shoulder Dia.	Base Dia.	Rim Dia.	Case Length	Ctge OAL

Cartridge	Case Type	Bullet Dia.	Neck Dia.	Shoulder Dia.	Base Dia.	Rim Dia.	Case Length	Ctge OAL
8mm Murata	Rimmed Bottleneck	0.329	0.361	0.485	0.492	0.558	2.060	2.900
8mm Hungarian M-89	Rimmed Bottleneck	0.329	0.365	0.473	0.491	0.554	2.200	3.020
318 Rimless Nitro Express	Rimless Bottleneck	0.330	0.358	0.445	0.465	0.465	2.380	3.350
375/303 Axite	Rimmed Bottleneck	0.330	0.343	0.390	0.457	0.505	2.470	3.480
33 Winchester	Rimmed Bottleneck	0.333	0.365	0.443	0.508	0.610	2.110	2.800
333 Rimless Nitro Express	Rimless Bottleneck	0.333	0.359	0.469	0.540	0.538	2.430	3.500
333 Jeffrey Rimless	Rimless Bottleneck	0.333	0.359	0.496	0.540	0.538	2.480	3.480
333 OKH	Rimless Bottleneck	0.333	0.365	0.443	0.470	0.473	2.490	3.370
333 Flanged Jeffrey	Rimmed Bottleneck	0.333	0.356	0.484	0.530	0.625	2.500	3.430
334 OKH	Belted Bottleneck	0.333	0.367	0.480	0.513	0.530	2.860	3.650
338-223 Straight	Rimless Straightwall	0.338	0.362		0.376	0.378	1.410	2.250
338 Whisper	Rimless Bottleneck	0.338	0.360	0.457	0.463	0.466	1.470	Varies
338 KDK	Rimmed Bottleneck	0.338	0.365	0.453	0.470	0.514	2.200	Varies
33 (Belted) BSA	Belted Bottleneck	0.338	0.369	0.453	0.534	0.527	2.400	3.100
338-06	Rimless Bottleneck	0.338	0.360	0.440	0.470	0.473	2.480	3.370
338 Winchester Mag	Belted Bottleneck	0.338	0.369	0.491	0.5127	0.530	2.500	3.340
330 Dakota	Rimless Bottleneck	0.338	0.371	0.530	0.545	0.532	2.570	3.320
338 Lapua Mag	Rimless Bottleneck	0.338	0.365	0.544	0.589	0.586	2.720	3.680
340 Weatherby Mag	Belted Bottleneck	0.338	0.368	0.495	0.513	0.530	2.825	3.600
338 Canadian Mag	Rebated Bottleneck	0.338	0.369	0.530	0.544	0.532	2.830	3.600
338 A-Square	Other	0.338	0.367	0.553	0.582	0.579	2.850	3.670
338 Excalibur	Rimless Bottleneck	0.338	0.371	0.566	0.580	0.580	2.990	3.750
338/50 Talbot	Rimless Bottleneck	0.338	0.380	0.748	0.774	0.782	3.760	4.250
348 Winchester	Rimmed Bottleneck	0.348	0.3757	0.485	0.553	0.610	2.255	2.795
Cartridge	Case Type	Bullet Dia.	Neck Dia.	Shoulder Dia.	Base Dia.	Rim Dia.	Case Length	Ctge OAL

Cartridge	Case Type	Bullet Dia.	Neck Dia.	Shoulder Dia.	Base Dia.	Rim Dia.	Case Length	Ctge OAL
9x71mm Peterlongo	Rimless Bottleneck	0.350	0.386	0.420	0.464	0.466	2.800	3.260
35 Winchester Self Loading	Semi-Rimmed Straightwall	0.351	0.374		0.378	0.405	1.140	1.640
351 Winchester Self Loading	Semi-Rimmed Straightwall	0.351	0.374		0.378	0.407	1.380	1.910
9mm Ultra	Rimless Straightwall	0.355	0.374		0.386	0.366	0.720	1.030/B
9mm Gilsenti	Rimless Straightwall	0.355	0.380		0.392	0.393	0.750	1.150
9mm Federal	Rimmed Straightwall	0.355	0.382		0.386	0.435	0.754	1.163
9mm Luger (+P)	Rimless Straightwall	0.355	0.380		0.392	0.393	0.754	1.160/B
9mm Browning Long	Rimless Straightwall	0.355	0.376		0.384	0.404	0.800	1.100
9x21mm	Rimless Straightwall	0.355	0.380		0.392	0.393	0.830	1.160
9mm Action Express	Rebated Straightwall	0.355	0.390	0.433	0.435	0.394	0.866	1.152
9mm Steyr	Rimless Straightwall	0.355	0.380		0.380	0.381	0.900	1.300
38-45 Hard Lead	Rimless Bottleneck	0.355	0.381	0.475	0.476	0.476	0.900	1.200
9mm Bayard	Rimless Straightwall	0.355	0.375		0.390	0.392	0.910	1.320
9mm Mauser	Rimless Straightwall	0.355	0.376		0.389	0.390	0.981	1.380
9mm Winchester Mag	Rimless Straightwall	0.355	0.379		0.392	0.394	1.160	1.545
380 Automatic (ACP)	Rimless Straightwall	0.356	0.373		0.373	0.374	0.680	0.980
38 Super Automatic (+P)	Semi-Rimmed Straightwall	0.356	0.382		0.383	0.405	0.900	1.280
9x57mm Mauser	Rimless Bottleneck	0.356	0.380	0.428	0.467	0.468	2.210	3.100
9x56mm Mannlicher	Rimless Bottleneck	0.356	0.378	0.408	0.464	0.464	2.220	3.560
357 SIG	Rimless Bottleneck	0.357	0.381	0.424	0.425	0.424	0.865	1.140
357 Maximum	Rimmed Straightwall	0.357	0.375		0.375	0.433	1.590	1.970
38 Long Colt	Rimmed Straightwall	0.357	0.377		0.378	0.433	1.030	1.320
38 Smith & Wesson Special (+P)	Rimmed Straightwall	0.357	0.379		0.379	0.440	1.155	1.550
357/44 Bain & Davis	Rimmed Bottleneck	0.357	0.383	0.454	0.455	0.515	1.280	1.550
357 Mag	Rimmed Straightwall	0.357	0.379		0.379	0.440	1.290	1.510

Cartridge	Case Type	Bullet Dia.	Neck Dia.	Shoulder Dia.	Base Dia.	Rim Dia.	Case Length	Ctge OAL

Cartridge	Case Type	Bullet Dia.	Neck Dia.	Shoulder Dia.	Base Dia.	Rim Dia.	Case Length	Ctge OAL
357 Automatic Mag	Rimless Bottleneck	0.357	0.382	0.461	0.470	0.473	1.298	1.600
357 Herett	Rimmed Bottleneck	0.357	0.375	0.405	0.420	0.505	1.750	2.100
35-30/30	Rimmed Bottleneck	0.357	0.378	0.401	0.422	0.506	2.040	2.550
360 Nitro for Blackpowder	Rimmed Straightwall	0.357	0.384		0.430	0.480	2.250	2.630
9x63mm	Rimless Bottleneck	0.357	0.384	0.427	0.467	0.468	2.480	3.280
400/350 Rigby	Rimmed Bottleneck	0.357	0.380	0.415	0.470	0.520	2.750	3.550
9x70Rmm Mauser	Rimmed Bottleneck	0.357	0.385	0.418	0.467	0.525	2.760	3.370
350 Griffin & Howe Mag	Belted Bottleneck	0.357	0.382	0.446	0.511	0.528	2.848	3.640
35 Remington	Rimless Bottleneck	0.358	0.384	0.4295	0.4574	0.460	1.920	2.520
358 Winchester	Rimless Bottleneck	0.358	0.386	0.454	0.4703	0.473	2.015	2.780
356 Winchester	Semi-Rimmed Bottleneck	0.358	0.388	0.454	0.4703	0.508	2.015	2.560
350 Remington Mag	Belted Bottleneck	0.358	0.388	0.495	0.512	0.532	2.170	2.800
358 JDJ	Rimmed Bottleneck	0.358	0.378	0.453	0.465	0.514	2.200	3.065
35 Winchester	Rimmed Bottleneck	0.358	0.378	0.412	0.457	0.539	2.410	3.160
35 Whelen	Rimless Bottleneck	0.358	0.388	0.441	0.470	0.473	2.494	3.340
358 Norma Mag	Belted Bottleneck	0.358	0.384	0.489	0.508	0.526	2.515	3.220
35 Newton	Rimless Bottleneck	0.358	0.383	0.498	0.523	0.525	2.520	3.350
350 Rigby Mag	Rimless Bottleneck	0.358	0.380	0.443	0.519	0.525	2.750	3.600
350 No. 2 Rigby	Rimmed Bottleneck	0.358	0.380	0.415	0.470	0.520	2.750	3.600
400/360 Nitro Express	Rimmed Bottleneck	0.358	0.375	0.437	0.470	0.590	2.750	3.590
358 Shooting Times Alaskan	Belted Bottleneck	0.358	0.484	0.500	0.532	NA	2.855	3.655
38 Smith & Wesson	Rimmed Straightwall	0.359	0.386		0.386	0.433	0.780	1.200
35-30 Maynard 1882	Rimmed Straightwall	0.359	0.395		0.400	0.494	1.630	2.030
35-40 Maynard	Rimmed Straightwall	0.360	0.390		0.400	0.492	2.060	2.530
35-40 Maynard 1873	Rimmed Straightwall	0.360	0.390		0.403	0.764	2.100	2.570
Cartridge	Case Type	Bullet Dia.	Neck Dia.	Shoulder Dia.	Base Dia.	Rim Dia.	Case Length	Ctge OAL

Cartridge	Case Type	Bullet Dia.	Neck Dia.	Shoulder Dia.	Base Dia.	Rim Dia.	Case Length	Ctge OAL
360 No. 5 Rook	Rimmed Straightwall	0.362	0.375		0.380	0.432	1.050	1.350
9mm Makarov	Rimless Straightwall	0.363	0.384		0.389	0.396	0.710	0.970
38-45 Stevens	Rimmed Straightwall	0.363	0.395		0.455	0.522	1.760	2.240
35-30 Maynard 1873	Rimmed Straightwall	0.364	0.397		0.403	0.765	1.630	2.100
9.3x53mm Swiss	Rimless Bottleneck	0.365	0.389	0.453	0.492	0.491	2.110	2.800
9.3x57mm Mauser	Rimless Bottleneck	0.365	0.389	0.428	0.468	0.469	2.240	3.230
360 Express	Rimmed Straightwall	0.365	0.384		0.430	0.480	2.250	3.00
360 Nitro	Rimmed Straightwall	0.365	0.384		0.430	0.480	2.250	2.800
9.3x62mm Mauser	Rimless Bottleneck	0.365	0.388	0.447	0.473	0.470	2.420	3.290
9.3x64mm Brenneke	Rimless Bottleneck	0.365	0.391	0.475	0.504	0.492	2.520	3.430
9.3x72Rmm Sauer	Rimmed Bottleneck	0.365	0.390	0.422	0.473	0.518	2.830	3.340
9.3x74Rmm	Rimmed Bottleneck	0.365	0.387	0.414	0.465	0.524	2.930	3.740
9.3x80Rmm	Rimmed Straightwall	0.365	0.386		0.430	0.485	3.140	3.500
9.3x82Rmm	Rimmed Straightwall	0.365	0.386		0.430	0.485	3.210	3.720
9.3mm JDJ	Rimmed Bottleneck	0.366	0.389	0.455	0.465	0.506	2.220	Varies
360 No. 2 Nitro Express	Rimmed Straightwall	0.367	0.384		0.430	0.480	2.250	2.980
9.3x65Rmm Collath	Rimmed Bottleneck	0.367	0.384	0.420	0.443	0.508	2.560	3.010
400/360 Westley Richards NE	Rimmed Bottleneck	0.367	0.375	0.437	0.483	0.572	2.730	3.440
350 Rimless Mag (Rigby)	Rimless Bottleneck	0.367	0.380	0.443	0.519	0.525	2.740	3.570
360 Nitro Express No. 2	Rimmed Bottleneck	0.367	0.393	0.517	0.539	0.631	3.000	3.850
9.3x53Rmm Hebler	Rimmed Bottleneck	0.369	0.398	0.462	0.484	0.550	2.120	2.920
35-30 Maynard 1865	Rimmed Straightwall	0.370	0.397		0.408	0.771	1.530	1.980
400/375 Nitro Express (H&H)	Belted Bottleneck	0.371	0.397	0.435	0.465	0.466	2.470	3.000
38-40 Remington	Rimmed Straightwall	0.372	0.395		0.454	0.537	1.770	2.320
38-45 Bullard	Rimmed Bottleneck	0.373	0.397	0.448	0.454	0.526	1.800	2.260
Cartridge	Case Type	Bullet Dia.	Neck Dia.	Shoulder Dia.	Base Dia.	Rim Dia.	Case Length	Ctge OAL

Cartridge	Case Type	Bullet Dia.	Neck Dia.	Shoulder Dia.	Base Dia.	Rim Dia.	Case Length	Ctge OAL
9.1x40Rmm	Rimmed Straightwall	0.374	0.385		0.404	0.446	1.600	2.000
380 Short	Rimmed Straightwall	0.375	0.379		0.380	0.430	0.600	1.110
380 Revolver	Rimmed Straightwall	0.375	0.377		0.380	0.426	0.700	1.100/B
38 Long, Center Fire*	Rimmed Straightwall	0.375	0.378		0.379	0.441	1.030	1.450
38-35 Stevens	Rimmed Straightwall	0.375	0.402		0.403	0.492	1.620	2.430
38 Extra Long Ballard*	Rimmed Straightwall	0.375	0.378		0.379	0.441	1.630	2.060
9.5x47Rmm	Rimmed Bottleneck	0.375	0.409	0.497	0.513	0.583	1.850	2.370
38-50 Maynard 1882	Rimmed Straightwall	0.375	0.415		0.412	0.500	1.970	2.380
375 Winchester	Rimmed Straightwall	0.375	0.400		0.4198	0.502	2.020	2.560
375 JDJ	Rimmed Bottleneck	0.375	0.396	0.451	0.465	0.514	2.225	3.130
375 Rimless Nitro Express	Rimless Bottleneck	0.375	0.403	0.456	0.468	0.468	2.250	2.960
9.5x57mm Mannlicher	Rimless Bottleneck	0.375	0.400	0.460	0.471	0.473	2.250	2.940
9.5x56mm	Rimless Bottleneck	0.375	0.400	0.460	0.471	0.473	2.250	2.940
400/375 Belted NE (H&H)	Belted Bottleneck	0.375	0.397	0.435	0.470	0.466	2.500	3.000
375 Flanged Nitro	Rimmed Straightwall	0.375	0.397		0.456	0.523	2.500	3.100
375 Whelen	Rimless Bottleneck	0.375	0.403	0.442	0.470	0.473	2.500	3.420
375 Dakota	Rimless Bottleneck	0.375	0.402	0.529	0.545	0.532	2.570	3.320
369 Purdey	Rimmed Bottleneck	0.375	0.398	0.475	0.543	0.616	2.690	3.590
375 Canadian Mag	Rebated Bottleneck	0.375	0.402	0.530	0.544	0.532	2.830	3.600
375 JRS	Belted Bottleneck	0.375	0.498	0.485	0.535	0.532	2.840	3.690
375 Holland & Holland Mag	Belted Bottleneck	0.375	0.402	0.4478	0.5121	0.530	2.850	3.600
375 Belted Mag	Belted Bottleneck	0.375	0.404	0.440	0.464	0.530	2.850	3.600
375 Weatherby Mag	Belted Bottleneck	0.375	0.403	0.495	0.513	0.530	2.860	3.690
9.5x73mm Miller Greiss Mag	Rimless Bottleneck	0.375	0.402	0.531	0.543	0.541	2.860	3.500
378 Weatherby Mag	Belted Bottleneck	0.375	0.403	0.560	0.584	0.580	2.920	3.690
Cartridge	Case Type	Bullet Dia.	Neck Dia.	Shoulder Dia.	Base Dia.	Rim Dia.	Case Length	Ctge OAL

Cartridge	Case Type	Bullet Dia.	Neck Dia.	Shoulder Dia.	Base Dia.	Rim Dia.	Case Length	Ctge OAL
375 Flanged Mag	Rimmed Bottleneck	0.375	0.404	0.450	0.502	0.572	2.940	3.690
380 Long Rifle	Rimmed Straightwall	0.376	0.379		0.380	0.435	1.010	1.330
9.3x48Rmm	Rimmed Straightwall	0.376	0.382		0.433	0.492	1.890	2.350
38-50 Ballard	Rimmed Straightwall	0.376	0.395		0.425	0.502	2.000	2.720
38-50 Winchester	Rimmed Bottleneck	0.376	0.403	0.447	0.506	0.6906	2.100	2.500
38-50 Remington	Rimmed Straightwall	0.376	0.392		0.454	0.535	2.230	3.070
9.3x57Rmm	Rimmed Straightwall	0.376	0.389		0.428	0.486	2.240	2.800
9.3x70Rmm	Rimmed Straightwall	0.376	0.387		0.427	0.482	2.750	3.450
9.3x72Rmm	Rimmed Straightwall	0.376	0.385		0.427	0.482	2.840	3.270
38-90 Winchester	Rimmed Bottleneck	0.376	0.395	0.470	0.477	0.558	3.250	3.700
9.8mm Automatic Colt	Rimless Straightwall	0.378	0.404		0.404	0.405	0.912	1.267
38-70 Winchester	Rimmed Bottleneck	0.378	0.403	0.421	0.506	0.600	2.310	2.730
38-72 Winchester	Rimmed Bottleneck	0.378	0.397	0.427	0.461	0.519	2.580	3.160
38-55 Winchester & Ballard	Rimmed Straightwall	0.379	0.392		0.422	0.506	2.128	2.510
41 Long Colt	Rimmed Straightwall	0.386	0.404		0.405	0.430	1.130	1.390
9.5mm Turkish Mauser	Rimmed Bottleneck	0.389	0.411	0.487	0.511	0.612	2.370	2.970
400 Nitro for Blackpowder (3)	Rimmed Straightwall	0.395	0.427		0.471	0.522	3.000	3.560
40 Smith & Wesson	Rimless Straightwall	0.400	0.423		0.423	0.424	0.850	1.135
10mm Automatic	Rimless Straightwall	0.400	0.423		0.423	0.424	0.992	1.260
401 Herter Powermag	Rimmed Straightwall	0.401	0.425		0.426	0.483	1.290	1.640
38-40 Winchester (WCF)	Rimmed Bottleneck	0.401	0.416	0.4543	0.465	0.520	1.300	1.590
40-50 Sharps (Necked)	Rimmed Bottleneck	0.403	0.424	0.489	0.501	0.580	1.720	2.370
40-50 Sharps (Straight)	Rimmed Straightwall	0.403	0.421		0.454	0.554	1.880	2.630
40-60 Marlin	Rimmed Straightwall	0.403	0.425		0.504	0.604	2.110	2.550
40-70 Sharps (Necked)	Rimmed Bottleneck	0.403	0.426	0.500	0.503	0.595	2.250	3.020
Cartridge	Case Type	Bullet Dia.	Neck Dia.	Shoulder Dia.	Base Dia.	Rim Dia.	Case Length	Ctge OAL

Cartridge	Case Type	Bullet Dia.	Neck Dia.	Shoulder Dia.	Base Dia.	Rim Dia.	Case Length	Ctge OAL
40-63 (40-70) Ballard	Rimmed Straightwall	0.403	0.430		0.471	0.555	2.380	2.550
40-65 Ballard	Rimmed Straightwall	0.403	0.435		0.508	0.600	2.380	2.550
10.15mm Jarmann	Rimmed Bottleneck	0.403	0.430	0.540	0.548	0.615	2.400	3.060
40-70 Sharps (Straight)	Rimmed Straightwall	0.403	0.420		0.453	0.533	2.500	3.180
40-90 Sharps (Necked)	Rimmed Bottleneck	0.403	0.435	0.500	0.506	0.602	2.630	3.440
40-85 (40-90) Ballard	Rimmed Straightwall	0.403	0.425		0.477	0.545	2.940	3.810
40-90 Sharps (Straight)	Rimmed Straightwall	0.403	0.425		0.477	0.546	3.250	4.060
40-110 Winchester Express	Rimmed Bottleneck	0.403	0.428	0.485	0.543	0.651	3.250	3.630
40-60 Winchester	Rimmed Bottleneck	0.404	0.425	0.445	0.506	0.630	1.870	2.100
10.25x69Rmm Hunting Ex.	Rimmed Bottleneck	0.404	0.415	0.480	0.549	0.630	2.720	3.170
40-70 Remington	Rimmed Bottleneck	0.405	0.434	0.500	0.503	0.595	2.250	3.000
40-70 Winchester	Rimmed Bottleneck	0.405	0.430	0.496	0.504	0.604	2.400	2.850
400 Whelen	Rimless Bottleneck	0.405	0.436	0.462	0.470	0.473	2.490	3.100
400 Purdey (3)	Rimmed Straightwall	0.405	0.427		0.469	0.516	3.000	3.600
450/400 Nitro Express	Rimmed Bottleneck	0.405	0.432	0.502	0.544	0.615	3.250	3.850
401 Winchester SL	Semi-Rimmed Straightwall	0.406	0.428		0.429	0.457	1.500	2.00
40-65 Winchester	Rimmed Straightwall	0.406	0.423		0.504	0.604	2.100	2.480
45-75/82 Winchester	Rimmed Bottleneck	0.406	0.428	0.448	0.502	0.604	2.400	2.770
40-72 Winchester	Rimmed Straightwall	0.406	0.431		0.460	0.518	2.600	3.150
40-70 Peabody	Rimmed Bottleneck	0.408	0.428	0.551	0.581	0.662	1.760	2.850
40-90 Peabody	Rimmed Bottleneck	0.408	0.433	0.546	0.586	0.659	2.000	3.370
450/400 Nitro (3)	Rimmed Bottleneck	0.408	0.434	0.518	0.545	0.613	3.000	3.750
41 Action Express	Rebated Straightwall	0.410	0.434		0.435	0.394	0.866	1.170
41 Remington Mag	Rimmed Straightwall	0.410	0.432		0.433	0.488	1.290	1.580
400 Jeffrey (450/400 3)	Rimmed Bottleneck	0.410	0.434	0.518	0.545	0.613	3.000	3.750
Cartridge	Case Type	Bullet Dia.	Neck Dia.	Shoulder Dia.	Base Dia.	Rim Dia.	Case Length	Ctge OAL

Cartridge	Case Type	Bullet Dia.	Neck Dia.	Shoulder Dia.	Base Dia.	Rim Dia.	Case Length	Ctge OAL
411 JDJ	Rimmed Bottleneck	0.411	0.425	0.455	0.465	0.506	2.235	Varies
10.15mm Serbian Mauser	Rimmed Bottleneck	0.411	0.433	0.515	0.520	0.592	2.460	3.130
405 Winchester	Rimmed Straightwall	0.412	0.436		0.461	0.543	2.580	3.180
40-90 Bullard	Rimmed Bottleneck	0.413	0.430	0.551	0.569	0.622	2.040	2.550
45-70 Bullard	Rimmed Straightwall	0.413	0.432		0.505	0.606	2.090	2.540
10.4mm Swiss Vetterli	Rimmed Bottleneck	0.415	0.437	0.518	0.540	0.630	1.600	2.200
40-40 Maynard 1882	Rimmed Straightwall	0.415	0.450		0.456	0.532	1.780	2.320
10.3x60Rmm Swiss	Rimmed Bottleneck	0.415	0.440	0.498	0.547	0.619	2.360	3.080
416 Barnes	Rimmed Bottleneck	0.416	0.432	0.484	0.505	0.608	2.112	2.950
416 JDJ	Rimmed Bottleneck	0.416	0.430	0.485	0.465	0.506	2.220	Varies
416 Taylor	Belted Bottleneck	0.416	0.440	0.489	0.512	0.533	2.500	3.330
416 Howell	Rimless Bottleneck	0.416	0.444	0.515	0.545	0.540	2.500	3.250
416 Remington Mag	Belted Bottleneck	0.416	0.447	0.487	0.509	0.530	2.850	3.600
416 Hoffman	Belted Bottleneck	0.416	0.446	0.491	0.513	0.530	2.850	3.372
416 Dakota	Rimless Bottleneck	0.416	0.441	0.527	0.545	0.540	2.850	3.645
416 Rigby	Rimless Bottleneck	0.416	0.4461	0.5402	0.589	0.586	2.900	3.750
416 Weatherby Mag	Belted Bottleneck	0.416	0.444	0.561	0.582	0.580	2.915	3.750
40-60 Maynard 1882	Rimmed Straightwall	0.417	0.448		0.454	0.533	2.200	2.750
40-70 Maynard 1882	Rimmed Straightwall	0.417	0.450		0.451	0.535	2.420	2.880
44 Evans Short	Rimmed Straightwall	0.419	0.439		0.440	0.513	0.990	1.440
44 Evans Long	Rimmed Straightwall	0.416	0.434		0.449	0.509	1.540	2.000
10.5x47Rmm	Rimmed Bottleneck	0.419	0.445	0.496	0.513	0.591	1.850	2.400
404 Rimless Nitro	Rimless Bottleneck	0.421	0.450	0.520	0.544	0.537	2.860	3.530
404 Jeffrey (10.75x73mm)	Rimless Bottleneck	0.421	0.450	0.520	0.544	0.537	2.860	3.530
10.75x73mm	Rimless Bottleneck	0.421	0.450	0.520	0.544	0.537	2.860	3.530
Cartridge	Case Type	Bullet Dia.	Neck Dia.	Shoulder Dia.	Base Dia.	Rim Dia.	Case Length	Ctge OAL

CHAPTER 29: CARTRIDGE DIMENSIONS

Cartridge	Case Type	Bullet Dia.	Neck Dia.	Shoulder Dia.	Base Dia.	Rim Dia.	Case Length	Ctge OAL
10.4mm Italian	Rimmed Straightwall	0.422	0.444		0.451	0.505	0.890	1.250
40-40 Maynard 1873	Rimmed Straightwall	0.422	0.450		0.460	0.473	1.840	2.340
40-70 Maynard 1873	Rimmed Straightwall	0.422	0.450		0.451	0.759	2.450	3.000
44 Henry (Center Fire)	Rimmed Straightwall	0.423	0.443		0.445	0.523	0.860	1.360
40-40 Maynard 1865	Rimmed Straightwall	0.423	0.450		0.458	0.766	1.750	2.240
425 Express	Belted Bottleneck	0.423	0.446	0.490	0.513	0.532	2.552	3.380
10.3x65Rmm Baenziger	Rimmed Straightwall	0.423	0.431		0.462	0.505	2.560	3.150
10.75x57mm Mannlicher	Rimless Bottleneck	0.424	0.448	0.465	0.468	0.468	2.240	3.050
10.75x63mm Mauser	Rebated Bottleneck	0.424	0.447	0.479	0.493	0.467	2.470	3.220
10.75x65R Collath	Rimmed Straightwall	0.424	0.451		0.487	0.542	2.560	3.020
10.75x68mm Mauser	Rimless Bottleneck	0.424	0.445	0.470	0.492	0.486	2.670	3.160
44-40 Winchester	Rimmed Bottleneck	0.427	0.443	0.4568	0.471	0.525	1.305	1.592
44-40 Extra Long	Rimmed Bottleneck	0.428	0.442	0.463	0.468	0.515	1.580	1.960
44 Smith & Wesson Russian	Rimmed Straightwall	0.429	0.457		0.457	0.515	0.970	1.430
44 Smith & Wesson Special	Rimmed Straightwall	0.429	0.457		0.457	0.514	1.160	1.620
44 Remington Mag	Rimmed Straightwall	0.429	0.457		0.457	0.514	1.285	1.610
44 Automatic Mag	Rimless Straightwall	0.429	0.457		0.470	0.472	1.298	1.600
444 Marlin	Rimmed Straightwall	0.429	0.453		0.469	0.514	2.225	2.570
10.4mm Italian M-70	Rimmed Bottleneck	0.430	0.437	0.517	0.540	0.634	1.870	2.460
10.75mm Russian Berdan	Rimmed Bottleneck	0.430	0.449	0.506	0.567	0.637	2.240	2.950
11mm Murata	Rimmed Bottleneck	0.432	0.465	0.526	0.542	0.632	2.360	3.130
44 Smith & Wesson American	Rimmed Straightwall	0.434	0.438		0.440	0.506	0.910	1.440
11mm Belgian Albini	Rimmed Bottleneck	0.435	0.472	0.535	0.580	0.678	2.000	NA
425 Westley Richards Mag	Rebated Bottleneck	0.435	0.456	0.540	0.543	0.467	2.640	3.200
44 Webley	Rimmed Straightwall	0.436	0.470		0.472	0.503	0.690	1.100/B
Cartridge	Case Type	Bullet Dia.	Neck Dia.	Shoulder Dia.	Base Dia.	Rim Dia.	Case Length	Ctge OAL

Cartridge	Case Type	Bullet Dia.	Neck Dia.	Shoulder Dia.	Base Dia.	Rim Dia.	Case Length	Ctge OAL
11mm Belgian Comblain	Rimmed Bottleneck	0.436	0.460	0.532	0.575	0.673	2.100	2.760
44 Long Ballard*	Rimmed Straightwall	0.439	0.440		0.441	0.506	1.090	1.650
44 Long Ballard (CF)*	Rimmed Straightwall	0.439	0.441		0.441	0.508	1.630	2.100
11.5mm Spanish Rem.	Rimmed Bottleneck	0.439	0.458	0.512	0.516	0.635	2.250	2.820
44 Bull Dog	Rimmed Straightwall	0.440	0.470		0.473	0.503	0.570	0.950
44 Extra Long Wesson*	Rimmed Straightwall	0.440	0.441		0.441	0.510	1.630	2.190
11.2x60mm Schuler (Mauser)	Rebated Bottleneck	0.440	0.465	0.512	0.512	0.465	2.350	2.860
11.2x72mm Schuler (Mauser)	Rebated Bottleneck	0.440	0.465	0.510	0.536	0.469	2.800	3.850
10.8x47Rmm Martini Target	Rimmed Bottleneck	0.441	0.463	0.512	0.516	0.591	1.750	2.230
11.15mm Werndl M-77	Rimmed Bottleneck	0.441	0.468	0.536	0.545	0.617	2.270	3.020
44-90 Rem Sp (Necked)	Rimmed Bottleneck	0.442	0.466	0.504	0.506	0.628	2.440	3.080
44-90 (44-100) Rem (Str)	Rimmed Straightwall	0.442	0.465		0.503	0.568	2.600	3.970
44 Colt	Rimmed Straightwall	0.443	0.450		0.456	0.483	1.100	1.500
44-95 Peabody	Rimmed Bottleneck	0.443	0.465	0.550	0.580	0.670	2.310	3.220
11.75mm Montenegrin	Rimmed Straightwall	0.445	0.472		0.490	0.555	1.400	1.730
44-70 Maynard 1882	Rimmed Straightwall	0.445	0.466		0.499	0.601	2.221	2.870
11mm French Gras	Rimmed Bottleneck	0.445	0.468	0.531	0.544	0.667	2.340	3.000
11x59R Vickers	Rimmed Bottleneck	0.445	0.468	0.531	0.554	0.667	2.340	3.000
44-75 Ballard	Rimmed Straightwall	0.445	0.487		0.497	0.603	2.500	3.000
44-100 Ballard	Rimmed Straightwall	0.445	0.485		0.498	0.597	2.810	3.250
44-100 Wesson	Rimmed Straightwall	0.445	NA		0.515	0.605	3.380	3.850
44-77 Sharps & Remington	Rimmed Bottleneck	0.446	0.467	0.502	0.516	0.625	2.250	3.050
11.15mm (43) Mauser	Rimmed Bottleneck	0.446	0.465	0.510	0.566	0.586	2.370	3.000
44-90 (44-100) Sharps	Rimmed Bottleneck	0.446	0.468	0.504	0.517	0.625	2.630	3.300
44-85 Wesson	Rimmed Straightwall	0.466	NA		0.515	0.605	2.880	3.310
Cartridge	Case Type	Bullet Dia.	Neck Dia.	Shoulder Dia.	Base Dia.	Rim Dia.	Case Length	Ctge OAL

Cartridge	Case Type	Bullet Dia.	Neck Dia.	Shoulder Dia.	Base Dia.	Rim Dia.	Case Length	Ctge OAL
44-60 Sharps Remington	Rimmed Bottleneck	0.447	0.464	0.502	0.515	0.630	1.880	2.550
44-60 Peabody & Winchester	Rimmed Bottleneck	0.447	0.464	0.502	0.518	0.628	1.890	2.560
11.43mm Turkish	Rimmed Bottleneck	0.447	0.474	0.560	0.582	0.668	2.300	3.120
11.43mm Egyptian	Rimmed Bottleneck	0.448	0.479	0.542	0.581	0.668	1.940	2.730
11.4mm Werndl M-73	Rimmed Straightwall	0.449	0.472		0.493	0.571	1.970	2.550
44-90/100/110 Maynard 1873	Rimmed Straightwall	0.450	0.490		0.497	0.759	2.880	3.460
11mm French Ordnance	Rimmed Straightwall	0.451	0.449		0.460	0.491	0.710	1.180
11mm German Service	Rimmed Straightwall	0.451	0.449		0.453	0.509	0.960	1.210
45 Winchester Mag	Rimless Straightwall	0.451	0.475		0.477	0.481	1.198	1.550
500/450 BP No. 2 Musket	Rimmed Bottleneck	0.458	0.486	0.535	0.576	0.658	2.360	2.900
45 Sharps (2.6)	Rimmed Straightwall	0.451	0.489		0.500	0.597	2.600	2.850
45 Sharps (2.75)	Rimmed Straightwall	0.451	0.489		0.500	0.597	2.750	3.000
45 Sharps (2.87)	Rimmed Straightwall	0.451	0.489		0.500	0.597	2.870	3.000
45-120 Sharps (3¬ʃ)	Rimmed Straightwall	0.451	0.490		0.506	0.597	3.250	4.160
45 Webley	Rimmed Straightwall	0.452	0.471		0.471	0.504	0.820	1.150/B
45 Automatic Short	Rimless Straightwall	0.452	0.476		0.476	0.476	0.860	1.170
45 Automatic Rim	Rimmed Straightwall	0.452	0.472		0.476	0.516	0.898	1.280
45 Automatic (+P) (ACP)	Rimless Straightwall	0.452	0.476		0.476	0.476	0.898	1.170
451 Detonics	Rimless Straightwall	0.452	0.476		0.476	0.476	0.942	1.170
45 Colt (Post WW-II)	Rimmed Straightwall	0.452	0.476		0.480	0.512	1.285	1.600
454 Casull	Rimmed Straightwall	0.452	0.476		0.480	0.512	1.385	1.600
11.4mm Brazilian Comblain	Rimmed Bottleneck	0.452	0.494	0.530	0.588	0.682	2.020	2.620
45-100 Remington (Necked)	Rimmed Bottleneck	0.452	0.490	0.550	0.558	0.645	2.630	3.260
45 Webley Revolver Mk-II	Rimmed Straightwall	0.454	0.476		0.480	0.535	0.770	1.230/B
45 Smith & Wesson Schofield	Rimmed Straightwall	0.454	0.477		0.476	0.522	1.100	1.430
Cartridge	Case Type	Bullet Dia.	Neck Dia.	Shoulder Dia.	Base Dia.	Rim Dia.	Case Length	Ctge OAL

Cartridge	Case Type	Bullet Dia.	Neck Dia.	Shoulder Dia.	Base Dia.	Rim Dia.	Case Length	Ctge OAL
45 Colt	Rimmed Straightwall	0.454	0.476		0.476	0.512	1.290	1.600
45-50 Peabody	Rimmed Bottleneck	0.454	0.478	0.508	0.516	0.634	1.540	2.080
45-60 Winchester	Rimmed Straightwall	0.454	0.479		0.508	0.629	1.890	2.150
45-75 Winchester	Rimmed Bottleneck	0.454	0.478	0.547	0.559	0.616	1.890	2.250
11.5mm Spanish Reformando	Rimmed Straightwall	0.454	0.466		0.525	0.631	2.260	3.060
45-100 Ballard	Rimmed Straightwall	0.454	0.487		0.498	0.597	2.810	3.250
450 Revolver	Rimmed Straightwall	0.455	0.475		0.477	0.510	0.690	1.100/B
455 Enfield	Rimmed Straightwall	0.455	0.473		0.478	0.530	0.870	1.350/B
455 Webly Automatic	Semi-Rimmed Straightwall	0.455	0.473		0.474	0.500	0.930	1.230
577/450 Martini Henry	Rimmed Bottleneck	0.455	0.487	0.628	0.668	0.746	2.340	3.120
500/450 Mag Nitro Express	Rimmed Bottleneck	0.455	0.479	0.500	0.570	0.644	3.250	3.910
450 No. 2 Express	Rimmed Bottleneck	0.455	0.477	0.518	0.564	0.650	3.500	4.280
45-125 Winchester	Rimmed Bottleneck	0.456	0.470	0.521	0.533	0.601	3.250	3.630
11mm Beaumont M-71	Rimmed Bottleneck	0.457	0.484	0.528	0.576	0.665	2.040	2.540
458x1 Barnes	Belted Straightwall	0.458	0.493		0.509	0.530	1.500	2.190
45 Silhouette	Rimmed Straightwall	0.458	0.477		0.501	0.600	1.510	1.970
458 Whisper	Belted Straightwall	0.458	0.485		0.506	0.525	1.750	Varies
458x2 American	Belted Straightwall	0.458	0.478		0.508	0.532	2.000	2.600
45 Sharps (2.1) Straight	Rimmed Straightwall	0.458	0.480		0.500	0.608	2.105	2.430
45-70 Government	Rimmed Straightwall	0.458	0.480		0.500	0.608	2.105	2.550
45-70 500 Government	Rimmed Straightwall	0.458	0.480		0.500	0.608	2.105	2.700
45-70 Sharps	Rimmed Straightwall	0.458	0.480		0.500	0.608	2.105	2.900
45-70 Van Choate	Rimmed Straightwall	0.458	0.480		0.500	0.608	2.250	2.910
45-78 Wolcott	Rimmed Straightwall	0.458	0.480		0.500	0.608	2.310	3.190
500/450 No. 2 Musket	Rimmed Bottleneck	0.458	0.486	0.535	0.576	0.658	2.360	2.900
Cartridge	Case Type	Bullet Dia.	Neck Dia.	Shoulder Dia.	Base Dia.	Rim Dia.	Case Length	Ctge OAL

Cartridge	Case Type	Bullet Dia.	Neck Dia.	Shoulder Dia.	Base Dia.	Rim Dia.	Case Length	Ctge OAL
45-80 Sharpshooter	Rimmed Straightwall	0.458	0.480		0.500	0.608	2.400	3.250
45-82/85/90 Winchester	Rimmed Straightwall	0.458	0.477		0.501	0.597	2.400	2.880
458 Winchester Mag	Belted Straightwall	0.458	0.4811		0.513	0.532	2.500	3.340
450 Howell	Rimless Bottleneck	0.458	0.480	0.515	0.545	0.532	2.500	3.250
460 Short A-Aquare	Other	0.458	0.484	0.560	0.582	0.579	2.500	3.500
500/450 No. 1 Express	Rimmed Bottleneck	0.458	0.485	0.530	0.577	0.660	2.750	3.250
458 Lott	Belted Straightwall	0.458	0.480		0.513	0.530	2.800	3.600
450 Ackley Mag	Belted Bottleneck	0.458	0.478	0.495	0.508	0.527	2.845	3.685
450 Watts Mag	Belted Bottleneck	0.458	0.481		0.513	0.530	2.850	3.650
450 Dakota	Rimless Bottleneck	0.458	0.485	0.560	0.589	0.568	2.900	3.740
460 Weatherby Mag	Rimless Bottleneck	0.458	0.485	0.560	0.584	0.580	2.913	3.750
450 Nitro Express	Rimmed Straightwall	0.458	0.479		0.548	0.626	3.250	3.850
500/450 Mag Express*	Rimmed Bottleneck	0.458	0.479	0.500	0.570	0.644	3.250	3.910
450 No. 2 Nitro Express12.1	Rimmed Bottleneck	0.458	0.477	0.518	0.564	0.650	3.500	4.420
450 Rigby Match	Rimmed Straightwall	0.461	0.472		0.507	0.598	2.400	3.700
11.4mm Danish Remington	Rimmed Straightwall	0.462	0.486		0.514	0.579	2.010	2.450
11.3mm Beaumont M-71/78	Rimmed Bottleneck	0.464	0.486	0.530	0.581	0.666	1.970	2.490
500/465 Nitro Express	Rimmed Bottleneck	0.466	0.488	0.524	0.573	0.650	3.240	3.890
476 Enfield	Rimmed Straightwall	0.472	0.474		0.478	0.530	0.870	1.330
475 Ackley OKH	Belted Straightwall	0.474	0.496		0.508	0.528	2.739	3.518
475 Wildey	Rimless Straightwall	0.475	0.497		0.500	0.473	1.295	1.580
475 Linebaugh	Rimmed Straightwall	0.475	0.495		0.501	0.600	1.500	NA
475 JDJ	Rimmed Straightwall	0.475	0.497		0.502	0.604	2.100	Varies
470 Capstick	Belted Straightwall	0.475	0.499		0.513	0.532	2.850	3.650
475 A&M Mag	Belted Bottleneck	0.475	0.502	0.560	0.584	0.533	2.900	3.750
Cartridge	Case Type	Bullet Dia.	Neck Dia.	Shoulder Dia.	Base Dia.	Rim Dia.	Case Length	Ctge OAL

Cartridge	Case Type	Bullet Dia.	Neck Dia.	Shoulder Dia.	Base Dia.	Rim Dia.	Case Length	Ctge OAL
470 Nitro Express	Rimmed Bottleneck	0.475	0.504	0.5322	0.572	0.655	3.250	3.860
476 Nitro Express	Rimmed Bottleneck	0.476	0.508	0.530	0.570	0.643	3.000	3.770
475 Nitro Express	Rimmed Straightwall	0.476	0.502		0.545	0.621	3.300	3.820
475 No. 2 Nitro Express	Rimmed Bottleneck	0.483	0.510	0.547	0.576	0.665	3.490	4.260
475 No. 2 Nitro (Jeffrey)	Rimmed Bottleneck	0.489	0.510	0.547	0.576	0.666	3.500	4.320
50 Action Express	Rebated Straightwall	0.500	0.540		0.547	0.514	1.285	1.610
577/500 Mag Nitro Express	Rimmed Bottleneck	0.500	0.526	0.585	0.645	0.717	3.130	3.740
12.17x44Rmm Rem M-67	Rimmed Straightwall	0.502	0.544		0.546	0.624	1.730	2.130
505 Gibbs	Rimless Bottleneck	0.505	0.530	0.588	0.635	0.635	3.150	3.850
500 No. 2 Express (577/500)	Rimmed Bottleneck	0.507	0.538	0.560	0.641	0.726	2.810	3.400
50 Remington Army	Rimmed Bottleneck	0.508	0.532	0.564	0.585	0.665	0.8775	1.240
577/500 Nitro Express (3.13)	Rimmed Bottleneck	0.508	0.526	0.585	0.645	0.717	3.130	3.740
50-90 Sharps	Rimmed Straightwall	0.509	0.528		0.565	0.663	2.500	3.200
50-140 (3¬∫) Sharps	Rimmed Straightwall	0.509	0.528		0.585	0.665	3.250	3.940
500 Linebaugh	Rimmed Straightwall	0.510	0.540		0.553	0.610	1.405	1.765
500 Jeffrey	Rebated Bottleneck	0.510	0.535	0.615	0.620	0.578	2.740	3.500
12.70x70mm Schuler	Rebated Bottleneck	0.510	0.535	0.615	0.620	0.578	2.940	3.500
500 A-Square	Other	0.510	0.536	0.668	0.582	0.579	2.900	3.740
500 Express (3)	Rimmed Straightwall	0.510	0.535		0.580	0.660	3.010	3.390
500 Nitro (3)	Rimmed Straightwall	0.510	0.535		0.580	0.660	3.010	3.680
510 Nitro	Rimmed Straightwall	0.510	0.535		0.565	0.665	3.245	4.185
50 Browning (BMG)	Rimless Bottleneck	0.510	0.560	0.714	0.804	0.804	3.910	5.545
50-115 Bullard	Semi-Rimmed Bottleneck	0.512	0.547	0.577	0.585	0.619	2.190	2.560
50-100/105/110 Winchester	Rimmed Straightwall	0.512	0.534		0.551	0.607	2.400	2.750
50-140 (3¬∫) Winchester	Rimmed Straightwall	0.512	0.531		0.565	0.665	3.250	3.940
Cartridge	Case Type	Bullet Dia.	Neck Dia.	Shoulder Dia.	Base Dia.	Rim Dia.	Case Length	Ctge OAL

Cartridge	Case Type	Bullet Dia.	Neck Dia.	Shoulder Dia.	Base Dia.	Rim Dia.	Case Length	Ctge OAL
50-50 Maynard 1882	Rimmed Straightwall	0.513	0.535		0.563	0.661	1.370	1.910
50-95 Winchester	Rimmed Bottleneck	0.513	0.533	0.553	0.562	0.627	1.940	2.260
50-70 Maynard 1873	Rimmed Straightwall	0.514	0.547		0.552	0.760	1.880	2.340
50-70 Government (Musket)	Rimmed Straightwall	0.515	0.535		0.565	0.660	1.750	2.250
50 Maynard 1865	Rimmed Straightwall	0.520	0.543		0.545	0.770	1.240	1.750
50-100 Maynard	Rimmed Straightwall	0.551	0.582		0.590	0.718	1.940	2.560
577 (14.7mm) Snider	Rimmed Straightwall	0.570	0.602		0.660	0.747	2.000	2.450

Cartridge	Case Type	Bullet Dia.	Neck Dia.	Shoulder Dia.	Base Dia.	Rim Dia.	Case Length	Ctge OAL
585 Nyati	Rimless Bottleneck	0.585	0.605	0.650	0.660	0.586	2.790	3.525
577 Tyrannosaur	Rimless Bottleneck	0.585	0.614	0.673	0.688	0.688	2.990	3.710
577 Nitro Express	Rimmed Straightwall	0.585	0.608		0.660	0.748	3.000	3.700
58 Berdan Musket	Rimmed Straightwall	0.589	0.625		0.646	0.740	1.750	2.150
600 Nitro Express	Rimmed Straightwall	0.622	0.648		0.697	0.805	3.000	3.590
700 Nitro Express	Rimmed Straightwall	0.700	0.728		0.780	0.890	3.500	4.200
75-150 Winchester	Rimmed Bottleneck	0.705	0.725	0.790	0.805	0.870	2.180	2.630

*Designates a heel-based design. Bullet diameter is approximately the same as neck diameter.

Photo credits: Hornady sign and bullets with rifle courtesy of the manufacturer. Winchester bullet boards and Laflin & Rand poster© Winfield Galleries, LLC, St. Louis, Missouri. Used with permission. To view current artwork and pricing, log on to www.WinfieldGalleries.com.

Cartridge	Case Type	Bullet Dia.	Neck Dia.	Shoulder Dia.	Base Dia.	Rim Dia.	Case Length	Ctge OAL

Index

"For Strenuous Sport" was a UMC promotional poster by an unknown artist. © Winfield Galleries, LLC, St. Louis, Missouri. Used with permission. To view current artwork and pricing, log on to www.WinfieldGalleries.com.

The 30-30 Winchester is the most likely chambering for the lever action the hunter holds in this Lynn Bogue Hunt painting. Hunt was born in 1878 in a small town south of Rochester, New York. An ardent hunter and fisherman, he also practiced taxidermy. While a staff artist at the Detroit Free Press, **he began submitting wildlife artwork to various national magazines such as** Field & Stream **in New York, and those works drew the attention of arms and ammunition manufacturers who bought his paintings for use in advertising. He died on October 13, 1960, in Williston Park, Long Island, New York. © Winfield Galleries, LLC, St. Louis, Missouri. Used with permission. To view current artwork and pricing, log on to www.WinfieldGalleries.com.**

The Original Winchester Horse & Rider Logo was a commissioned painting by Phillip R. Goodwin (circa 1919). © Winfield Galleries, LLC, St. Louis, Missouri. Used with permission. To view current artwork and pricing, log on to www.Winfield-Galleries.com.

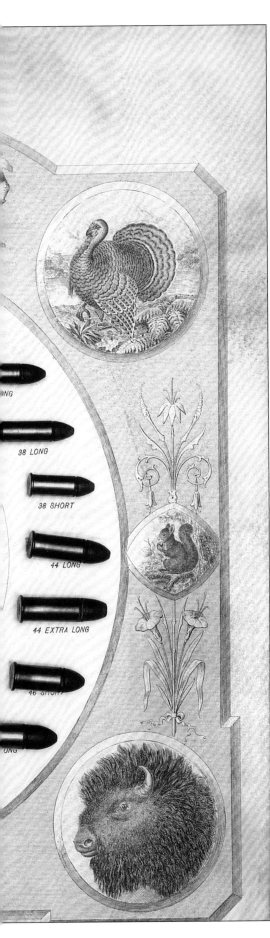

Cartridges (Metric)

The Winchester Rimfire Ammunition Cartridge Board dates to around 1870. The idea of placing a priming compound in the rim of the cartridge evolved from an 1831 patent, which called for a thin case with a priming compound coating the inside rim. The 22 Short, the second round below the stag head, was developed for Smith & Wesson's first revolver in 1857. It used a longer rimfire case and 4 grains of black powder to fire a conical bullet. More than 150 years later, rimfires are making something of a comeback. © Winfield Galleries, LLC, St. Louis, Missouri. Used with permission. To view current artwork and pricing, log on to www.WinfieldGalleries.com.

This Winchester calendar is called "Taking Aim," a painting by Fredrick Remington (circa 1892). © Winfield Galleries, LLC, St. Louis, Missouri. Used with permission. To view current artwork and pricing, log on to www.WinfieldGalleries.com.

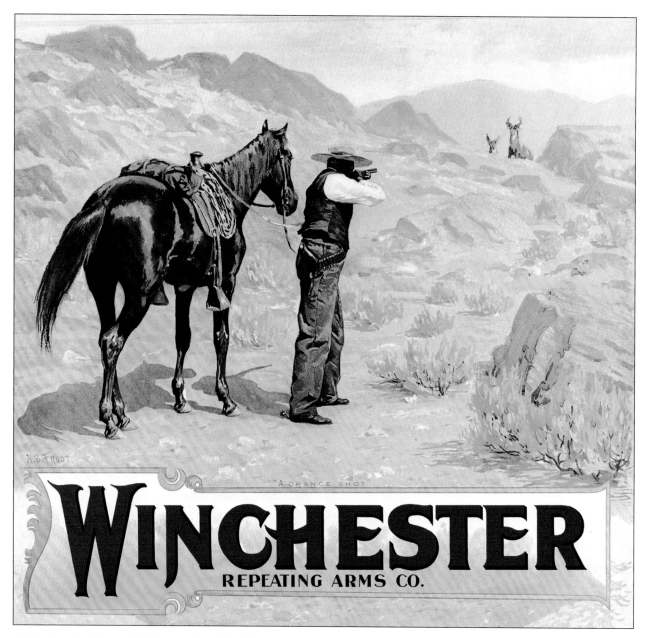

A.B. Frost (circa 1897) painted "A Chance Shot," a piece of Winchester calendar artwork. © Winfield Galleries, LLC, St. Louis, Missouri. Used with permission. To view current artwork and pricing, log on to www.WinfieldGalleries.com.

Factory Loads (A-B)

Factory Loads (C)

Factory Loads (D-E)

Factory Loads (F)

Factory Loads (G-H)

Factory Loads (K-P)